Why Social Justice Matters

Brian Barry

Polity

First published in 2005 by Polity Press
Reprinted 2005 (twice), 2006, 2007 (twice), 2008 (twice), 2012, 2013, 2015 (twice), 2017 (twice)

Polity Press
65 Bridge Street
Cambridge CB2 1UR, UK.

Polity Press
350 Main Street
Malden
MA 02148
USA

ISBN: 978-0-7456-2992-6
ISBN: 978-0-7456-2993-3 (paperback)

A catalogue record for this book is available from the British Library

Typeset in 10.5 on 12 pt Times
by SNP Best-set Typesetter Ltd., Hong Kong
Printed and bound in the United States of America by LSC Communications

For further information on Polity, visit our website: www.polity.co.uk

Contents

Preface

My last book was called *Culture and Equality*. Its (more informative) subtitle was *An Egalitarian Critique of Multiculturalism*.[1] As several reviewers noted, while the book delivered the promised critique, the egalitarian premises from which my criticisms were derived – equal opportunity, equal treatment and so on – were never systematically set out or explained. This was not an oversight on my part. Because 'multiculturalism' is an umbrella under which a number of different notions dwell – sometimes making messy bedfellows – I had to write a long book to separate out the ideas and to show how they worked in a variety of contexts such as religion and education. The underlying principles from which I criticized the implications of multiculturalism were expounded throughout the book on a 'need to know' basis, though I may add that I laboured mightily over the index so as to make it possible to assemble the theoretical framework by following through the entries under the main headings.

In fact, I originally envisaged a book in two parts; the first ('Culture') being critical and the second ('Equality') containing my own positive views. It soon became apparent, however, that this project, while in principle admirable, would not allow space for a discussion of multiculturalism that could hope to be convincingly thorough. This, then, is the second part of that projected book. It stands by itself, consisting of the ideas about social justice that I have developed over the years and their implications under contemporary conditions – for individual countries and also for the world as a whole. There will be nothing startling about the principles of social justice that I put forward: they are widely accepted by politicians, media pundits and the general public, at least nominally. Most of the book will be devoted to arguing that these ideas are being abused systematically to justify the massive inequalities that we can see all around us.

Thus, lip service is paid to the virtues of equal opportunity, but the usual incantation is 'equal opportunity to become unequal'. I shall show that this is incoherent, and that equal opportunity can be achieved only in a society that keeps the range of inequality within narrow bounds. Similarly, appeals to 'personal responsibility' are all the rage among political leaders, and inequalities are attributed to the different choices made by different people: those who do well have made choices that reflect their personal merits, while those who do badly have made choices that reflect their personal defects. I shall show that only a very small part of actually existing inequality can be explained in this way, and that choices are socially constrained in ways that are simply overlooked by those who play up the role of personal responsibility.

All this still leaves two questions that are bound to occur to anybody. The first is: if the diagnosis of what ails our societies is correct, what should actually be done to redress these injustices? I shall do my best to rise to this challenge by proposing some reforms that would, if adopted, bring the attainment of social justice much closer. The second question is: what reason is there for supposing that history is on the side of social justice? Inequality has got worse in the last twenty-five years, and the ideology justifying it has become more pervasive. Why should we expect the future to be any more favourable for social justice? I do not claim the gift of prophecy. However, one thing can be asserted with certainty: the continuation of the status quo is an ecological impossibility. The uncertainty lies in the consequences of this fact. It is quite on the cards that the response will be the further entrenchment of plutocracy within countries and an ever more naked attempt by the United States, aided and abetted by a 'coalition of the willing', to displace the costs onto poorer countries. Whether it succeeds or fails, any such attempt will be catastrophic. But I shall argue that there are some grounds for hope, which include growing discontent in rich countries with politics as usual. If discontent exhausts itself in protests, though, it will be ineffective. A theory of social justice can provide a systematic critique and a programme that follows from it. That is why social justice matters.

Before drawing these introductory remarks to a close, I feel that it is incumbent on me to say a little for the benefit of those who have followed my earlier work. I have not, either in *Culture and Equality* or in this book, called upon the apparatus for deriving principles of justice that I developed in *Justice as Impartiality*.[2] The reason for this is the same in both cases: doing so would have frustrated the purpose of both books, in which I have been concerned to argue for concrete conclusions in an accessible way. This does not mean that I have given up on the belief that the apparatus developed in *Justice as Impartiality* offers the best account of the grounds for adhering to principles of justice. It is simply that, if I am to arrive at my destination, I cannot afford to begin that far back. However, I do not think that any very elaborate chain of argument is called for to show that the principles appealed to in this book satisfy the 'reasonable rejectability' test put forward in *Justice as Impartiality*.

For a number of years now, I have been fending off kind enquiries about the likely publication date of the promised third volume of my *Treatise on Social Justice* (provisionally entitled *Principles of Justice*) by saying: when it is written. I think that now is a good time to say that it will never be written. If I had completed it, the third volume would have begun at the beginning, related the principles to the framework developed in *Justice as Impartiality* and refined them further. I would also have had the luxury of doing something that I have rigorously eschewed here, which is to analyse the relation between my interpretation of the principles of justice and those put forward by political philosophers working along parallel lines. But I would still come out in the same place, and the thought of getting there again with more philosophical trimmings is one that does not in the least appeal to me.

As I explained in the Preface of *Culture and Equality*, I suspended my work on the Treatise some way into the third volume because I became convinced that anything I could do as a political philosopher to discredit multiculturalism would be worth doing, given the failure of anybody else to produce a systematic refutation. This judgement has subsequently been borne out by a string of further illustrations of the toxic consequences of multiculturalism in exacerbating divisions within societies and reinforcing the traditional repression of women, children and nonconformists among immigrant minorities and indigenous peoples.[3] I did not follow that book with this one simply to fulfil the rest of the original plan, but because I again felt that nobody else had written the kind of book that was needed. I doubt if it will do anything for my standing among professional political philosophers, but it is not intended for them. To the best of my ability, I have aimed to reinforce the convictions of those who think things are bad and getting worse and to provide them with intellectual ammunition that will be of use in the fight for a better future.

I acknowledge with thanks comments from participants in seminars and lectures at Kansas University, Harvard University, MIT,

Nuffield College, Oxford and Berkeley. On the last occasion, Sam Scheffler's introduction to the discussion was especially probing and illuminating, explaining to me more clearly some things I had been trying to say. At the University of Wisconsin, I was fortunate, in addition to feedback from a public lecture, to spend a long afternoon with several faculty members who had read the entire draft, as it existed at that point, and came up with a wide-ranging set of penetrating questions. I should like especially, at the risk of being invidious, to thank Harry Brighouse, Dan Hausman and Erik Olin Wright. Towards the end of the process of writing the book, I had an opportunity to try out a condensed version of chapters 18 and 19 at a conference on global justice held in Pasadena, California, under the auspices of the Pacific Division of the American Philosophical Association, and am grateful for comments received there.

Columbia University provided me with several opportunities to try out my ideas on colleagues in seminars and also the good luck of being able to present the whole book to what happened to be the liveliest and brightest collection of graduate students it has been my pleasure to teach (and, equally, learn from) in a by now rather long time in the business. Not least of the contributions was made by my friend and co-teacher Jon Elster, whose complaint that normative political philosophy is too difficult for him echoes Nils Bohr's reaction to a few weeks of reading up on economics. Nevertheless, political philosophy with the breadth of applications to be found in this book is not so much difficult as impossible, because nobody can ever know enough to do it properly. This is why a cosmopolitan seminar and colleagues willing to have their brains picked are such advantages.

I also wish to acknowledge my indebtedness to Columbia University for granting me an extended period of sabbatical leave that enabled me to complete other projects and draft most of this book. During this period, I was able to take advantage of the leisure also enjoyed by David Heyd, Lukas Meyer and Jouni Reinikanen to round them up into a weekly seminar at which we discussed one another's work in progress. In the academic year 2002–3, I also gained from the presence of Leslie Green as a visiting scholar.

Having gone on to half time at Columbia, I spent the autumn of 2003 in London. Alas! So far from being a foretaste of retirement, the time was filled – and overfilled – by working on the penultimate draft of this book. I am deeply grateful to Helen Margetts, Director of the School of Public Policy, and Jo Wolff, Head of the Department of Philosophy, both of University College London, for generously co-sponsoring a set of lectures and seminars. This meant, among other things, that I was very fortunate in being able to present fairly advanced drafts of most of the chapters to a philosophy seminar. This gave me valuable feedback at a critical stage, especially from Jo Wolff, Michael Otsuka, Veronique Muñoz-Dardé, Brian Feltham and Alex Voorhoeve, who also found me some pertinent up-to-the-minute materials.

Included in the UCL package was an office in the School of Public Policy. This was used by Anni to turn a couple of new chapters and innumerable rewrites, many of them fundamental, into a typescript that was not only better written than the original but also took account of her (almost invariably well-founded) queries. Both of us are indebted to everyone at the School of Public Policy for their great helpfulness. Anni wants to particularly thank Aaron Crompton for invaluable computer assistance and Helen Daines, Scott Greer and Alan Trench of the Constitution Unit for helping to keep her spirits up.

I must also thank everyone at Polity Press, especially David Held and Louise Knight, for their support and understanding – and also for securing as readers of the first draft Harry Brighouse and Philip Kitcher, whose comments were enormously valuable. I should also like to thank Philip Kitcher for guiding me to the literature underlying chapter 9 and kindly agreeing to read a subsequent reworking of it. At my special request, Polity commissioned Howard Glennerster to comment on the second draft of the book, and he saved me from a number of errors within the (vast) area of his expertise. Keith Dowding and Matt Matravers also commented on this draft with their customary acuity, while Cheryl Schonhardt-Bailey provided me with some thought-provoking reactions to Part IV. David Miller pointed out that a claim I made was not quite right as it stood, and I hope I have clarified it now.

In the final stages, Reshma Varma helped keep the book on schedule by getting the first three chapters ready to send off, and Tim Waligore deployed his formidable fact-checking skills on the American material in Part II. He has also played an invaluable role in sorting out numerous computer glitches, sometimes literally dashing to the rescue. The final draft went directly into production, but saying that glosses over the painfulness for all concerned of the parturition of this book. Only a copy-editor as experienced and (justifiably) self-confident as Sarah Dancy could have coped. Grace under pressure is not, I am afraid, a virtue with which I am endowed, and I can only express my admiration for her ability to supply enough for two.

Those who have persevered through my previous books (or at least their prefaces) will not be surprised by my acknowledging the role played in writing this one by Gertie. Cats have been shown to lower blood pressure, and I am sure that she succeeded in doing this every time – and there were a lot of them – that I felt I had bitten off more than I could chew. Perhaps I had, but at least I finished the book, with Gertie keeping me company almost to the last iteration of the optimistically titled 'final draft'. However, she died at the age of 18 just before that, and this showed that I had if anything under-estimated the difference she had made.

Finally, what can I possibly say about Anni's role in this book? To say that it could and would not have been written without her is the literal truth, but falls far short of conveying the innumerable ways in which she has fought off distractions during its writing and rewriting at the cost of time and also peace of mind. Although I have toiled over the shaping of this book harder than ever before, I still feel that it was a one-sided collaboration and that whatever credit is due for the labour that has gone into it is owed more to her than to me. But I do not simply mean that without Anni the book would not have been finished. I mean that, without the assurance of her support and help, it would never even have been begun. I understand very well why most academics have given up writing books long before my age, and I could so easily have joined their number.

Fred Hesketh, the dedicatee of this book, who was my father-in-law, had an extraordinary ability to make a friend of everyone he met, quickly finding common ground with them whatever their position in society. He was never patronizing and never allowed himself to be patronized, treating all alike as equals. By behaving as if we already lived in a socially just society, he did as much as one man can to foster one. Nobody who knew him well failed to love him and to admire his shrewd good judgement and, above all, his unassuming but granite-like integrity. We all miss him very much.

Part I

Social Justice: The Basics

There exists today widespread propaganda which asserts that socialism is dead. But if to be a socialist is to be a person convinced that the words 'the common good' and 'social justice' actually mean something; if to be a socialist is to be outraged at the contempt in which millions and millions of people are held by those in power, by 'market forces', by international financial institutions; if to be a socialist is to be a person determined to do everything in his or her power to alleviate these unforgivably degraded lives, then socialism can never be dead because those aspirations never die.

Harold Pinter

Part I

Society, Space and Time

1

Why We Need a Theory

In 'Why I Write', George Orwell claimed that all writers were motivated by some mixture of four motives. The first was 'sheer egoism', which must to some degree be present if (as Orwell assumed) a 'writer' is someone who is not content to write but wants to publish. The second was 'aesthetic enthusiasm', which Orwell took to be some concern for the form (or perhaps even just the appearance) of one's work. The third was 'historical impulse' or, more broadly, 'the desire to see things as they are'. The last was 'political purpose – using the word "political" in the widest possible sense. Desire to push the world in a certain direction, to alter other people's idea of the kind of society they should strive after.'[1] Whether or not Orwell was correct in claiming that all these motives are present all the time in every writer, he would be right about the author of this book. I do want to get things straight and express myself effectively, as well as indulging in whatever egoism is called for to overcome the tendency to inertia that besets all writers. But I was also definitely led to write this book by the 'political' motive, as Orwell defined it.

But why produce a theory of social justice? In the poorest countries, people do not need a theory to tell them that there is something wrong with a world in which their children are dying from malnutrition or diseases that could be prevented by relatively inexpensive public health measures. Even in the richest country in the world, just north of the academic enclave in New York centred on Columbia University, lies Harlem, where it has been estimated that a black male born and brought up in some areas has less chance of reaching the age of 65 than a child born and brought up in rural Bangladesh. Some Americans (perhaps even a majority) purport to believe that this is not in some way a reflection on the way in which their society is organized, but only on the moral (and maybe also genetic) degeneracy of the denizens of the ghetto. I doubt if many people elsewhere would fail to draw the conclusion that all is not as it should be with American institutions. But is it that inequality is wrong or only that poverty is bad? Political philosophers and ordinary people disagree about that. They also disagree about what obligations, if any, the rich have towards the poor (either domestically or internationally), at any rate as long as the rich did not come by their wealth by manifestly illegitimate means such as theft or extortion. To answer questions like these we need a theory – a theory of social justice.

Even more importantly, of course, we need the right theory of social justice if we are to get the right answers. Having the wrong theory may bring about worse results, if it is acted on, than a simple feeling of goodwill towards the human race. For an ill-conceived theory may well have the pernicious effect of thwarting the natural impulse to feel that something ought to be done to save children in a rich society from homelessness and malnutrition, and in the world as a whole to relieve the absolute destitution that is the lot of at least a billion people. I believe that the theory of justice that I put forward in this book has universal validity, and I shall say something about its scope in chapter 3. But I shall lay out the theory primarily in relation to the most straightforward case of justice within a society.

Until about a century and a half ago, justice was standardly understood as a virtue not of societies but of individuals. The much quoted Latin tag to the effect that justice is 'the constant and perpetual will to give each his due' clearly presupposed that everybody had a 'due'. Justice consisted in not cheating, stealing or breaking contracts, within an established framework of property rights which might (as in the Roman case) include property in other human beings. Justice could, it was thought, also be ascribed to institutions, but only on a very limited scale. A verdict in a trial could be described as just or unjust, and the long-standing notion of retributive justice reflects persistent concerns about the appropriateness of the punishment to the crime. There was also the notion of 'natural justice' in a trial, which called for certain safeguards such as an impartial judge and the defendant's having the opportunity to hear the evidence and call witnesses in his defence. Perhaps the closest approach to the contemporary concept of social justice was the medieval notion of the 'just price', since this probed into the justice of a bargain that was not contaminated by force or fraud but entered into voluntarily by both parties. However, its scope was relatively narrow: its main concern was to condemn exploitation by sellers who took advantage of temporary scarcity or particular need. But such invocations of justice operate only at the margins of a system taken as given.[2]

The modern concept of social justice emerged out of the throes of early industrialization in France and Britain in the 1840s. The potentially revolutionary idea underlying the concept of social justice was that the justice of a society's institutions could be challenged not merely at the margins but at the core. What this meant in practice was that a challenge could be mounted to the power of the owners of capital, and to the dominance of the entire market system within which capitalism was embedded. The justice of the unequal relations between employers and employees could be called into question, as could the distribution of income and wealth arising from the operation of capitalist institutions and the part played in people's lives by money.

Social justice became the rallying cry of social democratic parties everywhere in Europe, but argument raged over the institutions that were required to realize social justice. These arguments took their most sophisticated form in Germany and Sweden, though it was in Sweden that the most fruitful developments occurred, because the task of creating a programme was seen by social democrats as collaborative rather than confrontational. Although no generalization can cover every case, it is broadly correct to say that in the period following the Second World War social democratic parties had converged on a handful of key ideas:

1 The power of capital must be curbed by strong trade unions (perhaps also worker representation) and by regulation to ensure that people come before profit. As far as public ownership was concerned, non-socialist parties had already, from the nineteenth century on, put public utilities and public transport under municipal ownership or control in most countries, but its extension beyond this was not essential to social democracy. (It is significant that the Swedish social democrats, who were the best exemplars, did not have public ownership as part of their core programme.)

2 The distribution of income and wealth created by capitalism was unacceptably unequal, and should be changed by appropriate measures of taxation and transfer. In particular, the market mechanism failed to provide support for those unable to earn enough to live on at a level consistent with social justice. Institutions (the 'welfare state') must therefore be created to provide adequate incomes.

3 Education and health services of uniformly high quality should be provided universally in such a way as to be equally available to

all, thus eliminating the market criterion of 'ability to pay'. Although housing was not treated in the same way across the board, it was universally recognized as too important to be left to market forces, though intervention might take different forms.

My object in this book is to elaborate a conception of social justice of a kind that will support the case for institutions of the kind that I have just outlined. I shall seek to show that the reasons that have been given for abandoning this analysis are flawed. Conditions have not changed in ways that make the social democratic prescriptions inappropriate: in some ways they have in fact changed so that social democratic institutions are more necessary than ever.

Although my lightning sketch of the development of social democracy has focused on Europe, many of the same ideas underlay Franklin Delano Roosevelt's 'New Deal', Harry Truman's 'Fair Deal' and Lyndon Johnson's 'Great Society', and their rationale was expressed in terms of justice. As is known, Roosevelt's inner circle of advisers felt that to describe their programme as 'social democratic' would be imprudent, and they therefore appropriated the word 'liberal' for it. This, however, makes no difference for my purposes, and it is a toss-up whether or not ambitious politicians in the United States are more keen to avoid being described as liberals than ambitious politicians in Europe are to avoid being described as socialists. In Britain, New Labour has quite explicitly repudiated the social democratic agenda that I have laid out. Indeed, a friend and ex-colleague who was recruited as a member of Tony Blair's team of special advisers told me that you could canvass any policy you liked, just as long as there was no possibility of its being branded as 'Old Labour' thinking.

I suggest that the most instructive way of tracing the peculiar evolution of the conception of social justice within the political elite of the Labour Party is to examine the work of the Commission on Social Justice that was set up by Tony Blair's predecessor as leader, John Smith, during his brief tenure in the position. When it reported, the Commission apparently felt obliged to retain the title *Social Justice*, but its real agenda was conveyed in its subtitle: *Strategies for National Renewal*.[3] One of the things that was going to have to be sacrificed in the cause of 'national renewal', as the Report repeatedly emphasized, was the pursuit of social justice understood in any way that retained a connection with the social democratic tradition.

The concept of social justice was disposed of peremptorily under four headings in a single paragraph.[4] The first two elements predated the modern conception of social justice. The first consisted of basic civil and political liberties and the second was the idea that 'basic needs' should be met – a claim recognized as far back as the Elizabethan Poor Law. The third element at first sight looks rather more promising in establishing some connection with the social democratic agenda: 'opportunities and life-chances'. But social justice is, and is normally understood to be, a question of *equal* opportunities. Significantly, however, that word does not appear. In relation to this book, the omission is important because I shall be arguing that, if the notion of equal opportunity is taken seriously, it generates implications inconsistent with just about everything in the Report. To say that you are in favour of *some* opportunities is not to say much, and we can see just how little it meant to the Commission by noticing that the Report did not even mention as a problem for social justice the competitive advantages conferred on children who attend expensive private schools.

As its final contribution to the definition of social justice, the Commission offered the proposition that 'unjust inequalities should be reduced and as far as possible be eliminated'.[5] Well, it would be hard to disagree with that – indeed logically impossible, on the assumption that injustice is a bad thing. The question is, of course, what makes an inequality unjust? Since the Report does not go on to say anything about this, we have to deduce what it thought from its recommendations about the taxation of income and wealth. The most remarkable thing here is that the Report does not even provide any information about the distribution of wealth, thus pre-empting the notion that its distribution of wealth largely defines the justice of a society. (See chapter 14 for a discussion of the crucial importance of the distribution of wealth and of possible ways in which it can be made more equal.) The Commission did concern itself with death duties, but seemed primarily concerned about the bad luck of having your parents die within seven years of giving away their money. Thus, it argued, the system created inequity *among* the very rich: 'a state-created gamble in which the state stands to gain at the expense of the less fortunate heirs'.[6] It had no suggestions for closing loopholes or raising rates.

As far as incomes are concerned, the Report gives a table showing their unequal distribution.[7] And it points out that 'the [income] gap between the richest earnings of the highest-paid and those of the lowest-paid workers is greater than at any time since records were first kept in 1886'.[8] But instead of concluding that the amount of tax collected from those making, say, £10 million a year should be vastly increased, its main concern turns out to be that old-fashioned adherents of social justice might want the rich to pay much more than the top rate of 40 per cent established by Margaret Thatcher (and retained by two New Labour governments). Thus, significantly, it buys uncritically into what – when left and right could be distinguished – was the typical cant of editorials in right-wing newspapers. So, to say that 'no one should pay punitive levels of taxation' is literal non-sense.[9] Even if the marginal tax rate on high incomes were 99 per cent, it would still be true that the more pre-tax income people have the more they would have after paying their tax. This is a kind of 'punishment' we would all enjoy being subjected to!

If the top marginal rate is high, the very rich will be less well off after paying taxes than they would have been if it had been lower. But the same could obviously be said of any tax rate – and was being said in the USA by Republicans even after the May 2003 tax cuts (of which more below).[10] Clearly, then, the truism that high tax rates are higher than low ones does not tell us what the top rate should be, and certainly does not justify the assertion that 'there can be no question of returning to the top rates of the 1970s'.[11] High marginal tax rates introduced during the Second World War were maintained after it by both the Labour and the Conservative governments that shared the period until Mrs Thatcher came to power in 1979. Furthermore, because tax brackets did not keep pace with inflation, the amount paid by the seriously rich actually increased after the war (see below). A policy endorsed by both parties for more than thirty-five years could scarcely be as outlandish as the Commission manages to imply.

Of course, if there is no question of returning to the high marginal tax rates of the pre-Thatcher era, there is presumably no need to explain why. It is curious, though, that the Report claims (only a page earlier) that 'taxes are not fairly shared', citing as evidence the fact that 'of the £31 billion which went in income tax cuts during the 1980s, £15 billion went to the richest 10 per cent of the population'.[12] But this was the inevitable consequence of cutting the top rate of tax to 40 per cent, so the disparity could be reversed only by going back to the earlier rates that are now said to be 'out of the question'. Although the Commission purports to find something objectionable in the growth of inequality in its initial analysis, its main message – constantly reiterated in a variety of (invariably tendentious) formulations – is that social justice does not, as some unregenerate Labour supporters might still think, have anything to do with taking away money from the rich and giving it to the poor so as to reduce the gap between them.[13]

Perhaps the most remarkable expression of the Commission's concern for the welfare of the rich is its axiom that, whatever the marginal tax rates may be, nobody should pay more than half of his or her total income in tax.[14] The Commission presents this 50 per cent rate as the absolute maximum that could be tolerated.[15] To put it into context, it is worth asking how much those earning ten times the average (which would have come to almost a quarter of a million pounds in 2004) would have paid in direct taxes – income tax plus national insurance contributions – in earlier years. The proportion of total income paid by such a person would have risen from 47 per cent in the 1950s to 70 per cent during the 1970s, fallen in Mrs Thatcher's first ten years to a bit over 50 per cent and then in the 1990s come down to the 38 per cent at which it remains after two terms of Labour. 'Fat cats have never enjoyed so much fiscal cream; even with the 50% tax rate [proposed by the Liberal Democrats] in place, someone with an annual income of almost £250,000 would still pay less than 45% of their total income in direct taxation – a lower rate than at any point between 1950 and 1987.'[16] Indeed, because somebody making £10 million a year could never pay more than £5 million in income tax, it is obvious that the implication of the Commission's proposal is that the very rich can never face an effective marginal tax rate above 50 per cent, even if the notional tax rate goes right up to 99 per cent.

The members of the Commission were not idiots – a couple of them were extremely intelligent, in fact – so how could they have reached the unanimous conclusion that social justice would be violated if those making £10 million were left with less than £5 million after paying their income tax? The only explanation that comes to mind is that, somehow, 'one for you, one for me' appears superficially equitable in contrast to the 'one for you, nineteen for me' that the Beatles sang about in a very different era. But if we take seriously the idea that social justice is about (among other things) what incomes people enjoy after taxes and transfers, the Commission's way of looking at it is simply frivolous.

Unfortunately for the Commission, it suffered from the same 'unseemly lottery with life' that attracted its sympathy for heirs who lost money as a result of the seven-year rule. By the time the Report was published, its sponsor was dead and his place had been taken by Tony Blair, who consigned it to the rubbish bin and created his own 'working parties' with members who were hand-picked to produce proposals that left the spirit of social democracy even further behind than those that had been made in the Report. I have exhumed it here simply because it constitutes the last sustained discussion of social justice sponsored by the Labour Party. It thus gives us some idea of the scale of the task ahead if social justice is to be restored as the guiding star of the party that we must (however wryly) call the party of the left. What we have instead are what the Commission called 'strategies for national renewal' or, in the New Labour lexicon, policies justified on the ground that they constitute 'modernization'. An invaluable guide with a glossary intended 'to help you talk bollocks and get ahead in Blair's Britain' explains: '*Modernization* should be used as if it is value-free, an objective process which cannot be resisted, especially if it is something highly contentious like taking away benefits.'[17]

The absence of an explicit conception of social justice in political life has the result that arguments about public policy are made without any attempt to explain from the ground up what is their justification. Instead, such arguments as are offered rest on tacit assumptions that would not withstand scrutiny if they were spelt out formally. Let me give two examples, one from Britain and one from the United States. The British one involves the place of universal cash benefits, that is to say benefits paid to anybody who falls into a certain category (e.g. having children, being over a certain age, being unemployed, being disabled, and so on), without regard to their incomes or assets. The extension of universal cash benefits is essential to social justice, as I shall seek to show in this book. Not surprisingly, therefore, they arouse the ire of New Labour. Why, it is asked, should money be paid to people who do not 'need' it? Instead of 'wasting' this money, it is said, it should go to the very poor (or kept by the very rich, if the very poor are considered well enough off already). At the least, the value of universal benefits for those who do not 'need' them should be reduced by lumping them in with other income and taxing them, so that the treasury claws a part back. This kind of thinking precisely reflects the archaic notion of the Commission on Social Justice that the obligations of the state extend only to meeting 'basic needs' – the thinking that informed the Poor Law and that the post-war 'welfare state' was supposed to have overcome.[18]

Social justice is about the treatment of inequalities of all kinds. Thus, the point of a disability allowance is to compensate for the financial disadvantage of disability. At any income level, therefore, a disability allowance will even out the position (economically at least) of those with and those without a disability. The relevant 'need' is for financial assistance to make up for the disability. If we think that the rich are too well off anyway, the answer is to tax them more highly – not to create an inequity between the disabled at any given level of income and others at the same level of income who are not disabled. Similarly, universal child benefit is not aimed at relieving poverty, though at an adequate level it does have the effect of lifting some families out of poverty. It is a way of recognizing that those who are rearing the next generation of citizens are performing an expensive task and that the cost should be shared by all citizens who can afford to contribute. There is therefore no case for linking it to parents below some income or for taxing it, since there is no case to be made for this allowance to be worth less to parents who are well off. Parallel points can be made about old age pensions and unemployment benefits, but I shall leave them until later.

My second example concerns the American tax cuts already mentioned, which lowered the capital gains tax, eliminated all taxes on dividends, and provided for the phased-in abolition of all death duties, at a time when inequality of wealth had increased faster than at any time since the 1920s. It also lowered income tax rates, but in such a lopsided way that a study found that 58 per cent of the benefits accrued to those making more than $100,000 a year (8.6 per cent of all taxpayers).[19] The defence of the tax cuts put out by the Republican National Committee on its website was that 'everybody who pays taxes [benefits] – especially middle-income Americans'.[20] If 'middle-income' means (as it should) those halfway down the income distribution (those at the median), it could hardly be further from the truth. For all taxpayers making $30,000 a year or less shared just 5 per cent of the total benefit between them, and over half of all households have incomes of $30,000 a year or less.[21] Moreover, it was not correct to claim that all taxpayers gained – even a pittance. Eight million taxpaying households gained nothing. In addition, needless to say, those too poor to pay direct taxes gained nothing from tax cuts, so that altogether there were '50 million households – 36% of all households in the nation – who [received] no benefit'.[22]

But even if everybody had benefited from tax cuts (even non-taxpayers by providing them with 'tax credits'), would this have told us anything about their contribution to social justice? Not a thing. We should first ask if taxes ought to be cut at all, or if they should actually be increased. Are there pressing demands for more public expenditure that should have priority? The architects of the tax cuts knew perfectly well what they were about. Like the Reagan tax cuts, these (and bigger ones still if the Republicans can get away with it) are deliberately designed to forestall such demands by ensuring that the tax base to fund them will have been abolished. The chairman of the Senate budget committee spelt it out: 'Members are talking about paying for prescription drugs [on Medicare] and expanding unemployment benefits. . . . But that's going to change because there will be less revenue available.'[23] (Although a lot of the tax cuts' boosters are born-again Christians from the South, their idea seems to be to take all they have and give it to the rich.) We must also, of course, look at the existing distribution of public expenditures, comparing the amount spent on the military, on agricultural subsidies and on prisons with the amount going on education, housing, medical care and income support.

If we leave all that on one side and simply ask about the fairness of the shape taken by the tax cuts – accepting their cost of $350 billion as fixed – we still cannot do that in a vacuum. We have to have some independently derived idea of what a just distribution of post-tax income would look like before we can ask whether any particular pattern of cuts contributed to the pursuit of social justice or detracted from it.

One apologist for the shape of the Bush tax cuts wrote in a letter to the *Wall Street Journal* that 'the top 1% of income earners constitute 20.8% of the total income earned and pay 37.7% of federal income taxes', so it was only reasonable that 'the richest 1% of tax-payers will get 29% of the benefits of the tax cut [excluding their gains from the abolition of death duties]. . . . Since the liberals' favourite mantra – fairness – is always lurking in the political wings, it's critical that responsible publications such as the [Wall Street] Journal do their best to dispel the myth that higher-income earners aren't already paying more than their fair share of income taxes, as a percent of their total income.'[24] Perhaps if the concept of fairness were at centre stage rather than 'lurking in the wings', it would be more clear that the correspondent's idea of fairness appears to be a tax system in which income taxes are paid on a basis strictly proportional to income. For why, otherwise, should it be assumed that the richest 1 per cent are paying more than their 'fair share', even after the tax cuts? An alternative way of looking at the position, for which I shall argue, is that there is something grotesquely wrong with a society in which 1 per cent of the population make off with more than a fifth of the entire national income, and that far *higher* marginal tax rates on very high incomes would be needed to approach some semblance of social justice.

The author of the letter concludes by contending that 'if the average American were made aware of these facts, the politics of economic envy and distortion, so shamefully peddled by the left, would be relegated to the wasteland where [etc.]'.[25] But what has to be emphasized is that the conclusions to be drawn from 'the facts' depend on one's theory of social justice. The author believes that, once made aware of them, the 'average American' would agree that the rich are paying more than their 'fair share'. But the same 'facts' can also support the opposite conclusion, that far tougher steps ought to be taken to address the monstrous inequality of incomes that (on the letter-writer's own 'facts') leaves the bottom half of the population sharing 13 per cent of the total income.[26] What the writer takes to be his trump card – that those in the bottom half of the income distribution pay only 3.9 per cent of federal income tax, so they can hardly be expected to benefit much from tax reductions – is, as far as social justice is concerned, insignificant.[27] It is the inequality of incomes that cries out as the key point. Perhaps the truth about the unequal distribution of wealth, with the top 1 per cent holding around 40 per cent of it, would have an equally galvanizing effect, especially since the benefits from the abolition of tax on dividends, the reduction in capital gains tax and the ending of death duties will accrue almost entirely to this tiny minority of extremely wealthy people.

No compilation of 'facts' can tell us about the fairness or unfairness of a tax system. For that we have to have a theory of social justice. As the eminent political economist John Roemer has put it: 'The major problem for the left today is a lack of theory. Where do we go from here? What kind of society do we wish to fight for? If we socialist intellectuals can provide some direction that will be of inestimable value for the transformation of society.'[28] Without claiming inestimable value for this book, it is certainly my intention to offer definite answers to the questions Roemer asks and provide a systematic rationale for them based on a theory of social justice.

2

The Machinery of Social Injustice

I take the expression 'the machinery of social injustice' from a Discussion Paper published for the Commission on Social Justice by David Donnison, one of Britain's most respected sociologists and public policy analysts. Funded independently from the rest of the project, its contents were comprehensively ignored by the Commission, since it actually bore on the Commission's titular subject, social justice.[1] What Donnison intended to convey was that 'the working parts of the injustice machine' are 'different patterns or dimensions of injustice, each of which has many causes'.[2] As a result of this interdependence among the causes of social injustice, he emphasized, 'none of [these patterns or dimensions of injustice] can be reversed if it is tackled in isolation from the others'.[3]

Since the Report cobbled together a package of unrelated recommendations, many of which could be traced directly to the hobbyhorses of various members of the Commission, it is scarcely surprising that Donnison's message was unwelcome to it. But Donnison's claim lies at the heart of everything that I have to say in this book. Anticipating evidence to be presented in later chapters, it can be said that morally arbitrary inequalities begin before conception, since the health and nutritional status of the mother at the time of conception is critical. In the womb, the future child is vulnerable to lack of essential nutrients (adequate folic acid can prevent most cases of spina bifida, for example), exposure of the mother to a toxic environment and her own use of tobacco, alcohol and drugs (whether prescribed – remember thalidomide – or not). The social structure is implicated in all of these events: as I shall explain, this is true of disadvantages arising from smoking, drinking and drug-taking as well as those imposed by the inability to afford nutritious food or to live in a non-toxic environment. For all these kinds of behaviour may well come about as responses to stress. And levels of stress increase as we go down the social hierarchy.

I need hardly follow the story through any further: the advantages of some new-borns and the disadvantages of others, which are likely to follow them through life, are only too obvious. Those who have seen Michael Apted's films, following a cohort of British children from the age of 7, can hardly fail to have been struck by the way in which their future courses were already foreshadowed at this young age. Of course, no prediction can be perfect: people may suffer from mental or physical illnesses or catastrophes in their personal lives that derail their careers, but from '7-Up' to '42-Up' there have not been many surprises. A similarly detailed study, this time of twelve American families, gives us a fascinating insight into the multifarious ways in which advantage and disadvantage are perpetuated over generations. The bottom line, however, is that 'parents' social class position predicts children's school success and thus their ultimate life chances'.[4] I shall trace the processes by which the transmission of class position occurs in chapter 5 and I shall show there that people's chances of falling or rising from their location at birth in the social order have declined in the last twenty years to such a degree that some sociologists have begun to talk about 'social closure'.

These deleterious changes within countries have been paralleled by the way in which the divergence between the life-chances of children conceived in different countries has increased even further in the past thirty years. Many of the losses inflicted on the poorest people are the results of deliberate policies adopted by rich countries and the international institutions that they control. Thus, when Indonesia was hit by an economic collapse, 'there were billions of dollars to bail out foreign creditors, but paying out far smaller sums to provide fuel and food subsidies for those thrown out of a job or who saw their wages plummeting was viewed as a waste of money'.[5] This is an inversion of justice. The foreign investors – 'Western banks [that] benefit from such bail-outs' and other creditors – chose to put their money into Indonesia and had no legitimate claim to be rescued by the IMF from speculative losses. (The IMF has no system for taxing speculative gains.) The situation of the workers was entirely different: their desperate condition was in no way a consequence of choices that they could have made differently. According to the theory of responsibility to be developed in this book, the creditors had no case for compensation, whereas the workers had an overwhelming one.

As I explained in the Preface, I shall focus in this book primarily on social injustice within countries, but in the next chapter I shall show the universal application of the ideas developed here by saying something about international injustice. At the end of the book, when I discuss the prospects of social justice, I shall again have to widen the scope, since the resolution (or non-resolution) of a number of global crises will have a profound effect on affairs within each country. It will therefore be essential to address these forces for change, as well as those generated internally by the self-destructive nature of capitalism. Taking the long view, the period 1945–75 was just a reprieve and the sands of time have been running out ever since. If this sounds absurdly alarmist, let me point out that it is in the pages of the *New York Times* – not the *Socialist Worker* – that one finds articles with titles such as 'Could Capitalists Actually Bring Down Capitalism?' and others containing quotations such as this one from the famous financier Felix G. Rohatyn:

> Only capitalists can destroy capitalism. . . . When you have senior people walking away with millions, leaving everyone else in the dirt, that is hugely depressing and very dangerous. . . . Does the system work to spread the wealth in some way that's reasonably fair? . . . Clearly at this point the answer is no, and that's not tolerable.[6]

For the purpose of this chapter, then, I shall leave on one side the global reach of justice and focus on justice within a single country. If we ask what is the subject of social justice, we shall find an influential answer in the work of John Rawls, who defined it in *A Theory of Justice* as 'the basic structure of society'.[7] This 'basic structure' can be understood as being constituted by the major institutions that allocate (or bring about an allocation of) rights, opportunities and resources. Thus, we can ask how the political system allocates the right to vote and what opportunities it provides for firms or wealthy individuals to finance political campaigns. We can ask if there are different grades of citizen with different legal rights. We can ask what rights people have to criticize the government, practise their religion freely, and so on. How far are employers constrained by legal obligations concerning hours, working conditions or dismissals? Are there laws against monopolies and cartels? Does the law make it easy or difficult to form trade unions and what rights do they have (e.g. the right to strike)? How are taxes raised and what is the basis on which cash benefits are paid? What are the systems (public and private) through which health care, education and housing are provided? The answers to these and many other questions along the same lines will tell us a lot about the mechanisms that generate the differences between different countries in the ways in which rights, opportunities and resources are distributed.

There is much to be said for putting the basic structure at the centre of the picture. It has the advantage of keeping us in contact with reality – a virtue not as common as one might hope for among political philosophers. The reality that underlies the relevance of the basic structure for social justice is one to which I have already alluded. The rank of somebody in the pecking order at the age of 25 will be a good predictor of their position within the social hierarchy at the age of 50. Moreover, there is a strong tendency for positions in the hierarchy to be inherited: we can predict that the child of professional parents is likely to occupy a higher position as an adult than the child of school drop-outs. How far either of these facts can be taken as symptoms of social injustice remains to be discussed. But their existence emphasizes the importance of the basic structure. The justifiability of inequalities would surely be of less pressing importance if somebody's position in the social hierarchy at a certain time bore no relation to their likely position ten years later. Similarly, it would matter less if knowing the position of the parents gave us no ability whatever to predict where in the hierarchy their children would finish up.

Institutions that play a role in providing people with different life-chances will be the main focus of this book. But this is not to say, as Rawls does, that they are the *subject* of justice. Institutions are obviously key to the realization of social justice. They also have the crucial feature that they can (to varying degrees) be changed simply by passing a law. Of course, there may be great political difficulties in changing the law so that the resulting institutions will implement social justice. But this does not affect the case for focusing on the institutions demanded by social justice. Nevertheless, institutions are not an end in themselves: they are a means to getting things done. If we want to ask how far a society's institutions work together to produce social justice, we shall have to look at the distribution of individual rights, opportunities and resources these institutions bring about. In other words, we have to work back to the justice of institutions from their contribution to just *outcomes*, which are assessed by their contribution to a just distribution of rights, opportunities and resources.

Once we see that the primary subject of justice is not institutions themselves but the distribution of rights, opportunities and resources that exists in a society, we can recognize that institutions often have a rectificatory function. For example, a racially homogeneous society would not need measures against racial discrimination, nor would a racially mixed society in which race discrimination did not occur. Thus, we cannot say whether or not justice requires a society to have anti-discrimination laws (together with enforcement mechanisms, permanent commissions to monitor and advise on policy, and so on) unless we know what would happen in their absence. Furthermore, acts of injustice can be perpetrated by individuals (as sellers of houses, providers of services, and so on) or corporate entities such as firms, hotels, housing agencies or clubs. But the aggregate effect of individual acts of injustice is very unlikely to be random. Normally, the individual acts will form part of a pattern that creates a systematically unjust distribution of rights, opportunities and resources. To offset this unjust allocation arising from individual decisions, the society's institutions will need to be changed.

Individual just acts, in contrast, will normally operate in such a way as to make the overall allocation of rights, opportunities and resources more just. For example, a firm that provides disadvantaged minority employees with extra training opportunities, even when these are not legally mandated, will be reinforcing the beneficial effects of anti-discrimination measures. It is true (as I shall emphasize later in this chapter) that the pursuit of profit has an inevitable tendency to induce a 'race to the bottom' among firms; but it is also true that the money spent on grotesque financial rewards to directors and on-the-job perks such as lunches for a dozen top executives cooked by a full-time chef could be diverted to worthier causes while leaving profits just the same. Public policy should not be built on the assumption that directors will behave better than they are made to; but the conceptual point that I am making here remains valid: we can ascribe justice and injustice to actions by individuals as well as to institutions, in both cases judging them by their effects on the distribution of rights, opportunities and resources.

A just distribution of rights, opportunities and resources may be achievable by a variety of alternative instruments. We have concluded, let's say, that a just distribution of earnings must enable anybody working normal hours in a full-time job to make at least 60 per cent of the average income in the society. How might this come about? One way would be for a strong and unified trade union movement to negotiate with employers for wages satisfying this condition. (The 'solidaristic' wage policy pursued by the Swedish unions in the 1970s exemplified such an approach.) This would require legislation giving unions a strong bargaining position as well as a disposition by unions to use it so as to extract a high minimum wage. Supposing these conditions were met, it would not be necessary for the government to enact a minimum wage law. Under normal conditions, however, the desired end can be achieved only by making a high minimum wage mandatory.

Until now, I have been using the terms 'rights', 'opportunities' and 'resources' without defining them. This will do well enough for a general discussion. But these are the three key ideas around which this book is organized, so it will avoid difficulties later if I pause here to explain precisely how I intend them to be understood. Let me start, then, with rights. In order to distinguish them from opportunities, I intend for the purposes of this book to define rights narrowly. On this conception, to say that people have a right to do something is to say only that they are not prohibited from having it or doing it. A woman's right to appear in public dressed as she chooses and in the company of anybody she likes is simply the absence of any prohibition (of the kind quite common around the world) on doing such things. Again, the right to make a contract or a will is the absence of any prohibition on exercising a certain kind of legal power. It is important not to take such legal powers for granted. Traditional legal doctrine concerning marriage in England (as elsewhere) was summed up by the saying that 'in law, man and woman are one, and the man is the one'. Only in the second half of the nineteenth century did a married woman acquire the right to own property and sign contracts, and, as a consequence, have any money to leave in a will. The plots of many Georgian and early Victorian novels depend on the right of a man to run through his wife's inheritance by gambling, speculation or riotous living.

The problem that I face in this book is that the language of rights has become the lingua franca of the United Nations, and pretty much any demand will get framed by saying that people have a right to it. In the United States, too, we find a whole variety of logically distinct demands lumped together under the umbrella of 'rights'. This causes confusion. For example, when United Nations declarations assert that education is among the 'rights of the child', they mean to assert that it should be the responsibility of parents – and, ultimately, the state – to ensure that children actually get an education. But this employs a stronger sense of 'right' than that which I am using. It has the consequence that we are left with no language in which to make the separate point that children should not be *prohibited* from receiving a formal education. Yet exactly that right was formally denied to girls by the Taliban (who merely codified a practice that preceded them and has in fact succeeded them), while in the nineteenth century a number of states in the South made it a criminal offence to teach a slave to read or write.

I shall say that the right to education is constituted by its not being illegal. Of course, the right to education is of no practical use to a child if schools charge fees and its parents cannot afford them. But the lack of a right to education and the lack of an opportunity to be educated are still quite different matters. Again, the existence of a right to an abortion means only that, if a woman has one, neither she nor the person who performed it will be prosecuted. Manifestly, such a right is not worth anything in the absence of qualified people who are prepared to carry out abortions, and even then it is not worth much to poor people unless the public hospitals offer them without charge. But we are inviting confusion if we skip over the absence of a prohibition and equate a universal right to an abortion with the universal opportunity for any woman who wants one to have one.

Let me take a last example, with which I shall be able to introduce a discussion of the concept of opportunity. When Americans talk about the rights of disabled people – say, those who are wheelchair-bound – to have access to public places, they do not mean merely that there should be no law forbidding them access. They mean that it should be physically possible, thanks to ramps and elevators, for dis-abled people actually to get to offices, shops, educational institutions, places of public entertainment, and so on. I shall say that this is the demand not for a right but for an opportunity. To put it formally, then: an opportunity to do or obtain something exists for me if there is some course of action lying within my power such that it will lead, if I choose to take it, to my doing or obtaining the thing in question. We must not oversimplify the idea that something is an opportunity for me if getting it depends on my will. This can sometimes mean nothing more demanding than my stretching out my hand, as when I have the opportunity to take either an apple or an orange from a bowl. But taking advantage of an opportunity usually requires more than that.

If I am wheelchair-bound, it is obvious that I do not have the opportunity to attend a theatre that is not wheelchair-accessible. But even if the theatre is wheelchair-accessible, that means only that it will be physically possible for me to get to a place in the theatre once I arrive. I still have to get there. The background assumption in saying that the theatre's wheelchair-accessibility gives me the opportunity to attend performances there is that it is already within my power to set in train a series of events that will end up with my being in the theatre's lift, and from there to somewhere from which I can watch the show. To take a more challenging example, suppose that you have won a scholarship that pays for the fees at an expensive school for as many years as it takes to complete the course. Then we can say that you really do have the opportunity to graduate from it. But you might, of course, behave in a way before that which results in your being expelled. This need not alter our judgement that you had the opportunity at the start to complete the course. Provided we were right in thinking that it was within your power to do that, making full use of the opportunity was your responsibility: you still had the opportunity.

Since I shall have a lot more to say about opportunities in the course of the book, let me leave the discussion of them there for now and move on to resources. We ordinarily think of resources as consisting of things external to themselves that people own or to which they have access – things with the characteristic of enabling them to achieve their ends, or at least of improving their chances of doing so. Money is a generic resource, a car is a more specific resource, and so on. But when we describe people as 'resourceful', we commonly mean that they are ingenious in finding ways of realizing their ends *without* being able to call on large material resources. Thus, you may inherit some money from your parents. This is a resource. But another form of good fortune is to have parents who command a large vocabulary, plenty of books around the place, and a home environment that encourages curiosity, intellectual agility and the acquisition of educational qualifications. This kind of home environment constitutes an educational resource for a child, and so does a good school. Educational qualifications themselves are a resource, because they open up the possibility of getting jobs that would otherwise be unattainable. A good job is a resource because it makes available other resources – not only money but also benefits that flow from the social status associated with it.

Let me confess that the category of resources is a bit of a rag-bag. This heterogeneity would be a problem if I had any intention of aggregating different kinds of resource and talking about the justice or injustice of the distribution of this composite. But I shall not be doing this. Rights and opportunities are also of very different kinds, and it would obviously be crazy to ask about the distribution of all rights together or all opportunities together and ask how far they were justly distributed. Perhaps resources are liable to arouse different expectations because justice may require a shortfall in one resource to elicit a greater supply of some other. Thus, a deficit in health can (to a greater or smaller degree) be cancelled by the expenditure of resources on medical care. But we at no point need to suggest that we are trying to equalize some composite score made up of each person's initial state of health and the quantity of resources devoted to his or her medical care. Similarly, equal opportunity for education requires a child with learning difficulties to have access to more generous teaching resources than one who learns easily. But we again have no need to invent a unit whose components are learning ability and resources devoted to education.

Perhaps the notion that resources can be reduced to a common denominator arises from the idea that there is some generic stuff (called 'utility', 'advantage' or whatever) whose distribution is the subject of social justice. This idea has a long history but has in recent years been revived by an academic debate about 'the currency of egalitarian justice'. It was initiated by asking 'Equality of what?' The presupposition of this question is that we are in favour of equality of something and all we have to do is find out what it is whose distribution we want to be equal. This seems to me about as foolish as Tony Blair's announcing that he was in favour of 'the third way' and then inviting a bunch of academics and academic hangers-on to suggest what it might be. We have to discuss each right, each opportunity and each resource separately and ask what principles of social justice can tell us about it. There is no need for surprise that the hunt for 'the currency of egalitarian justice' was as unsuccessful as the hunt for the Holy Grail.[8] The problem in both cases is that there is no such thing.

The idea that the justice of a society can be assessed by its distribution of (some) rights is older and less controversial than the claim that the distribution of opportunities and resources within a society also makes for a society's being just or unjust. Social justice – concerned with the distribution of opportunities and resources – should be conceived of as building on the foundation of liberal rights. Unquestionably, there is a conflict between certain rights claimed by traditional liberals (today often distinguished by calling them 'libertarians') and the demands of social justice. Thus, if the right to private property includes the right to appoint people to jobs in the firm you own on any basis you like, it is obviously incompatible with the demand that jobs should be filled without discrimination or nepotism. (I shall discuss the relation of this demand to social justice in chapter 4.) And it goes without saying that it would be a complete waste of time to talk about the just distribution of resources unless the redistribution of property by the state was on the agenda.

During the nineteenth century, a number of people who saw the critical importance of opportunities and resources denigrated negative rights altogether: in the ideal socialist or communist state, to insist on rights would be an expression of egoism and would actually be pernicious. Fatefully, Karl Marx was numbered among those who took this line. We cannot know if the course of the history of the Soviet Union (and after 1945 its Eastern European satellites) or of

China would have been different had Marx emphasized the permanent importance of individual rights. But we have only to call to mind the horrors unleashed by Stalin and Mao to recognize that Marx was tragically mistaken. Social justice must subsume liberal justice. Unfortunately, however, a contempt for social justice does nothing to guarantee liberal justice. The American judiciary has granted the government unfettered discretionary power to lock people up indefinitely; the government also admits to using methods of 'interrogation' that fall within the internationally recognized definition of torture, and this is no doubt just the tip of the iceberg.[9]

The demand for social justice can best be seen as a response to the inadequacies of liberal justice. Thus, the foundation of the liberal conception of justice is that all citizens should be treated equally. The French Revolution resulted, for example, in the abolition of the system of three 'Estates', under which the nobility and the clergy had legal and political privileges denied to the rest of the population (the Third Estate). It may seem obvious that no state can be just if it has different grades of citizenship, but that does not prevent many states in the world from having first-class and second-class citizenship. Apartheid South Africa had an elaborate system, with the whites as first-class citizens and several categories below this. But many states systematically advantage the members of the dominant ethnic or religious group over others, both legally and as a result of the way in which decisions are made within institutions that do not have the prohibition of discriminatory practices written into their rules.

When the classic statements of liberal rights were promulgated, their scope was limited despite the breadth of their language. The American Declaration of Independence held it self-evident that all men are created equal and had rights to life, liberty and the pursuit of happiness. Yet it was drafted by a slave-owner, Thomas Jefferson, and signed by a number of other slave-owners. The French Declaration of the Rights of Man was thought by most of the revolutionaries to be compatible with laws that privileged men over women. These inconsistencies did not go unnoticed at the time. Samuel Johnson wrote: 'How is it that we hear the loudest yelps for liberty among the drivers of negroes?'[10] And in France the clearest thinker among the revolutionaries, the Marquis de Condorcet, wrote a pamphlet arguing that equal citizenship must demand the equal treatment of women.[11]

During the nineteenth century, the gross violation of equal rights represented by slavery became intolerable to most people except the beneficiaries, with the result that it was abolished first in the British Empire and then in the United States. Similarly, the argument that unequal rights for women violated the basic premise of liberal justice gradually gained ground, with women's position under marriage law improved and their access to higher education and the professions opened up in Britain, though (as in many other countries) equal rights in voting had to wait until the twentieth century – in some cases well into it. But parallel with these movements was a growing sense that, however perfectly liberal justice might be realized, it could do nothing in itself to address problems that cried out for drastic changes of some kind. Most of this concern was not expressed in the language of justice: the 'condition of England question' preoccupied writers as diverse as Thomas Carlyle, Benjamin Disraeli and Charles Dickens, none of whom posed the question in terms of justice.

There are still those who wish to maintain that whatever distribution of opportunities and resources exists is just as long as it came about without force or fraud – and even then that force or fraud establish a clear title today as long as they occurred far enough in the past. Those who take this position may still be concerned about poverty in the midst of plenty. But they lack any proposals for redressing the situation beyond appealing to the rich to be charitable and the powerful to behave compassionately. As the spokesman for 'Young England', Disraeli's answer to the existence of 'two nations' was not a social revolution but a stronger sense of *noblesse oblige* among the landed aristocracy. Dickens was undeniably a critic of existing conditions: 'In every page of his work one can see a consciousness that society is wrong somewhere at the root.'[12] Yet, as George Orwell pointed out in his essay on Dickens, 'it would be difficult to point anywhere in his books to a passage suggesting that the economic system is wrong *as a system*'.[13] Even in his most direct attack on the consequences of unfettered capitalism, *Hard Times*, the 'whole moral is that capitalists should be kind, not that workers should be rebellious'. If those with the power 'were better men, the system would work well enough'.[14] The *deus ex machina* in Dickens's plots 'is always a superhumanly kind old gentleman who "trots" to and fro, raising his employees' wages, patting children on the head, getting debtors out of jail and, in general, acting the fairy godmother'.[15] Thus, for example, the moral regeneration of Scrooge is exhibited by his raising Bob Cratchit's pay, 'endeavour[ing] to assist' his 'struggling family', and giving a big donation to a charity dedicated to 'mak[ing] some slight provision for the poor and destitute, who suffer greatly at [Christmas] time' – and presumably have to get by without for the rest of the year.[16] We may also presume that he became less of 'a tight-fisted hand at the grindstone' by driving less hard bargains and not enforcing those he had made so as to avoid 'ruining' those who were unable to pay their debts.[17]

This remains as much a fantasy as it was when Dickens created it. If things are better now, it is not on the whole because those with economic power are nicer people, but because they are forced by law to behave better. Firms still tend to squeeze everything they can out of employees unless limited by trade unions operating in a favourable legal environment, and (unless the unions are enormously powerful) by laws limiting hours, imposing safety requirements and setting a minimum wage. Landlords and lenders make the most they can unless limited by laws protecting tenants and prohibiting usury. As for charity, it is bound to be as capricious as the Dickensian provision of Christmas treats for the poor: billions of dollars showered on the families of the victims of the September 11 attacks, while a third of the nation's children are growing up in poverty. An official in one of the organizations deluged with money after September 11 explained a lot of the motivation as 'vengeful giving'.[18] Perhaps the lack of charitable contributions for the relief of hunger and homelessness might be described as 'vengeful non-giving'. What is, at any rate, clear is that this arbitrary way of moving money around cannot possibly, even under the most favourable conditions, add up to a systematic attack on social injustice.[19]

Social democracy, as we saw in the previous chapter, challenges the assumption that whatever distribution of opportunities and resources arises within a framework of liberal rights is necessarily just, and its implication that any departure from the inequalities thus generated must depend on the good will of the beneficiaries. One way in which social justice can be seen as an extension of liberal justice is quite simple. Liberal justice rests on the presupposition that all citizens are equal before the law. But why should equal treatment be confined to liberal rights? Surely, we should also be concerned about equal opportunities to exercise those rights. In a traditional liberal society, there will be a universal right to education, but only a right in the sense in which I have defined the term: the absence of a law prohibiting education. In many countries today (as was the case in England well into the nineteenth century), a child's opportunity to go to school depends on the ability and willingness of its parents to pay for it to do so. It is hard to see how this inequality of opportunity for education can fail to be unjust, rather than merely unfortunate. (This is, of course, only the grossest denial of equal opportunity: I shall take up the whole question of the meaning of equality of opportunity in chapter 4.)

A parallel argument can be made about medical care. The absence of a prohibition on its being supplied to anybody does nothing to guarantee that everybody has the opportunity to receive it. If the opportunity depends on the ability to pay for it, some will get good medical care, some will get basic medical care and some will get none. That people with the same medical condition will have such unequal opportunities to obtain treatment again seems to raise issues of justice. Equal rights to employment suffer the same limitation. Certainly, it is important that there should not be laws prohibiting members of certain ethnic groups from holding particular jobs, as in Nazi Germany, apartheid South Africa and contemporary Israel. But the right to a job, in the negative sense, is very different from an opportunity. The absence of legal exclusion is quite consistent with exclusion practised by employers. As I noted earlier, the unmitigated rights of private property include the right of an employer to make a labour contract on any basis, however arbitrary or discriminatory. Equal opportunity, even understood simply as non-discrimination, therefore requires state intervention to curb the rights of employers.

The absence of discrimination in the job market constitutes fairness among the applicants. But there may have been discrimination at an earlier stage, in that many (perhaps most) members of the society were legally prohibited from acquiring the qualifications necessary for entering the competition. Even if there was no formal discrimination, there are in every country unequal opportunities for acquiring the qualifications that lead to the best universities and the best jobs. I shall explore in Part II the implications of taking equality of opportunity seriously when it is construed in this way.

3

The Scope of Social Justice

The theory of social justice put forward here applies to all countries and provides a universal standard against which they can be judged. Although I shall focus in this book on wealthy countries, and especially Britain and the USA, it has to be said that the worst cases of social injustice within countries occur outside the relatively affluent western liberal democracies. If the victims are forced to appeal to 'local norms', they will be in the absurd position of having to invoke norms that are characteristically antithetical to the rights of women, children, ethnic and religious minorities and the poor. The whole point of a universalistic conception of justice is that it provides a basis on which both those inside and those outside a country can criticize practices and institutions that reflect local norms, which typically endorse discrimination, exploitation and oppression.

In every society, the prevailing belief system has been largely created by those with the most power – typically, elderly males belonging to the majority ethnic and religious group, who also run the dominant institutions of the society. It is notable, for example, that almost all religions rationalize a subordinate position for women and explain that inequalities of fortune are to be accepted as part of God's great (if mysterious) plan. Although those who lose out may not fully accept these ideas, because they too obviously conflict with their own experience, few societies in history have ever offered a fully articulated alternative belief system. The eighteenth and nineteenth centuries produced two important bases for a systematic critique of the status quo. One was the Enlightenment, which paved the way for the French Revolution and for the spread of liberal institutions through Western Europe; the other was socialism in various forms, including, of course, Marxism.

Since the adoption in 1948 by the United Nations of the Universal Declaration of Human Rights, we can add another important contribution: the idea that every human being can claim certain fundamental rights against his or her state. But the demands that can be made on the basis of human rights do not rest there. A country's failure to respect the human rights of its own inhabitants is now clearly understood to be the common concern of all, and opens its government to universal condemnation. What is less well understood, though it follows equally clearly, is that the Universal Declaration of Human Rights has implications – and very important ones – for the international community as a whole, not just for individual states. If governments simply do not have the means of supplying everyone with such things as adequate nutrition and housing, pure drinking water, sanitation and a generally healthy environment, education and medical care, then the wealthy countries, individually or in any combination, have an obligation to ensure that, by one means or another, the resources are forthcoming. This can take the form of direct economic aid. But, as we shall see later in this chapter, it may in the longer term be more a matter (for all but the poorest countries, anyway) of changing the rules governing international trade so that poor countries can export under more advantageous conditions and protect their own economies from ruinous foreign competition and speculative raids on their currencies.

By now, the Declaration of Human Rights has been supplemented by a number of covenants and other declarations, all claiming universal validity. United Nations agencies, NGOs such as Amnesty International and Human Rights Watch and the governments of some countries are among those who constantly appeal to human rights as a standard for judging the conduct of states. Dissidents within countries whose governments violate human rights typically appeal to the idea of human rights as the ground of their complaints. This is all to the good. The trouble is, however, that to claim a right is simply to assert a conclusion. What is still needed is some argument for that conclusion. The principles of social justice put forward in this book can provide what is needed: a rationale for almost all of the individual rights against states claimed in these documents. (There are a few cultural and religious rights that cannot be derived; that does not show the framework to be inadequate, but the claims to be unfounded.)

As I have already hinted, the principles of social justice laid out here also apply to the world as a whole. It is sometimes objected that the present dispensation has arisen within an international system in which there is no equivalent of a state, so there is no organization with the authority to implement principles of social justice. The most straightforward response is to deny this claim. There is in fact already an international economic order – a set of institutions such as the World Trade Organization, the International Monetary Fund and the World Bank. Their rules are open to assessment according to the criteria of social justice. For example, the WTO has enacted strong 'intellectual property' rights, which force poor countries to pay the prices charged by western companies for drugs under patent and to pay high prices for new plant varieties.[1] There are provisions for compulsory drug licensing in an 'emergency', but third world countries are in a permanent emergency, and in 2003 the United States vetoed a proposal supported by 143 other countries to recognize this and waive patent protection across the board.[2]

The primary mission of the IMF is to prevent countries from defaulting on loans, regardless of the deprivation among the most vulnerable caused by its 'structural adjustment' packages, which force debtor countries to slash their already inadequate programmes for public health and education and to open their markets to cheap foreign exports, thus destroying the kinds of local employment on which many workers rely for a living.[3] Countries are also compelled to sell off their public services to the highest bidder – usually a foreign company which proceeds to make its profits by supplying essential public services such as water and electricity only to those who can afford its prices, while making no effort to ensure that supplies are even available in poor areas that do not promise the prospect of a good return on capital.

In addition, despite all the evidence that poor countries need to control financial transactions to avoid having their economies wiped out by the withdrawal of capital and by speculative raids on their currencies, the 'Washington consensus' imposed by the IMF and World Bank as a condition of aid demands that countries should not impose controls on the movement of capital. This dogma has taken hold during the twenty years in which the volume of money sloshing around the world looking for the highest possible return has increased so much that on any given day only a fraction of the currency transactions corresponds to trading of goods and services.

Not accidentally, the net result of these policies is to hamstring the efforts of reforming governments to get anything significant done by way of equalizing the distribution of wealth and income or providing high-quality public services to all their citizens. Moreover, with their ability to set their own fiscal and monetary policies constrained by 'agreements' that have actually arisen from coercion, governments can do almost nothing to deliver on promises to their voters to reduce the rate of unemployment – often appallingly high in third world countries.

The case of Brazil is, in fact, highly instructive in this context. Luiz Inácio 'Lula' da Silva assumed the presidency of Brazil on 1 January 2003. More than a year later, bitter disappointment reigns among those who supported him. 'The promises in his inaugural speech . . . were . . . inspiring. Hunger would no longer be a factor in Brazilian society, hundreds of thousands of landless people would be given land, millions of jobs would be created', and so on. Instead, 'critics say that he has sold out, abandoned decades of struggle against poverty, against international bankers and ruling elites, and embraced neo-liberal politics.'[4] The explanation is external to Brazil: 'Before his election Lula's socialist reputation had frightened the markets. A run on the real [the currency] threatened a financial crisis. To calm the markets the PT [Partito dos Trabalhadores – Workers' Party] was forced to agree to a fiscal straitjacket.'[5] The 'agreement' entailed 'a self-imposed budget surplus of 4.24%'. As a result of the budgetary cuts and high interest rates that were required to meet this constraint, 'the economy ground to a halt, and prized social programmes stumbled. Unemployment . . . rose to around 13% . . . In Rio de Janeiro, 160,000 people applied for only 1,000 jobs as rubbish collectors. The queue of applicants stretched miles.'[6] Ironically, governments nominally of the left have to work harder to demonstrate their orthodoxy.

> Possibly people are surprised at how far they have bent over to satisfy international investors. . . . The buck stops with the IMF and international capital unfortunately so the government has, perhaps, gone much further than people might have imagined they could have done to show what good boys and girls they are.[7]

Consider a specific example, the key programme that went under the name of 'Zero Hunger'. Lula announced when he took office, 'that his administration's top priority would be to guarantee that every Brazilian could eat three meals a day'.[8] However:

> the aid for hungry families has . . . been scaled back, reflecting the austerity measures he has been forced to put into effect as part of an agreement with the International Monetary Fund. On the campaign trail, he talked of stipends of as much as $70 a month, but the Zero Hunger effort will, at least initially, be limited to a $15 monthly payment.[9]

That's some cut back!

The obvious question is why paying off debts should require 'austerity' on the part of the poor rather than slightly less obscene luxury among the rich. 'Soak the rich' would be an appropriate response anywhere, but it is especially applicable to Brazil, which, 'according to statistics from the United Nations, has the third most unequal distribution of wealth in the world, trailing only Swaziland and Nicaragua [which, put together, have only a tiny fraction of Brazil's population]. The wealthiest ten per cent of the people ... take in more than half of the national income, while the poorest tenth receive less than one per cent.'[10] A tiny part of the gap (measured by the difference between $70 and $15 a month) is being filled by corporate philanthropy. As the director of Ford's truck division said, it's 'good for brand image'.[11] Since what they are giving is far less than they should be paying in tax, corporations are, morally speaking, in the position of a thief who expects your gratitude for returning a tiny fraction of his haul. Even if you could not get any of it back by your own efforts, gratitude is still not the right response, as against anger at his keeping the rest.

As far as the World Bank is concerned, its own research department has concluded that 'much of what counts as aid in official statistics isn't aid at all. Huge loans that the bank and other donors made to African dictators were political bribes for lining up with the West during the cold war. The amount of money that actually trickles down to the poor has been negligible for decades.'[12] Moreover, a UN report says: 'Aid disbursements have increasingly been allocated to ensure that official debts are serviced.'[13] Quite often, nothing gets done at all: in many cases, including notoriously Russia, official loans have been immediately recycled by politicians and public servants into foreign bank accounts, thus increasing the country's debt with no benefit to its people. Even when money does actually get used for development projects (whether given by the World Bank or by individual countries), much of it has gone on financing large projects (especially dams) whose effects are to displace poor and indigenous people while the beneficiaries are those affiliated with the government.[14]

In any case, official aid is trivial beside the increase in income that third world countries could derive from trade in the absence of barriers to their staple exports and the distortion of the market arising from the enormous agricultural subsidies provided by' the EU and the USA.[15] The Director-General of the WTO from 1999 until 2002, Michael Moore, gave a remarkably frank interview in 2003. Asked what he thought about the influential Oxfam Report, *Rigged Rules and Double Standards*, which argued that 'trade rules today are still structured in favour of the rich',[16] he replied: 'I agree with a lot', adding that 'by and large . . . the accusing fingers should point to the rich countries'.[17] Expanding on this, he said:

> The reality is that global trade is not yet fair nor free and it is a matter of enormous shame that rich countries have blocked poor countries where they have a competitive advantage. If the OECD removed its protectionist barriers in agriculture, you could do 4 or 5 times more for Africa than existing official development aid. Look at the story of sugar, cotton, coffee, cocoa. . . . If you got rid of the cotton subsidies, it would generate a $250m boom in West Africa. Coffee is a disgrace, you know. What is wicked is a thing called tariff escalation. You can't put that on a placard. But every time a grower [of coffee] in Ethiopia, which is 70% of their exports, or Kenya, which is 60% of their exports, wants to roast his beans, grind them, put them in a box, get those jobs, his tariffs go up. So he has to sell the raw product. So those other jobs go to Europe and the United States. I think that's something we could fix in a trade round.[18]

No doubt it could be fixed, in principle, and so could all the defects of the United Nations, its agencies and the other two international economic organizations whose records I have savaged. However, Moore ignores the possibility of changing the existing distribution of power. He is therefore reduced to pinning his hopes on a recognition by the rich countries that it would be prudent, taking the long view, to give the poor ones a better deal. This fatalism about structures leads him to say:

> The leaders of the G8 will be discussing security and not development issues in the main when they meet this year. It is going to be a cost, but it also provides, surely, a determination that we are going to do something about terrorism and the poverty in which it breeds. A more just world can do that and trade has a significant role to play in this.[19]

As we now know, Moore's hopes that enlightened self-interest would lead the rich countries to act in such a way as to reduce the amount of misery and desperation in the world proved naive. Efforts were indeed made by the leaders of some European countries (especially President Chirac) to focus on constructive moves to reduce the size of the pool of radically disaffected people around the world who support (morally and materially) the tiny fraction who are recruited to engage in attacks on western targets. But these efforts to introduce a note of rationality were treated with scarcely disguised contempt by President Bush, who was interested only in lining up supporters for his own 'war on terror', a purely military 'solution' that has predictably created additional misery and desperation and fuelled a (perfectly justifiable) hatred of the United States and its accomplices – the so-called 'coalition of the willing' – a tragic outcome for all parties.

I shall offer in Part VI some powerful additional reasons appealing to self-interest for rich countries to make radical changes in the international economic regime. But for the purposes of this chapter, the crucial point, which I hope I have established abundantly, is that there does exist an elaborate and interlocking set of international institutions. These institutions have a well-defined power distribution, which gives the United States a privileged position within the World Bank (whose Director it appoints by convention) and the IMF (where the voting rules give it a veto), and both institutions rest formal control entirely in the hands of the rich countries. The WTO has a different formal structure in that each state has a vote and unanimity is required for a decision. Until the Cancun summit in 2004 (whose implications I shall analyse in chapter 20), it was nevertheless in practice run by the rich countries, whose representatives concerted in drawing up the agenda for its meetings and succeeded to an outrageous extent in getting through their proposals in the face of a collection of fragmented and leaderless countries many of which were in addition susceptible to threats and promises made by rich countries (especially America).

It seems to me that, taken together, this network of international institutions surely constitutes a basic structure in the sense defined in chapter 2. For it gives rise to much of the rapidly increasing inequality between countries and also to increasing inequalities within them – within poor countries, where the human cost is the highest, but also in rich countries. There may be some stick-in-the-muds who insist that the framework of global governance that I have described still cannot count as a basic structure because it lacks a sovereign power. Even if I were to concede this, it would do nothing to impugn my claim that it is appropriate to talk about global justice and injustice. For we can do this without having to refer to institutions at all. The key move here is the one that I made at the beginning of the previous chapter. It may be recalled that I stipulated there that the subject of social justice is the distribution of rights, opportunities and resources. Since there is, trivially, a global distribution of rights, opportunities and resources, it must be permissible to enquire into the justice or injustice of this distribution. Thus, we can compare the rights, opportunities and resources enjoyed by the average inhabitant of (say) Mali or Burkina Faso with those enjoyed by the average inhabitant of (say) Norway or Sweden. We can ask if the inequality between the first pair and the second pair can be justified on any plausible theory of justice. Is the explanation for the differences in resources between the first pair and the second that they all have the same opportunities but that the Norwegians and Swedes make better choices? The entire pattern of global inequality can be probed in the same way. If we conclude that the pattern cannot be squared with elementary principles of justice, we can then shift to a focus on institutions and ask what system of governance, and what kinds of rules, would be required to bring about a more just world.

We can also go back to another point made in chapter 2: the possibility of actions that are intended to make things more just even where they are not required by any binding rule. People can give money to Oxfam, Amnesty International and dozens of other NGOs. States or entities such as the EU as a whole can act unilaterally to improve matters. Thus, even if the restrictions by rich countries on imports of food and textiles from third world countries are permitted by the WTO, that is quite compatible with getting rid of them: they are not *required* by it. Similarly, the massive subsidization of agriculture by the USA and the EU could be phased out unilaterally. Currently, the USA dumps corn, soybeans and rice on the world market at half the cost of producing it. Farmers in poor countries are ruined and are driven out into the already overburdened cities, while whole countries that were formerly self-sufficient for foodstuffs become importers. Of course, if the billions of dollars and euros wasted on these subsidies were converted into foreign aid, that would be even better than simply scrapping the programmes. For increasing foreign aid is, again, a decision that countries can take unilaterally. Thus, if we once have in place a clear conception of the requirements of global justice, we have the basis for judging the status quo and starting to think of ways in which it can be improved, both by changing international institutions and by actions on the part of rich countries to discontinue harmful policies and introduce beneficial ones.

Part II

Equality of Opportunity

Semper pauper eris, si pauper es, Aemiliane.
dantur opes nullis nisi divitibus

(If you're poor now, my friend, then you'll stay poor.
These days only the rich get given more.)

Martial (*c*.40 AD–*c*.104 AD), trans. James Michie

4

Why Equal Opportunity?

In chapter 2, I said that filling a job in a way that is non-discriminatory and non-nepotistic is fair. What makes it fair? The simplest explanation is that a job is a scarce resource. (It must be scarce if there is more than one applicant for it.) And the way in which this scarce resource is distributed should not depend on irrelevant characteristics such as race or 'pull'. A society in which the best-qualified applicant gets the job is more just than one in which other factors enter into the appointment – as long, at any rate, as we keep our attention focused narrowly on the field of applicants. The proviso is crucial, however, because it may be that a society would be more just overall if this rule were departed from and preference were given to candidates who were less qualified but had faced greater obstacles in acquiring the relevant qualifications. In other words, if the opportunity to acquire qualifications is unjustly distributed, it may be worth compensating for that injustice even at the cost of departing from the rule for the fair allocation of jobs among applicants.

It will be noticed that neither in chapter 2 nor here have I invoked the value of equality of opportunity to explain why, focusing strictly on the applicants, it is fair for the best qualified to get the job. Yet many people and institutions actually define the notion of equal opportunity in such a way that it consists in precisely this. The usage is so familiar that we probably let it slip by without subjecting it to scrutiny. Yet it is actually rather baffling, if we understand an opportunity in the way that I proposed in chapter 2. I said there that an opportunity to do or obtain something exists for me if there is some course of action lying within my power such that it will lead, if I choose to take it, to my doing or obtaining the thing in question. What could it mean, if we start from this definition, to say that two people have the same opportunity to obtain some resource that both want and only one can have? Surely, it must mean that both have the capacity to make the right choices or exert the extra efforts that will result in success. But there is no connection, on the face of it, between this and a situation in which the choice of the successful candidate is uncontaminated by discrimination or nepotism.

Consider an extreme but by no means fanciful case. Suppose that the employer believes in a version of 'meritocracy' according to which the job should go to the candidate with the highest score on some test that is supposed to measure 'aptitude'. If the test is a standard one (corresponding to the American SAT and GRE examinations for admission to undergraduate and graduate study), and has already been taken before the job is advertised, the die is cast when the list of applicants is closed. The point is that there are *no* choices or efforts that any of the candidates can make after the job is advertised that will affect their chances of getting the job. Not very much changes in this analysis if the employer administers a test to all the applicants, since the opportunities to improve one's score by last-minute study or by extra effort on the day are not likely to be very large compared to the differences that existed already between the candidates when the job was advertised. Anyone with enough information about the candidates at that point should be able to make a pretty accurate prediction of the rank ordering of scores on the test.

Of course, the employer can add other procedures, such as interviews, that will make more turn on choices and efforts after the job is advertised. Indeed, formal qualifications or test scores might be used as a cut-off for shortlisting candidates but made no further use of. This would make everything turn on the candidates' performance in interviews. The problem with this is that there is a wealth of evidence showing that impressions gained at interviews are even worse predictors of future job performance than more impersonal criteria. This is scarcely surprising when we bear in mind that 'in studies of job interviews, investigators have found that potential employees have less than one minute to make a good impression'.[1] Even after that first minute, the chemistry between the candidate and the interviewing panel may be decisive but irrelevant. To a large extent, interviews simply add 'noise' – random departures from any semblance of rational decision-making. To the extent that they have a systemic effect, however, it is to advantage middle-class applicants over working-class applicants with equal ability and potential. 'Researchers stress the importance of eye contact, firm handshakes, and displaying comfort with bosses during the interview.'[2] These traits are typically middle-class ones, so interviews are to that degree a form of class discrimination. Even more obvious class bias in interviews arises from the tendency in England for interviewers to be favourably disposed to people with a 'good' accent – what used to be called a 'public school' or 'Oxford' accent and was then formalized as the 'BBC accent' used by announcers and newsreaders. Such an accent has in the past been used quite explicitly as an appointment criterion: 'Its possession was, among other things, a criterion for selecting young men as officers during the First World War, and throughout much of the 20th century was the favoured accent for recruits to the Foreign Office and other services representing the United Kingdom, including for many years the British Council.'[3]

This leaves us with a paradox. Let us stick for a moment to the common idea that 'equality of opportunity' requires the successful candidate to be the one who, on the basis of the best available information, holds out the most promise of performing the job well. Then it follows that an appointment procedure that offers the candidates little or no chance to change the outcome by their own efforts between the closing date for application and the decision is the most likely to satisfy the criteria for equality of opportunity. The candidates thus have a very unequal opportunity of getting the job, if we understand opportunity as the ability to achieve something by your own choices and efforts. In the limiting case, in which the sole criterion is the score on some test already taken, the identity of the person who will be offered the job is determined once all the applications are in. The second-ranked candidate will be offered the job if the first refuses it, and so on. Although this adds an element of indeterminacy, it is one that leaves the appointment of lower-ranked candidates subject to factors over which they have no control.

How, then, can the idea of equal opportunity have come to be associated in such a routine and unquestioned way with that of appointing the best candidate? It can be squared with my definition of 'opportunity' only if, lurking somewhere in the background, there is the presumption that at some prior stage (maybe a long way back) many of the candidates for the job had the possibility of being the most highly qualified applicant. Thus, what made the difference between the candidate who was successful and the others was that he or she made superior choices from a set of options that was equally open to all of them: chose the right subjects to study, worked harder, and so on. But we should not confine our attention to those who had the minimum necessary qualifications at the time at which the job was advertised. Unless the claim of equal opportunity is to be a cruel hoax, we must also believe that there are millions of other people who could at some earlier stage have acquired the qualifications needed to get the job by making the right choices from a common set of options.

Let us put this point in the language of resources. At the time at which the job came up, there was a very unequal spread in the distribution of the personal resources required to get appointed to it. But we have to imagine that there was some earlier stage at which many people had equal personal resources, and that what made the difference was entirely what they did with them. The opportunity to develop personal resources depends on other resources such as education, quality of family background and neighbourhood, and so on. Presumably, then, it has to be imagined that there was equal access to those too. To sum up: appointing the best person constitutes equal opportunity only if there was an earlier time at which millions of people had an equal opportunity to be the best candidate.

The classic statement of the idea of equal opportunity that is at work here is the one made by the restored Bourbon king, Louis XVII, to the cadets at St Cyr: 'Remember that there is not one of you who does not carry in his cartridge-pouch the marshall's baton of the Duke of Reggio; it is up to you to bring it forth.'[4] What we have here is an ideology: it cloaks the status quo with legitimacy through a process of mystification. For it has the effect of building into the limited claim that some appointment was fair the far more grandiose claim that the successful candidate was distinguished from very many others only by pursuing a course of action that it was equally open to any of them to have taken. R. H. Tawney aptly christened this 'the Tadpole Philosophy':

> It is possible that intelligent tadpoles reconcile themselves to the inconvenience of their position by reflecting that, though most of them will live and die as tadpoles and nothing more, the more fortunate of the species will one day shed their tails, distend their mouths and stomachs, hop nimbly on to dry land, and croak addresses to their former friends on the virtues by means of which tadpoles of character and capacity can rise to be frogs.[5]

To pursue the issue further, let me introduce, as a quasi-technical term, the concept of a starting gate. The metaphor is drawn, of course, from the turf. A race is fair if the best combination of horse and jockey wins, the next best comes second, and so on down the field. The point about the starting gate is that we look forward from it to the race, but not back from it to ask how there came to be these particular horses and jockeys in the race, how they came to be in whatever condition they are in, and so on. How do we assess the extent to which the result of a race reflects different uses made by the jockeys of the resources they brought to it? With great difficulty. Each horse has its 'form', based on its past record, and each jockey also has his 'form'. If betting were an exact science, everybody would agree on which horse is going to win and everybody would be right. As we all know, however, favourites can and do lose. The *maximum* effect on the result that we can attribute to variable effort by the jockeys is the extent of the departure of the result from the best prior estimate. (Notice that the relative *skill* of the jockeys is already incorporated in this estimate.) But it would be vastly implausible to rule out other explanations. The horse could be 'off form' (a racing expression whose use has been generalized) for any number of reasons. Luck may well also have entered into the course of the race. For example, the horse with the best prospects may have got boxed in at a certain point. Sometimes, other jockeys gang up on the favourite to improve their own chances. If they can do this in a way that avoids disqualification, we can say that they exercised skill. But is this the kind of effort that we hoped would be rewarded?

If we take a horse race as a simple model of competition among people, there are two points we can draw from the analysis. First, picking up the final point, the efforts that get some of the biggest rewards may not be particularly virtuous: unpunished corporate crime or financial finagling just outside the reach of existing law can be thousands of times more lucrative than any amount of honest toil. Second, wherever we put the starting gate, the different resources that people bring to it are liable to overwhelm the significance of the differential use they may make of those resources. 'Obviously, people cannot have completely equal opportunities unless the net results of *all* economically relevant factors beyond their control are equalized. Such factors are legion.'[6]

Children start with, and grow up with, an enormous variety of different resources. On the basis of just a few facts about a child, such as its social class and its race or ethnicity, we can make a good prediction of where it will finish up in the distribution of earnings, the likelihood that it will spend time in jail, and many other outcomes, good and bad. There will, of course, be some departures from our predicted outcomes: some children will do better and some worse. An obvious response is to say that a child's resources depend on more factors than we have picked out.

However many factors we include, though, our predictions of final outcomes will still, we may be sure, be somewhat wide of the mark in a number of cases. How are we to explain this remaining difference in outcomes? The most obvious – and quite likely the most important – reason is that only a small proportion of the factors that make a difference to opportunities can be measured. Among these will be a variety of contributions from the home. Factors that have been treated as relevant by sociologists include the existence in the home of magazines and newspapers, the possession of a library card and the number of siblings.[7] Other things being equal, the more siblings the less attention each individual child gets – but other things are not equal, since parents with the same number of children give different amounts of time to them. Similarly, the relation between the items counted and the amount and quality of intellectual stimulation and emotional support that children receive is inevitably loose.

A second factor is luck. This can be divided into environmental and genetic luck. Environmental luck that will fall outside any individual measure includes such things as hanging out with one set of peers rather than another (this often happens even among siblings), striking up particularly good rapport with a teacher, or being in the right place at the time to hear about some job opportunity. Genetic luck is often thought of as some kind of 'native ability' that can be treated as an independent resource, measurable by something like an IQ test. I shall show in chapter 9 that this is, generally speaking, nonsense. But there is, undeniably, some genetic bad luck, such as Down syndrome and fragile-X syndrome.

We are left with 'effort' as a justification for inequality. Despite all the difficulties in establishing that opportunities are equal, we can say that, wherever they are equal, it is possible for differential outcomes arising from choices made among a common set of options to give rise to just inequalities. To illustrate, let us take as our starting gate a condition in which a number of workers are doing the same job in the same firm, and that there is some qualification possession of which leads to promotion. The firm provides free instruction in the course that prepares people for the examination that leads to the award of the qualification, so all workers have an equal opportunity in that respect. Now let us compare two workers, Able and Baker, and suppose that Baker has to put in twice as much effort as Able to acquire the same increment of attainment. Say, for example, that Able has the option of passing the course by spending ten hours a week on homework and ten hours in the pub, whereas Baker could pass it only by spending twenty hours a week on the homework and none in the pub. On the assumption that both prefer the pub to homework, the fact that Able gets twice the return for each hour of homework gives him a much stronger incentive to do it. Baker is therefore much more likely to drop out of the course.

To put it in terms of resources, one worker began the course with more personal resources – that is to say, more ability. If Baker drops out (or works more hours per week than Able but not enough more), he finishes up further behind Able because one has the qualification needed for promotion and the other does not. We can say that Baker chose not to get the qualification. But he did not choose the circumstances in which that choice was made. Compare this case to one in which Able and Charlie have the same level of ability, defined as the rate at which they can turn hours of study into gains in attainment. Able, as before, spends ten hours on homework and ten in the pub, while Charlie puts in all his time at the pub with the result that Able passes and Charlie fails. Let us now introduce a fourth worker, Doug, who believes correctly that he could not gain the qualification however much work he put in on it. (To tie up a loose end, add that additional coaching would not help.)

If we were asked why Baker, Charlie and Doug failed to qualify, we would give very different answers for each of them. We would say that Doug didn't gain the qualification because he couldn't. In the case of Charlie, we would focus on the reason for his failing despite his high ability: he didn't do the work because he preferred the pub. What about Baker? We would be inclined to say that he gave up because it would have taken an enormous amount of work and he did not think it was worth it. If we liked, we could say that the opportunity costs of gaining the qualification (the things that had to be given up to get it) were too high.

The difference in outcome between Able and Charlie can be justified according to the principle of equal opportunity because they both faced the same set of options: for any given amount of effort they could get the same results. We could, of course, say that Able and Charlie did not really face the same costs in studying. We can deduce from their choices that (even if they valued the qualification equally highly), Charlie must have found an hour of homework more irksome than Able did, or that he suffered more hardship from cutting down on his visits to the pub than did Able. (Perhaps, for example, it would have entailed giving up his much-sought-after place on the pub's darts team.) Something of the sort has to be true to explain why they behaved differently. But the whole idea of equal opportunity becomes inoperable unless we are prepared to count this as a case of it. In effect, we take an equal ability to turn time into results as sufficient. Perhaps I should qualify this by saying that this equal ability produces only a strong assumption of equal opportunity. If we knew that Charlie suffered from repetitive strain injury, so that getting as much done in an hour as Able cost him a lot of pain and a risk of further injury, we would no doubt think again. But the point is that, if we are ever to employ the concept of equal opportunity, there has to be a limit to the amount of fine-grained detail we consider relevant in order to declare that two people had equal opportunities.

As long as we are prepared to overcome our scruples about the possibility of equal opportunity, we can say that it underwrites Able's getting the promotion and Charlie's not doing so. But Able's claim to greater material rewards in virtue of that is limited by three factors. The first is that his success depended on his starting with an advantage over Baker and Doug, so that they did not have an equal opportunity of success. This is, of course, a specific case of the potential for abuse inherent in the concept of equality of opportunity. The second limitation is that, as I shall show in the rest of this book, approximate material equality is a necessary condition of a socially just society, so the spread of unequal rewards must be constrained. The third is that initial inequalities typically give rise to further inequalities: Able's promotion, for example, puts him in a position to move further ahead of the others by getting additional promotions.

To see why this matters, we should envisage a series of starting points, with choices being made from different sets of options after the first stage. To illustrate the process of cumulative advantage and disadvantage, imagine a version of the Tour de France in which at the start of the race each competitor is made to carry a twenty-pound weight. At the end of the first stage, the packs of the leaders are lightened and those of the rest are made heavier according to some formula that relates weight to time taken to complete the stage. At the next stage, the process is repeated on the basis of the combined times for both stages, and so on until the end of the race. Even if the contestants had an equal opportunity at the start in the sense that they had equal ability, we could complain that the system is unfair. For it will be virtually impossible for any rider who is not among the leaders at the end of the first few stages to win. Even those who might have caught up under the usual rules will be unable to do so. I wish to maintain that a just system would have to give people second (or more) chances, so that losing out at the beginning does not permanently close doors that might be opened by extra effort later. Contemporary societies have regressed in this respect. Formal qualifications have become such pervasive conditions for getting almost any desirable position (even if they are irrelevant) that the possibility of getting your foot in the door and then proving yourself on the job has virtually disappeared.

Initial advantages cumulate, then. Those with the best school results will tend to go to the best universities and go on to the most desirable jobs. The same cumulative process operates for disadvantage as well as advantage. Margaret Thatcher's famous assertion that 'there is no such thing as society' actually occurred in response to the suggestion that 'society' might have something to do with taking up a criminal career: as far as she was concerned, people were responsible for their own choices, and some people with bad characters were simply disposed to criminality. As against this, however, Oliver Letwin, when in 2002 he was Conservative Shadow Home Secretary, acknowledged that people are much more likely to drift into crime than to choose it and that the tendency to become career criminals arises from a series of cumulative disadvantages: 'The individual passes through successive stages on the conveyor belt: neglected or abused child, disruptive pupil, anti-social teenager, young offender, first time prisoner, repeat offender, hardened criminal.' And, in an implied repudiation of Thatcher, he added that 'society' has to find 'easily accessible exit points' and 'a helping hand to make those exits'.[8] In my terms, a neglected or abused child brings few positive resources for learning to school. This makes him or her more likely to be disruptive (or at best inattentive) than pupils whose homes provide them with more resources.

As a good Conservative, however, Letwin focuses on the responsibility of individual parents for the initial disadvantage: the only source that he acknowledges is 'neglect and abuse'. The allocation of rights, opportunities and resources is thus let off the hook, since Letwin makes it sound as if the cause is randomly distributed personal deficiencies. This leaves it utterly mysterious why criminals are drawn mostly from a relatively narrow social stratum, why they tend to have appalling reading and mathematical abilities, and so on. Clearly, there are other processes of disadvantage at work, and I shall illustrate the operation of these in chapter 7. Before that, however, I shall take up two major examples of cumulative advantage and disadvantage. Chapter 5 will deal with education and chapter 6 with health.

5

Education

In the previous chapter, I introduced the case of Able and Charlie, who had the same capacity for turning an hour of study into an increment of attainment. Able, it will be recalled, gained a certain qualification while Charlie did not. Why should we regard this outcome as fair? Ultimately, I suggest, the answer turns on the idea of responsibility. Able freely chose differently from Charlie out of the same set of options, and this makes them responsible for success and failure respectively. Because the notion of personal responsibility has been made so much of in recent years, I shall devote the whole of Part IV to it, illustrating its convenience to politicians who want to avoid accepting the responsibilities that should be shouldered by governments. For the present purpose, it is sufficient to make the point that a new-born baby cannot possibly be responsible for the material and social conditions into which it is born, and that whatever 'decisions' a child may make for a number of years after that cannot be its responsibility. It is doubtful how far decisions taken even by older children can be said to be autonomous in a way that generates responsibility for outcomes. There is something very unrealistic about a model of choices from choice sets which abstracts from parental encouragement and discouragement, peer pressure and the attitudes of other children in the school, for example. Admittedly some of the same forces may influence choices made by adults, but it is more reasonable to hold them responsible for choosing how far to act in accordance with them. If we are not prepared to do that, the whole principle of personal responsibility collapses. Perhaps it should – but I shall postpone the discussion of that question until chapter 10. Until then, let us simply go along with it and see where it takes us.

To cut the Gordian knot, I propose that we should regard the demands of social justice as being met to the extent that there are equal educational attainments at the age of 18. Nobody in the contemporary world is equipped to understand it or get around in it without education to the age of 18, so it is a personal resource that is of great value to everyone. And in as far as educational attainments provide the route to chosen careers, we can say that their equalization constitutes equal opportunity. It would, undeniably, be possible to complicate matters by saying that children start acquiring some responsibility from the age of, say, 14. But I believe that the social determination of outcomes is so powerful that adding this kind of nuance would make very little difference in practice to the implications of social justice for educational policy or the implications of unequal attainments for social justice.

Before I go any further, let me make it clear that 'equal' should not be understood rigidly as 'identical'. It simply means that attainments should be equivalent. For example, in the British context, similar (university entry level) scores can be counted as an equal level of attainment regardless of the subject in which they were received. In the United States, the parallel is graduation from equally well-regarded high schools with equally impressive records. Equal attainments so understood constitute an ideal benchmark, which we know can never be achieved, if only because there are children suffering from congenital handicaps who would be incapable of doing so. But these ineliminable inequalities are in fact the clearest evidence for the proposition that those who achieve the most desirable jobs cannot claim that they owe it all to their personal merits. (I shall return to this point at the end of chapter 9.)

My subject in this chapter is cumulative advantage and disadvantage. I want to emphasize how early the process of differentiation between the potentially successful and the potentially unsuccessful starts and how pervasive it then continues to be. 'The socio-economic gap in education has been shown to start as early as 22 months. Traditionally, it has widened throughout the education system, culminating in skewed access to higher education.'[1] Instead of taking these inequalities as God-given, let us trace some of the paths leading to them, beginning with the period between conception and birth. The development of the foetus depends on the state of health of the mother at the time of conception and through pregnancy. One of the ways in which income affects health is via nutrition. But the adequacy of the mother's nutrition during pregnancy is especially significant, so if there are some mothers who cannot afford a healthy, balanced diet, equal opportunity requires them to be provided with the necessary funds. A dramatic illustration is cretinism, which has among its symptoms mental retardation: this arises from lack of iodine during pregnancy, and there are estimated to be three million cretins in the world from this simple cause.[2] There are many other dietary deficiencies that are known to have deleterious effects on foetal development, but the most widespread is simply protein-energy malnutrition. This 'has a decided impact on mental development, and with an estimated 150 million children suffering from the affliction worldwide, its potential cost in human, as well as social and economic, terms is staggering.'[3]

Exposure to metals such as lead, arsenic and mercury, and also to an enormous variety of chemicals, has a deleterious effect on foetal development, including mental development.[4] The poor are the most likely to be exposed to hazards such as these. A study by the Columbia Center for Children's Environmental Health found that, in the poorest areas of New York City, exposure to a high level of air pollution caused low birth weight and smaller than normal head circumference, both of which 'have been linked with lower IQ and poor cognitive functioning, such as learning disabilities'.[5] The tendency for the poor to be the victims of contaminated air and water has both economic and political causes. Land for siting a toxic waste dump or a noxious factory is cheaper in areas where the poor live, and, even if it was not cheap before, the affected area will become cheaper, so that the inhabitants will be people who cannot afford to live elsewhere. In addition, the poor tend to be a weak force politically, so they are less likely to be able to form an effective NIMBY ('not in my back yard') lobby than the well-to-do. 'Zoning, as a body of law, is supposed to be applied and enforced to protect all portions of the population equally.'[6] But the reality is far different. As one New York expert said: 'No question that zoning protects some people better than others. Zoning is responsive to wealth, property, [and] political power.'[7]

The key is the designation of 'M' zones. 'M' stands for 'manufacturing'. With the decline of manufacturing in New York City, however, in practice it means more and more 'waste facilities – private solid waste transfer stations, marine transfer stations, waste-water treatment plants, combined sewer overflow outfalls, junkyards, auto salvage yards, scrap metal and construction debris processing sites, and medical waste disposal plants'.[8] The most damning evidence for the discriminatory nature of zoning is that, from the 1950s on, 'the city was rezoning to increase M zones in areas with higher than average minority populations, lower than average incomes, and lower than average rates of home ownership. Conversely, the city was rezoning to decrease M zones in areas with lower than average minority populations, higher than average incomes, and higher than average rates of home ownership.'[9] Notice that the disadvantage attaches to being poorer than others: the absolute level of incomes in the society makes no difference. In the past half century, the average income in the United States has risen enormously; and, although the gains have been unequally distributed, even the poor are better off in terms of income. But inequality has increased in the same period (especially the second half of it), so it is hardly surprising that the connection between relatively low income and living in a zone designated 'M' has become tighter.

Quality of prenatal care and quality of medical care in childbirth are obviously of crucial importance, so a society that does not provide the same quality to everybody is necessarily unjust: among the rich countries, the most extreme case is represented by the United States, where many pregnant women do not see a doctor at any time during pregnancy. As a result, by the time the child is born it may also have acquired preventable handicaps. Prenatal care includes classes covering pregnancy and early childcare. For women to have an equal opportunity to attend classes, these have to be free (to avoid deterring those with no money left over for optional expenses), they have to be accessible (which may be difficult for someone without a car in the absence of good public transport), and the mother must have the time available to go to them. This is inconsistent with having to work long, inflexible hours (or even have two jobs) to make ends meet.

In the absence of paid leave both before and after giving birth (whether provided mandatorily by an employer or in the form of a state benefit), poverty is also likely to mean that a mother cannot take off the time she needs from paid employment. The USA is extraordinarily poor at giving women any kind of financial support either from employers as a matter of right or from the state. Only since 1993 have workers had a right to twelve weeks' leave in a year for birth or adoption, and even then only the half of the workforce in firms with more than fifty employees are covered, and the leave is unpaid. 'The Congressionally established US Commission on Leave reports that 64 per cent of employees who need but do not take [this unpaid] leave indicate that they cannot afford the loss of wages.'[10]

All the factors that I have referred to (or their obvious post-partum analogues) continue to act so as to differentiate the abilities (cognitive and other) of children according to the different circumstances in which they find themselves. Thus, the health (including the actual survival) of the parents obviously contributes to the child's development. (I shall talk about 'parents', intending to subsume within this the case of a single custodial parent.) Similarly, the child's nutrition is important for its mental as much as for its physical development. Protein-energy malnutrition has deleterious effects on both throughout childhood, for example. The deleterious effects of exposure to heavy metals and toxic chemicals continue to affect development, as does poor quality housing. The two are, indeed, closely associated, not simply because poor housing tends to be in hazardous areas, but also because poor housing is itself liable to be hazardous.

> Research in the 1990s demonstrated how the pipes and paint of slum housing – major sources of lead – damage the developing brains of children. Youngsters with elevated lead levels have lower IQs and attention deficits, and – according to a study published in the New England Journal of Medicine – were seven times more likely to drop out of school.'[11]

Quality of medical care continues to be relevant to equal educational opportunity, because it makes a difference to health, and ability to learn depends on the state of health of children and their parents. The capacity to understand and act on advice (written or oral) on the part of the parents is of critical importance, so one of the ways in which poor education is transmitted from one generation to the next is via health. Social workers often say that much of the child abuse that they are called in to deal with does not arise from any bad intentions on the part of the parents but from failure to understand what they are supposed to be doing.

One of the prenatal disadvantages that I mentioned was lack of parental time. This is if anything more important with a child than with a foetus. Raising a child (as against propping it up in front of the television set) is an extremely time-consuming business, so if both parents (or the single parent) have to work long hours to make enough to live on, their children will suffer from the lack of this resource. A lot also depends on what happens in that time. The early years are of critical importance here: 'Neurologically, infancy is a critical period because cortical development is influenced by the amount of central nervous system activity stimulated by experience.'[12]

This point is worth emphasizing simply because MRI (magnetic resonance imaging) machines have now spread beyond hospitals, enabling anybody who can get a grant to point one at people's heads while they solve problems and announce that the brains of those who are good at this activity are different from the brains of those who are not. As far as it goes, this is no more than an expensive glimpse of the obvious: barring miracles, every difference in mental capacity must correspond to some neurological difference. However, such findings become pernicious when they are seized on by right-wing ideologues as evidence that differences in ability are 'innate'. As the quotation above reminds us, they show nothing of the sort, because cortical development arises from environmental stimuli. In fact, the more we learn about the power of the early environment, the more plausible it becomes that, in the absence of some definite neurological deficit, all children have the same cognitive potential.

On the whole, better-educated parents do a better job of providing their children with the stuff that will later turn up in measured ability. This is partly because they are more likely to have read about how to do it (or associate with people who have), and have absorbed 'the idea that parents should talk to children at length, read to them, and take a proactive, assertive role in medical care'.[13] However, it is also true that this kind of thing is likely to happen anyway with middle-class parents. For example, they tend to talk more to their children, and talking to the child (even before it can speak itself) is advantageous to its intellectual development. Indeed, stimulus of this kind even at the foetal stage has been found to be important for subsequent ability, so the children of lone parents or parents who work long hours (especially if they are not the same hours) tend to be at a disadvantage right from the outset.

Some stunningly painstaking and sophisticated American research has shown just how large the gradient of class inequality in talk is: 'The longitudinal data showed that in the everyday interactions at home, the average (rounded) number of words children heard per hour was 2,150 in the professional families, 1,250 in the working-class families and 620 in the welfare families.'[14] There was also a sharp gradient in the complexity of the language used. 'To ensure their children access to advanced education, [professional] parents spent time and effort developing their children's potential, asking questions and using affirmatives to encourage their children, to notice how words refer and relate, and to practice the distinctions among them.'[15] Both quantity and quality of parents' speech correlated very strongly with children's measured linguistic ability at the age of 3.[16]

Finally (at any rate for the purposes of this drastic summary), there was also an extremely sharp class gradient in the ratio of encouragement to discouragement that children received.

The average child in a professional family was accumulating 32 affirmations and 5 prohibitions per hour.... The average child in a

working-class family was accumulating 12 affirmatives and 7 prohibitions per hour. . . . The average child in a welfare family, though, was
accumulating 5 affirmations and 11 prohibitions per hour, a ratio of 1
encouragement to 2 discouragements [as against 6 to 1 among professional and 2 to 1 among working-class parents].[17]

The results show up clearly in achievement at the age of 3: 'We
saw the powerful dampening effects of development when relatively
more of the child's interactions began with parent-initiated impera-
tives ("Don't", "Stop", "Quit") that prohibited what the child was
doing.'[18]

The effects of parents' unequal cultural resources are by no means
beyond the reach of social policy, because the advantages of children
with better-educated and more articulate parents can be offset. In
Britain, the 'SureStart' scheme that has been created in (pitifully
few) poor neighbourhoods encourages parents to follow the simple
recipes for success in preparing children to learn at school: talking to
them, reading to them and inviting curiosity rather than suppressing
it. Even if this is successful, however, the gap between vocabulary and
discursive ability between middle-class and working-class parents will
still remain. But this gap can to a considerable extent be filled by
high-quality professional child care. In the United States, though, this
is hard to come by: 'child-care workers earn[ed in 2001] an average
of $15,430 per year', usually without benefits or paid leave, whereas
garbage collectors earned an average of $25,020.[19] 'The low salary
and lack of benefits generate high turnover rates among child-care
providers. Nationwide, about one-third of staff leave their centers
each year.'[20] Further, 'child–staff ratios in many states allow child-care
centers and family child-care homes to operate with far too many
children per staff member to ensure that children receive adequate
supervision and support.'[21]

The qualifications of those entrusted with child care are, not
surprisingly in view of the pay, dismal: 'Some 22 per cent to 34 per
cent of teachers in regulated child-care centers and family child-care
settings do not have a high school diploma', while 'in unregulated
family-and-relative child-care settings, between 33 and 46 per cent of
caregivers have not completed high school.'[22] In addition to their lack
of education, these child-care workers are unlikely to improve the
cultural and linguistic capital of their charges beyond that which they
acquire at home. The family and relative carers are likely to be similar
culturally to the parents. And 'many [of the paid carers] are immi-
grants from developing countries' who are hardly likely to provide
what is lacking.[23]

Furthermore, leaving aside family-and-relative child care, there are only eleven states that require even those who take care of children in their homes as a profit-making activity to have 'any early childhood training prior to serving children in their homes',[24] whereas 'hairdressers and manicurists must attend 1,500 hours of training at an accredited school in order to get a license'.[25] Regulations seem to be little guarantee of even the absolute minimum: 'one four-state study found fully 40 per cent of the rooms serving infants in child care centers to be of such poor quality as to jeopardize children's health, safety or development.'[26] In the mainly unregulated home-care system, a national study found more than a third of the programmes 'inadequate, which means that poor quality was enough to harm children's development'.[27]

Even this primitive kind of care does not come cheap: 'In more than half of the urban areas surveyed [in 2000], the average cost of [home] child care for a 4-year-old is $4,500 per year. Generally, this cost of child care is even higher for infants.'[28] As far as care in a centre is concerned, the absence of available publicly subsidized places means that 'the average annual cost of child care for a 4-year-old in an urban area center is more than the average annual cost of public college tuition.'[29] In a quarter of states, it is twice the amount: 'Child care can easily cost an average of $4,000 to $6,000 per year. In certain parts of the country, families may be spending more than $10,000 a year on child care. . . . Among the cities surveyed, the average cost . . . for infants is generally about $1,100 a year [more].'[30] As a result, the cost of child care for an infant exceeds the average cost of public college tuition in every state.[31]

In the year to which these figures apply, the average child-care worker was making only $14,820, so one of them in a stable relationship with a garbage worker – a member of the aristocracy of manual labour by contemporary standards – would have had only about $40,000 pre-tax gross between them. With an infant and a toddler, they might be looking at a bill of over $13,000 for *average* quality child care. If they were both working full time at the federal minimum wage (making a total of $21,400), this would amount to about two-thirds; but even for the better-off couple it would still be a third, and out of the question. Yet, as we have seen, even beginning to close the gap between their children's linguistic competence and that of a professional couple's would require interaction with highly educated and well-trained teachers, much of it on a one-on-one basis – the kind of pre-school education that, ironically, only professionals can afford. Even more ironic (but no surprise to anyone who knows anything about American politics) is that there is a Dependent Care

Tax Credit, which is useless to those too poor to pay income tax and has a value that increases according to the marginal tax rate of the couple and thus pays most to the richest.

The scale of the problem of unaffordability of child care can be seen by noting that, in the year following that covered by the cost figures I have given, more than one in four families with young children earned less than $25,000 a year.[32] There existed when this was written a programme of child-care subsidies, but 'nationally, only 12 per cent of eligible children who need[ed] help [were] getting any assistance.'[33] No amount of computer-jockeying has succeeded in turning up figures later than 2001. Given the massive federal tax cuts since then and the increase in the military's share of the remaining budget, plus the fiscal crisis faced by most states as well as the increasing amount of their budgets absorbed by prisons, it is hard to see where the money could have come from to fund George W. Bush's promise to 'leave no child behind'.

Britain does better with child care than the USA, but a lot worse than Sweden: the inadequate provision of publicly funded places and their failure to cover the whole working day mean that a lot of the children whose parents both work and cannot afford better are subjected to minimally stimulating child-minding.[34] New Labour makes a lot of fuss about the 'SureStart' programme already mentioned. This is intended to provide comprehensive child care, 'but the promise was painfully modest. Labour has created only 88,000 childcare places in six years – and now there are only to be another 43,000 by 2008: SureStart gets a lot more self-congratulation from Labour than its tiny weight will bear.'[35]

Once children are in school, the odds are very high that the differences in environment to which they have already been exposed will continue to exist, providing the already advantaged children with continuing advantages that compensatory education is unlikely to be powerful enough to reverse. How well a child is fed, for example, is intimately connected with its ability to benefit from school attendance. There is a well-established finding that children who go to school without having had breakfast learn less well than others, and that this effect is stronger among children who are generally malnourished.[36] Even a programme of free school lunches for poor children will not eliminate this disadvantage. Parental time continues to be a critical resource once children are in school. Children lose out if their parents cannot afford to take time off to look after them when they are sick or to deal with crises. This requires paid leave for parents, except for those who are well-off enough to take unpaid days off. But even if they can afford it, parents may well be reluctant to do so out of fear that this may jeopardize their jobs in the feral work environment that British and American economic and social policies have created.

Because of the enormous variability in working conditions in the USA, it is easy to study the difference to a child's development that the availability of parental time makes. In a study done in 2000, it was found that those children who scored in the bottom quarter on reading and mathematics were significantly more likely to have working parents who lacked paid holidays, sick leave and job flexibility. Further, 'even controlling for differences in family income and in parental education, marital status, and total hours parents worked, the more hours parents had to be away from home after school in the evening, the more likely their children were to test in the bottom quartile on achievement tests.' More remarkably still, perhaps, 'after controlling for other differences, parents who had to work at night were still 2.7 times as likely to have a child who had been suspended from school'.[37] Needless to say, the parents who were unable to care for their children at home were far more likely to have low incomes: for example, only half as many parents in the bottom quartile of the income distribution could take time off for sick children as could parents in the top quartile, and the gap for flexible working hours was almost as large.[38] Those who already have the disadvantage of being poor have it compounded by Dickensian conditions of work.

Manifestly, in a society dedicated to the pursuit of social justice, intensive research efforts would be devoted to finding out the best ways to overcome the disadvantages that children carry with them into the school system – and continue to suffer from – as a consequence of their home and neighbourhood environment. In fact, the conventional (and convenient) wisdom has been 'that there is almost nothing that money spent on schools can do to improve outcomes'.[39] This would suggest deep irrationality among generations of parents who have paid for more expensive education either by buying it directly or paying a premium to live in an area that spends more on schools. Nevertheless, the US Supreme Court cited research along these lines to deny that school funding within a state should be equal.[40] And in Britain, successive governments of both parties have cited similar findings to explain why large class sizes (the worst student–teacher ratio in Western Europe) do not put children in state schools at a disadvantage. Fortunately, however, research has now caught up with the real world. It has been discovered experimentally that really small class sizes do help, and studies have shown that 'a number of variables including total expenditure, student–teacher ratio, teacher experience, and teacher education were significantly related to student test score outcomes'.[41] Despite this, as we shall see, social disadvantage tends to be compounded by poor schooling, rather than compensated for by superior schooling.

It is instructive to contrast the tendency to write off the socially disadvantaged as 'ineducable' with the intensive and expensive interventions that are undertaken in both Britain and (especially) the USA in relation to those whose learning disabilities are more severe – serious enough for them to be counted as 'retarded'. The simple explanation is that retardation for the most part has causes in which the socioeconomic environment of the foetus and the child does not play a significant part. Even environmental causes operating at birth or shortly after, such as asphyxia, infection and trauma, can happen to anybody's children, though as a matter of fact they happen more to those of poor people. Non-environmental causes of moderate and severe retardation, such as Down syndrome and some genetic disorders, are distributed more or less randomly across the socioeconomic hierarchy. In short, 'mental retardation knows no boundaries. It cuts across lines of racial, ethnic, educational and social background. It can occur in any family.' This fact is opportune for persons with retardation: many of their most effective advocates have become involved 'because they happened to have a child or sibling with retardation'.[42] Indeed, 'President Kennedy's initiative, inspired by his own family's experience with mental retardation, marked the beginning of "a new positive philosophical approach to understanding and managing mental retardation as a chronic handicapping disorder".'[43] This was backed up by a newly created lobbying organization, called the American Association of Mental Deficiency.[44]

Another example of the phenomenon that has been described as 'the sharp elbows of the middle class' is the way in which privileged parents are reluctant to accept that their child is simply 'bad at reading' or 'disruptive' and instead shop around until they can get it certified as suffering from dyslexia or 'attention deficit disorder' and therefore as requiring special treatment. I recall reading somewhere (before I started to collect materials for this book) that there are some schools in affluent neighbourhoods in Los Angeles where up to half the children have achieved an official diagnosis of some kind of 'learning disability', which gives them advantages – such as turning in less work, turning it in later, taking longer in tests, and so on – that are denied to their classmates with parents who are less persevering or cannot afford to go on consulting experts until they get the answer they want.

The point is not that such quasi-medical diagnoses are *necessarily* bogus, but that they could doubtless be made of a far larger proportion of children with poor, marginalized parents. But among these children, it is simply regarded as normal that they will often be ill-disciplined and read poorly. Whereas moderate and severe retardation are distributed roughly randomly across a society, and can (as we have seen) frequently be attributed to some fairly specific neurological abnormality, mild retardation is clustered at the bottom of the social hierarchy. Thus, mild mental retardation is 'associated with "sociocultural or psychosocial disadvantage" in a child's home environment'.[45] Specifically, 'children in disadvantaged areas may be deprived of many common cultural and day-to-day experiences provided to other youngsters. Research suggests that such understimulation can result in irreversible damage and can serve as a cause of mental retardation.'[46]

I shall treat at some length in the next chapter the relation between inequality and stress – in both parents and children. But it is important to add this as a factor not only in health outcomes (especially in relation to asthma in children) but also in learning ability.[47] Material conditions also, as I have been emphasizing, have a direct effect on the intellectual functioning of children. To sum up in the words of Gary Orfield, the United States has 'many regions with schools overwhelmingly occupied with residents who are economically marginalized and experiencing the kinds of problems of health, joblessness, family crisis, community decay and powerlessness that supposedly characterize the Third World'.[48] It is scarcely surprising if all this expresses itself in abysmally poor academic attainment among the children who attend these schools.

It is important to recognize that a school in such a neighbourhood is itself necessarily an extremely negative environment. They look bleak from the outside, and are no doubt equally bleak inside. Razor-sharp barbed wire around the perimeter and armed police patrolling the halls are scarcely propitious. And, of course, a child in such a school will find it full of others with the same problems, the same cultural deficits and the same limited horizons. Hence, there is nothing surprising in the finding that the 'additional basic skills instruction' given to 'students attending concentrated poverty schools' produced smaller improvements than were achieved by 'similar students receiving no programs but attending less isolated schools'.[49]

Children 'with mild mental retardation . . . are capable of learning academic skills to approximately a sixth grade level.'[50] It is significant that, despite their having a normal capacity to learn in a nurturing environment, this low level of attainment is characteristic of the *average* black child in the USA – not just those from the inner-city ghettoes, whose average is well below that. Thus, in 1999, the average black score in mathematics at the age of 17 was 283.3; that of the average white 13-year-old was 283.1. In reading, blacks did a little worse even than that: the average 17-year-old black scored 263.9, whereas the average white scored 266.7 at the age of 13. To put this into perspective, scores between 250 and 300 in mathematics denote 'numerical operations and beginning of problem solving', whereas above 300 (average white score at the age of 17 was 314.8) we get to 'moderately complex procedures and reasoning'. (The interpretation of the different reading scores at the age of 17 is of a similar kind.)[51] Perhaps even more depressing than these scores themselves is that they had peaked in the mid-1980s and then declined to these levels.[52] Depressing as this may be, it is hardly cause for surprise when we bear in mind the cumulative effect of changes in public policy reducing incomes and economic security for the poor as well as the huge increase in the male black prison population in this period. (I shall return to this last phenomenon and its effects in chapter 7.)

The first demand of social justice is to change the environments in which children are born and grow up so as to make them as equal as possible, and this includes (though it is by no means confined to) approximate material equality among families. The second demand – which is more pressing the further a society fails to meet the first demand – is that the entire system of social intervention, starting as early as is feasible, should be devoted to compensating, as far as possible, for environmental disadvantages. Thus, the authors whose discussion of the acquisition of linguistic competence I discussed earlier wrote that 'the accomplishments of the higher-SES [socioeconomic status] children are hardly surprising when we consider their cumulative experience'.[53]

Just getting the authors' so-called welfare children up to the average working-class level 'would have to start at birth and run continuously all year long. There are no extra hours available to make up for the 60,000 words of experience that may have been lost in some past week. . . . We can see why our brief, intense efforts during the War on Poverty did not succeed.'[54] Equal opportunity for all regardless of parentage, as I defined it, cannot be achieved in one generation. But it would not be unrealistic, as long as the resources were committed to it, to aim for every child not reliably diagnosed as retarded to complete secondary education with respectable results. This would provide a platform for a further move in the next generation towards equal opportunity (provided the same efforts were maintained), while at the same time enabling people to play their role as citizens and providing them with a prospect of participating in the mainstream economy.

The possibilities and the limitations of maximum intervention under the most unpromising conditions are illustrated by a programme in Milwaukee, Wisconsin that enlisted seventeen mothers whose IQ tested at 75 or below. Initially, 'the para-professional who would become the infant's individual caregiver [spent] 3–5 hours, 3 days a week, in the family home with the mother' as an adviser; then, 'at 6–8 weeks of age', the infants 'were enrolled in out-of-home, full-time day care', while the mothers received remedial education and job training. These children, 'unlike children from comparable families not enrolled in the project and unlike children in less time-consuming intervention programs, were equal to the national average at age 8'.[55]

Echoing what I said earlier, the authors point out that this involved 'beginning at birth and integrating all the technology routinely available to families in crisis and children with special needs' to help children whose parents were no more than extremely ill-educated in the usual boring way.[56] Even then, it got the children only up to the average, though as an achievement this is by no means to be underestimated. At the same time, the Wisconsin Program raises almost as many problems as it solves, since it is fairly clear that it formed part of a 'welfare-to-work' system under which participation was a necessary condition of receiving welfare benefits. It goes without saying that this set-up is infinitely preferable to the one following the 'end of welfare' under which mothers with no other means of support are required to take any job, however ill-paid and loathsome, when their children reach the age of six weeks and are forced into whatever makeshift child-care arrangements they can manage, even if these put at risk their children's development and perhaps physical safety. Allowing for all the bells and whistles, however, the compulsory nature of the programme still makes it questionable.

An IQ of 75 does not by itself abrogate the moral claim of a mother to have some control over the upbringing of her children.[57] On a simple-minded view of the matter, this is a conflict between social justice and other values, if we assume that any programme less strongly interventionist would lower the children's attainment at the age of 8. But there is more to social justice than equal opportunity. As I shall emphasize especially in chapter 14, the usurpation of power by the state – and, thanks to state policies, by employers – to control the poor is itself a crying injustice that disfigures Britain only to a lesser degree than America. There is, however, an alternative perspective. Regardless of their reliance on public funding, children under the age of 18 should not, I have argued, be held fully responsible for their choices about staying in school or working hard. But by the same token, they are too immature to take responsible decisions about their own children. I would suggest, therefore, that something along the lines of the Wisconsin Program should be a requirement for children whose parents are minors.

As far as the parents are concerned, there would surely be a large take-up rate if all the elements of the Wisconsin Program, and other forms of intervention as well, were made available free of charge. Suppose that mothers with children under the age of 2 were all paid reasonable subsistence (say, two-thirds of the median wage) unconditionally. Provided social policy assured that paid work produced more than this, many mothers would choose to take full-time or part-time employment voluntarily, and would thus avail themselves of child care which we are stipulating to include a good deal of one-on-one interaction. Moreover, there is a lot of evidence that the vast majority of parents sincerely want to do well by their children.[58] If they were convinced by seeing results, they would be attracted by the options of high-quality child care supplemented by (middle-class) 'parent aides . . . the extra pair of hands that extended family once provided' and mentors (who might be retired people) chosen to provide advice on child-rearing.[59]

Any such programme would, of course, cost a great deal of money, which would have to come out of the pockets of those who have it. In addition to middle-class resistance to paying higher taxes, paying for this particular purpose would run into a further political roadblock. For it would, to the extent that its purposes were realized, be contrary to the interest that middle-class parents have in passing on their privileged position to their children. Early, multidimensional high-quality child care sustained over several generations is the only possible route to the real equalization of opportunity. This makes it more of a threat than any amount of fiddling around with the school system, since it is clear that, by the time children reach school, middle-class advantage is already so entrenched under existing conditions that nothing can overcome it later. Not that reassurance of this kind prevents middle-class parents from a fanatical concern with schools, as we shall see.

Through most of the twentieth century, class conflict over social mobility was muted by the fact that gains for some did not have to correspond to losses by others. The expansion of middle-class occupations meant that middle-class parents could pass on their status to their children while still leaving room for working-class children to move into the middle class. This expansion could not continue, and it has not. In April 2004, the Prime Minister's Strategy Unit produced a report on the situation in Britain entitled 'Life Chances and Social

Mobility: An Overview of the Evidence.' Its key point was that 'the expansion of the middle class has halted in recent decades'.[60] Social mobility has thus become a zero-sum game: working-class children can rise only if an equal number of middle-class children fall, and this is barely occurring. 'A middle-class child is 15 times more likely to stay middle class than a working-class child is likely to move into the middle class.... Only the USA has less upward social mobility than the UK among western nations.'[61] A study completed in 2002 showed how social mobility had declined: those born in 1970 were more likely to stay in the quartile of the income distribution they had been born into than those born in 1958. Among the 1958 cohort, 34 per cent of children with parents in the top quartile of incomes attained a similar position; among the 1970 cohort it was 43 per cent. At the other end of the scale, 30 per cent of children in the 1958 cohort with parents in the bottom quartile of incomes inherited the same position; the corresponding figure for the 1970 cohort was 38 per cent.[62]

There are other forces intensifying this undeclared but very real class war. Those who fail to have middle-class jobs are increasingly finding themselves not with the stable working-class jobs of the past (in steel mills, car factories, and so on) but either unemployed or employed in temporary jobs at the margins of the economy that do not carry with them the occupational benefits that trade unions used to insist on in labour contracts. At the same time, as the middle class has grown, it has become more differentiated. The enormous increase in the inequality of earnings that has occurred in Britain and the USA has been almost entirely concentrated in the top quarter of the income distribution; and, within that, the increase has been greater the higher we move up the scale. Both of these shifts in the structure of employment and earnings have made the stakes higher. For the child of a middle-class parent to finish up in a non-middle-class occupation represents a much bigger fall than before; and within the middle class 'it is a question of who is filling the best opportunities'.[63] For an ambitious middle-class parent, such as Tony Blair, what used to be thought of as good jobs are no longer good enough. Asked by a journalist why he did not send his sons to an ordinary state school, he said: 'Look at Harold Wilson's children.' 'The journalist demurred and said that one son had become a headmaster and the other a professor at the Open University. To which Tony responded, startlingly, "Well, I certainly hope my children do better than that." '[64] To me what is surprising is that Robin Cook (in whose diaries the anecdote occurs) found the remark startling, given that Blair has both expressed and acted on the maxim that no mere 'ideology' (equal opportunity, perhaps) should stand in the way of his 'doing the best' for his children.

Increasing the proportion of those who go to university does not do anything to ameliorate the struggle, since it simply means that the level of qualifications to get the fixed number of middle-class jobs – and especially the most desirable ones – will increase to keep pace. More working-class children are going to universities, it is true, but the lion's share of the expansion has been absorbed by middle-class children. In 2002, 'only 15% of children whose parents are manual workers went to university, compared with 81% of the children of professionals'.[65] The significant competition today, however, is not to get into *a* university, but to get into the *right* university. Thanks to ever-more concentrated funding of universities on the basis of their research records, gaps in resources between them are wide and growing. For example, the student–staff ratio at Oxford, Cambridge and Imperial College London (three elite institutions) is about twice that of three typical ex-polytechnics, North London, London Guildhall and Thames Valley.[66] These resource differences are paralleled by the difference in the quality (measured by A-level grades) of incoming students.

'Students from low income families may be going to college in increasing numbers – but to attend lower ranking institutions leading to jobs lacking in status.'[67] For example, comparing the same six universities, we find that Oxford and Cambridge take 9 per cent of their students from the lowest three social classes, Imperial 17 per cent, North London 41 per cent, Guildhall 36 per cent and Thames Valley 34 per cent.[68] 'The existence of such stark divisions between universities' and 'the widening gap between the elite and the rest' increase 'the pressure on middle class parents to choose private or selective schooling for their children'.[69] Private schools, which account for only 7 per cent of the school-age population, provide half or more of the entrants to elite universities. Studies have found that parents are more likely to use private schools the better off they are, but that, other things being equal, they are less likely to do so if the local authority expenditure on schools is high. By Western European standards, Britain spends relatively little per head on its state schools.[70] At the same time, it also has very unequal incomes and the role of private schools in its educational system is unique.

What is particularly outrageous is that private schools are subsidized to the tune of an average of £2,000 per pupil per annum by the taxpayer.[71] This subsidy comes about because private schools, despite actively contributing to the perpetuation of social injustice, are afforded charitable status and get other advantages as well. Thus, private schools are able to get tax relief on interest from bank deposits and income from investments and obtain tax-free charitable donations. They also enjoy a reduced contribution to local taxation based on their property value.[72] This anomalous charitable status had been left in place by five Labour governments with majorities before Margaret Thatcher showed how a government seriously committed to social engineering could enormously increase its value. For example, the 1980 Finance Act (her first) allowed for tax to charities to be deducted from the higher rate of tax rather than only the standard rate. The limit on the amount that could be given 'was raised in 1983/4 and 1985/6 and removed in 1986. Firms can, since 1986, set single donations against corporation tax [whereas individuals have to take out a seven-year covenant to qualify]. The 1986 Finance Act also introduced tax relief on payroll giving [i.e. deductions from pay before tax].'[73] Another example is that the 50 per cent reduction in rates for charities (local government tax) that already existed was raised to 80 per cent when the community charge ('poll tax') was introduced.[74] The average private school fee in 2002 was £6,250 per annum; the average amount spent by the state on a secondary school student was around £3,000.[75] Thus, the effect of the £2,000 handout is that private schools can outspend state schools by an average of more than two to one; without it, the ratio would be reduced to only half as much again, which is a gap that could be bridged by bringing up the expenditure on the state schools to that in the Western European countries with the best schools.

Another example of the purchase of privilege is private tuition. A rapidly increasing number of parents with children attending state schools are paying for private tuition. At primary school level, this operates as a way of improving the middle-class grip on the still flourishing 11+ examination for selective schools within the system and in the competition for the most desirable schools that are notionally non-selective but are in fact selective because they are oversubscribed. Parents are thus able to gain all the benefits of the state system at its best at secondary level without having to pay the cost of private schools at the primary stage. 'In some schools [in London], more than half of the 11-year-olds have had at least 18 months of private tuition in English and maths before they sit their tests at 11.'[76] This is buying advantage on the cheap only, of course, if the relevant comparison is with private school fees: one researcher found 'one primary school where 65% of 11-year-olds were being tutored. A significant minority of their parents spent more than £100 a week on tutoring – more than many of the black and working class families were living on.'[77] Needless to say, this disadvantages working-class children and 'undermines any pretensions to a comprehensive school system'.[78] But what is less obvious is that it makes the situation of children without tutors where they are in a minority absolutely as well as relatively worse. 'The mother of a 10-year-old asked one teacher why the class rarely had any maths homework. "Oh, I don't tend to give homework any more because most of the children are being tutored," she replied cheerfully.'[79]

In a sane world, it would be the children who could really benefit from one-on-one help with basic skills such as reading and mathematics who would be getting personal tuition, not those who are already the best prepared. However, it would be both politically and practically very difficult to prohibit private tutoring. The only solution that can give equal opportunity a look in is to improve public education – by hiring tutors for all children if that is what it takes – and to reduce inequality in wealth and incomes to the point at which buying a higher quality of education than that which is provided publicly is feasible only for a small minority. At the same time, greater equality would reduce the importance of being just a little better than the next best candidate, because people's positions in the rank order of incomes would correspond to smaller differences in income. (I shall return to this in chapter 13.)

Within the state system, money can also buy school quality. The phenomenon, which was discovered only in 2001 by Tony Blair's private think-tank, the 'Performance and Innovation Unit', is that 'wealthy parents are buying access to good schools by being able to afford the higher prices in the school's local catchment area'.[80] One of the things that makes a school 'good' is having middle-class children in it, because of the personal resources they bring to it: middle-class articulacy, middle-class ambitions, and so on. Any country whose housing policy fails to prevent economically homogeneous areas from developing and then draws school catchment boundaries round them is automatically producing inequality of opportunity, even if the other educational inputs are the same as elsewhere. It is worth bearing in mind here that the quality of teachers is a resource. If pay is the same in all schools, better teachers will tend to be drawn to middle-class schools. 'Equal inputs' therefore require rationing or whatever pay differences are needed to get enough of the best teachers into schools that have predominantly working-class and minority children.

Increased inequality of income and wealth, combined with the pressures felt by middle-class parents to transmit their class position to their children, have resulted in a more and more self-conscious manipulation of the system. A 'survey of more than 1,200 parents suggested that 59% would consider moving house to be in the catchment area of a successful school. A recent Barclays [Bank] survey found that parents were willing to spend up to a third more for a property near a good primary [school].'[81] The poisonous effects of the frantic search for educational advantage combined with the inequalities between schools are illustrated by some other findings in the first survey: almost one in seven families would consider using a fake address to get their child into a good school, one in ten would fake a divorce for the same purpose and one in five would 'lie about or exaggerate their religious commitment' in an area in which a religious state-financed school was the best bet.[82]

The remaining strategy is to exploit the possibilities of 'choice' that have been created within the cities, and especially London. As Gary Orfield has said, 'choice mechanisms, if not limited by other policies, tend to have a clear tendency toward social stratification along socioeconomic lines, because of the way markets work for people with very different information, skills and resources'.[83] This holds true across countries and spheres of public policy: more choice means more inequality. Rather than worry about inequality between schools, New Labour has seen the solution to middle-class defection from the state system (13 per cent in London as against 7 per cent nationally) in making inequality among state schools greater. As one minister put it: 'we haven't the range of quality of secondary schools in London that often exists elsewhere in the country.'[84] In pursuit of precisely this objective, the government is busy creating 'city academies', with extra funding, which will be able to choose their own pupils.

In fact, what exists already is 'a complex mosaic of procedures and local practice, riddled with overt selection, covert selection and huge inequalities'.[85] Oversubscribed schools – those with the best results – choose their pupils rather than being chosen, and every school is looking for children who are likely to do well. This process is even more biased towards the middle class than the old 11+ examination – which was at least objective – because it makes heavy use of interviews 'to ascertain that parents have the right motivation'.[86] Thus, even middle-class children who do not satisfy other conditions can be dragged in as 'motivated'.

The result is that 'schools in London are becoming increasingly segregated along class and racial lines, with working-class and ethnic-minority children concentrated in the lowest achieving schools, and white and middle-class children dominating the highest-scoring ones with increasing polarization in the past four years under the aegis of New Labour'.[87] That was written in 2002, but a special report by the government's Office for Standards in Education (Ofsted) in 2003 showed that forces making for increased polarization could not be reversed without a complete revamp of government policy, and in particular the policy (carried over from Margaret Thatcher) of allowing the more popular schools to expand. The additional places tend to go to middle-class children, thus 'mak[ing] matters worse for the remaining unpopular schools', which are liable to enter into a 'spiral of decline'.[88] The remaining middle-class parents are – reasonably enough – anxious to rescue their children from a 'sink school', and 'are willing and able to transport their children to alternative schools further away from home'. But 'parents who are themselves trapped in a cycle of acute deprivation are more likely to have low aspirations for their children and lack the motivation or knowledge to seek places in more successful schools.'[89] In addition, of course, the obverse of the point made about middle-class parents applies here: you need both a car and a flexible work schedule to be able to get your child to some awkwardly located school and back every day reliably.

Whereas a socially just education system would minimize the effects on children's opportunities of their parents' social and economic position, the current set-up in Britain operates at every point to expand the advantages of parents with education, money and high aspirations. 'School choice' is just the final straw, in which the effects of parental advantages and disadvantages are multiplied by placing an enormous premium on know-how and resources. In the wake of the Ofsted report on 'The Influence of School Place Planning on School Standards and Social Exclusion', the chief inspector of schools 'urged local education authorities to take action "to prevent unpopular schools from sinking further"'.[90] But this is, as he no doubt realized, a pointless piece of advocacy because, as 'Ofsted concedes', local authorities are 'constrained by the fundamental principles of parental preference and school autonomy'.[91] As long as the government insists on retaining the Thatcherite market model, embodied in these two New Labour mantras, the inequality of school provision and the segregation of school children by class and ethnic background cannot but continue to run their course.

The United States, as I mentioned earlier, is the only country with less social mobility than Britain among western countries, and there too it has declined. Attending college has become more than ever the preserve of the children of parents who are well off. 'In contrast to the peak of access when the top quartile of families, in terms of income, were six times more likely than the bottom group to send their children to college, the ratio is now ten to one.'[92] Part of the explanation is that between 1980 and 1996 the federal government's grant for poor university students lost 57 per cent of its value.[93] Supplementing education in school with tutoring to improve test scores is widespread, though it should be added that in a market system you get what you pay for. At one end are hints about how to guess the answer to a multiple-choice test when you don't know it and exhortations not to spend time on any one question. (That advice of this kind and practice in following it do actually raise SAT scores illustrates the relative triviality of the tests.) At the other end are highly paid experienced coaches who push their charges through work on substantive school subjects.

As far as private education is concerned, this is more prevalent in the USA than in Britain (10 per cent), but this figure has to be treated with caution because about half of it is in Roman Catholic schools that would be state schools in Britain, and $3\frac{1}{2}$ per cent is in 'other Christian' schools that mostly teach whacky stuff of a fundamentalist nature: that Genesis is all true, the United Nations is sinful as an attempt to rebuild the Tower of Babel, and so on.[94] The Roman Catholic schools are not well funded and the 'other Christian' schools discourage their products from attending mainstream universities, so the equivalent of British private schools are 'non-sectarian' schools, which account for less than 2 per cent of the school population.[95] In relation to their numbers, these schools do extraordinarily well. Among the undergraduates admitted at Princeton, for example, public schools were slightly overrepresented (55 per cent) but 35 per cent were from non-sectarian private schools: over 20 times their 1.7 per cent in the school population. This figure may be a little above the average for elite universities (which are pretty coy, so that scraps of information have to be gathered where they can be), but not a lot out of line with the others.

Nevertheless, the majority of admissions are from the graduates of the public schools (in the American sense), and here the key is the way in which finance in most states is local. The average spent on a child in a state school is $6,000, but

> levels of spending vary considerably, both across and within states, from more than $8,000 per student to less than $4,000. Because most schools are financed primarily by property taxes, rich communities have rich schools. In comfy suburbs with rising real estate values, even relatively low tax rates can generate high revenues.[96]

Carrying even further the principle that the local public school is really a private club for the subscribers, this extraordinarily inequitable system of funding is extended even further down, to school districts. Thus, within Westchester County, a generally affluent dormitory suburb in New York State, the amount that is spent on the schools depends on the wealth of each school district. The result is that, even within this one county, wealthy districts such as Scarsdale spend around $18,000 per pupil while Mount Vernon, with more poor people and minorities, spends only $11,000 per pupil.[97]

Segregation by income and class has increased in America concomitantly with the increased inequality of incomes and the virtual disappearance of social programmes (except, of course, punitive ones) for poor blacks. The increase in black poverty in the 1970s and 1980s was

> absorbed by a small set of racially homogeneous, geographically isolated, densely settled neighbourhoods packed densely around the urban core; and because class segregation was increasing as well . . . a disproportionate share of the economic pain was absorbed by neighbourhoods that were not only black but also poor.[98]

Meanwhile, 'the typical affluent person (defined here as someone with an income of more than four times the poverty level) lived in a neighbourhood that was 39 per cent affluent in 1970; by 1990, the figure had risen to 52 per cent.'[99] On a stricter definition of 'affluence', the degree of homogeneity would be higher.

Even where spending per head is equalized across states (as it is in some), each jurisdiction within the state takes exclusively the children within its borders – extraordinarily, the Supreme Court has gone so far as to declare it unconstitutional to shift children from one jurisdiction to another in order to create balance in the schools. The result is to concentrate poor racial minorities in cities such as Chicago, Cleveland and Hartford, Connecticut, while around them are affluent, almost entirely white, suburbs. In more heterogeneous cities such as Boston, the collapse of busing to overcome exclusion, combined with the extreme division within cities by wealth that I have already mentioned, results in racially homogeneous 'neighbourhood schools'. Since, as we know, the children in a school are a major resource for the other children and, as I have pointed out, teachers prefer (if salaries are the same) to teach middle-class children in middle-class areas, the result is still that educational inputs are very unequal. Finally, it is not enough, even financially, to equalize spending per head within states because there is no mechanism for equalizing expenditures across the United States, and these are very unequal.

The point of this chapter has been to illustrate the process of cumulative advantage and disadvantage for the case of education up to the age of 18. I think I have demonstrated that the courses of different children are already set to some degree by the time they are born, and that at every stage those who already lag behind tend to fall behind further. I want to conclude, however, by pointing out that this is not a deterministic process but one that could be prevented, ameliorated or reversed by appropriate public policies. The problems of poverty and work scheduling could be overcome in a wealthy society. Over time, land planning policy could aim to create socially mixed neighbourhoods, rather than (especially in the United States) used to create homogeneous ones. The advantages that children gain in stimulus from their parents could be evened up by the large variety of methods I have discussed. If all schools were required to have a socioeconomic and ethnic mix typical of a wide area around them, there would no longer be the segregation characteristic of London between schools full of articulate and 'motivated' children and schools populated by poor and minority children. Children who were having trouble with their work would get extra help, instead of the personal tutoring going to those who are already ahead. This list could be extended indefinitely, but its object is to show how it is social institutions that perpetuate cumulative inequality. If there is any determinism involved, it is political: the range of powerful interests that would be mobilized in opposition to moves designed to disturb the process by which the advantages of one generation are transmitted to the next.

6

Health

'Eliminating health inequities is important as a matter of social justice because health is an asset and a resource critical to human development' and because of 'scientific evidence that health inequalities are the outcome of causal chains which run back into and from the basic structures of society'.[1] Of course, public policy cannot determine how healthy or long-lived any given individual will be. But public policy does not determine individual educational attainments or earnings, either, and this does not stop its making all the difference to the justice or injustice of their distribution. The distribution of ill-health and long life in the population depends on relative incomes, on racial and ethnic stigmatization, on autonomy or powerlessness in the workplace and on a multiplicity of other aspects of the basic structure of the society. Virtually every significant feature of a society has differential effects on health, according to its impacts on people in different locations within the social structure. By the same token then, there will be very few areas of public policy that do not have implications for the justice of the distribution of health. 'Because health inequalities are multi-determined, policies need to exert leverage at multiple points.'[2]

All the quotations in this chapter so far have been from a collection of articles entitled *Health and Social Justice* that was published in 2003. Apart from its existence, what is interesting about this book is that its contributors are drawn from the fields of public health (a majority), social epidemiology, sociology and (in one case) political science; but there is not a single contribution by a political philosopher. This may seem curious in a book about social justice, and the absence of such a contribution reveals itself in the lack of any systematic discussion of the concept of social justice and its relevance to health. There is, however, a good explanation: as far as I am aware, no such discussion exists. To the extent that political philosophers write about social justice and health, they confine themselves to the distribution of health *care*. The underlying assumption appears to be that everything to do with social justice and health has been included when health care has been discussed, whereas the truth is that this is only a small part of the picture.

We can see this equation of health with health care at work in an article by Ronald Dworkin, which sets up as a premise for an argument (whose content is irrelevant here) 'that health care is, as René Descartes puts it, chief among all goods: that the most important thing is life and health and everything else is of minor importance'.[3] No citation is offered, but if Descartes really said that health care (as against health) was the chief good, then he must have had extraordinarily poor judgement. It is certain that until some time late in the nineteenth century, when bleeding and prescribing (literally) poisons had gone out of fashion and antiseptic surgery was creeping in, medical care was more likely to kill than cure. Descartes's contemporary, Thomas Hobbes, exhibited sterling good sense in saying he would sooner trust his health to the care of a wise old woman than to a qualified doctor.[4] Few people, it has been asserted, would wish to insist 'that medicine's effectiveness went back much before the advent of antibiotics in 1940 or sulphonamides in the 1930s'.[5]

Go round any English churchyard and you will see pathetic tombstones from the mid-nineteenth century recording the death of perhaps a dozen children in infancy. By the end of the century, they have disappeared. This cannot have been due to any significant improvements in the quality of health care: the technology did not change a lot and access to it was just as hit and miss:

> There is evidence that modern preventive and therapeutic medical care can account for only a minor fraction of the dramatic improvements in individual and population health over the past 250 years. . . . Even analysts admiring the impact of medical science on health, for example, estimate that only about five years of the 30-year increase in life expectancy in the United States in the twentieth century has been due to preventive or therapeutic medical care. . . . The remainder is attributable primarily to increasing socioeconomic development and associated gains in nutrition, public health and sanitation, and living conditions.[6]

Scourges such as typhoid fever and cholera were wiped out in Britain in the nineteenth century by the provision of pure drinking water and the safe disposal of human wastes. Another public health measure – the use of quarantining – virtually eliminated scarlet fever and diphtheria long before there were any effective drugs. An important contribution to 'living conditions' was the improvement in housing, thanks to city codes (as in New York) mandating ventilation standards and the reduction in overcrowding. This did much to reduce the spreading of pulmonary tuberculosis among families.

A vivid illustration of the role played by housing is that tuberculosis has reappeared in New York City in recent years. It is associated with 'an upsurge of family homelessness' because, when people lose their homes, the only alternative to the street or a temporary shelter is 'doubling up with other families'.[7] This deterioration is the direct effect of public policies aimed against the poor, especially those suffering from the concentrated disadvantages found in the ghetto, such as a real reduction in the value of welfare benefits (especially in relation to housing costs) and the inadequate supply of subsidized public housing. (I shall return to the issue of responsibility for homelessness in chapter 12.)

The relative insignificance of health care can be established by plotting the proportion of the GDP spent on health care against expectation of life for OECD countries: we find a distribution of points that looks more like currants in a Christmas pudding than the kind of linear relationship that might be naively expected. Japan, with the greatest longevity, is a below-average spender, whereas the USA, which spends by far the most, has a rather mediocre average expectation of life.[8] On the most generous estimate, 'the benefits provided by each of the main areas of medical services, including screening, immunisation and the main areas of treatment . . . added at the most five years to the life expectancy of Americans'.[9]

To put this in perspective, it will be useful to contemplate figures such as the following: 'Americans in the top 5 per cent of the income distribution can expect to live about nine years longer than those in the bottom 10 per cent.'[10] This gap is not atypical. 'These health inequalities usually account for differences of five to ten years in life expectancy between rich and poor within countries – and occasionally for as much as a fifteen-year difference.'[11] In Britain, 'professional men now live nine-and-a-half years longer than unskilled manual workers, the widest gap on record. The death rates for under-65s in our poorest urban areas are two-and-a-half times higher than in our richest areas.'[12]

What matters most, apart from being alive at all (and arguably matters more than that) is being in good health, in as far as this is the necessary condition for achieving many of one's goals. It makes a difference to job opportunities, to abilities to have and raise children, and generally to the chance of enjoying life – at least given a minimally decent physical and social environment. But those who live less long are also dogged by ill-health from an earlier age. This may, indeed, be an even more pronounced inequality:

> In East Surrey, Kingston and Richmond, wealthy suburbs of London, the average expectation of life is 79. The expectation of a healthy life unaffected by disability or poor health is 67 years. In Barnsley [a relatively poor town about twenty miles north-east of Manchester] the expectation of life is 76, with only 52 years of healthy life.[13]

Moreover, while few people can be aware of the way in which psychosocial processes lead to early ill-health and death, they do affect 'the real subjective quality of life among modern populations'.[14] As Richard Wilkinson puts it:

> If the whole thing were a matter of eating too many chips or of not taking enough exercise, then that would not in itself mean that the quality of life which people experienced was much less good. You can be happy eating chips. But sources of social stress, poor social networks, low self-esteem, high rates of depression, anxiety, insecurity, the loss of a sense of control, all have such a fundamental impact on our experience of life that it is reasonable to wonder whether the effects on the quality of life are not more important than the effects on the length of life.[15]

I shall explain the way in which stress has deleterious physiological effects later. Before that, it is high time for me to deal systematically with the fundamental question: what constitutes social justice in health?

I suggest that, if 'health inequalities are the outcomes of causal chains which run back into and from the basic structure of society', then wherever we find groups defined by class (however measured), ethnicity, race or any other structural characteristic that experience differences in the quality of their health, the society has a prima facie unjust distribution of health. How can the prima facie injustice be shown not to be a real injustice? The only way consistent with the principles of justice laid out in this book is to trace the whole of the inequality between the average health of two groups to systematically different choices made by members of these groups under circumstances that generated personal responsibility. I shall take up the question of personal responsibility at the end of this chapter. But I can anticipate the result of that enquiry now by saying that 'lifestyle' is very largely a red herring in the context of health and social justice.

The reason for this is, to put it intuitively, as follows: if two groups systematically behave differently in ways that affect their health, it is overwhelmingly likely that these differences will in turn have their basis in the social locations of the two groups. If this is so, we are still looking at the effects on health of the basic structure of society, but this time mediated by structurally induced differences in behaviour.

Since, as I showed in chapter 3, there exists a global basic structure, what I have said here for justice within countries extends naturally to justice in the world as a whole. To the extent, for example, that people (especially infants and young children) are dying of lack of nutrition and simple cost-effective public health measures, they are to a large degree being killed by the policies of the IMF, the World Bank and the WTO, exacerbated by the dismal record of rich countries in supplying economic aid. Of course, if a large part of a poor country's income (however derived) is syphoned off by its rulers or spent on instruments of domestic repression and external aggression, these rulers bear a heavy responsibility too. But we must recognize that these regimes themselves are an element in the overall system of international politics, and are very often sustained (sometimes actually brought into being) because they serve the interests of governments and firms in rich countries. What is at first sight a paradox – that the countries in sub-Saharan Africa with the most natural resources have had the worst economic records since independence – dissolves once we see how the possession of natural resources invites political manipulation.[16] The insurgents in Sierra Leone, for example, maintained themselves with money from diamond companies. And the chaos in the Congo suits international firms just fine, since there is nobody capable of taxing or controlling them.

Let me now return to systematic health inequalities within wealthy countries. How can the big gaps that I have cited be accounted for? Notwithstanding what I have said about the relatively small impact of medical care, it is still worth observing that those in the more advantaged social positions tend to get more expensive care. This is notoriously true in the United States, though the overtreatment of the well-insured in that country may undo a lot of the good done by health-improving treatments. (I shall return to this.) In Britain, within the National Health Service, resources are quite closely matched to *demands*, but 'minority ethnic groups and very low income groups [make] *less* use of health services for a given level of morbidity (illness)'.[17] A British study published in November 2003 found that 'affluent achievers from the middle class were 40% more likely to get a heart by-pass than the "have-nots" from lower socioeconomic groups, despite the much higher mortality from heart disease in the deprived group. Poorer people were 20% less likely to get a hip replacement, although they were 30% more likely to need one.'[18] Similarly, a report published 'by Cancer Research UK revealed [in March 2004] that it is the affluent who are profiting the most from faster diagnosis and better treatment, while the prospects for the poor lag years behind'.[19]

The explanation hypothesized by the research team was that 'rich people are quicker to go to the doctor when they suspect something is wrong and know how to demand attention'.[20] This is the sense of entitlement, articulacy and self-confidence in pushing doctors that middle-class parents pass on to their children, as we saw in the previous chapter. Needless to say, New Labour's vaunted extension of 'patient choice' within the National Health Service will inevitably widen the class gap by increasing the advantages of pushiness and know-how. A further point (analogous with the school case) is that the choice of a distant hospital is much more feasible for those whose family have flexible hours and the ability to afford the means of travel to inaccessible places. This explains differential take-up of formally equal options by saying that they are not really equal, because many of these options are infeasible to those outside the middle class or feasible only at greater cost in time and effort. But the larger number of visits to a doctor by middle-class people for any given degree of illness has also been attributed, at least partially, to cost: they usually have enough flexibility in their work schedules to visit a doctor without facing loss of pay. Again, it has been found that doctors are very poor at conveying what they intend to say to any patients except middle-class ones, with the results that others often fail to follow the regime prescribed for them.[21]

It is important to recognize, however, that lack of knowledge, articulacy and pushiness also have origins in the class structure. There is no reason for thinking that the poor value health less than the rich. If a large proportion of the poor were Christian Scientists and only a few of the rich, it would be a different matter. Medical care should not be imposed on adults against their will, so that those who spurn it as a result of religion or cultural beliefs are responsible for any adverse consequences for their health.[22] This sort of difference is totally implausible as an explanation of the actual phenomenon. The technology for overcoming the transmission of disadvantage in getting the most out of institutions (including the health care system) is known, as we saw in the previous chapter. All that is needed (all!) is the political will to commit the necessary resources. Injustice in the distribution of health care has tangible consequences: lives blighted or truncated by preventable or curable disease because treatment goes to the pushy rather than the needy.

Having said all that, it still has to be added that differential quality of medical care cannot possibly explain more than a fraction of the class gap in health. One way of seeing this is to imagine that the richest 5 per cent of Americans got no health care whatever, while the poorest 10 per cent benefited from every possible form of intervention: the richest would still live on average about four years longer than the poorest. The key to a long and healthy life is not getting sick in the first place. But what are the determinants of staying well? Confronted with the finding that 'health inequalities are wider where income differentials are larger', our first thought is likely to be that this is because a more unequal society will tend to have more poor people in it, and poverty is bad for health.[23] This is undoubtedly true, but primarily for societies that have a low average income: life expectancy and gross domestic product are significantly related, but the best-fitting curve relating them shows expectation of life increasing sharply with average income up to about $5,000 per head, then flattening out up to about $10,000 per head, after which it almost levels off.[24] This curve gives us an increase of only four years (from 74 to 78) as we go from $10,000 a head to $25,000, which is pretty small beer when we compare it with the gain in expectation of life from a little over 50 to a little over 65 between $1,000 a year and $5,000.

At low average incomes, it must be added, the best-fitting curve does not fit very well.[25] Around $2,000 per annum, average longevity ranges from a little over 45 to a little under 75 – close to the average expectation of life in the United States. This is consistent with the idea that in a poor country an unequal distribution of income will leave a large proportion of the population in destitution, with a devastating effect on average mortality rates. In rich countries, however, the class gradient of longevity must be explained mainly in some other way. For if it were mediated through absolute deprivation, we would expect the effects of inequality on expectation of life to become smaller and smaller as we moved up from $10,000 to $25,000, whereas differences of ten years or more from top to bottom persist even in very wealthy countries. Furthermore, 'the usual pattern is a continuous gradient across the whole society, with death rates declining and standards of health improving step by step, all the way up the social hierarchy. In this way, even people who are comfortably off tend to be less healthy than the very well off.'[26]

Anyone who lives in Manhattan and looks at a map of zip codes (post codes) will instantly recognize that they are drawn up to make life easy for marketers by demarcating each zip code area so that it is as economically and ethnically/racially homogeneous as possible. Why should the age-adjusted mortality of men who lived in an area with an average income (in 1980 dollars) of $33,000 or more have been higher than that of men with an income of between $30,000 and $32,999?[27] Surely, there could be no form of nutrition, housing, access to a gym or any other directly health-improving product that was within reach of the first group but not the second. Again, a division of men in England and Wales between the ages of 20 and 64 into four social classes showed a sharp increase in standardized mortality rates from the lowest class to the highest in 1989. A similar division of Swedish men showed a fairly large decrease between the top class and the next down (though less than in Britain), but only relatively small differences among the other three.[28] This is, if we place our bets on direct material effects, profoundly counterintuitive.

The answer is that anxiety and stress tend to increase as we move down the social scale. I shall give a number of reasons for this in a moment, but let me first explain how chronic stress leads to ill-health and premature mortality. Stress in short bursts contributes to survival in emergencies, which is why human beings (in common with other primates) are equipped with the ability to produce

> glutcocorticoids [which] are steroid hormones released during stress as part of the 'fight or flight' mechanism. As such, they are a major component of the system by which the body's resources are diverted from non-urgent tasks, such as growth, tissue repair and the immune system, to preparing the body for immediate action and mobilising the necessary energy resources for muscles.[29]

The effect of stress on the immune system is illustrated by 'a study which examined throat swabs from medical students during exams'. It found that 'exam stress weakened their immunity'.[30] An experiment comparing the rate at which high-stress and low-stress people developed colds when dosed with nasal drops containing the cold virus found that the former had a 75 per cent higher chance of contracting a cold than the latter.[31]

Cortisol, though beneficial in short bursts as a response to stress, is very bad for you if you live in an environment that generates chronic stress, because the feedback mechanism that controls its production is destroyed.[32] Constantly elevated levels of cortisol result in underweight babies and stunted growth, as well as a depleted immunity system and a high concentration of lipoproteins of the kind that give rise to cholesterol deposits.[33] Fibrinogen, another stress product, makes the blood clot more readily – an obvious gain in coping with a glancing blow from a sabre-toothed tiger, but a recipe for coronary heart disease and other ills when it becomes too much of a good thing.[34] Finally, chronic stress creates high blood pressure.[35] This was something I discovered for myself when I spent four years near the University of Chicago in a constant (and justifiable) state of apprehension about the risk of violence from people who, if they did not accost you in the street, were quite capable of smashing your door down and helping themselves after immobilizing you.

The more materialistic a society – the more that it is generally believed that money is the only significant goal in life – the more that people with a lot of money will feel like winners and those with a little will feel like losers. This feeling will intensify if those who are better off than others believe that they are more virtuous and those who are worse off share this belief. As we shall see in chapter 10, the idea that countries such as Britain and the United States are 'meritocracies' has been propagated with great effectiveness even though it is wildly contrary to the facts. There is no reason why this association of money with superiority and inferiority should not ascend all the way up the scale: a cottage, Marx said, shrinks to a hovel if somebody builds a castle next to it; but the castle shrinks to a cottage if someone builds an enormously larger castle next to it. (I shall take up the wasteful and mutually destructive nature of the competition unleashed by invidious comparison in chapter 13.) We are not talking about a subjective sense of success or failure alone. Almost all everyday interactions are mediated by the parties' estimates of their relative social standing. Even those who do not acknowledge their class position are affected by it:

> [A]mong groups of teenagers from high school, all of whom are doing equally well academically, working-class kids showed prolonged rises in cortisol under any kind of stress while upper-class kids showed a quick spike and then a decline. The physiology of working-class youngsters was altered by their social location, whether or not they acknowledged their working [class] status.[36]

In Britain, inequalities of income are interwoven with the subtleties of social status. The *locus classicus* for the anatomy of snobbery among the toffs is Proust's *A la recherche du temps perdu*, but the true poets of the phenomenon among the middle of the middle class (where what Freud called the 'narcissism of minor differences' reaches its apogee) are playwrights such as Alan Ayckbourn and numerous writers of British sitcoms in which such amusement as there is derives heavily from their exploitation of the minutiae of class differentiation. In the United States, outside some long-established cities such as Boston and Philadelphia, money and status are tightly connected, with one huge exception: race. The black–white gap in average life expectancy holds up even when we compare blacks and whites in the same range of incomes. Using figures for 1979–89, it was found that the gap at the age of 45 was more than three years for women and two for men in the lowest two of the four income groups into which the population was divided. In the upper two, the gap was almost two years for women and more than one for men.[37] (To put a gap of this size into perspective, bear in mind that eleven of the thirty-three countries with incomes over $10,000 a year fall within the two-year interval of 74–76 and another eleven within that of 76–78.)[38]

Two explanations can be offered for black–white differences in longevity among people in the same income group. One is that a key component of American racism is the belief that blacks are 'naturally' inferior – a belief not-so-subtly reinforced by the kind of 'scientific' racism that I shall dissect in chapter 9. 'A few studies have opera-tionalized the extent to which African Americans internalize or endorse' these stereotypes, and 'found that internalized racism is pos-itively associated to psychological distress, depressive symptoms, sub-stance use, and chronic physical health problems'.[39] The other cause of stress is the everyday experience of racism: snubs, slights, social exclusion, and the like. This can explain why there is a black–white gap at the top end of the income scale as well as the bottom. Black professionals may be well treated at work and by their neighbours in their professional-dominated neighbourhoods. But in the impersonal transactions that are such a large part of everyday experience, they are much more likely to be exposed to the common fate. A distin-guished (and no doubt well-paid) professor at Harvard complained in a television documentary aired in spring 2004 of his frustration in often seeing cabs sail past him and pick up a white passenger a few yards further along the road.

He might be better off if they *always* did, because random occur-rences create uncertainty and hence stress. This is a point with general application. The direct health effects of being born, living and dying on the street in Mumbai are doubtless bad compared to those of living in a house in a rich country. But if you spend all the time worrying about losing the house because interest rates or rents go up or because you become unemployed, you are probably worse off from the psychosocial angle. It is now well established that 'a large part of the link between health and unemployment is related to job insecurity and the anticipation of unemployment'.[40] Hence, your health starts to deteriorate when redundancies are announced, regardless of whether it turns out that you are going to lose your job or not.[41] Job insecurity is most extreme among those with ill-paid, marginal jobs, but it extends all the way up the scale, helping to explain the continuous health gradient. A further point is that wealth is highly correlated with income (though far more unequally distributed), so a bigger income is likely to go with a bigger cushion against economic adversity, thus making the prospect of a sudden loss of income less threatening.

Finally, control over working conditions makes for better health and longer life. When we bear in mind how much time people spend at work and how significant for their sense of self-worth their job is for many people, this is scarcely surprising. Earnings are a pretty good proxy for power (or lack of it) at work. Thus again, we have a case in which the continuous gradient of health and longevity is not actually caused by income but by a source of stress strongly associated with it. The most conclusive evidence comes from a study carried out on '17,000 civil servants working in government offices in London [which] found that death rates were three times as high among the most junior office staff as they were among the most senior administrators'.[42] None of those studied was a manual worker, so this large health difference was contained in the upper part of the income hierarchy in Britain.[43]

A further refinement, which points to stress resulting from lack of autonomy is that 'although . . . seniority . . . is closely related to the amount of control people have over their work, control over work was significantly related to health, even after controlling for employment grade and a number of other risk factors'.[44] Similarly striking results have been obtained in the United States. For example, 'women who reported having a heavy workload and limited job control were at three times greater risk for coronary heart disease than women who had heavy workloads combined with control over their work.'[45] The link between stress and coronary heart disease is also illustrated by the study of British civil servants. It may be recalled that 'bad' lipoproteins and fibrinogen are concomitants of stress that contribute to coronary heart disease. Significantly, elevated levels of these 'accounted for about one-third of the increased heart disease among low-ranking civil servants.'[46] The rest remained unexplained, but it is hard to see how anything except stress could be the cause. We can only conclude that stress kills in more ways than have yet been nailed down.

To sum up so far: extreme poverty kills directly through malnutrition, poor housing, and so on, but it also kills, especially in rich countries, because the extremely poor constitute a stigmatized minority. The power of stigmatization as an independent factor in ill-health is demonstrated by the lower expectation of life among American blacks at all income levels. *Relative* poverty, however, has psychosocial effects that help to account for the continuous gradient of longevity from the bottom to the top because of the relation between income and status in materialist societies. Differences of income also serve as markers for other factors implicated in early death. In this context, I looked at anxiety about becoming unemployed and control or lack of it over working conditions. But there are other forces at work that relate relative poverty, as conventionally measured, to shorter life.

A very important link is political. Those who have more disposable resources are able to manipulate public policy in their favour at the expense of those with fewer: 'inequality kills because it affects public policy, altering the distribution of education, health care, environmental protection, and other material resources.'[47] This is true in rich countries and poor ones, and regardless of the existence of elections and political parties. Cuba produces better outcomes in education and health than the United States on a fraction of the income. By way of contrast, in India 'about four-fifths of healthcare spending . . . is effectively private medicine. Spending on universities rather than schools sees the country produce 2 million graduates a year and leaves more than half the country's women illiterate.'[48] This arises because 'India's development is one born of policies that have been skewed in favour of the rich and the aspirational since independence'.[49] With very little change, all this could equally be said of the USA.

The irrelevance of absolute income is illustrated by a case I discussed earlier: the larger the income gradient, the more likely the society is to be one in which those who are relatively poor will be incapable of resisting the siting of toxic waste dumps where they live. The point is that this is entirely a matter of *relative* income. In New York the concentration of toxic wastes in poor areas has gone hand in hand with increased inequality. It makes no odds that at the same time the United States has become far wealthier. If anything, this makes things worse, because, in the absence of government regulation, a wealthy society will produce more rather than less toxic waste from chemical plants and hospitals as well as more domestic rubbish. The absence of government regulation to cut down on the production of toxic wastes as a by-product is itself much more likely if the wealthy and powerful can avoid coming into contact with them.

If everybody were liable to exposure to toxic wastes, 'not in my back yard' would soon be transformed into 'not in anybody's back yard'. 'Much of noxious industry need not exist at all. . . . Many adverse impacts could be ameliorated or eliminated altogether by the use of industrial best-management practices, application of waste reduction measures at the source', and so on.[50] The German system in which the cost of disposal is built into the price of a car could be extended to all products with great advantage. Gratuitous rubbish could be stopped by taxing everything down to toothbrushes on the cost of disposal – including environmental costs in the calculation. Faced with a tax on the unnecessary cardboard and plastic in which they are encased (which is a bother, anyway), manufacturers of toothbrushes would doubtless rediscover the virtues of simplicity, while, at the other end of the scale, creating toxic wastes would be very expensive and nuclear power an economic impossibility.

If high inequality is associated with 'systematic underinvestment across a wide range of human, physical, health and social infrastructure', it will also tend to kill through psychosocial effects.[51] Participation in common institutions makes for increased social solidarity, which has been shown to be good for everybody's health.[52] But the absence of universal high-quality public services has especially malign effects on those who are at the bottom end of the social scale. For they are as a result liable to find themselves excluded from many mainstream activities in their society and forced into the use of stigmatizing services that are shunned by those who can afford better. However, social exclusion can also be experienced by a majority, when members of a rich minority are able to pull out of common institutions and resort to private education and health care, ultimately isolating themselves completely from the common fate by shutting themselves up in gated communities and providing all their own services.[53]

This has a bearing on health care. Although, as we have seen, its quality does not make a great difference to health, the form that it takes may still do so through its psychosocial effects. It has been suggested that 'the common lament that 15 per cent of Americans [currently more] are "uncovered" by health insurance' may be misplaced. 'The uninsured are treated in public clinics and in emergency rooms, which (although they lack the conveniences of insured care and may have long queues) provide competent services both standard and high-tech.'[54] Also, by being treated only when they actually become ill, the non-insured have the advantages of avoiding unnecessary treatment that may be debilitating or even lethal. Nevertheless, this antiseptic description of the public facilities fails to bring home their demoralizing and stigmatizing quality within a system where medical care covered by insurance is the norm:

It is an ordinary enough afternoon at Highlands public hospital in Alameda County, California [i.e. no multiple crashes or shoot-outs] ... and yet ... in the shabby concrete building on the outskirts of Oakland ... patients are told to expect a four hour delay [in the acute care clinic]. In the emergency room ... any rush of critical cases can mean the rest must wait into the night. .... 'Emergency tests take too long, x-rays take even longer,' said a senior administrator.[55]

A British reader may be forgiven for thinking that this just sounds like the NHS but a bit worse. Remember, however, that these patients have no equivalent of a GP (primary care physician in America) and – this is the crucial point – only a small minority of the British population can afford to opt out of the public service. As a result, the political pressure for improvement in health care is extremely strong. In contrast, this kind of inferior treatment affects only a minority of Americans, so 'there have been few political points to score by imposing any change'.[56] That was written in 1990, but the main thing that has happened since is that the number of people not covered by insurance has increased, while political points have been scored for immiserating the poor further, not for improving their lot. My hypothesis is that, even if the care received by the 'medically indigent' is technically competent (eventually), it still raises mortality rates because of the adverse effect on health of being excluded from the society's common institutions in such an unignorable way. In other words, being forced to use a public hospital may make little difference to your chance of being cured once you are ill, but it may make you much more likely to become ill.

This raises the question of the compatibility of private health care with social justice. Of course, even if private health care were prohibited within a country, there would be nothing to stop those with enough money from travelling to another that had high-quality private health care. The same might be said, quite accurately, about schools; but sending one's children abroad to school is a far bigger step than travelling abroad for a major operation. Leaving that on one side, it does not seem to me that private health care is a straightforward breach of equal opportunity in the way that private education is, in virtue of its buying an unfair advantage for a child in the competition for places in elite universities and for desirable occupations. Health care is not inherently zero sum in the same way. In a market society, a higher income gives its recipients the opportunity to consume more of everything whose sale is not prohibited (and maybe some of that). But in a society in which the extent of inequality was consistent with social justice, there would on the face of it be no more objection to those who were better off spending it on medical care than to their spending it on, say, expensive holidays. If, however, private care lures away qualified doctors and nurses from the public system, it does constitute an abuse of wealth: the rich are now making the poor worse off.

Even if a system of private health care is considered to be compatible with social justice, it is still important that the standard of publicly provided health care must be found adequate by a large majority of the population. Only in this way can the stigmatization of those who use the basic service be avoided. This is partly a question of funding the service adequately but it is equally a matter of convincing people that the funding is going on the right things. Mammograms, for example, are still being pushed hard by the medical industry in the USA and women are having them at ever higher rates, despite screening programmes of this kind having been shown (to the satisfaction of just about everybody without a vested interest) to be on balance harmful, because aggressive treatment of tiny clusters of cancerous cells kills as many women as it saves, while subjecting a much larger number of others to distressing, disabling surgery, chemotherapy and radiotherapy.[57] The size of the vested interest in the USA must not be underestimated: 'almost three-quarters of all women are screened, at a cost of $3 billion a year' – enough to transform public health in the whole of sub-Saharan Africa.[58] Only the naive will be surprised to learn that 'the National Committee for Quality Assurance, an independent agency that sets standards for the health care industry, wants to increase [the proportion of women screened] to 81 per cent'.[59] Britain's National Health Service does not have anything approaching the perverse financial incentives for overtreatment inherent in the American system.[60] But it still persists with expensive procedures such as mammograms that do more harm than good.

To keep people satisfied, emphasis would need to be put on 'running repairs' to knees, hips, varicose veins, and so on. At the same time, people might become less willing to entrust themselves to hospitals if they were made aware that in the United States as many as 100,000 patients a year may be being killed because the wrong person is operated on or medicated.[61] There must be very many non-fatal cases of mistaken identity for every fatal one: amputating the wrong leg, so that the victim becomes a double amputee for example, or – a case known to me – operating on the wrong eye so that the victim becomes blind. So perhaps a million Americans are being injured or killed every year by American hospitals just through this one sort of error. Since there are many other sources of error, one might conclude that, unless the hospitals are doing a remarkable amount of good to the other patients whom they manage not to harm, closing them down might improve America's health. This thought is reinforced by profit-driven overtreatment and response to profit-driven advertising: 'We [in the USA] kill nearly two hundred thousand a year through improper medical interventions. Many more die due to misuse of heavily advertised prescription medicines, over-the-counter remedies, and other preparations.'[62]

One day after the report on errors in the *New York Times*, the *Guardian* carried a report saying that a million patients per year – a tenth of the total admitted – 'will suffer some accidental harm, from a minor fall to serious injury or death' in NHS hospitals.[63] Since hospitals absorb the lion's share of the health care budget, a more realistic estimate of potential benefits and costs would help to save money. A bigger contribution would be to make it compulsory for doctors to act on 'living wills' specifying treatments people did not want in the event that they were incapable of deciding for themselves and also, of course, if doctors were required to respect patients' wishes about the withholding of treatment if they could indicate them. Whether in advance or at the time, patients should be able in addition to specify euthanasia so as to avoid the pointless suffering and degradation of terminal illness. Since about half the hospital budget goes on people in their last six months of life, this measure in conjunction with the others would probably make it possible to afford a health service that avoided arbitrary limits on treatment and was perceived by the great majority as acceptable.

Finally, let me return to the question of personal responsibility for health. It is highly convenient for defenders of social and economic inequality to suggest that class and race differences arise from good and bad lifestyle choices:

> If social and economic inequalities are as powerful in determining health expectancies as current research indicates they are, then [governments that accept a responsibility for health] would seem obligated to narrow these inequalities, or to find ways to reduce their effect on health and longevity. But if we assign responsibility for the excess mortality and morbidity associated with economic inequality to individuals (on the premise that these misfortunes stem from differences in lifestyles that reflect different personal priorities, tastes and character traits), then we cannot demand remedial action by [such] states.[64]

Since 'none of the principal studies of health inequalities linked to socioeconomic status points to differing lifestyles as the key explanation', the potential role of individual responsibility is limited.[65] But the residual link between different choices and different outcomes could be made a question of personal responsibility only if a lot of other things could be established. To begin with a very simple point: do social class differences in behaviour have the same impact on health? They do not. There is a class gradient with regard to smoking: its incidence increases as we go down the social scale. But smoking (say) a pack of cigarettes a day will on the average impair your health more the lower your socioeconomic status. 'American smokers of high social status are less likely to contract cancer and are more likely to live longer when they do contract it than Americans near to the bottom of the pecking order.'[66] If this is so, the stress that (as we shall see) causes the class gradient in smoking also exacerbates the ill-effects of smoking.

A poor physical environment can make the effects of contracting a disease much worse than they would be in an environment that was more conducive to good health in the first place. For example, the HIV virus impairs the immune system, so those whose environment contains more sources of infection are more liable to become sick and die than are others with a safer environment. Such sources (arising from, among other things, lack of pure water and sanitation) are much more common in Africa than in wealthy countries, so the effects of becoming HIV positive will be worse there even if medical care were equally good. Again, nutritional deprivation in childhood directly produces poor health in later life. But it also makes controlling weight difficult by impairing metabolism in a way that results in storing fat rather than burning it up. Of two adults with different backgrounds who eat the same diet, take the same exercise, and so on, one is liable to gain weight while the other does not.[67]

To generalize: wherever adverse conditions exacerbate the bad effects of 'unhealthy' choices, a class gradient in such behaviour will turn into a bigger class gradient in health outcomes. Even if we hold people fully responsible for their choices, therefore, we still have to say that members of different classes are only partly responsible for differential outcomes. But is it reasonable to hold that 'unhealthy' choices have 'all the attributes – informed, voluntary, uncoerced, spontaneous, deliberated, and so on – that, in the ideal case, are conditions for full personal responsibility'?[68] Even the British and American governments have recognized that meeting these conditions is the last thing that tobacco companies want. On the contrary, when tobacco companies started worrying about people giving up smoking, they responded by spiking cigarettes secretly with extra nicotine on the strength of scientific advice that this would make them more addictive. Governments have therefore insisted on their supplying health warnings and information about tar content and have exerted control over advertising and sponsorship. Yet in both Britain and America, as we shall see, they remain passive in the face of the enormous increase in the incidence of obesity.

One obvious way of 'blaming the victim' is to hold poor people responsible for choices that arise directly from the relatively limited set of options that poverty (by definition) gives rise to in the market. Faced with the same limited set of alternatives – between eating, keeping warm and avoiding having the water cut off, for example – people who are currently wealthy might very well make exactly the same decisions as do those who actually face this range of options. You may be perfectly well aware that a healthy diet requires plenty of fresh fruit and vegetables. But if you live on one of the big post-war housing estates built outside big cities, you simply will not be able to find them without travelling (by non-existent public transport) to the city centre. And in any case, if you have a hungry family to feed and are living on state benefits or a job at the minimum wage, you will have to fill their bellies with the cheapest food you can buy, which means carbohydrates. It would not be a bad place to start to take it as axiomatic that nobody actually desires chronic ill-health and early death. There must, if that is so, be some reason for people making choices that have a tendency to lead to this result. Among the candidates are two already given: lack of resources and lack of information (or false information) – much of which is deliberately disseminated by companies to sell their products. The differences in health and life expectancy that are left over after allowing for the effects of choices cannot all be accounted for – recall the large unexplained variation in death from coronary heart disease among British civil servants – but they must arise from some way or other in which the better off enjoy a more favourable environment than the less well off.[69]

I want to concentrate here on one way in which an environmentally induced killer – stress – gives rise to 'unhealthy' behaviour as a way of coping with it. The evidence suggests that 'smoking, heavy alcohol consumption and eating for comfort may . . . be responses to anxiety'.[70] Barbara Ehrenreich reports that her fellow workers in high-stress/low-pay jobs found her ability to get through a shift without smoking incomprehensible.[71] If she had been serving a life sentence rather than taking a quick dip into the underside of work to gather copy, there is no reason for thinking she would not have behaved in the same way:

Smoking increases inversely with the degree of freedom one has at work. . . . The unhealthy choices people make are not irrational choices. We have to see them as constrained rationality, making the best of a bad situation . . . so it is unlikely that their behavior will change by lecturing to them. You have to change the context within which the choice is made.[72]

Smoking has a very steep class gradient, alcohol and illegal drugs somewhat less and the immense number of psychiatric drugs obtained on prescription even less so. Overall, it appears that anxiety and stress are dispersed throughout society (even if not evenly), again illustrating that the primary causes of bad health in rich countries have to be looked for outside material deprivation. Eating 'comforting foods', which 'usually have high sugar and fat content', is 'one of the many ways people respond to stress, unhappiness and unmet emotional needs'.[73] Epidemiological studies have shown that this works. 'There are now a number of studies showing an association between low plasma cholesterol and higher risks of suicide, violence and accidents.'[74] Richard Wilkinson had the evidence for the association but could only speculate on the explanation. However, in 2003 a study reported the identification of a 'biological mechanism' forming the basis for 'comfort foods actually help[ing to] block the effects of high levels of stress'.[75] The author of the report suggested that 'in the short term, if you're chronically stressed', it might be worth fighting the ill-effects in this way, 'perhaps at the expense of a few pounds'.[76] For those who suffer from chronic stress, this solution is obviously a recipe for unlimited weight gain, and 'fixing the source of the stress' is easier said than done.[77] As we know, it would require profound social changes to reduce insecurity and to promote social solidarity in place of stigmatization and competitiveness – in a word, to create a society of equals.

Wilkinson remarked that 'it is interesting to note that there were dramatic increases [in Britain] in the numbers of obese men and women of working age during the later 1980s while income differences were widening so rapidly.'[78] Since then, inequalities of income – and even more, of wealth – have increased further to an enormous degree in both Britain and the United States and have been accompanied by what has been described as literally an obesity epidemic. With the exception of some South Sea islanders, Americans are the fattest people on earth. In the last twenty years, the proportion of overweight Americans – 'overweight enough to begin experiencing health problems as a direct result of that weight' – has risen from 25 per cent to 61 per cent, while the rate of (life-threatening) obesity is now 20 per cent.[79] In Britain, the adult obesity rate has tripled in the last twenty years, so that it now challenges the American figure.[80] Child obesity is particularly worrying, both because it sets the stage for a lifetime of ill health and because it has grave immediate risks: in both countries, doctors are seeing rapidly increasing numbers of children with Type 2 diabetes – normally a disease of adults – in grossly overweight children. 'Obesity in British children has doubled in two decades.' 'Among six year olds it . . . increased [between 2001 and 2003] from 8.5% to 10% and among 18 year olds from 15% to 18%,'[81]

It will hardly come as a surprise that obesity is not evenly distributed across the population:

> Poverty. Class. Income. Over and over these emerged as the key determinants of obesity and weight-related disease. True, there was a new trend that saw significant numbers of the middle and upper class also experiencing huge weight gains. But the basic numbers were – and are – clear and consistent: the largest concentration of the obese, regardless of race, ethnicity, and gender, reside in the poorest sections of the [American] nation.[82]

Among the explanations is one that I have already mentioned as undermining responsibility: asymmetry of information. A study of twelve thousand obese adults discovered that fewer than half were advised by their doctors to lose weight, but that there was a class bias: 'Patients with incomes above $50,000 were more likely to receive such advice than were those with incomes below.'[83] Indeed, the whole notion of having 'a doctor' does not apply to those who are not covered by medical insurance. Indigent blacks, another study found, have 'a remarkable lack of perception about obesity'.[84] Why do not schools address the information gap? The answer to this question illustrates the way in which the public agenda in the United States is driven by middle-class concerns, as a result of their control over public policy.

'Most anorexics come from the middle class', and their numbers are far smaller than their lobbying group maintains.[85] Moreover, anorexia as a disease of middle-class girls preceded current preoccupations with thinness.[86] (A number of female saints were clearly sufferers but found a creative way of using it.) Finally, 'the data – and the experience of physicians, health workers and others in the field – consistently indicate' the falsity of the common assumption 'that too much fat awareness somehow causes eating disorders'.[87] In spite of all this, and the immensely greater significance of obesity, measuring body fat and counselling in schools are stymied by the anorexia scare. As a professor of nutrition says about this, 'the number of kids with eating disorders is positively dwarfed by the numbers with obesity. It side-steps the whole class issue.'[88]

It is instructive to contrast this situation with that of France, where for a century (since the Public Health Act of 1904), the state has been actively involved in the nutrition of children through clinics and schools. The attitude was that 'raising a child could be a rational act, but only if the parents were given the encouragement, facts and tools to do so'.[89] In recent years, the incidence of child obesity in France has doubled and the level of overall obesity has risen to 10 per cent – half that of Britain and the United States. This has been enough for 'the French health authorities [to] have launched a vigorous effort to reinforce the old attitudes [that parents must control their children's diets] while addressing the needs of new immigrant groups'.[90] Needless to say, 'You will not find Coca-Cola in a French middle school', as you may in Britain and America.[91] 'There is already a comprehensive set of public health goals, including the training of all school nurses in screening for obesity and its prevention, special care for obese children and rigorous control of advertisement messages about food products aimed at children.'[92]

The United States lies at the other extreme, with Britain, as usual, somewhere in between: benighted by the standards of the rest of Western Europe but more enlightened than America though moving towards it. Both in Britain and the United States, fast-food chains and soft-drink manufacturers have got themselves inside the schools, but companies have succeeded in exploiting the financial plight of many schools in America to gain an extraordinary degree of leverage, so that the schools themselves become co-opted as pushers. For example, back in 1996 Colorado Springs School District 11 negotiated a deal with Coca-Cola that required it to shift seventy thousand cases of the product within the first three years for the contract to be lucrative. By the beginning of the 1998 school year, sales were lagging behind schedule, so a school district administrator sent a memo to all school principals suggesting that they should allow students to bring Coke into the classrooms and should reposition the machines to increase sales: 'Research shows that vendor purchases are linked to availability. . . . Location, location, location is the key.'[93]

That was only a harbinger of the corporate takeover of American schools. The man who negotiated the Colorado Springs deal moved on to a school district in Texas to solicit advertisements 'not only for [its] hallways, stadiums, and buses, but also for its rooftops – so that passengers flying into Dallas-Fort Worth airport could see them – and for its voice-mail systems. "You've reached the Grapevine-Coleyville school district, proud partner of Dr. Pepper" was the message [he] proposed.'[94] The deputy superintendent told the *Houston Chronicle* that the school district would not have lent itself to this 'if it weren't for the acute need for funds'.[95]

The same desperation has driven 'thousands of school districts to us[ing] corporate-sponsored teaching material'.[96] The largest group producing this stuff boasts that its publications get to more than sixty million schoolchildren. It is remarkably frank in explaining the value of its wares. 'Now you can enter the classroom through custom-made learning materials created with your specific marketing objectives in mind', ran one of its pitches.

> 'Through these materials, your product or point of view becomes the focus of discussion in the classroom,' it said in another, '. . . the centerpiece in a dynamic process that generates long-term awareness and attitudinal change.' The tax cuts that are hampering American schools have proved to be a marketing bonanza. . . . The money that these corporations spend on their 'educational' materials is fully tax-deductible.[97]

The same tax dollars could have been used instead to buy real textbooks, instead of this kind of thing:

> Procter and Gamble's *Decision Earth* program taught that clear-cut logging was actually good for the environment; teaching aids distributed by Exxon Educational Foundation said that fossil fuels created few environmental problems and that alternative sources of energy were too expensive; a study guide sponsored by the American Coal Foundation dismissed fears of a greenhouse effect, claiming that 'the earth could be benefited rather than harmed from increased carbon dioxide.'[98]

As if this were not enough, there is a 'commercial television network whose programs are now shown in classrooms, almost every school day, to eight million of the nation's middle, junior and high school students – a teen audience fifty times larger than MTV'.[99] Needless to say, the fast-food chains are well represented among the advertisers. More all-pervasive is advertising on children's television programmes. In notable contrast to the attitude of the French government, the Federal Communications Commission has exerted no control over advertising on American television, with the result that by the late 1980s, 'there was so much money for youth advertising that entire new ad agencies were formed simply to handle the "Saturday A.M. buy"', and a study in 1993 found that '41 per cent of all Saturday morning kids show ads were for high-fat foods', with firms such as McDonald's and Pizza Hut driving their advertising agencies to ever greater efforts.[100] In Britain, too, no regulatory body has intervened to prohibit the same kind of targeting: 'Nearly 40 per cent of commercials shown during children's programmes are for food products, most of them high in fat and sugar.'[101] The first five places are taken by three chocolate bars, McDonald's and Kentucky Fried Chicken. Even the healthier-sounding cornflakes that follow them are in fact laden with sugar: the top one is 49 per cent sugar and the next two 40 per cent.[102] In response to the proposal that such advertising should be banned, Tessa Jowell, the UK Minister of Culture, ruled it out on the ground that it would cause the commercial television companies to lose too much advertising revenue.

If the core of social democracy is encapsulated in the slogan 'people before profits', it would be hard to find a clearer indication of the way in which New Labour represents the antithesis of social democracy. The contributions of the junk-food manufacturers to television stations are not, after all, a form of charity. They spend the amount they do because market research has told them that this level of advertising expenditure increases sales so much that their increased profits more than cover the costs. The people running advertising agencies exult in the ease with which children can be manipulated. The president of one agency said: 'Advertising at its best is making people feel that without their product, you're a loser. Kids are very sensitive to that. . . . You open up emotional vulnerabilities, and it's very easy to do with kids because they're the most emotionally vulnerable.'[103]

Children are not the only victims of a major source of obesity, which is the enormous increase in the number of calories in 'super-sized' fast foods and soft drinks. It is instructive that the McDonald's French operation has actually advised the public not to eat its product more than once a week – presumably to pre-empt tough government measures – while the American corporation's objective is to have as many families as possible eating three meals a week.[104] Someone who had been eating the 'same' meal at McDonald's for many years would have been consuming more and more calories – with no warnings, of course. A serving of french fries constituted 200 calories in 1960 and has grown steadily to 610, while a 'meal' has grown from 590 to 1,550 calories.[105] Helping to explain the rapid rise of obesity in Britain is the increasing penetration of American ice-cream parlours, and the staggering number of calories and grams of fat in their typical offerings. Whereas a standard British-style ice cream has 65 calories and 2 grams of saturated fat, a cone of Haagen-Dazs or Ben and Jerry's with toppings can contain 1,000 calories and 30 grams of fat – as against a recommended total daily intake of 20 grams.[106] One of the nutritionists who undertook the research into these new products pointed out that a seemingly innocuous frozen yoghurt had been dosed up to have 'the calories and saturated fat of two pork chops, a caesar salad and a buttered baked potato'.[107] It is hard to see how any responsible government could resist calls for tobacco-style labelling of junk foods, 'warning about high-fat diets causing obesity and increasing the risk of cancer, heart disease and diabetes'.[108]

So far from acting to stem the obesity epidemic, the British government is instead enthusiastically cheering on efforts to increase the incidence of child obesity even further. In 2003, a scheme under which 'children as young as seven [were] to be targeted in a multimillion pound campaign by Cadbury to encourage them to buy chocolate bars in exchange for new school sports equipment' received 'the backing of the government' and the strong endorsement of the Sports Minister.[109] Schools that sign up will thus actually do Cadbury's work for it, encouraging children to acquire tokens by eating exactly the kind of sugary, fatty snack food that is already contributing to the epidemic. A spokesman for the Prime Minister declined to comment, except to say: 'This is an independent campaign by a private-sector organisation.'[110] This extraordinary statement is not an aberration: it is simply an application of the dogma that government concern for what goes on in the private sector is to be shunned as 'Old Labour' thinking. Addressing the national conference of the CBI (the employers' organization) in November 2003, in a speech to which the delegates 'responded warmly', Tony Blair said: 'We have to free Europe away [sic] from the idea that the modern social agenda is about regulation. . . . The issue today is not to get rid of the social agenda but redefine it so that it becomes about jobs and skills.'[111] Obviously, there is no room here for the idea that jobs should not exist unless they can survive regulation to protect workers, the environment or (as in the case at hand) public health.

I began this chapter by referring to the book *Health and Social Justice*. Let me end by drawing attention to the title of one of the articles in it: 'Is Capitalism a Disease?'[112] It seems hard to deny by now that its author was right in concluding that it is. It should be added that it is a disease whose severity can be reduced by government intervention to equalize the distribution of wealth and income, insulate all public services (including health and education) from the market, control firms to make the workplace and the environment safer, prohibit the sale of dangerous products while monitoring the labelling and advertising of others, and making use of all the other methods that successful social democracies have employed to tame the beast.

Unfortunately, however, it is in just the countries that are most in need of strong government action that rich individuals and corporations, directly or through foundations that they finance, have gained the most pervasive grip over the commonly shared ideology and the public agenda. The lying propaganda disguised as information disseminated through textbooks and televisions in American schools may perhaps be the most repulsive manifestation of this, but it is only the tip of the iceberg. I shall explore the phenomenon more fully towards the end of the book in chapter 17 and then in the remaining chapters ask what forces may nevertheless bring about change.

7

The Making of the Black Gulag

In this chapter, I shall describe a particularly striking case of cumulative disadvantage, which can be illustrated best by following the typical career of a black male raised in an American inner-city ghetto. I shall move quickly through the early stages, simply pointing out the way in which the poverty and poor education of the parent(s), plus the multiple social pathologies of the ghetto, combine with wretched schools to produce terrible educational outcomes. In Chicago, for example, 'half of the city's high schools place in the bottom one per cent on the American College Test, two thirds of the city's ghetto students fail to graduate, and those that do graduate read, on average, at an eighth grade level' (out of twelve grades).[1] This, together with the disappearance of blue-collar jobs in the ghetto, sets the stage for large-scale unemployment or at best casual or insecure jobs carrying no benefits (such as health care insurance, sick leave or paid holidays) and paid so poorly that it is impossible to afford minimally decent housing, adequate nutrition and other necessities with a full-time job at the legal minimum wage, while a lot of casual employment pays even less.

Many of those in these marginal positions get involved in behaviour classified (reasonably or not) as crime. But cumulative disadvantage continues here. The high level of police surveillance (backed up by a network of informers) in the ghetto, combined with a discriminatory use of police discretion, results in a very high rate of arrests among African Americans in large cities: with 15 per cent of the population, they accounted in 1994 for 43.4 per cent of arrests for vagrancy, 34.2 per cent for disorderly conduct, 39 per cent for prostitution and slightly over 40 per cent on drug abuse charges.[2] The very definition of 'disorderly conduct' is discretionary: whether 'hanging out on the front steps of a building or loitering with neighbours' counts as criminal behaviour or not depends on who does it where.[3] Soliciting and street drug-dealing is more likely to be detected in areas of high intensity policing, and in any case prostitution in the suburbs tends to be more discreet while drug distribution is carried on by word-of-mouth contact through bars, athletic leagues and so on.[4] A suburb with its own jurisdiction can make it clear to the police that their future depends on turning a blind eye to legal offences that arouse no complaint from the neighbours.

In the whole country, 75 per cent of drug users are estimated to be white and around 15 per cent black, yet blacks account for '35 per cent of all drug arrests, 55 per cent of all drug convictions, and 74 per cent of all the sentences for drug arrests'.[5] Prosecutors make discriminatory use of their discretion in deciding what offence to charge the defendant with. Especially in relation to drugs, they can also decide whether to put the case before a federal or a state court, and this makes a big difference. Federal mandatory sentences for drug offences are much more severe than typical sentences in state courts for the same verdict: in California, for example, sentences were frequently eight years less than those for the same offence in a federal court in 1988–99, during which period no whites were convicted in federal courts, whereas hundreds were in state courts.[6]

The discrepancy between outcomes for blacks and whites can be further explained by the way in which 'jury commissioners and lawyers have long engaged in discriminatory practices that result in disproportionately white juries.'[7] If all else fails, the venue can be changed, as in the example of a particularly brutal assault on a black prisoner by white policemen: on the ground that everybody in New York City would be 'biased', the case was moved to upstate New York. The point is that, even if white jurors are not guilty of crude racial prejudice, their experience of the police is likely to have been far more benign than that of blacks, so they are strongly inclined to believe them. Where the defendant is black, the views of a black juror are a good deal more relevant than those of a white one. These different perceptions of the police no doubt underlay the belief of a big majority of whites that O. J. Simpson should have been convicted, while a big majority of blacks supported his acquittal.[8]

What made Simpson's case distinctive was that he was one of the relatively few blacks in the country who could afford expensive representation. 'The way in which a wealthy defendant's resources could purchase DNA testimony, pursue investigative leads regarding police misconduct, and assemble an all-star defence team' illustrates the comparative burdens borne by any 'indigent defendant, or even defender of limited means'.[9] Almost any other black man accused of killing a white woman and a white man would have to rely on a defence provided by the state or federal government. The priority this expenditure receives is indicated by its running on 2 per cent of total state and federal justice expenditures. In fact, the national average per capita spending on indigent defence (at state and federal levels) in 1990, the latest year for which figures are available, was $5.37; Arkansas spent eighty-eight cents and Louisiana an even more derisory eleven cents.[10]

Public defenders, salaried employees of the state, are normally so overburdened that they can offer only a perfunctory service, often meeting the accused for the first time in the courtroom, having glanced at the papers on the way to it.[11] But most of the accused are represented by court-appointed counsel, and cannot be expected to get much for the amounts offered. For example, Mississippi sets an arbitrary limit of $1,000 per case, including capital ones. Two experienced attorneys who did a thorough job (though falling far short, no doubt, of an all-out Simpson-style defence) calculated that they had been working for two dollars an hour.[12] An especially significant point, which adds further to the defendant's disadvantage, is that the court has complete discretion in choosing who to appoint, with no obligation to favour counsel who sometimes get their clients acquitted or those with any knowledge or experience of trying such cases, as long as they have a bar qualification.

In fact, diligence and competence are viewed as positive drawbacks: courts prefer to appoint counsel who can be counted on not to waste their time by mounting a serious defence. A study in 1986 'concluded that assigned counsel "were court functionaries . . . who comply with its goals by providing cost-efficient, expeditious dispositions, and [that the system] alienates those who view the defence function in adversarial terms"'.[13] Courts have held the constitutional right to 'effective assistance' as satisfied when counsel slept through part of the trial, was drunk throughout the proceedings, admitted in evidence to not being prepared on either the law or the facts or, in a capital case, could not name a single Supreme Court decision on the death penalty.[14]

The net result of the discrepancies between the treatment of black and white adults is that blacks are three times more likely than whites to be imprisoned if arrested and get on the average a six-month longer sentence for the same offence.[15] As far as juveniles are concerned, their treatment does not lend itself to such simple summarization because more discretion exists with regard to them; but this discretion is very clearly exercised in a highly discriminatory fashion. We can begin with the enormously disproportionate rate at which blacks are arrested for crimes, especially drug-related ones, which is even more pronounced among juveniles and has got worse as the political climate has become harsher. In Baltimore, for example, five times as many blacks as whites were arrested for selling drugs in 1980; in 1990, the number of white juveniles arrested fell from 18 to 13, while the number of blacks arrested grew from 86 to 1,304, a rate of more than a hundred to one.[16] Following arrest, 'black youth are . . . treated progressively more severely than whites at each stage of the juvenile justice process'.[17] Summarily: 'black teenagers were more likely to be detained, to be handled formally, to be waived to adult courts, and to be adjudicated delinquent.'[18] They are then 'placed outside the home almost twice as often as white youths'.[19] Furthermore, 'if removed from their home they were less likely to be placed in the better-staffed and better-run private-group home facilities and more likely to be sent into state reform schools.'[20] They were also more likely to be jailed. The same behaviour that is seen in black youths as evidence of incorrigible criminal traits is more likely to be diagnosed among whites as 'troubled', with the result that they are 'channeled into private psychiatric clinics and drug abuse programs. . . . In California 70 per cent of drug-related sentences went to blacks, while whites got two-thirds of the treatment slots.'[21]

The notion that prison should 'help to resocialize individuals and thus reduce the possibility of further offences' was still popular in the late 1960s: 'as late as 1968, a Harris poll showed that 48 per cent of the public thought that the primary purpose of prison *was* rehabilitation and that 72 per cent believed the emphasis *should be* on rehabilitation.' This idea was replaced in the 1970s by the currently orthodox one that the only job of prison is 'to neutralize offenders – and individuals thought to be likely to violate the laws, such as parolees.'[22] 'In California, the word "rehabilitation" was expunged from the penal code's mission statement in 1976.'[23] The logic of 'incapacitation' as the object of the criminal justice system is that 'habitual offenders' should be locked up for very long periods even for offences that carry relatively short sentences. The idea of 'three strikes and out' – life sentences for a third felony conviction – caught on with amazing speed in the mid-1990s. 'Between 1993 and 1995, twenty four states and the federal government' adopted this policy.[24]

The notion that this incapacitates habitual violent criminals is quite false:'[I]n its first two years, California's law led to life sentences for twice as many marijuana users as murderers, rapists and kidnappers combined.'[25] Furthermore, '85 per cent of those sentenced under the law were convicted most recently [i.e. their 'third strike'] of a non-violent crime'. Some of these crimes are as minor as stealing a slice of pizza or five bottles of liquor.[26] When a man was sentenced to sixteen years in jail for stealing a candy bar, the prosecutor, 'asked if the sentence might be excessive . . . replied "It was king-size"'.[27]

The result of the policy has been to increase the jail population even more rapidly than before, and it will continue to do so: 'third strikers comprised 8 per cent of the prison population in 1996, but . . . by 2024 they will amount to 49 per cent.'[28] It can be imagined what this will cost. Already, in the last fifteen years, prison spending in California has gone up from 2 per cent of the state budget to 10 per cent. It now exceeds the amount spent on higher education.[29] Despite the obvious inequality, as well as the cost, of this fantastic form of cumulative disadvantage, the laws creating it have remained sacred to the Governor and the legislature. At the beginning of 2003, California faced a massive budget crisis, leading to the gutting of social services and arbitrary elimination of a number of items (such as prostheses) from the public medical programmes. There were also savage cuts in the budget for schools, resulting in their having to dismiss up to a quarter of their teachers. Yet nobody appears to have suggested slashing the prison population, or even halting its automatic increase, as a way of reducing the deficit.

Similarly, the Governor of New York proposed a budget in which a variety of public services were cut.[30] But there was no suggestion of relieving the crushing financial burden imposed by the prison system. The huge number of prisoners is to a considerable degree generated by the state's insane drug laws, under which 'selling two ounces of cocaine received the same sentence as murder'.[31] (Drug legislation, 90 per cent of whose victims are black or Hispanic, accounts for three-quarters of the huge increase in federal and state prisoners since 1980.)[32] Altogether, by the end of 2002 the US prison population had quadrupled in twenty-odd years to 2,166,260.[33] Despite the enormous programme of prison-building in that period, 'state prisons were operating between 1 per cent and 16 per cent over capacity . . . while the federal system was 33 per cent over'.[34] The number of inmates had increased tenfold since 1973.[35]

Since blacks are convicted of more felonies than whites (for all the reasons we have seen), they are by far the most affected by 'three strikes' laws. Thus 'in California . . . blacks make up 7 per cent of the general population, yet as of 1996 they accounted for 43 per cent of the third-strike defendants sent to prison.'[36] The consequence of the cumulative disadvantages suffered by blacks is an astonishing rate of incarceration: it is 'higher than the total incarceration rate in the

Soviet Union at the zenith of the Gulag and in South Africa at the height of the anti-apartheid struggle'.[37] 'On any given day upwards of one third of African-American men in their twenties find themselves behind bars, on probation or on parole. And at the core of the formerly industrial cities of the North, this proportion often exceeds two thirds.'[38] 'One [black] male out of every twenty-one [is in prison] and one out of nine between [the ages of] twenty and thirty-four'.[39] The proportion went on rising since that was written in 2002, and a year later stood at 12 per cent for this age group, compared to 1.6 per cent for white men.[40] Ominously for the future of black communities, 'one of every fourteen black children [had] a parent who [was] behind bars' even several years ago, so the proportion must be higher now.[41]

'The American prison system disgorges 600,000 angry, unskilled people each year – more than the populations of Boston, Milwaukee or Washington.'[42] Yet as a result of punishment having become an end in itself, there is no political mileage in proposing that the prisons should 'prepare prisoners for their release better and earlier, train them for jobs that pay more than the minimum [and] teach them all to read and write'.[43] The substitution of mindless incarceration for rehabilitation is remarkably clear in the case of higher education. There are 'numerous studies showing that higher education reduces recidivism'.[44] Despite this, 'Congress eliminated Pell grants [federal grants for poor people] for prisoners in 1994. . . . As a result, almost every prison college program was shut down.'[45]

The process of cumulative disadvantage rolls on after release from prison. So far from getting a helping hand, ex-prisoners are given a vicious boot to keep them down. 'Without a college degree, former prisoners have little chance of earning much more than the minimum wage. Even low-skill jobs are difficult to obtain for anybody with a felony record.'[46] Discrimination is easy and perfectly legal: in many states, the prison administrations have 'put their entire databases on line, thus making it possible for employers and landlords to discriminate against ex-convicts with full legal impunity'.[47] Convicts may be specifically prohibited from getting any of a list of jobs such as plumbing or barbering.[48] They are also prohibited by federal law from living in public housing, or even visiting friends and relatives who live in public housing. A woman living in decaying public housing on the South Side of Chicago had to tell her son that he could not come to live with her or even come to visit her or she could be evicted.[49]

The 'Work Opportunity and Personal Responsibility Reconciliation Act' of 1996 clearly works on the assumption that those who suffer disadvantage should be disadvantaged further, excluding most ex-convicts from Medicaid, the federal system of health care for the poor and other forms of assistance.[50] Those convicted of drug offences (a large proportion) suffer a lifetime ban on receiving welfare or food stamps, which leaves only crime as a means of subsistence unless (an unlikely event) they can find a job that pays well above the minimum wage.[51] Again, however, 'more than 45,000 students have lost their financial aid this year because of a law, passed by Congress, that strips assistance from college students who have been convicted of possessing or selling drugs.'[52] Typically, those affected wish to enrol in institutions such as urban community colleges. Thus, the financial aid director of Long Beach City College, California, has said:

> I thought our purpose here was to try and help pull people out of bad situations and help them make changes in their lives and give them better choices so that they won't end up where they started. . . . But this law is saying 'You messed up so we're not going to help you.'[53]

The system of parole – which now extends on the average to about two years after release – is a powerful instrument for putting ex-prisoners back in prison even if they have broken no law. It has been said that the parole system 'functions like a circular conveyor belt, delivering recently freed people straight back to the penitentiary. . . . About 40 per cent of ex-prisoners are behind bars within three years of their release.'[54] Looking at it another way, those guilty of breaking the terms of their parole make up 'a third of all those admitted to state penitentiaries each year (two-thirds in California)'.[55] Parolees can be sent back to jail if they 'stay out past curfew (usually 9 or 10 p.m.), skip appointments with their parole officers, hang out with anyone who has a criminal record, leave the state without permission or spend the night anywhere except in their approved residence'.[56]

It would be interesting to know what proportion of the readers of this book would not violate these onerous impositions within a period of two years. Certainly, the 16 per cent of ex-prisoners suffering from severe mental illnesses such as schizophrenia or manic depression have little chance of staying out of trouble, since they are not eligible for medical care. Parole officers, fearing that they may do something to hit the headlines, routinely send them back to jail for technical violations of parole.[57] About half of all parolees returned to jail have committed no new crime: the system manufactures its own prisoners.[58]

Finally, having survived jail and parole, ex-prisoners in fourteen states are denied one of the basic rights of citizenship – the right to vote – *for the rest of their lives*. In this, the USA is 'far out of line with international norms: no other democratic nation bars ex-offenders from voting for life'.[59] The impact of this on blacks is, of course, grossly disproportionate to their numbers: '[F]elony disenfranchisement among black males is seven times the national average, and in Alabama and Florida, 31 per cent of black men are permanently disenfranchised.'[60]

What is even worse is that these voteless citizens are included in the tally of residents for purposes of local and national elections. At the Constitutional Convention, the compromise was settled on to count slaves as only two-fifths of a white, so as to prevent the South from being too grossly over-represented in virtue of its number of additional votes. (Bear in mind that a number of states had more slaves than white residents.) Yet in the contemporary USA, not only are blacks excluded from voting, but the votes of the remaining voters are, in effect, cast as proxies for them. Similarly, the electoral rolls of the mainly sparsely populated areas in which prisons tend to be located are swollen by counting all the prisoners as residents. 'With both political reapportionment and federal and state funding formulas relying on these figures, the expanding prison population has essentially resulted in a transfer of wealth and influence from urban to rural communities.'[61]

These proxy voters obviously have interests diametrically opposed to those of the people whose votes they have appropriated, and equally contrary to the interests (as well as the political positions and party affiliations) of those people's communities. The economic interest in maintaining and increasing the incarceration rate extends well beyond that of the more than 600,000 guards and other prison employers (plus their families) to all those who depend on them for jobs and business: almost everybody for miles around the jail, in other words.[62] It is also worth bearing in mind that, in most states, there are elected judges, so candidates who run on a 'tough on crime' platform start with a big advantage.

In addition to voting, and quite likely more important, is the fact that the prison industry can afford to make substantial financial contributions to politicians – in return for which they expect (and normally get) favourable treatment. Privatization of prisons has increased the size of the stakes. 'In the words of one industry call to potential investors: "While arrests and convictions are steadily on the rise, profits are to be made – *profits from crime*. Get in on the ground floor of this booming industry now." '[63] On the other side, advocates of the victims and the communities devastated by 'tough on crime' policies have no financial clout: of the hundred largest contributors to national-level politicians and parties, not one represents the poor or minorities.

We can therefore begin to see how the cost of prisons escalates at the expense of education, health care and the social services. Yet, even in terms of dollars and cents, the taxpayer is being taken for a ride. One study reached the conclusion that 'every dollar invested in substance abuse treatment generated seven dollars in savings, primarily through reductions in crime and reduced hospitalizations'.[64] Again, 'a 1996 Rand Corporation study found that programs offering incentives to disadvantaged youth to finish high school ... dollar for dollar, reduce crime three to four times as effectively as California's three-strikes-and-you're-out legislation.'[65]

Even the most obviously sensible changes to reduce reconviction (which, as we have seen, is the rule rather than the exception now) are taboo. For example, the former executive director of the New York parole agency has proposed scrapping parole and replacing it with 'halfway houses for newly freed people and set[ting] up a voucher system that would enable them to purchase the services they need, like drug treatment'.[66] 'Most experts' dismiss this proposal as not 'practical' – but by this they do not mean that it would not work, but that it would be politically impossible.[67]

As we have seen, three-quarters of the spectacular growth in the prison population can be attributed to the 'war on drugs', which is a complete failure on its own terms: it has been estimated that the availability and purity of cocaine and other drugs are greater than before it started.[68] At the same time, 'the rate of murder, robbery, assault and other types of violation has declined in the last decade'.[69] Yet in that same period, 'there has been a marked increase in accounting and corporate infractions, fraud in health care, government procurement and bankruptcy, identity theft, illegal corporate espionage and intellectual piracy'.[70] One really good corporate fraud can net the lifetime proceeds of many thousands of those who are currently serving long jail sentences for theft. But 'Enron's chief executive hasn't gone to Sing Sing as the head of the New York Stock Exchange did in 1938 ... for market abuses originated in the 1920s.'[71] Notice, though, that it took until the heyday of the New Deal for him to be treated as a criminal: taking corporate crime seriously had to wait for a new ethos, new prosecutors and new judges. The ethos, the prosecutors and the judges today are much more like those of the 1920s: sympathetic to business and contemptuous of blacks.

Financial malfeasance on a massive scale is, of course, the preserve of those in relatively privileged positions – some, like company directors, already immensely rich, but greedy enough to manipulate the prices of their stock so as to maximize the value of their share options. If there were ever a group of people of whom it could be said that they chose to commit crimes voluntarily – free of financial necessity, well educated and fully aware of the nature of their acts – it would be the perpetrators of these swindles. But they either get off scot-free or are given punishments that are extraordinarily light (often no more than paying back their ill-gotten gains), in relation to the scale of their misdeeds and the number of lives ruined by their actions: those, for example, whose life savings have been lost, like the employees of Enron whose occupational pensions simply disappeared. As the founder of the Association of Certified Fraud Examiners said: 'The message is clear in the mind of the better-educated public that, if you want to commit a crime, fraud is the way to go. . . . The take is better, and the punishment is generally less.'[72]

It is worth adding in conclusion that, as so often with New Labour, Britain follows where America leads. When the government came into office in 1997, the prison population in England and Wales was 61,100; in March 2004 it was 75,191 – more than 8,000 higher than the official capacity of the prisons.[73] Within that overall increase was a much sharper increase in the number of Afro-Caribbean prisoners: between 1997 and 2003 it rose from 7,585 to 11,710, one in a hundred of all black adults.[74] Young Afro-Caribbean men are also following the track described earlier: 'Studies indicate many young men involved in street crime are those who underachieve or have been excluded from school. Afro-Caribbean pupils are four times as likely as others to be suspended or expelled.'[75] This naturally shows up in the youth jail population. Three-quarters of prisoners had been excluded from school, a report observed, adding: 'The ethnicity of excluded pupils is reflected in the prison population.'[76] The pattern of discriminatory treatment described in America also occurs in Britain: blacks are more likely to be arrested, more likely to be charged and likely to be prosecuted for a more serious offence than others.[77]

Since coming into office, New Labour has passed a dozen criminal law bills. The Lord Chief Justice, Lord Woolf, gave a succinct account of the result: 'There has been political initiative after political initiative that has led to the increase in the use of custody. There has been no trust in judges to impose the right sentence. The judges' hands are tied.'[78] Mandatory prison sentences have been responsible for a lot of the increase in the American prison population, and they are doing the same in Britain. Prison has enormously destructive effects, as we know. 'While in prison, one third lose their home, two thirds lose their job, over a fifth face increased financial problems and two fifths lose contact with their families.' It is hardly surprising that two out of three are reconvicted within two years, with the proportion among males aged 18–20 rising to seven out of ten.[79] But once a society has gone so far down this self-defeating road, the only way back is for the government to turn its back on populistic punitive measures and start to move in the direction of other countries. But I can see no sign of that.

Part III

What's Wrong With Meritocracy?

In the early 1970s, on a visit to England, I went to see a distant cousin. One of her children had just failed the eleven-plus. . . . Like many children before her, the girl had been promised a new bicycle if she passed the eleven-plus. Like many parents before them, her mother and father had given her the bicycle anyway. The daughter was visibly depressed. She felt that she had failed her parents, and she was not looking forward to the beginning of the school year, when she, together with the other 'failures', would transfer to a new school. Still the bicycle was there, a small consolation to her and a token of her parents' continued support. As she wobbled down the sidewalk (the bicycle was somewhat too big for her), pride in her new possession temporarily overcame her sense of inadequacy. As I watched her, I remembered many of the children I had known, and the ways in which the educational system had narrowed their horizons at an early age. Those whose aspirations have been mangled and whose lives have been reduced through the application of misguided science direct us to look closely at any theorizing that might lead us to further mistakes. Their descendants deserve better. A bicycle is not enough.

Philip Kitcher

8

The Idea of Meritocracy

The word 'meritocracy' was introduced in 1958 by Michael Young in his book, *The Rise of the Meritocracy, 1870–2033*.[1] Supposedly written in the year 2033, in which the process of advancement by merit had been perfected, it described a Britain in which those with the most merit ruled, 'meritocracy' thus being constructed on parallel lines to 'democracy' (rule of the many) and 'aristocracy' (rule by the well-born, in the traditional sense). The trappings of democracy would remain in the form of an elected House of Commons and ministers mostly drawn from it. But the real power would lie with the House of Lords (which Young presciently foresaw as being appointed – on the basis of merit, of course) and the higher civil service, the preserve of the best brains in the country. Although the term 'meritocracy' caught on, its emphasis on rule by the meritorious was downplayed in popular usage, and its originally negative connotations forgotten. A meritocracy was therefore thought of as a kind of society in which there would be inequalities, but in which those who got the best positions would have achieved them 'on the basis of individual merit' rather than these positions having been 'allocated randomly, or by ascriptive characteristics such as race and gender, or by the machinations of the already powerful'.[2]

By 2001, the point of Young's spoof had been so thoroughly forgotten that Tony Blair had no qualms, during the run-up to the election of that year, in announcing his fervent belief in meritocracy. This provoked Young into returning to the subject in an article entitled 'Down with Meritocracy!' In this he picked up on the consequences of a belief among the successful that the mere absence of discrimination or patronage is sufficient to justify any degree of inequality:

If they believe, as more and more of them are encouraged to, that their advancement comes from their own merits, they can feel they deserve whatever they can get. They can be insufferably smug, much more so than the people who knew they had achieved advancement not on their own merit but because they were, as somebody's son or daughter, the beneficiaries of nepotism. The newcomers can actually believe they have morality on their side. So assured have the elite become that there is almost no block on the rewards they arrogate to themselves. ... As a result, general inequality has been more grievous with every year that passes, and without a bleat from the leaders of a party who once spoke up so trenchantly and characteristically for greater equality.[3]

From the position taken in this book, meritocracy understood in this way – even supposing it to have been achieved – cannot by itself justify large rewards because the opportunities to achieve 'merit' are so unequal.[4] If that were the only conception of meritocracy, there would be no more to be said. But there is a more subtle one that is worth a good deal more attention. I can introduce it by quoting from a piece published by Michael Frayn in 1964, before he became known as a playwright and novelist. With almost uncanny foresight, he anticipated the invention of New Labour, imagining the Modern Living Party – 'the new centre party founded with the go-ahead people of today in mind', whose leader proclaimed that 'at the very heart of our political thinking' is '*Equality of Opportunity*'.[5] Unlike the Conservatives, it would see to it that 'the old school tie and the right accent' ceased to be the road to success.[6] But it also rejected 'the [Old] Labour Party's vested interest in dragging us all down to the same level'. It had no plans 'to mess about with the foundations of society' in that way, no 'high-falutin' theory about paying surgeons the same as roadsweepers'.[7]

The quality shared by the party's members was, its leader said: *successfulness*. By that I mean we are the sort of people who are good at passing exams ... at winning scholarships to the university ... and, in general at doing well for ourselves in a highly competitive world. ... In short, the sort of people who join the Modern Living Party are men and women who enjoy certain natural advantages which they've inherited from their parents, and which they confidently expect to hand on to their children.[8]

If we left the word 'natural' out of that last sentence, we would simply have the idea discussed so far: that people should advance by 'individual merit' – here contrasted with nepotism, patronage, discrimination or other irrelevant factors. That would have left it open that this merit could be transmitted from generation to generation by parents who exploited all kinds of social, cultural and economic advantages, as it actually is now. Once we add the notion that the privileged can pass on competitive success to their offspring only through 'natural advantages', however, we get a very different picture of the process. 'Natural' is to be contrasted with 'social': the idea now is that 'individual merit' resides in some kind of heritable innate ability. The confidence of the members of the Modern Living Party in passing on their advantages to their offspring now has to depend on their being able to pass on to them genes for success. This assumes, of course, that there are such things as genes for success that can be inherited.

There does seem to be support for the idea that people can properly lay claim to advantages derived from natural abilities. In 'common perceptions of fairness . . . the line [is] often drawn between innate qualities of the individual, which are mostly seen as true merits, and inherited economic and social advantages, which are not.'[9] The implication of this would appear to be that unequal rewards arising from innate ability can be justified only against a background of equality of opportunity. But for this purpose equal opportunity must be defined in a special way that ties in with a new idea of meritocracy:

A recurrent theme in discussions of meritocracy is *equality of opportunity*, which means that family origins should not constitute a significant advantage or handicap in pursuing economic success. One intuitive measure of this is the fraction of variance in income that is attributable to an individual's own qualities, or lack thereof, rather than to his or her background.[10]

But how much of the reward arising from natural ability can people justly claim to be deserved? Adam Swift describes what he calls 'the conventional view' in the following terms:

[Tiger Woods] deserves to earn more than [a social worker]. Not because he currently works harder, or worked harder to get where he is, but simply because his having been blessed with exceptional golfing ability enables him to do something more valuable – at least as measured by other people's willingness to pay – than what she is able to do.[11]

But does Woods deserve all of his enormous earnings because his natural talent was a necessary condition of his achievements, or should some of them be attributed to his good fortune in having a father who dedicated his life to developing his son's golfing prowess?

To sharpen up the point by relating it to social class, consider tennis-playing. Although Britain scarcely shines in this sport, those who do fairly well, like Tim Henman, still make a lot of money. Yet the opportunity to play tennis at a competitive level is essentially a middle-class preserve, because (given the climate) it is necessary to have access to an indoor court to practise year-round and do a lot of training. State schools and local authorities do not provide such facilities, so only the children of fairly affluent parents have an opportunity to develop high-level tennis ability. This might suggest that Henman's earnings should be somehow apportioned between the share arising from his natural talent and that arising from his advantages in utilizing it.

In *The Rise of the Meritocracy*, Young equivocated about the basis of unequal rewards. One formula was this: 'Intelligence and effort together make up merit $(I + E = M)$.'[12] This would suggest that the superior education that is to be bestowed on the most intelligent in the society of the future should be regarded as an undeserved bonus. For it falls under neither of the relevant categories: in itself, it is neither intelligence nor effort. However, the tenor of the book as a whole runs in a different direction. Thus, Young has his narrator write:

> Today the eminent know that success is the just reward for their own capacity, for their own efforts and their own undeniable achievement. ... They know ... that not only are they of higher calibre to begin with, but that a first-class education has been built on their native gifts.[13]

This suggests that achievement is itself a basis for the totality of its rewards to be deserved, but only as long as the superior education that makes it possible has been given only to those with superior 'native gifts'.

We are thus confronted with two competing meritocratic views of the appropriate basis for rewarding achievement, though (as the example of Young himself suggests) they are seldom clearly distinguished, despite their potentially very different distributive implications. However, the institutions themselves would be the same on either basis of remuneration. We can therefore conveniently define a meritocratic society in terms of its institutions: (1) equal opportunities for those with equal native talent and (2) positions in the society awarded on the basis of actual attainments. These institutions can even be supported by those who accept the proposition that rewards based on (native) intelligence and skill are a matter of luck. For it can be suggested that they are the best that can be achieved practically. This bluff position was taken by one of the leading boosters of genetically derived ability, Arthur Jensen, who wrote in 1968: 'We have to face it: the assortment of persons into occupational roles simply is not "fair" in any absolute sense. The best we can hope for is that true merit, given equality of opportunity, will act as a basis for the natural assorting process.'[14]

An obvious gap in this formulation is that it does not specify what is to count as 'true merit'. On the face of it, any innate qualities that help their bearers to get ahead in life should be included. As in Swift's example, if there is an innate physical basis (though it needs a lot of developing) to being a star golfer, then that should be 'merit'. In practice, however, the innate qualities that are peculiarly thought to be meritorious in the writings of meritocratic theorists are cognitive ones. The explanation may have something to do with the fact that people who write in favour of meritocracy probably believe that they have a lot of innate cognitive ability, whereas it may be all too apparent to them that they have few other plausibly innate characteristics related to success. (This is, indeed, one of the major reasons for people becoming academics.) In any case, I shall for now follow the trail where it leads, which means that the supposedly innate component in occupational success that will dominate the scene is cognitive ability.

Jensen's statement of meritocracy in the sense we are now examining makes it clear that the key concepts are 'true merit' and 'equality of opportunity'. 'True merit' is to be understood as 'innate ability': a capacity that can be affected very little by the environment. It can be measured by subjecting children to a battery of tests. There will be a common factor that can be extracted from the separate test scores. We call this factor IQ: Intelligence Quotient. According to Jensen: 'The term "intelligence" should be reserved for . . . the general factor common to standard tests of intelligence. . . . [I]t is probably best thought of as a capacity for abstract reasoning and problem solving.' Taking a further leap, Jensen goes on to call it 'a biological reality', whose existence has been scientifically established.[15]

We know now what 'true merit' is: a genetically derived ability for abstract reasoning and problem solving. 'Given equality of opportunity', this 'will act as the basis for the natural assorting process.' Against the background of a century of talk about 'nature versus nurture', we can have no difficulty in identifying the 'natural assorting process' with one that produces an ordering of outcomes that corresponds to the relative amounts of 'biological' IQ, give or take a bit for effort. It is mediated, as we have seen, by equality of opportunity.

On the face of it, equality of opportunity is an exceedingly strong demand. The only way in which we can be assured that the ordering of success is the same as the ordering of IQ (assumed to be genetic in origin) is to ensure that children have environments that are equally conducive to developing this innate talent. If there are powerful environmental effects on its development, and these are correlated with the parents' wealth and education, the implications of a serious attempt to ensure equal opportunity will be radical. But meritocrats of Jensen's stripe are able to avoid this subversive implication of their ideas by insisting that IQ is more or less fixed from the earliest years, and that differences in home or neighbourhood environments have little effect on it. Equal opportunity therefore can be reduced to equal educational opportunity. The relevant sense can be defined as follows: 'Children of different classes but the same level of natural talent should receive roughly equal educational resources.'[16]

This principle does not say anything about the relative resources to be bestowed on children with different IQs. One possibility would be to say that, the higher a child's IQ, the less that should be spent on it, so as to compensate those who are disadvantaged through no fault of their own. But this would be contrary to the spirit of meritocracy, which tells us that inequalities in innate abilities should express themselves in due course by underwriting unequal attainments and unequal positions. Suppose that a higher IQ produces a bigger gain in attainment for any given educational input. Then the most efficient use of resources would be to concentrate them on those with the highest IQs. Take an analogy with raising pigs. Different breeds of pig put on different amounts of weight for each pound of food they eat. If you have a variety of breeds and a fixed amount of feed, and you want to maximize the total porcine avoirdupois, you will obviously start by feeding the breed that most efficiently converts food into weight. At some point, either the pigs cannot eat any more or severely diminishing returns to additional food set in. You will then start feeding the next most efficient converters, and so on down the list until either you run out of feed or have as much total weight of pig as you can use. The pigs left over will get nothing.

I need not labour the application of the analogy. Suppose you think that what really matters is to identify those with the potential to become the best and the brightest, and shovel educational resources at them. You may think that everybody benefits from this, because the writers, the scientists, the top civil servants, the top managers in business, and so on will be so marvellous that the society will have high achievements in all areas, including the economy, so that there will be enough to distribute to those who are both untalented and (as a consequence) uneducated. In *The Rise of the Meritocracy*, the key to the creation of a society stratified according to 'natural ability' was to put far more resources into schools for the intellectual elite: already by 1989, Young predicted, the staffing ratio in the selective grammar schools had become (according to his narrator in 2033) twice as high as that in the secondary modern schools to which the failures were allocated. The secondary modern schools, meanwhile, would prepare children for low-grade jobs – including the revival of domestic service, which Young presciently foresaw as a by-product of increasing inequality.

All this was no more than a projection forward from 1958 of the system set up after the Second World War. The creation of a system that segregated children by ability, measured by IQ tests at the age of 11, arose from a widespread acceptance among politicians and educationalists of the ideas that I have described as underlying the theory of meritocracy. This virtual consensus crossed party lines: indeed, the Butler 1944 Education Act implemented by the 1945 Labour government took its name from the Conservative politician under whose acgis it was passed in 1944 while the country was governed by a Conservative-dominated coalition.

The man chiefly responsible for the dominance of the idea of IQ as a measure of a genetically endowed (and therefore unmalleable) capacity to benefit from education was Sir Cyril Burt. Burt was a 'single factor' man as regards IQ and a tireless propagandist for the notion that IQ was almost entirely heritable, which was taken then (and still is by a lot of people) to mean that it was genetically determined. He was so enthusiastic, in fact, that he fabricated data to support his theory and even invented research assistants whose work he acknowledged. This did not come out until a lot later as a result of ingenious detective work on the origins of various peculiarities in Burt's published data.[17] At the time, Burt was riding high, as educational adviser to the London County Council (by far the biggest local education authority in the country) and the generally accepted authority on psychology.[18]

The state school system set up in 1945 tested children at the age of 11 (the '11+ exam') and on the basis of this assigned them to schools appropriate to their native abilities. Proportions varied somewhat from one local education authority to another, for largely accidental reasons, but it was always a minority who went to the selective grammar schools. The rest went to schools that many of them left as soon as they were legally free to do so, which at that time was at the age of 15. Of the three possible models for relating educational inputs to IQ, this system followed the one that put its money on 'the best and the brightest'. The low expectations of the teachers, the demoralizing effect of having 'failed', and the general inferiority of resources in the 'secondary modern' schools, combined with the rigidities in the system, ensured that for almost all children the results of the 11+ test were irrevocable. 'Perhaps one or two pupils per school per year succeeded in showing that they had been wrongly categorized.'[19] Yet even on its own premises as a perfect test of ability, the test could not possibly have been that accurate, if only because many children were bound to have turned in an uncharacteristically good or bad performance on the day of the examination.

Within the selective schools, the process of sorting by IQ was carried to a further stage: at my grammar school (a run-of-the-mill state school which I have no reason to suppose was atypical) the boys were assigned to one of four forms, not, as at Hogwarts, by a magic hat (a far more attractive alternative) but by scores on tests. There was very little movement between forms after this on the basis of achievement. This stratification system produced enormously unequal outcomes within the school, even though all the boys were in the top 20 per cent of measured IQ. At the time I was at school (the late 1940s and early 1950s) about 3 per cent of each age cohort went to university. One quarter of 20 per cent is 5 per cent, and roughly half of the top form did go on. I am not at all sure that a majority of the bottom form even stayed to the age of 18. These results could have been (and I believe were) an artefact of the assumptions underlying meritocracy. If you act on the assumption that a set of tests at the age of 11 establishes an innate ability to learn, which has a dominant effect on the amount that different children can learn, your prophecy will be a self-fulfilling one.

In my epigraph, I quoted Philip Kitcher celebrating the end of the 11+ examination and the segregation of children into schools with 'academic' and 'non-academic' missions. On the basis of the analysis in chapter 5, however, one might conclude that, with all its faults, it might be preferable to the current system, especially in London, where manipulation of the system has been allowed (in fact encouraged) to run riot. Of course, the test scores themselves reflected, and would still reflect, all the advantages that middle-class children had had up to the time of the examination. But at least the test scores were definitive: children were allocated to schools and the schools had nothing to say about it. Let me make it clear, however, that I am not buying into the bogus psychological theories that underlay the 11+. In the next chapter, I shall explain what is wrong with them.

9

The Abuse of Science

I have already dismissed the broad conception of meritocracy as appointment by merit. In this chapter, I shall address the narrower one, according to which inequalities of outcome are just as long as they arise from conditions of equal opportunity, understood to mean that those with equal native abilities have equal access to the means of developing them. Whether all the rewards thus arising are supposed to be deserved or only those that can be attributed to the element of native talent has been left as an open question. The premises required for both versions are the same, and I hope to show that they are untenable, so the question of choosing between them does not arise.

Let me start, then, by listing a number of empirical propositions that the theory of meritocracy has to maintain. The first is that IQ is genetically determined to a large degree. 'Genetically determined' means that it is not open to much change from the environment, and that measures of IQ are reliable measures of what Sir Cyril Burt called 'innate, general, cognitive ability'. A corollary of the resistance of IQ to environmental change is, of course, that it is resistant to change through schooling. In fact, it is supposed that this genetically derived IQ sets strict limits on how much any given person can ever learn, however favourable their environment (in school and out of it) may be. It is also held that what we might call 'raw IQ' provides its possessor with advantages in addition to educability. (This is the old 'diamond in the rough' idea.) Thus, of two people with equal educational attainment, the one with the higher IQ will be better at everything with a cognitive element in it, such as remembering who ordered which meal. He or she will therefore be able to get a job with more pay and status. The authors of *The Bell Curve*, launched with a great deal of ballyhoo (whose origins I shall analyse in chapter 17) as the last word in genetic determinism, are particularly keen on this idea.[1]

Another proposition in genetics is that IQ is largely inherited. Characteristics can be genetically determined but not inherited: the distinctive characteristics of Down syndrome arise from an error in the process of creating a single set of chromosomes from the two sets (mother's and father's) available. As we shall see, the concept of heritability has very odd properties, but the idea it is intended to capture is that of traits that 'run in families' like the Hapsburg chin or congenital deafness. Taken as a whole, 'the meritocracy thesis strikes at the very heart of the humane-egalitarian ideal. . . . The abolition of inequality [of opportunity] and privilege produces a class-equals-caste society with high status the inheritance of a few, dependency and low status the inheritance of many.'[2]

The transmission of 'genes for intelligence' from generation to generation depends on what is called 'assortative mating': the tendency of couples who have children to be similar in some respects. There is strong evidence that members of the same educational level and social class tend to pair up, and that this tendency is getting stronger in time in Britain and the USA. One explanation is that, the longer people wait before having children, the more likely it is that they will be mixing almost exclusively with their own kind. As the author of a British study said: 'It is not that the middle class set out to insulate themselves. It's just that they don't meet people from different backgrounds, either at university or work. So the partners they consider are socially restricted.'[3] The greater material inequality between classes, the greater this effect is bound to be, because the ways of life of people belonging to different social strata will diverge more. The system of 'coming-out parties' (not in the contemporary sense) was designed to ensure that young women from the aristocracy or near-aristocracy (debutantes) met only 'suitable' young men socially. The (good) university, the law firm and the squash club now serve a similar function for a broader elite group.

Of course, assortative mating on the basis of social status will result in transmission of genes for success only if it is true that there is a high correlation between social status and the assumed genetic basis of success, which is standardly taken to be IQ. In *The Bell Curve*, it is asserted that, ever since 1940, at an accelerating pace, sorting by cognitive ability has been occurring in the USA, primarily through admission to universities on the basis of merit and the expansion of the numbers going to university. As a result, 'bright were more likely to marry bright, encouraging cognitive partitioning in terms of the occupational status of the family'.[4] Hence 'genes for intelligence become more and more segregated by class'.[5] The authors of *The Bell Curve* asserted that this had already happened to such a degree that 'most people at present are stuck near where their parents were on the income distribution in part because IQ ... passes on sufficiently from one generation to the next to constrain economic mobility'.[6]

It is interesting to notice that all these propositions were accepted by Michael Young in *The Rise of the Meritocracy*.[7] Thus, it was assumed that IQ is unaffected by the environment, and can in principle be assessed at birth on the basis of information about heredity. It can change somewhat over time (e.g., it declines with age), but this is a purely biological phenomenon and its course can again in principle be predicted. Education is more productive when given to those with high IQs, at any rate if economic return is the criterion. Given that education is channelled to those with the highest IQs, their rise to the top will be assured. Young also predicted assortative mating on the basis of IQ, which, he wrote, was going to be a fact about people made publicly available. This tendency for like to pair with like would arise for two reasons. The first was that the disparities in developed intellectual ability between those with different IQs (widened by their different qualities of education) would make them incompatible company for one another. The second was that a high IQ person would not want to take an unnecessary chance of becoming the parent of a low IQ child and suffering the humiliation that this would bring with it. The meritocracy would therefore increasingly become a caste because of the high correlation between the IQ levels of parents and children.

Remarkably, Young still apparently retained a belief in these propositions until the end of a very long life: in 'Down with Meritocracy!', he claimed that what he had predicted in the book had indeed occurred. Thus he said that the working class had been 'deprived by the educational selection of its natural leaders', and he made it clear that by 'natural leaders' he meant those with high innate IQs. In the past, he suggested, when barriers to social mobility had been high, 'ability' had been 'distributed between the classes more or less at random'. But today all those with high levels of innate ability have been educated, leaving nobody with any ability in the working class. This, he maintained, explained why the Labour cabinet no longer contained men who had risen through leadership of a trade union (Ernest Bevin) or local government (Herbert Morrison).[8] This strikes me as a remarkable invocation of a genetic factor to explain something that can readily be explained by other means. Without going too far into this historical byway, let me simply point out that the destruction of the powers of trade unions and local councils under Margaret Thatcher made leadership of them a far less likely path into national politics. (Nothing has changed, it need scarcely be said, under New Labour, which is equally hostile to all potential rivals for power, and has completely abandoned the notion that the party is the political arm of the labour movement.) Be that as it may, Young was doing no more in his article than echo the prediction in *The Rise of the Meritocracy* that already by the 1960s the 'outstanding children of manual fathers' could get to the top, so that the 'lower classes' were becoming 'progressively denuded of ability'.[9]

I shall seek to show that all the propositions underlying the theory of meritocracy are flawed. Let me begin with the claim just discussed, that over the last century, and at an accelerating pace, western societies have undergone a filtering process that has concentrated those with high IQs more and more in the top jobs and those with low IQs at the bottom. If the genetic assumptions of meritocracy were correct and this had been happening, we should find that, in each succeeding generation, there will be a bigger gap between the average IQ of the children of those in the high status occupations and children with parents in low status occupations. In fact, however, the gap in the USA between the average IQ of children whose parents are in the top third of the occupational hierarchy and the average IQ of those whose parents are in the bottom third has stayed the same. It stood at almost exactly ten points in 1948, 1972 and 1989.[10]

I know of no comparable study in Britain, but there is no need to invoke inherited IQ to explain the tendency of middle-class parents to have children who in turn stay in the middle class. As Philip Kitcher has written, 'it is possible to develop a model of transmission of culture from parents to children that makes no use of the idea of genetic transmission' and produces analogues of 'the usual theorems of population genetics'.[11] I have already shown in chapter 5 how middle-class parents are succeeding, to a greater and greater extent, in transmitting their advantages to their children and keeping others out. We should therefore not expect genetically transmitted IQ (if there is such a thing) to be becoming more concentrated at the top of the income distribution.

Let me now turn to the psychological propositions. It is quite true that IQ has quite a strong connection with academic attainment, but this is hardly surprising since it is the kind of test that children who do well at school will do well at. IQ is simply a common factor extracted from the results of a battery of tests. It correlates highly with examination results in particular academic subjects because it calls for the same abilities. To the extent that IQ tests do differ from tests of attainment in specific subjects, they focus on 'abstract questions and puzzles with right or wrong answers'.[12] However, 'a score that measures only intelligence at that level of abstraction' simply favours those with a certain kind of puzzle-solving ability over others who may be just as intelligent in any ordinary sense of the word and do just as well or better at real academic subjects.[13]

If IQ does not cause academic success, does it cause success irrespective of formal attainments, as the meritocratic theory claims? In fact, IQ is not a very good predictor of success, at any rate as measured by income: in the USA, IQ differences explain 'only about 12 percent of the [overall] variation in income'.[14] Even this degree of association is partly an artefact: if employers believe that high IQ makes people good at jobs, those with high IQs will get the most desirable jobs. It is well established in a whole variety of settings that measured IQ has only a very limited relation to successfully performing a job.[15] This means that establishing a 'testocracy' is actually unfair, if our criterion of a fair appointment is that it should depend on ability to do the job. Filling jobs on the basis of test scores for IQ or anything like it is a form of discrimination against those who perform relatively poorly on such tests. For many who could actually do the job as well as or better than those appointed will be excluded from consideration.[16]

I now need to assess the genetic basis of the theory of meritocracy. Here we can make progress only by following the (real) geneticists and talking about norms of reaction. A norm of reaction tells us about the way a given genotype reacts to a given environment. A certain kind of grain, for example, will grow taller with more watering (holding other environmental factors constant) up to a certain point, but somewhere beyond that point it will simply rot. A different grain will react differently to different amounts of water. In the same way, two (non-identical) twins, Peter and Paul, will have different genotypes. If these have interacted with a common environment, we might be tempted to conclude that, if Peter has a higher IQ than Paul, he must have possessed more 'innate intelligence'. But the same genotypes might have reacted with a different family environment so as to produce the opposite effect on IQs. For example, if there is a genetic element in introversion and extroversion (the best-supported claim for the psychological effects of genes) then in one family the extrovert Peter might be rewarded with more attention than Paul; in another, Peter might be sat on and Paul encouraged. In either family, the differences in IQ are genetic in origin, since we are in each case postulating that the two children are faced with identical environments. But there is also a sense in which the differences depend on the environment, in that the different environments could also be described as causing the differences in IQ, given the different geno-types. All this is perfectly comprehensible within the framework within which we talk about norms of reaction, yet it falls outside the purview of those who still adhere to the terms of the stale 'nature versus nurture' debate.

None of this need worry the true believers in the meritocratic theory, who hold that different environments can do little to change the 'innate' level of IQ. The trouble is that this is not so. Stephen Jay Gould has cited as evidence against it 'impressive gains for poor black children adopted into affluent and intellectual homes . . . and the failure to find any cognitive differences between two cohorts of children born out of wedlock to German women, reared in Germany as Germans, but fathered by black and white American soldiers'.[17] There are examples of even bigger gains: in the Netherlands, the cohort of 18-year-olds gained an average of twenty-one IQ points between 1952 and 1982.[18] The genetic characteristics of the Dutch can scarcely have changed much in thirty years, and we can no doubt account for the change if we bear in mind that the earlier cohort lived under Nazi occupation between the ages of 7 and 11, and that this was associated with very poor nutrition at times and no doubt in addition generated all kinds of problem for children growing up in that period. The average level of measured intelligence across a variety of countries increases by about three points per decade.[19] This is inexplicable on a basis of genetic determinism – especially since the tendency for the more intelligent to have fewer than the average number of children ought to lower the level of IQ in the population in each successive generation.

Despite all this, I suspect that there is still in many readers the lurking feeling that it must, in principle, be possible to assign to every-body a score for 'native ability' that can then be modified by the environment. But this idea of an 'underlying' level of ability that can be ascribed to every child does not stand up when confronted with the point that what children are born with are 'norms of reaction'. To see the implications of this, I invite readers to examine the table opposite (I promise that there are no more to come), which sets out the norms of reaction for two children, Adrian and Beryl, to three possible environments: good, middling and poor. If the numbers represent IQ scores, which is more 'naturally' intelligent? With a middling environment, they are equal. But saying this seems arbitrary and loses a lot of information about what happens in other environments. We might be tempted to say that Beryl best fits the idea of the

Table 1: Norms of Reaction to Three Environments

	Adrian	Beryl
Good	110	105
Middling	100	100
Poor	90	95

kid who comes through relatively well even in adverse circumstances. But we may also be pulled in the opposite direction by the thought that Adrian has the most potential in a good environment. The simple answer is that there is no answer to the question: which of the two has the most 'innate' ability?

This illustrates the folly, even in its own terms, of picking 'the best and the brightest' at some age such as 11 for hothouse treatment. Suppose that a 'good' scholastic environment after the age of 11 counts as a 'good' environment. Who should be picked for this privilege? To make a selection at the age of 11, we have to assume that IQ at this age is a valid predictor of future academic capacity. This may be quite false: some children may peak at the age of 11 while others are late developers.[20] But the whole business of selection depends on assuming that this possibility can be ignored. Suppose we say, then, that a child with the best IQ score at the age of 11 should get the place in a selective school. If the table is taken as representing possible IQ scores at this age, it is clear that the choice will turn on the kind of environment to which the children have been exposed up to that point. Beryl will get the place if her environment has been good and Adrian's middling or poor. She will also win if both have been exposed to poor environments. Adrian will win if and only if he has had a good environment. (As we have seen, there will be a tie if both have had middling environments.) Whatever is going on here, it is surely clear that it has nothing to do with the simple-minded notion that a test at the age of 11 will reveal which child has the most 'natural' academic talent.

The points I have been making are in no way esoteric. They have been the merest commonplaces of genetics for many years. The basic argument was set out classically by Richard Lewontin in 1974.[21] Yet I am not aware of a single political philosopher (and I have read a lot of them) who discusses issues involving equal opportunity without assuming that it makes sense to ascribe to each person some measure of 'native ability' or 'native talent', understood as cognitive ability or talent. Some may have doubts about our chances of actually assigning scores for this innate ability, and some think that it is morally insignificant anyway. But they all take it for granted that it is there somewhere. The popular conception of equal opportunity as equal educational inputs to children with the same 'native ability' clearly presupposes the existence of such a thing.[22]

The second proposition in genetics is that IQ is heritable. No doubt most (though not all) genetic traits are transmitted from parents. But now we have seen what 'the genetic basis of IQ' comes to, this loses a lot of its interest. It becomes even less interesting when we understand what 'heritability' means. 'Heritability is defined as a fraction: the ratio of genetically caused variation to total variation (environmental and genetic).'[23] The variation in question is the amount occurring within a certain population, so heritability is a characteristic of a population, like the proportion owning DVD players. The heritability of some trait therefore depends on the extent to which the environment varies within that population. Height, for example, is a function of genetic factors (tall parents tend to have tall children, and so on) and also nutrition: on the average, children born in the 1960s in most western countries were distinctly taller than their parents, who had experienced the Great Depression and the Second World War. If all the children in the population had received nutrition of equivalent quality, heritability of height would be high. If they had received greatly different amounts, heritability would be low. It is hard to see why we should attach any significance to an estimate for the heritability of heights in a population once we understand how it is arrived at.

When we apply the same apparatus to IQ, heritability becomes an even more elusive concept. Imagine that all the children in a population are exposed to an identical environment. Then the heritability of IQ will necessarily be high, because non-genetic sources of variation have been eliminated by stipulation. But we are not entitled to say that this environment is 'equally good' for all the children: recall my case in which a child genetically disposed to be pushy is encouraged in one environment and suppressed in another. If the uniform environment is favourable to children with the pushy tendency, then the genes responsible for pushiness are 'good' genes in that they predict relatively high IQ. But if the environment favoured the other kind of child, the same genes would be 'bad'. The case of Adrian and Beryl bypassed this problem: we stipulated that we could define 'good', 'middling' and 'poor' environments so that each of them did better the better the environment. But this still does not get us round the predicament posed by the fact that Beryl does better than Adrian if they are both in a poor environment while the positions are reversed if both are in a good environment. The implication of both examples is that any talk about the 'genetic component' in each person's IQ is doubly misguided: first, heritability is an attribute of a population, not an individual; and, second, whether or not a genotype interacts with the environment in ways conducive to high IQ (or any other character trait) depends on the environment.

Remember that a person's complement of genes is simply a basis for that person's norms of reaction. We have no direct access to these norms, so we have to infer what they are by observing what actually happens within a given environment. Since we have very little idea what features of the environment are relevant, and certainly cannot measure the environment except on certain gross dimensions, about all we can say is that, within the normal range, IQ is brought about by some interaction between genetically based norms of reaction and the environment. But we have no way of guessing what the maximum IQ of each person might be with an optimal environment. As Ned Block has written: 'perhaps in ideally favourable environments most genotypes yield more or less the same phenotype, that is to say, in this context, IQ.'[24]

It should hardly be necessary to point out that measures of the inheritance of IQ (i.e., correlation between that of parents and children) tell us nothing about the role played by genes. For children inherit their environment (much of which consists simply of the characteristics of the parents) as well as their genes. The highest correlation between parents and offspring for any social traits in the United States are those for political party and religious sect. The Public Health Commission that originally studied the vitamin-deficiency disease pellagra in the southern United States came to the conclusion that it was genetic because it 'ran in families'.[25] Pulmonary tuberculosis might similarly have been regarded as genetic because parents tended to infect their children. We know that these connections were in fact environmentally generated (same food, same bacillus), and we are reluctant to envisage the same for IQ only because the relevant environment is too pervasive and multifarious. Anyone who starts with the methodological principle that any differences in ability that cannot be attributed to the environment must be genetic in origin is bound to conclude that the lion's share of the differences arise from genes, simply because we know so little about what features of the environment are relevant and have no way of measuring most of those that we do surmise to be relevant. Genetic determinism, in other words, is simply an expression of ignorance.

We are left with the meritocratic theory of social justice. I left it open that this could take either of two forms: it might be taken to justify all inequalities arising from differences in natural talent against a background of equal opportunities. Alternatively, it might be taken to justify only the element of inequality that can be traced directly to genetic advantage or disadvantage. But, as we now know, this is in general an incoherent idea, so it does not make any difference which version we adhere to.

The only instances in which we can really apply the principle that people should gain or lose from genetic advantages or disadvantages and not from environmental ones are those of severe retardation, because there it is usually possible to establish causation. The arbitrariness of the meritocratic conception of equal opportunity becomes starkly apparent here. Suppose that the mothers of Frank and Graham are exposed to the same environment *in utero*, which arises from their mothers' exposure to the same amount of some toxin at the same point in the pregnancy. And suppose that Frank escapes injury while Graham suffers severe retardation, as a consequence of their different genetically based norms of reaction to the same amount of this toxin. Now imagine a society in which all foetuses are exposed to the same toxic threat, and are divided into F and G types. Then we can say that the Fs derive their higher intelligence from their genetic advantage. They will be able to claim credit for whatever differences in reward their differences in productivity give rise to, as long as there is equality of opportunity after birth. But in a society in which no foetus is exposed to this toxic threat it will make no difference to their intelligence whether people have F or G genotypes. We shall be back with the usual interplay between norms of reaction and environment which, as we have seen, defeats the application – indeed the intelligibility – of the meritocratic conception of justice.

Here is a second illustration of the way in which the meritocratic theory of justice works in a case in which it makes sense and can be applied in the real world. Down syndrome children are always retarded, but how well they learn to cope with life depends on the environments in which they grow up and then live. Suppose all Down syndrome children with IQs below 50 are warehoused in an institution where they are all equally neglected. This would be consistent with the conception of social justice that I am considering because the special treatment was genetically triggered: it would simply be the obverse of sending children with IQs of 150 or more to far better schools than the rest of the population on the assumption that a high IQ was genetically determined. According to the conception of justice advanced in this book, however, what is going on here is that a genetically derived lack of equal opportunity is being compounded by a socially created one, which makes for double injustice. I hope that anyone who has been resistant to the line of argument pursued in this chapter will be given pause for thought by these implications of the idea that people can legitimately claim the fruits of whatever advantages they happen to be born with.

Part IV

The Cult of Personal Responsibility

Rights and responsibilities have always been at the heart of my politics.... The New Deal is a symbol of this mission. It explicitly seeks to provide new opportunities in return for new responsibilities. It reaches not only the unemployed but single parents and sick and disabled people.

Tony Blair

Never use *rights* without mentioning *obligations* (or, conceivably, *duties* or *responsibilities*) in the same sentence. If you started using *rights* on its own, people could get the idea that rights are somehow automatic and inalienable.

Alistair Beaton: Glossary in
The Little Book of New Labour Bollocks

10

Responsibility versus Equality?

Monotheistic religions are, we all know, confronted with the conundrum: if God is good and omnipotent, how come there is so much suffering in the world? And we are all familiar with the answer: because God endowed us all with free will, so we, rather than God, are responsible for everything bad about the world. To the response that this seems a pretty rotten trick to play on people, the standard reply is that free will was endowed on human beings as a punishment. Undoubtedly, the most famous expression of this idea is the opening lines of Milton's *Paradise Lost*, in which he promised to tell us the story

> Of man's first disobedience, and the fruit
> Of that forbidden tree, whose mortal taste
> Brought death into the world and all our woe
> With loss of Eden . . .

Hobbes said: '[I]t is with the mysteries of our religion, as with wholesome pills for the sick, which swallowed whole, have the virtue to cure; but chewed, are for the most part cast up again without effect.'[1] But many of those who have earnestly tried to swallow the lot have still gagged on the difficulty of explaining how human sin can account for plague or smallpox, for example. Charles Darwin, while still struggling to retain some form of deism, if not Christianity, expressed the problem well in correspondence with the eminent American biologist Asa Gray, who adhered to a version of creationism, writing: 'I own that I cannot see, as plainly as others do, and which I should wish to do, evidence of design and beneficence on all sides.

There seems to be too much suffering in the world.'[2] Darwin was as concerned with the suffering of non-human animals as with that of human beings. But at least with regard to the latter some prominent American divines have diagnosed AIDS as God's punishment – though more selective this time around – for the increased incidence of the sins that led to the destruction of Sodom and Gomorrah (though we can only speculate about what they did in Gomorrah). So, since God moves in mysterious ways, we have to trust that there is some parallel explanation for plague and smallpox: we are merely too ignorant to know what it is.

The implication is, then, that the power to employ our free will to commit sins (and thus qualify for eternal torment) is God's savage revenge for 'man's first disobedience'. That being so, should we not show human solidarity by doing what we can to help our errant brothers and sisters? Unfortunately, many of those who believe that we all suffer from Original Sin are very far from drawing such humane conclusions. Rather, they take the view that it would be frustrating God's intentions if we did not do our best to ensure that the sinful should suffer for their sins in this life as well as the next – perhaps because of some residual doubts about the reality of heaven and hell. Immanuel Kant expressed this dismal notion of retribution for the sake of retribution by saying that, even if a society were to dissolve, its last act (before turning out the lights, presumably) should be to execute every last inmate of death row.

In the past quarter century, this approach has been adopted not only in the treatment of prisoners (as we have seen) but has also become the driving force behind social policy generally, especially starkly in the USA but with Britain very clearly moving in the same direction. It has become a premise of such ideological power that no ambitious politician nowadays dares to challenge it. Its previous high point was the period running from the last quarter of the nineteenth century up to the First World War – another period of rapidly increasing inequality. Thus, unmarried mothers were treated with gratuitous harshness so that they could expiate their sin. Their children, conceived in sin, were also made to suffer in about as many ways as human ingenuity could devise. Charities distinguished between the 'deserving poor' and the 'undeserving poor', leaving the latter to the only state-funded institution, the workhouse, whose conditions were deliberately designed to be as repellent and degrading as possible. Old age and feebleness were no bar to the offer of the workhouse or nothing. (Those adjudged insane were the only exceptions, and, in the absence of private means, were condemned to their own special hells in the form of 'lunatic asylums', popular destinations for amusing week-end excursions to observe the inmates.)

The charities could not be counted on even where the family's lack of income could not possibly be regarded as the responsibility of its members. For to be 'deserving', it was not enough to be destitute through no fault of one's own: it was also necessary to satisfy tests of sobriety, sexual 'morality' and frugality. Perhaps the most nauseating aspect of the whole business was the legion of comfortably situated ladies who visited their wards to check that their miserable pittance was not being spent on anything that might make life worth living, rather than on merely subsisting. I shall trace in the next chapter the recrudescence of such thinking in the development on both sides of the Atlantic of the idea that any kind of non-universal government payment is a sort of gift to which arbitrary conditions, in addition to need, can be attached by the donors (i.e. the taxpayers).

Arthur Hugh Clough had already by 1862 spotted the implications of a society in which wealth was worshipped and poverty despised. For in 'The Latest Decalogue' published in that year, he added glosses on the ten commandments to reflect current attitudes. The best known couplet was:

> Thou shalt not kill; but need not strive
> Officiously to keep alive.[3]

The point I want to make here is that many people since, missing the satirical intention, have quoted these lines as an admirable explanation of the purport of the fifth commandment. Any society in which Clough is taken as clarifying the will of God is well on the way to comprehensive moral collapse.

As religious belief declined in the last quarter of the nineteenth century, some alternative justification had to be found for systematic inequality. The next move was therefore to assert that human beings are 'naturally' unequal. The idea of natural inequality saturated ancient Greek thought. In *The Republic*, Plato postulated that there are three types of human being with different capacities and personal characteristics: gold, silver and bronze. Thanks to interbreeding among the members of each group, most children will belong to the same class as their parents, but a few will exhibit the signs showing that they belong to a different group. These will be promoted or demoted accordingly. It is impossible not to be reminded of Michael Young's scenario in which, despite a high degree of assortative mating, rigorous IQ tests will on occasion reveal a few cuckoos in the nest, who will be despatched to an environment appropriate to those either more or less intelligent than their parents. Although I have been talking about Plato's idiosyncratic development of the notion of hereditary characteristics, the basic idea on which he built it was commonplace:

> The ancient world was . . . concerned with the relation between heredity and behaviour. The Greeks anticipated eugenics with their belief that young men who distinguished themselves in war or socially valued activities should be encouraged to breed, whereas depraved persons should not.[4]

The triumph of Darwinism brought with it a revival of the idea that differences among human beings might have their origins in qualities that were inborn and largely hereditary. Sir Francis Galton, Darwin's cousin, was inspired by '*The Origin of Species* . . . to study, by measurement, the influences of heredity upon the mental and physical characteristics of human beings'.[5] In the process, he spawned the whole industry of measuring IQ. He also wrote a book, *Hereditary Genius*, arguing for the genetic transmission of genius – taking his own family as a leading example.[6] In addition, he has the questionable honour of having 'invented the word "eugenics"' for 'a body of scientific knowledge by which men could rationally direct the future course of human evolution'.[7] In his autobiography, published in 1908, he wrote with high-minded passion about this elevating new religion of scientific breeding to improve the quality of human beings, which he saw as the only available substitute for the discredited supernatural religions.[8] The constantly recurrent panic about the deterioration of the 'racial stock' due to the tendency of the intelligent to have fewer children than the stupid dates from this period, and duly resurfaces in *The Bell Curve*, despite the constantly increasing levels of measured IQ that I pointed to in the previous chapter.

The line from Galton runs straight through to Sir Cyril Burt and it has been noticed by others that the original plan of the 1944 Butler Education Act, inspired by him, reproduced the Platonic division of the human race into three grades. There were the brainy minority, destined for grammar schools, and the dim majority whose fate was to be to attend the residuary 'secondary modern' schools until the minimum school-leaving age (then 15). But in between it was postulated that there lay a set of children who could be trained in useful skills at 'technical schools'. In practice, these were never popular (as a result, I surmise, of the idea that academic achievement was all that mattered), with the result that Britain suffered a lack of skilled workers that contributed to its relative economic decline.[9]

Within this framework of genetic determinism, it is scarcely surprising that eugenics flourished. At one end of the scale, it underwrote a system of tax relief for parents, which constituted a child benefit whose value was greater the higher the tax bracket of the parents (and worth nothing to non-taxpayers). At the other end of the scale, workhouses (both in Britain and the USA) segregated men and women and thus prevented the 'unfit' from having children. With the breakdown of this system, compulsory sterilization of the 'congenitally feeble-minded' was introduced in order to prevent them from propagating their tainted genes.[10]

I hope that I have destroyed the reputability of all the components of this crude 'new-Darwinism'. Of course, genotypes interact with environments to produce everything from height to the ability to pass examinations. But Galton's idea that there is a 'natural order of inequality' can safely be laid to rest. And with it we can bury any notion that the division between the successful and the unsuccessful – with the concomitant differences in wealth and privilege – reflects 'natural' inequalities.

Defenders of inequality are therefore still faced with the challenge: if people are born equal, how can we justify the enormous inequalities that are common in capitalist countries? The answer is to accept that people are in principle equal in potential, but to attribute inequalities to unequal merits. The rich owe their wealth to hard work, enterprise and frugality, while the poor have a bad moral character, which leads to laziness, fecklessness and the kind of behaviour that (as we saw in chapter 7) is liable to land them in prison.

I have referred to the dominance of such ideas among the political class today. But the political efficacy of such ideas has over the decades had its ups and downs in both Britain and the USA, though not quite in lockstep. Thus, the Great Depression in America made manifest nonsense of the notion that the unemployed could all get jobs if they tried harder, and resulted in the election of Roosevelt on a programme that assumed the government, rather than the individual, to have responsibility for unemployment. In Britain, the sense of common fate generated by the Second World War (including the obviously uncontrollable effects of conscription, direction of labour and air raids) helped to produce a remarkable shift in public opinion since the previous (pre-war) election, which resulted in the election of the first majority Labour government in the hope (largely vain) that it would advance the cause of social justice. George Orwell pointed out in mid-1943 that 'the chances of war' had mixed up the classes, and argued that 'the old line about sturdy individualism and the sacred rights of property is no longer swallowed by the masses'.[11]

It is a matter for speculation how much the swing back to the notion that people are personally responsible for their own social positions, as a result of good or bad choices, owes to the rise of politicized religion. In America, we can hardly overlook the increasing grip of the religious right on the Republican Party, which is now imposing on the whole country – and, as far as it can, the whole world – values prevalent in the south of the USA. As far as President Bush himself is concerned, his unshakeable confidence in his own judgement, regardless of all rational argument, appears to derive from his daily sessions with God.[12] Moreover, he has shown no signs of wondering if he has a wrong number, despite his views about the admissibility of invading Iraq having been contrary to the 'almost universal conviction of religious leaders, with the most notable exception of a few spokesmen of the Southern Baptist Convention who are greatly influenced by their commitment to Israel based on eschatological, or final days, theology'.[13] According to this, a necessary precondition for the Second Coming is Armageddon, and anything that helps to bring that about is therefore to be welcomed. Although those who believe this are a small minority, they were solid for Bush in 2002.[14]

In Tony Blair, Britain probably has the only Prime Minister since William Gladstone who is a devout Christian (not all have even professed nominal Christianity), and it may well be that his substitution of 'conviction' for the ability to convince others may also have a religious basis. (There is an interesting parallel in Gladstone's pressing ahead with Home Rule for Ireland at the cost of splitting his party and putting the Conservatives in power for a quarter of a century.) More pertinent to the present discussion is Blair's having declared on a number of occasions that his religious beliefs lead him to a strong sense of individual responsibility, which must be reflected throughout the entirety of social policy, criminal law, and so on.

I have already accepted that people who made different choices from the same set of opportunities can be held responsible for different outcomes. Why, then, do I not accept that it has the implications drawn from it by the defenders of the status quo – or those pressing in the United States for even more inequality by cutting tax rates, eliminating death duties, abolishing taxation on share dividends, and so on? The general lines of my answer should already have become apparent. But in the next two chapters I want to tackle the abuse of the notion of personal responsibility more systematically.

One obvious but crucial point is that there are quite stringent conditions for a choice to count as a voluntary one for whose consequences the person taking it can legitimately be held responsible. Thus, a child's 'decision' not to go to school cannot be held to be its responsibility, whatever the cause, because this is not the kind of choice that a child can make in a way that gives rise to responsibility: knowing the consequences and being able to weigh them up, for a start. The mother of two children who disclaimed any responsibility for her children's persistent truancy was jailed in Britain in 2002, and this was not an unreasonable application of the principle of personal responsibility. Even at the age of 16, a child's 'decision' to leave school at the minimum age possible cannot make it responsible for the outcome if its earnings are needed to keep the family in basic necessities. It would be absurd to say that this child's truncated career prospects are just in comparison with those open to a child who benefits from parental support and encouragement while attending a school in which proceeding on to a university is a norm among the students. Neither child could be said to have much choice: certainly, one cannot be held responsible for leaving, while for the other staying on is simply following the line of least resistance.

Inadequacy of information also reduces responsibility for the outcomes of choices among adults. To choose between options sensibly, you need to understand the nature of the options. There will normally be a range of possible outcomes arising from each choice, and you need to have at least some estimate of their relative likelihoods. Each of those contingencies will then open up a further range of options, and so on. A good deal is known about the difficulties most people find in dealing with calculations of this kind. It is also immediately apparent that the ability to acquire and manipulate information, and the leisure to do so, are very unequally distributed. This is a large part of the explanation for the finding that the introduction of choice into public services invariably slants provision towards the better placed and better educated members of the society.

I shall say more later about the limits of personal responsibility. But this is, perhaps, a good point at which to pause and ask the basic question: can people *ever* properly be held responsible for choices made from a certain choice set? Those who believe (for religious or other reasons) that we have 'free will' are, I take it, going to have no difficulty with the notion of personal responsibility. They will, I hope, be capable of being persuaded that the principle of personal responsibility does not legitimize large inequalities, as long as they have a sensible idea of the limits of 'free will'. Thus, I shall need the assumption that people have certain mental and physical capacities at any given time and that no 'effort of will' can overcome the limits imposed by these capacities. I shall also assume that people cannot, by an 'effort of will', completely transform their personalities. It is interesting, indeed, to observe that, when people start acting in a way that is wildly 'out of character', the normal response is to look for some pathology that leads to a lack of self-control. This may be permanent or temporary. An example of the second is intoxication: this reduces responsibility for acts done under its influence, though people can still, of course, be held responsible for getting drunk in the first place, unless we assign them the longer-run pathology of alcoholism. There are more exotic excuses such as automatism or post-hypnotic suggestion and also other mundane ones such as provocation. In all such cases, 'free will' is regarded as diminished rather than superabundant.

There are, and always have been, two chief arguments for free will, if it is taken to mean that 'we' (situated in some sort of non-locatable black box that is somehow capable of controlling our brains) can decide what to do in a way that is somehow outside the realm of causation to which the rest of the universe is subject. The first was put forcefully by Dr Johnson: 'Sir, (said he,) we *know* our will is free, and *there's* an end on't.'[15] But everything we 'know' from our own experience is entirely compatible with determinism. We are not automata, although (as I have just mentioned), automatism is possible. People whose spouses are strangled by them while they are asleep (though not, as is normal, immobilized by sleep) are regarded very differently from those whose spouses are strangled by them in the full awareness of the nature of the act. The point is that we can in principle distinguish automatism from usual behaviour. (In practice, of course, a defence of automatism is hard to sustain if the killing is cited as the only instance of it: a long-established pattern of sleepwalking and the like will make the defence far more plausible.) The essential requirement is that the process of deliberation plays an essential role in decision-making, and it makes no difference to responsibility for action that the medium through which the process occurs is the electro-chemical system of the brain. If an electronic calculator is wired up right, it will produce the correct answers to arithmetical problems. We can be trained (starting with our existing neural equipment) to think logically and act on reasons. This is a large part of successful child-rearing.

The second argument for free will is that we simply have to hang on to the doctrine because the consequences of widespread disbelief in it would be disastrous. This, however, depends on the assumption that determinism is incompatible with assignment of responsibility, and there are plenty of reasons for thinking this is not so. The most obvious is that when we say somebody did something 'of her own free will', we mean only to rule out certain alternative explanations such as coercion or mental abnormality. In other words, we are asking if her action had the wrong sort of cause to give rise to responsibility. The issue of its forming part of some overall causal chain does not arise. To expand the point, the notion of *mens rea* (guilty mind) as a condition of legal responsibility asks again if the action flowed from the actor's will in the right kind of way, and is unaffected by any questions about determinism in general. Thus, mistake and accident are at least excuses (the person may still be guilty of not taking due care) because the outcome was manifestly different from the actor's intention: we can distinguish a mistake from a case in which a nurse deliberately gave a patient the wrong medicine or dosage and we can distinguish an accident from one in which somebody deliberately smashed a valuable vase. The defence of provocation works rather differently: the claim is that the actor was impelled by causal forces that bypassed the normal processes of deliberation and self-control. Again, though, the point is that the act occurred because the wrong sort of cause was operative. Somebody who did the same act (say, punched another person on the nose) but could not plead provocation would not be able to say 'Well, there must have been *some* cause or I wouldn't have done it.' Evidence of having planned the whole thing ahead ('malice aforethought') is especially damning because it shows that the act was the conclusion of a resolution settled and maintained over time.

Of course, this appeal to common practices in assigning responsibility may be rejected as irrelevant: somebody might say that, if we once took seriously the implications of determinism, we would realize that the assignment of responsibility is a charade. This book is addressed primarily to those (determinists or not) who do regard personal responsibility as a potential justification of inequality. My object is to show that it can justify much less inequality than is usually supposed. But anyone who rejects personal responsibility altogether will be led to the conclusion that has panicked so many people into promoting 'free will' – i.e., that there is no basis in justice for differential outcomes.[16] Of course, it can still be accepted that we shall have to have incentives to get people to do things and punishments to prevent them from doing others, but these arise from purely pragmatic considerations. In fact, the same issue arises (or may well be thought to arise) in relation to the conclusions about social justice that I draw from a principle of social justice that includes the principle of personal responsibility: how far must we sacrifice social justice to provide incentives, produce an efficient labour market, and so on? I shall take these questions up in chapter 16.

The principle of responsibility, as applied to incomes, has wide support, or did around 1991. An ambitious cross-national survey that included countries in Eastern and Western Europe plus Japan found widespread agreement on the proposition that 'it's fair if people have more money or wealth, but only if there are equal opportunities'.[17] Of course, the interpretation of these findings depends on how strong a conception of 'equal opportunity' is at work here. We can gain some illumination on this point, at least as far as the United States is concerned, from a discussion of this point in 2002 by Samuel Bowles and Herbert Gintis:

> Survey data shows that people – rich and poor alike – who think that 'getting ahead and succeeding in life' depends on 'hard work' or 'willingness to take risks' tend to oppose redistributive programs. Conversely, those who think the key to success is 'money inherited from family', 'parents and the family environment', 'connections and knowing the right people' or being white support redistribution.[18]

Notice that, although the last two items on the list would be inconsistent with equal opportunity understood merely as the best qualified person getting the job, the other two items would be consistent with it. We can explain the illegitimacy of 'money inherited from family' and 'parents and the family environment' only by adopting the position taken in this book: that we have equal opportunity only if different outcomes depend on decisions that are (or are taken to be) within people's control. 'Hard work' and 'willingness to take risks' would then fall into place as open to choice.

The idea that qualities for which people can be held responsible make all the difference is deeply ingrained. It has been most vociferously pressed in the USA in periods when it has been most manifestly false. Thus, more than one observer has compared the past twenty years in America to the 'gilded age' of robber barons and a widening gulf between rich and poor. It was in exactly this period – between 1867 and 1899 – that Horatio Alger Jr. wrote more than a hundred novels 'whose aim was to teach young boys how to succeed by being good'.[19] Thus, in the final paragraph of *Struggling Upward*, Alger summarizes the career of his hero, Luke Larkin: 'He has struggled upward from a boyhood of privation and self-denial into a youth and manhood of prosperity and honour. There has been some luck about it, I admit, but after all he is indebted for most of his good fortune to his own good qualities.'[20] In the eulogistic introduction to the 1945 reprint of two of Alger's books describing their objective, the author calls Alger 'a good influence on the Gilded Age; it needed a touch of old-fashioned principle. You furnished it and displayed its benefits.'[21] An alternative take on the phenomenon is that a hundred or so tales such as the one about 'Ragged Dick' turning himself from an illiterate bootblack to a respectable citizen were somehow supposed to legitimate the fortunes of the Rockefellers, Goulds and Carnegies.

11

Rights and Responsibilities

In 1888, during the passage of the Liberal budget, Sir Henry Harcourt said: 'We [i.e. the political elite] are all socialists now.'[1] Political leaders today can say 'We are all conservatives now.' By an almost too delicious irony, it was Harcourt who, in his 1894 budget, imposed death duties (estate taxes) at a significant level, while in 2003 the ultimate triumph of conservatism (so far) has been approval for the abolition of these taxes in the United States – with bipartisan support.[2] In Britain, nothing has been done by New Labour to raise the rates of inheritance tax or to plug the loopholes that make it largely a voluntary contribution. As we have seen, the ideology that underlies the acquiescence in or actual enthusiasm for inequality is the principle of responsibility. Thus, George W. Bush has called this 'the age of responsibility'. Yet it is unquestionable that his admission to Yale had nothing to do with his demonstrated abilities and everything to do with his being the son of a rich and famous alumnus. Again, despite the insistence that poor people can make up for their disadvantages by trying harder, Bush notoriously failed to make up for his lack of intellectual capacity by applying himself diligently to his studies. On the contrary, his 'gentleman's C' was a throwback to an earlier age in which studiousness was not expected of those who were guaranteed success later in life without the need for academic credentials.

Bush's confidence that he would somehow be looked after despite his modest attainments turned out to be well-founded. As a director of Harken oil, he sold his stocks in it on 22 June 1990 – 'a transaction that catapulted him to massive wealth and on to the political stage in Texas and thereafter the world'.[3] In July 2002, 'at the end of the week in which Bush went to Wall Street to launch a crusade to clean up business', documents emerged showing 'that, despite his claims to the contrary, Bush was advised that [the shares were] about to plummet'.[4] In fact 'two weeks before Bush moved to sell, on 7 June, [company president Mikel] Faulkner' provided him with minutes of an executive committee meeting warning of a 'shutdown effective 30 June unless third-party funding is found'.[5] Bush made a profit of $835,807; two months later 'Harken posted quarterly losses of $23.2 m'.[6] There remains 'one great mystery', said Knut Royce, who discovered the internal memos. 'Who was the "institutional client" who bought Bush's shares? Who the hell bought such a large block of crummy stock? . . . Someone out there was sure looking after George W.'[7]

There is also a puzzle, though not a mystery, about the way in which Bush acquired the stock in Harken to begin with. He was in fact a remarkably bad business man – the kind of person who, according to his own views about personal responsibility, ought now to be holding out a paper cup on Broadway and begging for small change. 'Harken had come to Bush's rescue after he had failed in a series of ventures in the oil business. It offered to buy out his sinking Spectrum 7 oil company, give him a seat on the board and a consultant's salary of $120,000.'[8] Given his sorry record, why would anybody want to hire him as a consultant? '"It helps to be the son of the President," said the firm's founder, Phil Kendrick, explaining the otherwise senseless splash-out for Bush's Spectrum. "He's worth $120,000 a year just for that."'[9] It also helped when the Securities Exchange Commission appointed by his father declined to prosecute him for the criminal offence of insider trading and not fulfilling disclosure requirements.

The second stage of Bush's climb to riches was also achieved by skulduggery rather than honest toil.

> While Bush claims publicly to 'do everything I can to defend the power of private property and private property rights', he and his partners in the Texas Rangers [baseball team] arranged for the Texas authorities to expropriate private land to allow the investors to build their new stadium. When some owners resisted, or balked at the low prices being offered, their land was condemned and expropriated by force of law. This occurred on 270 acres of land, even though only about seventeen acres was needed for the ballpark. The rest was used by Bush and Co for commercial development and has provided the basis of Bush's personal fortune.'[10]

So much for Bush's 'personal responsibility' for his wealth. In Britain, as the epigraph to Part IV indicated, the mantra of New Labour is that 'with rights and opportunities come responsibilities and obligations.'[11] Now, there is one understanding of the link between rights and responsibilities that is, as far as it goes, an honourable one. It would have been recognized by Conservatives from Disraeli to Harold Macmillan as *noblesse oblige*: the idea that (as the OED puts it) 'privilege entails responsibility'. In the United States, too, an early generation of the wealthy,

> [such as] the Kennedys and the Rockefellers . . . display a sense of noblesse oblige – what one might call an urge to repay, with charitable contributions and public service, their good fortune. The Bushes don't have that problem; there are no philanthropists or reformers in the clan. They seek public office but, if anything, they seem to feel that the public is there to serve them.[12]

Those who have benefited most from the existing system of rights – the rich and powerful – are those who bear the heaviest responsibilities, because the way in which they use their advantages has such a large impact on the lives of everyone else. Thus, political office should not be abused by turning it into a means of personal enrichment, nor should the political power of the wealthy be deployed to further unjust public policies, slanted towards their interests. Those running companies should not use the discretion this gives them to pay themselves inordinate amounts of money. Nor should they seek loopholes in the rules protecting consumers, workers or the environment. Still less should they simply fail to comply with them if the fines or payments for damages are estimated to be less than the money saved by ignoring pollution, unsafe working conditions, unsafe maintenance procedures, and so on.

Instead of accepting their responsibilities, the current business elite both in Britain and the United States appear to be interested only in the 'bottom line' – how much profit they can generate for the company and how much (even if the company loses money) they can carry off themselves. Thus, for example, the government agency with responsibility for the environment has been publishing the names of the companies with the worst records for 'careless, avoidable neglect of environmental responsibility'.[13] But 'a distressing number of well-known companies are continuing to cause pollution despite the name and shame policy', said Barbara Young, its chief executive. Although she expressed surprise that 'multi-million pound businesses are still prepared to risk their reputations', this is naivety because 'naming and shaming' works only if the people responsible are liable to shame.[14] Until recently, it was often said that the only sin in business is being found out. Now, being found out makes no difference either, as long as the transgression generated a net profit. As Ms Young complained, 'with irreplaceable environmental damage and risk to public health, penalties often fail to match up to the costs avoided'.[15] Similarly, illegal share price manipulation and the exploitation of inside knowledge are usually still profitable even when detected. Our societies have become ones in which your standing among your peers (the very rich) is unaffected by evidence of greed, corruption, illegality and knowingly ruining thousands or hundreds of thousands of people – just as long as you stay rich.

This is a class that is, let us hope, in the process of destroying itself. The robber barons – the unscrupulous monopolists and oppressors of labour – are the closest analogy.[16] It has been said of them that 'by exercising their unparalleled economic power without a corresponding sense of public responsibility they undermined the moral prestige of the leading capitalist country in the world to an extent that is almost incalculable'.[17] At the end of this book, I shall offer reasons for hoping that (among other factors) the greed and abuse of power shown in recent years by private companies will undermine the moral basis for capitalism still further and help to open up the political possibility of radical change.

At its best (and, as we have seen, it is now virtually non-existent), paternalism was always open to the social democratic critique that the welfare of workers, consumers and residents should not depend on the goodwill of the rich and powerful for protection. There should be no need for gratitude. The rights granted to property owners should indeed be made correlative to responsibilities to all those whose well-being is affected by their actions: responsibilities imposed by law. Associations of workers, consumers and residents must be given legal standing to ensure that enforcement does not depend on some administrative body at best lackadaisical and at worst (which all experience shows to be common) seduced by the very people it is supposed to be regulating. Those who suffer have the most urgent motive to intervene, and should be given every opportunity to do so.

Sadly, however, New Labour talk about rights and responsibilities is notably vacuous when it comes to the responsibilities that should be imposed on the privileged. As Martin Kettle has said:

New Labour's strong doctrine of personal responsibility has always made it extremely clear that the poor are expected to make changes, in some cases sacrifices, in order to be able to claim the benefits and rewards of the new opportunity-orientated economic policy. But there has never been any equivalent responsibility placed on the rich. Few changes, much less sacrifices are demanded from them in New Labour's moral economy.[18]

A good example of the double standard in both Britain and the United States is the contrasting treatment of 'welfare cheats' and people who defraud the Treasury by not paying their taxes. Most so-called 'welfare cheats' are very poor people making a bit of money for themselves and not losing it as a result of declaring it. This is not to deny that there are a few people who commit fraud on a large scale by collecting benefits under a number of aliases. But even the amount that this yields is minuscule compared with a piece of successful tax evasion by somebody making, say, ten million a year. Despite this, in both Britain and the USA, there is a great deal of effort put into enforcement, 'hot lines' to encourage informing on neighbours are set up, and those who are caught are almost always subjected to criminal proceedings.

As far as tax evasion is concerned, although criminal penalties are possible, evasion that is discovered is almost invariably treated as a civil matter, settled by payment of the amount owing plus some penalty. This, in addition to all its advantages of avoiding a criminal record, also means that it can be kept a secret between the guilty party and the tax authority – and usually is. Although these discrepancies are routinely pointed out by academics, they are rarely made much of in the mass media. Clearly, what is at work here is a deep-seated notion that stealing 'our' money is a heinous offence, whereas the desire to keep 'your own' money, even by breaking the law, is an understandable peccadillo. Somehow, the notion that 'we' (the citizens) are being robbed blind by the wealthy – deprived of the money that, under the tax code should belong to us – has little resonance with the public.

It may be recalled from the epigraph that the people singled out by Blair to have new responsibilities imposed on them were the unemployed, single parents, the sick and the disabled – in other words the most vulnerable members of society. There was a conspicuous absence of any mention that in return for their privileges the wealthy should have new responsibilities placed upon them. 'New Labour has no framework for discovering how the rich ought to behave. . . . If you . . . asked whether there was a moral or rational case for anyone to earn more than, say, £250,000 a year, they would dismiss the idea as ridiculous.'[19] Ministers occasionally make disparaging noises about especially egregious examples of huge payments to company directors whose firms have lost money or gone bankrupt, or enormous 'compensation' paid to those who have been dismissed. But this is entirely in line with the 'meritocratic' ideology denounced by Michael Young (see chapter 8), in that these are cases of conspicuous failure to match rewards to 'merits'. The significant point is that no suggestion has been made of legislation to deal with the increasing divergence between the pay of directors and other workers, or even to control the admitted abuses.

The most dramatic illustration of the reeking hypocrisy of the rhetoric about rights carrying personal responsibilities is that those who have the biggest rights to take decisions affecting others (present and future) are virtually immune from personal responsibility for the consequences of their actions. Some of the pollution that I described, by contaminating water supplies and emitting toxins into the air, was a threat to health and even life. Yet not only were the corporate fines inadequate, punishment of those personally responsible was non-existent. Similarly, even when it can be proved that decisions by management aimed at increasing profits led directly to unsafe working conditions and consequent injury or death, the individuals responsible have never until now been punished. Belatedly and reluctantly, only 'six years and hundreds of deaths on from the election pledge whereby Labour promised to introduce the crime of corporate responsibility, [was] the Government moving to give the offence some teeth'.[20]

Even then, having the law on the books does nothing unless prosecutions for manslaughter are routine in cases of egregious management failure. For example, Thames Trains, one of whose trains was responsible for a crash outside Paddington that left '31 people dead and hundreds injured', pleaded guilty to safety charges, admitting 'inadequacies in the way it trained drivers'. The driver of the train, who went through a red light and crashed head-on with another doing 130 mph, had been qualified for only thirteen days and had received no training about the automatic warning system of 'signals passed at danger' (SPADS). He had not been warned against this particular red light, which had been passed at red by eight drivers in five years, had not been given a map of black spots of this kind, and 'the company had not tested [his] knowledge of the labyrinthine route that led into the west London station'.[21] Not surprisingly, 'safety campaigners said they were still frustrated that it was the company, rather than individual directors, that was facing prosecution'. More bluntly, 'whatever the size of the fine, the company has got away with bloody murder'.[22]

If managers sincerely believed that their rewards stemmed from their own personal merits – the ideology of 'meritocracy' – one might suppose that they would welcome the only implication that could possibly support it: that they should suffer personally for wrong-doing. If you thought so, think again. The Confederation of British Industry remains implacably opposed. 'As a spokesman put it: "A director who faced the possibility of prison would be very reluctant to take decisions." '[23] Reluctance to take decisions that will endanger life and limb is, of course, what managers should feel. As Deborah Orr has commented: 'Faced with the possibility of multi-million pound pay-offs, bad decisions can be taken by directors without any reluctance at all. But there doesn't seem to be much of a problem with that.'[24]

So far from placing new obligations on employers, the government is obsessed with the United States economy as a great 'success' and is promoting ever-greater 'flexibility' in the labour market: more people on short-term contracts and workers forced to work at hours that suit employers rather than those that fit in with their own responsibilities. The human cost does not enter into its calculus. Yet a dramatic example of workers' priorities was provided by a mass walk-out by British Airways staff when the management proposed to introduce, without consultation, a computerized system for clocking in and clocking out. Needless to say, newspaper editorials thundered against the 'irresponsibility' of the staff in stranding thousands of passengers. But it turned out that concern for their own ability to fulfil their own responsibilities was at the core of their resistance.

> Currently, shifts are organized three months at a time and women can arrange childcare around their working hours. What they fear is a system in which a computer will decide on a day-to-day or hour-to-hour basis when they should come to work. A computer won't understand that this happens to be Samir's first day at school and his mother needs to be there; it won't be able to organize shifts so that Joanne can take her elderly mother to hospital.[25]

It seems that BA and the unions both expected the women to give up convenient, predictable work schedules in return for more pay. But this ignored their own priorities. 'If split shifts are introduced, and they cannot be fitted around the needs of the children, then they will give up their jobs. They literally have nothing to lose by refusing to budge on this issue.'[26] Of course, the 'flexibility' valued by the workers is the precise opposite of the 'flexibility' promoted by the government.

This ordering of priorities also sheds light on the very limited success of New Labour's 'welfare to work' policies, which are designed to coerce mothers of young children into paid employment. While '46% of lone mothers now go out to work compared to 29% 10 years ago', this still means that a majority do not.[27] 'If they had partners who could care for their children while they worked part-time, then they would go out to work. In the absence of a partner, they will prioritise the needs of the children', which entails that 'child-care [must be] as good as, or better than, they themselves can provide'.[28]

At least these mothers still have a choice (though for how much longer?). In the United States, they used to as well, under the Aid to Dependent Children Act (later Aid to Families with Dependent Children), passed as part of Roosevelt's 'New Deal'. But

> by 1996, when Congress passed the Personal Responsibility and Work Opportunity Act and repealed the federal guarantee of income support for parents and children living in poverty . . . a fundamental shift in public debate had taken place: instead of believing it was impossible for most single parents to care for their children adequately while earning enough money for subsistence, the public insisted that nothing other than insufficient willpower was stopping single poor parents from working full-time and caring for their children as well.[29]

This was 'personal responsibility' with a vengeance. It was not matched by any recognition that at the least such a draconian measure must require corresponding responsibilities by the state: to provide all-day high-quality daycare free of charge and to write tough legislation requiring employers not to require parents to work anything except day shifts and to give them paid time off (unless the state paid it) to allow them to carry out their responsibilities to their children in cases of sickness, problems at school, and so on.

But nothing of the sort was done, and it was not made the task of any government agency to discover the real consequences of the Act for people's lives. The only criterion for 'success' was the size of the reduction in the welfare rolls. 'We now know that welfare reform works', President Clinton trumpeted a year after the Act came into effect, citing the 1.4 million people who had left welfare since 1996.[30] Clinton chose to make his triumphant claim in Missouri, the state that pioneered the system (subsequently adopted by most states) euphemistically known as 'Direct Job Placement'. What this meant in practice in Missouri was that all welfare claimants were directed to apply for jobs 'working in poultry plants or in hog slaughterhouses, where assembly-line jobs involve processing animal parts at a feverish pace in a dirty and dangerous environment'.[31] Anyone who refused to apply was eliminated immediately: all those who did apply could easily be given jobs because nobody with any alternative would accept the pay and conditions. But if they refused the job or left as a result of stress, exhaustion or injury within a few months (as almost all did), they constituted another success story by being cut off the welfare rolls. The attitude of those in charge of the task of slashing the number of welfare recipients is illustrated by just one incident:

> As one woman on welfare discovered, even having a newborn baby and no means of transportation is no excuse. When the thirty-year-old mother . . . informed her case managers of these extenuating circumstances, they were not sympathetic. 'They told her she had to work at Tyson's [the closest processor] even if she had to walk to get there [a six-mile trek]. They sanctioned her while she was pregnant' and then ordered her to work at Tyson when her baby was just eleven days old, [the informant] recalls. 'She hasn't had any income for six months. How are they supposed to live?'[32]

The stability of the society depicted in *Nineteen Eighty-Four* was sustained by Doublethink:

> To tell deliberate lies while genuinely believing in them, to forget any fact that has become inconvenient, and then, when it becomes necessary again, to draw it back from oblivion for just as long as it is needed, to deny the existence of objective reality and all the time to take account of the reality which one denies – all this is indispensably necessary.[33]

Hence, 'in our society, those who have the best knowledge of what is happening are also those who are furthest from seeing the world as it is. In general, the greater the understanding, the greater the illusion: the more intelligent, the less sane.'[34] It would be hard to imagine a more perfect exemplification of Doublethink than the rhetoric surrounding 'welfare reform'. One of the chief architects of the current consensus, Lawrence Mead, claimed: 'Underclass poverty stems less from absence of opportunity than from the inability or reluctance to take advantage of opportunity.'[35] Of course, if the 'inability' is real, there is no opportunity. But what 'opportunities' were being turned down? The proposition would be interesting only if the jobs rejected had come with high-quality child care and medical insurance, while also paying enough to live on, offering paid holidays, sick leave and time off to deal with responsibilities to dependants, and not being disgusting or degrading. A manager at Tyson's explained that they could easily accommodate 'direct job placement' because they always had vacancies. Should that be taken to mean that anybody with enough willpower could get a job?

Furthermore, current economic orthodoxy maintains that there is a 'natural rate of unemployment' that has to exist in any given economy to avoid runaway inflation. The implication is, of course, that some employable people have to be sacrificed on the altar of economic stability. Clearly, only a complete mastery of Doublethink could permit anybody who holds this view to combine it with the notion that the able-bodied unemployed must bear the full responsibility for their situation. They could more aptly be compared with the crew member who is thrown out of the basket so as to keep the balloon on course for a round-the-world trip. Desmond King sums up the shift from obvious well-established objective explanations of unemployment to ones sustainable only by Doublethink as follows: 'Neoliberal politicians [in both countries] adopted critiques of welfare programs, which stressed the deficiencies of individual recipients and dismissed explanations based on social structural . . . or economic . . . factors.'[36]

Ultimately, as in the gloss provided by *New Labour Bollocks* in the epigraph to Part IV, the doctrine of 'rights and responsibilities' entails that what have previously been thought of as rights are not rights at all. This was spelt out in 2002 in Blair's 'Vision for Britain':

> From the 1940s to the 1970s, government sought to address social and economic planning. Social democrats in Britain and the US who held a liberal view of the 'permissive society' divorced fairness from personal responsibility. They believed that the state had an unconditional obligation to provide welfare and security. The logic was that the individual owed nothing in return.[37]

This is, of course, totally tendentious in that no countries, including the most elaborate and generous 'welfare states', have ever offered unconditional subsistence incomes. There have always been conditions: that the recipients of state benefits must be unemployed, must have caring responsibilities that preclude paid employment or must be sick or disabled. Subject to those conditions being met, however, cash benefits were indeed regarded as entitlements as solid as state pensions – or for that matter earned incomes and inherited wealth. Blair's intention, which is not immediately apparent in the passage I quoted, is to attack the idea that means-tested benefits are unconditional in the sense that no further conditions have to be met beyond those establishing eligibility. It will be recalled that his hit-list of people who were going to have to take on 'new responsibilities' consisted exclusively of the unemployed, single mothers and sick and disabled people.

Blair's 'Vision' is one in which benefits paid to those eligible in virtue of their circumstances should not be regarded as a right – an elementary demand of social justice – but as charity, to be dispensed in return for good behaviour. Going back a century, Blair's 'Vision' is for the return of the Charity Organisation Society, with its distinction between the deserving and undeserving poor. Of course, the money is raised by taxation rather than voluntarily, but this, as far as he is concerned, makes no difference to the point that it is 'our' money going to 'them', and we can make any demands we like on the behaviour required in return for it. I pointed out earlier how the moral status of 'welfare cheats' is sharply distinguished from that of tax evaders, even though the sums involved in tax evasion are much larger and the evasion is carried out by people who do not have the excuse of penury. What we are looking at here is the logical conclusion of the idea that taking 'our' money is criminal while to hang on to more of 'your' money than you should deserves no more than a slap on the wrist.

The notion that benefits must be 'deserved' has, not surprisingly, been enormously popular in the United States. Many states have enacted a whole string of requirements that those who would otherwise be destitute have to meet in order to receive welfare benefits, thus attaching responsibilities to rights in precisely the way approved of in Blair's (nightmare) 'Vision'. What somebody who would otherwise be destitute is supposed to do if their benefits are cut off because, say, their children miss some school days, nobody seems to care about. And, of course, since the 'success' of the 'Personal Responsibility Act' is, as we have seen, measured solely by the number of people it gets off the welfare rolls, the more vexatious the demands that are made on recipients the more 'successful' it is bound to be. Blair himself proposed that in order to deal with truancy, money could be taken away from recipients of means-tested state benefits. What possible rationale could there be for tackling truancy in this way? Is truancy uniquely a problem among those in receipt of means-tested benefits? Of course not. A system of fines, which could be graduated so that the better off paid more and those on the bare minimum paid little, would obviously have the advantage of being fairer in every respect. But fines would involve taking 'our' money from 'us', whereas cutting benefits saves 'us' from having to give money to 'them'.

A parallel proposal – contained in a consultation paper on rights and responsibilities, no less – was that those in receipt of housing benefit should lose it, or some of it, if convicted in a criminal court or 'if a tenant had twice been warned by a local government officer'.[38] Thus, those who dare to draw on the largesse of the state are not even to be allowed any semblance of due process, since 'two warnings' could be issued arbitrarily. By contrast, 'wealthier anti-social tenants who did not receive benefit would face only punishment in the courts'.[39] Housing pressure groups complained that this constituted an unfair distinction, since those on housing benefit would be 'at risk of double jeopardy – punished for their behaviour by the courts and then forced to suffer a financial penalty through loss of benefits'.[40] The response of the Housing Minister, Malcolm Wicks, to this irrefutable objection ran as follows: 'There is something specifically wrong about someone being able to make the life of their neighbour hellish and doing it courtesy of a subsidy from the taxpayer in the form of housing benefit.'[41] However, despite enthusiastic support from Tony Blair, this proposal was unceremoniously dropped in early 2004 after a 'consultation exercise' carried out by the Department for Work and Pensions discovered that '75% of people and organizations that expressed a view were against [it]. This included 81% of local authorities.'[42] The public has still, it seems, not caught up with the forward march of New Labour.

12

Irresponsible Societies

If bad things that happen to people are their responsibility, then a 'nanny state' is not merely unnecessary but encourages irresponsibility by creating 'dependence'. Thus, it is possible to rule out, without knowing anything about the facts, the whole social democratic agenda. We can forget the notion that states have a duty to ensure decent material conditions for everyone and to protect their safety, autonomy and human dignity, either by provision or by regulation. Moreover, we can rule out as contrary to the principle of responsibility the idea that the state should set strict limits to the consequences of good and bad choices and ensure that all choices with non-trivial consequences are made in a well-informed way from a range of options that is not unjustly limited.

The convenience of the cult of individual responsibility for those who wish to contract the role of government is easy to see. If the only source of homelessness is lack of prudence and initiative, there is no need to worry about the supply of 'affordable' housing. The embarrassing class gradient in longevity and state of health can be attributed to a failure to adopt 'healthy lifestyles'. If those low in the social hierarchy smoke more and weigh more and have less healthy diets, that is just another illustration of their lack of willpower. Almost every set of bad outcomes lends itself to two contrasting approaches: one that calls on individuals to adapt and one that demands changes in the environment. Corporations spend a lot of money on promoting the 'personal responsibility' approach, while being at the same time acutely conscious of their ability to manipulate individual choices and suppress information that is essential to responsible choosing. Unless they believed this to be true, the invasion of schools by 'liquid candy' and fast food companies would not have been so aggressively pursued, nor would advertising aimed at children consume such a large amount of their money. It would be hard to comprehend how they could resist proposals to label foods as high in salt, sugar and calories.

Individual responsibility can always be manufactured by throwing on to individuals the responsibility for avoiding the potentially bad consequences of a hazardous environment. Thus, to return to a case discussed in the last chapter, if there are certain red lights that train drivers consistently tend not to notice, there are two possible reactions: one is to bemoan the drivers' lack of attention and the other is to accept that the light is poorly sited and fix it – something that Railtrack had had at least five years to do with the crucial red light that caused the Paddington disaster. The correct answer here may seem obvious, but it is inevitable that a 'culture of blame' inhibits the flow of information about hazards. Thus, most plane accidents are partly or wholly due to 'human error', but for every error that causes an accident there are hundreds of others that do not. Pilots have, for obvious reasons, been reluctant to report these to their employers. But a scheme enabling pilots to report errors anonymously revealed that they occurred in systematic ways, and could be reduced by changes in procedures and in the physical environment of the cockpit. Similarly, many deaths in hospitals are due to 'human error' in the form of giving patients the wrong amount of medicine or the wrong one altogether. Again, there are many more such errors (especially involving injections and drip-feeds) that do not have devastating consequences and are, again, liable not to be reported. Yet a study of these errors, carried out under the condition that nobody would be identified, found that a number of quite simple changes, involving the design of equipment, the labelling and location of drugs, and standard routines, could dramatically reduce the incidence of errors.

For example, one anti-cancer drug 'is fatal if administered spinally'.[1] This has happened in Britain thirteen times in the last fifteen years, and in most cases the patients died. These errors could be easily avoided by 'the introduction of incompatible connectors for intravenous syringes and special catheters', a course of action that was most recently recommended to the National Health Service in 2000 by the chief medical officer. Instead, what he has described as a 'climate of blame, acrimony and confrontation' pervades the NHS.[2] When a doctor who ordered the incorrect procedure was sentenced to eight months in jail (having already served eleven on remand), the lawyer defending him said: 'Medical deaths are often the result of system error, but it is the individual doctor who is made responsible.'[3]

Doctors in the NHS work long hours under constant time pressure, so that such tragic mishaps are bound to occur unless changes are made (often simple ones, as in this case) that would render them impossible. The doctor's defence – 'I am a human being' – was the only possible one. It should have been sufficient. Of course, if prior to this he had already acquired a record of unusual negligence, the hospital should have stopped him sooner. As it was, the only result of criminalizing negligence was to deprive the doctor of his liberty, and the NHS of a doctor, for a year. Instead, the people to be prosecuted (for corporate manslaughter) should have been those who took the decision against following an obviously sensible safety recommendation. For there can be no question that they deliberately and knowingly followed a course of action that would predictably cost lives. Of course, an inquiry into responsibility for the decision is always liable to be lost in the mire somewhere between NHS managers, civil servants and ministers. But a formal inquiry into the cause of every system failure would sometimes succeed in locating culpability precisely, and in any case would create greater concern about failures to create safe conditions.

Any system that relies for safety on 100 per cent vigilance by everybody 100 per cent of the time is unjust, because it creates a standard that cannot reasonably be met. We must start from the assumption that lapses of concentration will occur, and try to ensure that they are not critical. Nowhere is this better illustrated than in the workplace, where profit and the safety of workers are in constant tension. Jobs can always be completed faster by cutting corners – speeding up, bypassing safety mechanisms, omitting safety checks, and so on. Death and injury are the wholly predictable consequences of these practices. Even if in almost every case the immediate cause can be traced to 'human error', the point remains that work practices can be more or less dependent on perpetual vigilance and making the right call every time.

Hardly surprisingly, the United States and Britain have relatively poor work safety records. Unionization has been shown to improve safety, and both countries are poorly unionized; New Labour also followed the Conservatives in refusing to accept provisions in the Social Charter that would give employees more control over the workplace. In addition, the enforcement of what standards there are is extremely inadequate due to the lack of inspectors. Even when detected, infractions are rarely punished. When they are, fines tend not to be big enough to make dangerous practices unprofitable, as we have seen to be equally true of fines for pollution. Finally, the prospect of individuals responsible for the death or injury of workers facing prosecution is remote – despite their demonstrable guilt.

In the United States, anyone who professes beliefs about the responsibilities of employers is liable to fail to get even an ill-paid job – perhaps an ill-paid job especially. According to Barbara Ehrenreich, 'tests' administered as a condition of employment include questions such as 'Do I think safety on the job is the responsibility of the management?' or 'Is management to blame when things go wrong?'. She is surely correct to conclude that questions such as these (and others, such as one about conflict between the interests of workers and management) have such obviously 'right' answers that their function 'is to convey information not to the employer but to the potential employee'.[4] The management of Wal-Mart (and the same goes for other firms that administer such tests) is not content with your body: it wants your soul as well. In return for $6 an hour, this is such a bad bargain that only those with no alternative would accept it. (Faust got a much better offer, and had no need to take it.)

Institutions should shield individuals from exposure to danger rather than creating a dangerous environment and demanding that individuals adapt to it. This can be broadly termed the 'public health' approach, because the promotion of public health measures has been such an important aspect of it. Despite its obvious advantages, the alternative remains: leave the danger and make individual safety depend on individual conduct.

> This way of thinking about public health might recommend that the individual undertake disease reduction measures (such as installing mosquito netting in her home to guard against malaria) when they exist as alternatives to measures made at public expense (such as eradication of mosquitoes, or the treatment of malaria).[5]

This is no doubt intended as a *reductio ad absurdum*. But it has been proposed seriously in the United States that, where the source of the water supply is heavily contaminated, no attempt should be made to make tap water safe to drink and instead every household should be given an adequate supply of bottled water. The rationale is, of course, that only a tiny fraction of the water supply is used for drinking and it is a waste of money to purify it all: providing bottled water would be much cheaper. This shifting of responsibility for health from the provider to the customer would create an onerous burden for everybody and an intolerable one for parents, who would have to be watchful all the time. It would also require the premature institutionalization of old people whose memory and ability to concentrate were going. The object of public policy should much of the time be to reduce the significance of choice rather than enhance it. As here, the effects of unskilful or unlucky decisions on people's health should be eliminated, and where that is impossible they should be minimized.

The point can be generalized. Instead of accepting their responsibility for providing adequate health care coverage and pensions (in the absence of adequate state-run schemes), employers can transfer the responsibility to employees. If an employer provides a single kind of health care policy for all its employees, everybody knows who to complain to if it turns out to have holes in its coverage. But increasingly in America employers offer the choice between a whole raft of insurance companies offering different kinds of policies. 'And within these plans, there are more options – the level of deductible, the prescription drug plan, dental plan, vision plan, and so on.'[6] There are two objections to this proliferation. First, it creates impossible decision-making burdens: 'I think I've met only one person in my entire life who fully understands what his insurance covers and what it doesn't and what the statements that come from the insurance company really mean.'[7] And, second, it encourages people to blame themselves rather than their employer if it turns out that some gap in their insurance is financially devastating – as can and does happen.

Similarly, employers used to provide '"defined benefit" pension plans, in which retirees get whatever their years of service and terminal salaries entitle them to'.[8] Although these are still common in public service occupations, private firms have increasingly 'switched . . . to "defined contribution" plans, in which employee and employers each contribute to some investment instrument. What the employee gets at retirement depends on the performance of the investment.'[9] Faced with a wide variety of options – money market, bond market, real estate and a number of alternative stock market alternatives (defined by countries, sectors, 'growth' versus 'yield', and so on), almost everybody feels incompetent. Moreover, even those who were supposed to be competent – the advisers of universities, foundations and insurance companies, for example – almost all succeeded in losing money for their clients when the prices of shares fell in the USA and the UK. Instead of companies having to bear the risks in providing guaranteed pensions, these are transferred to employees. 'Choosing wisely among these options becomes the employee's responsibility.'[10] The result is anxiety, inability to plan for the future and a tendency for people to reproach themselves when their choices turn out badly instead of blaming their employers for 'creat[ing] more individual responsibility for failure'.[11]

New Labour has in the same way recognized what a wonderful cop-out 'choice' offers the government. No wonder 'choice is a New Labour mantra'.[12] Instead of being saddled with the responsibility for providing a uniform high quality of public services, it can substitute 'choice', thus transferring responsibility for their own fate to the users of those services. As I pointed out in chapters 5 and 6, this is completely phoney. If some schools and hospitals are good while others are bad, the government's responsibility for that inequality is exactly the same if children and patients are randomly allocated by a central authority as it is if children and patients arrive at their destinations as a result of some sort of opaque decentralized process.

The only difference from the individual's point of view is that the first constitutes a pure lottery, whereas the second is a quasi-lottery with the addition of possibilities for those with the know-how, self-confidence and time to manipulate the system to their advantage. In as far as the existence of these possibilities buys off the middle class, it reduces the pressure for uniformly high standards that a lottery is bound to bring about. If it can lead people to hold themselves responsible for being treated by poorly qualified staff in a dilapidated and unhygienic hospital, that is even better. Unfortunately for this policy of obfuscation, the public sees through it. In April 2004, it was reported that 'private polling by the government . . . found that parents want their local schools to be decent rather than have a range of schools from which to choose'.[13] Similarly, since (apart from those who favour the Royal Homeopathic Hospital) everybody wants the same things from a hospital, it is scarcely surprising that surveys have found people wanting their local hospital to be good rather than having a choice between good and bad hospitals.

Instead of admitting that their whole approach is a bust, New Labour ideologues insist with ever-growing stridency that the answer is more choice rather than more equality. In response to the private poll whose results I cited, Stephen Byers, one of the most fanatical propagandists, said that the 'scope and scale' of choice 'needs to be expanded if we are to secure social justice'. Among his many bright ideas is that the sick and elderly should be able to choose their suppliers of home meals and their home helps, thus relieving local authorities of the responsibility for their quality.[14] When his loss of contact with reality becomes too obvious to ignore, I hope that he has a choice of men in white coats to carry him away.

Let me offer in the rest of this chapter a couple of case studies that illustrate the power of the 'public health' approach and the shoddiness of the 'personal responsibility' alternative. The first case is home-lessness. If an epidemic of homelessness breaks out in a city, the natural thought might be that the cause is some combination of people at the bottom of the heap getting poorer and the stock of affordable housing shrinking. But this conclusion can be avoided with a sufficient effort of will. Ronald Reagan once announced that most homeless people are that way because they choose to be homeless. In contrast to this view, 'in the 1980s, advocates presented the problem [of homelessness in New York] as a failure to do right by the most vulnerable: people who were just more unlucky than others, not different or less deserving'.[15] And the advocates were successful: more public housing was built, and the homeless were allocated a share of it.[16] But this was not how the next Mayor of New York, Rudy Giuliani, saw it.

Giuliani embraced the ethic of the Work and Personal Responsibility Reconciliation Act with such fervour that he actually instructed city employees not to tell welfare recipients that they were also eligible for food stamps. His first homeless service commissioner, Joan Malin (who resigned in 1996),

> recalled that in 1995 the Mayor had determined to shrink the soaring shelter population the way Richard J. Schwartz, his senior policy adviser, was shrinking the welfare rolls: tighten eligibility rules, deter applicants at the front door, and eject those who failed to meet new work requirements. . . . 'What Richard's done in the welfare system is what you need to be doing', she was told by Giuliani. 'It became his mantra.'[17]

To back up this policy, he 'reduced subsidized housing placements from the shelters to a 10-year low, and let the pipeline of city-owned apartments dry up'.[18] Unfortunately, Giuliani's theory that the homeless were responsible for their own plight did not seem to be borne out by reality. 'By February 2001, the number of people lodging nightly in the shelter system equalled the 1980s peak of 28,737, and Mr Giuliani's last commissioner of homeless services . . . exclaimed in an interview, "I can't screw the front door any tighter".'[19]

In the end, it turns out that the simple-minded explanation of homelessness – that it is due to lack of affordable housing – was right all along. 'A New York University study that followed homeless families who entered city shelters in 1988 and a random group of families on public assistance who had not been homeless found that only one factor – subsidized housing – determined whether a family in either group was stably housed five years later.'[20] The author of the study found that education, work history, mental illness, childhood trauma, substance abuse, experience with the criminal justice system – nothing we could measure made any difference. . . . The basic message is that subsidized housing was both necessary and sufficient to create housing stability. . . . We conclude that housing cures homelessness for families.[21]

What this showed is that drug abuse did not cause homelessness in New York. The popular impression of a link between drug addiction (including alcoholism) and homelessness may still have a basis, however, if homelessness causes addiction. This has been found to be so in Britain: a study reported in July 2002 found that 'drug dependence rose steadily the longer a person remained homeless. If a housing crisis lasts more than three years, there is a two-in-three chance that the person will have become dependent on their main drug of choice.'[22] The mechanism underlying this is not hard to understand: 'On a typical day, four in five [homeless people] spent time with other homeless people, and half these had similar levels of drug use to their own.'[23] This is the familiar cycle of cumulative disadvantage at work: you suffer from job loss or household break up and become homeless, in the absence of any system for ensuring affordable housing for everybody. You then deteriorate precisely as a consequence of being homeless, which in turn makes it harder for you to get a job or be reintegrated socially.

Homelessness is the most extreme form of social exclusion (with the possible exception of being in prison) in contemporary western societies. Those with 'no fixed abode' (whether sleeping rough or in temporary shelters) have no mailing address, which is a minimum condition of participation; they have no way of exchanging hospitality (so it is hardly surprising that they hang out with other people in like circumstances) and they occupy the most despised social status. They thus illustrate strikingly the dependence of behaviour on circumstances. Faced with a bleak and meaningless existence, can it be wondered at that homeless people resort to some reliable means of attaining oblivion? 'The research will exacerbate concern that it may be almost impossible for homeless people to kick addictions to drugs and alcohol.'[24] So once again, instead of holding individuals responsible, we should apply the public health model and change the circumstances in which they find themselves.

A beautifully documented and presented illustration of the abuse of individual responsibility as an excuse for system failure concerns the death in Chicago, between the 14th and 20th of July 1995, of about 740 people as the result of a severe and prolonged heat wave. Contrary to one comforting view of the disaster, these were not people who 'were about to die anyway': if that had been the case, mortality rates would have dipped below normal in the following months, but they did not.[25] On 21 July, the US Centers for Disease Control and Prevention threw a team of eighty people into a project to identify 'the personal characteristics that proved most consequential during the catastrophe.'[26] They did this by having each investigator go to the place of residence of someone who had died, then find the nearest person who 'matched' the deceased in age and find out about both.

The results showed what differentiated the people who died from those in the same location and of the same age who did not. Thus, they were more vulnerable to the effects of the heat wave 'if they did not leave home daily, had a medical problem, were confined to bed, lived alone, or lacked air conditioning, access to transportation, and social contacts nearby'.[27] However, the design of the study – comparing matching pairs in the same location, 'ruled out the possibility that their study would capture neighborhood or regional differences in heat wave mortality or the broader social context of the catastrophe'.[28] The analogy would be to look at an outbreak of cholera and concentrate on trying to find out why, of two people identically situated, one succumbed to the disease and the other did not. Fortunately, the Victorians, for all their belief in individual responsibility, did not approach cholera epidemics in this way, but asked what caused the epidemic and why those who fell victim to it lived predominantly in poor neighbourhoods.

The totally inappropriate use of the clinical model instead of the public health model played into the hands of those, such as the Mayor and the newspapers, who suggested that victims came from all over the city and every social class. It is true that some did, but deaths were in fact concentrated in the poor black South Side. Thus, of two people too poor to run an air-conditioner (a problem exacerbated by federal and state funding of the programme to help poor people with energy costs having been cut to bits), it is hardly surprising that the one who was bedridden was more likely to die of heatstroke. But another way of looking at the issue is to say that the primary cause of vulnerability was poverty, and then to add that among equally poor people some were more fortunately placed than others to cope.

Indifference to deaths from heat exemplifies a pattern: 'Heatwaves kill roughly 1,500 Americans a year – the combined toll from hurricanes, tornadoes, earthquakes and floods is less than 200.'[29] But these destroy property on a large scale, so that 'potential victims of other extreme weather' can get prevention and compensation treated as a public responsibility – even where the victims are in fact responsible for their own losses by building on flood plains and on land known to be unstable. Heat waves, in contrast, are most likely to affect 'the poor, aged and isolated residents of cities' – the orphans of American public policy.[30]

Eric Klinenberg, in his 'social autopsy' of the Chicago disaster, demonstrates a variety of ways in which the neglect of the old and vulnerable had its roots in a variety of public policies. For example, extreme social isolation among those whose relatives had died, moved away or were in jail (about half of Chicago residents over the age of 65) was exacerbated by a variety of acts and omissions by the city that had left most of the elderly poor in hotels whose proprietors had no responsibility for their well-being or in public housing with such levels of violence as to inhibit movement, let alone gathering in common spaces.[31] (Thus, 'not going out' was for many a rational response to the environment.) Even then, the heat wave would not have been so lethal if the city had employed an adequate staff of qualified social workers, who would have been able to contact people especially at risk and gain the trust of those too terrified to open the door to strangers. But 'while the Police Department expanded to historic levels, the Department on ageing reduced its full-time staff and hired less expensive part-time and temporary employees.' It also 'outsourced' more and more of its work, inviting bids that 'provide[d] perverse incentives for agencies to underestimate the costs of services and overestimate their capacity to provide them'. Thus:

> competition can undermine the working conditions for human services providers if it fosters efficiency yet compromises the time and human resources necessary to provide quality care. . . . Regular communication, if only by phone, was crucial for maintaining the lines of social contact and the loose bonds of trust. The problem was that [one typical 'outsourced'] organization's contract with the city has left them with a small staff and, in the words of one case manager, 'about two times more clients than we can possibly handle.'[32]

Of course, in labour-intensive occupations such as social work, you get what you pay for. 'Efficiency' merely means less service for less money.

Similarly, 'the city's supply of fifty-six ambulances and roughly six hundred paramedics is inadequate to meet either regular or exceptional demands for care.'[33] Even so, the city could have expanded the supply, but 'the "reinvented" city government has cultivated an ethic of fiscal austerity among administrators that trumps even the most urgent requests for resources to combat a health crisis'.[34] The city could have put fifteen more ambulances on the streets by calling in off-duty staff, and could then have supplemented these with seventy more ambulances from the suburbs by activating an emergency system designed for the purpose, the 'mutual aid boxed alarm system'.[35] As a senior paramedic said, 'we could have had enough people to get them, to put fluids in them and cool them down', so that 'lives could have been saved'.[36] But all that would have cost money.

Instead, all the effort went into spin. The Mayor's first reaction was to deny that there were any excess deaths and to order city employees to suppress the statistics that would have shown this to be false.[37] This cover-up became impossible because 'the Cook County Morgue, with hundreds of dead bodies, a parking lot full of refrigerated trucks containing even more corpses, and frenzied emergency workers, was a spectacle waiting to happen.'[38] The press and television duly seized on these powerful (and easily obtained) images. Thereafter, the Mayor and his senior officials focused on dodging responsibility.[39] The official response was (among other obfuscations) that the victims were 'people who die because they neglect themselves'.[40] The local newspaper helped out by reporting 'that casualties of heat "rejected any kind of help" – even though all the evidence pointed to the reverse'.[41] The failure of the ambulance service to respond to calls because it was overwhelmed and the desperate wish of old people for more contact with social workers are sufficient to show where the problems lay. Yet this attempt to shift the responsibility from the public authorities to the individuals who died was successful in saving the Mayor from recrimination or retribution.

The Mayor appointed a commission of inquiry whose title – 'Commission on Extreme Weather Conditions' – already defined the event as a natural disaster rather than a public policy failure, and its report (edited in the Mayor's office), 'rather than recommending new programs . . . exhort[ed] individuals and communities to take care of themselves'.[42] This conclusion fitted in perfectly with the ethic of the irresponsible society. By way of contrast:

> after floods in Nicaragua killed nearly ten thousand people in 1998, citizens gathered and screamed "murderer" to their president as he drove through towns to offer symbolic support for regions whose vulnerability the government had long tolerated. But in Chicago and other US cities hit hard by crises, the dominant political culture of individual responsibility does not promote such understandings of disaster.[43]

The stages of response to a crisis through which the Mayor of Chicago passed are the hallmark of an irresponsible society: first, deny that there is any problem; second, play down its importance; and then, when all else fails, invoke personal responsibility. Corporations can play the game as well as governments. If the stink rises to a critical level, however, elected officials will seek to deflect it by blaming firms for irresponsible track maintenance, corrupt corporate accounting practices, grotesque directors' pay, and so on. This blithely ignores the way in which an economic system built on greed has incentives for lying, cheating and stealing built into it from the base up, so that only intelligently designed and rigorously enforced government regulation can hold in check the constant abuses that such a system generates by its own nature.

The British government's response to the obesity epidemic (discussed in chapter 6) illustrates perfectly these processes at work, though with a twist. Back in November 2003, when it still believed that reality could be completely buried by 'spin', it tried to make it impossible even to raise the question of government responsibility. At that time, it set up a so-called 'consultation exercise' in which the prescribed agenda simply omitted topics that might prove embarrassing (such as Iraq and inequality) and in other cases, such as obesity, prejudged the answer in the formulation of the question. The topic was announced as 'individual personal responsibility for health, including the sudden rise in obesity'.[44] Get people arguing about that and you are home and dry!

This strategy was blown away by a report from the House of Commons Select Committee on Health in May 2004, which constituted a scathing indictment of the government's failure to act even though 'obesity had grown by almost 400% in 25 years, with three quarters of adults now overweight or obese'.[45] Without actually denying the facts, one minister's immediate reaction to the report was to dismiss it as 'hysteria'.[46] Tony Blair simply moved on to the next step, appearing on the radio to say that 'we can get this issue in the wrong place' – the place that holds the government responsible for subservience to corporate interests. 'The prime responsibility for people looking after themselves is people.'[47] This is, of course, a tautology but (as with the 'consultation exercise') it defines the framework for thinking about the question in a tendentious way. Are we to suppose that people have become only a quarter as good at looking after themselves in twenty-five years or is something else going on? That question is, again, ruled out. What the government can do is 'to encourage, for example, sport in schools' – by backing the Cadbury's chocolate scam that I described in chapter 6, I suppose.

Finally, if anybody is to blame except suicidally disposed individuals, it is still not the government: 'we can try to get the food industry to behave responsibly' – which implies that it is now behaving irresponsibly.[48] Of course, the government is not really reduced to pure exhortation, which simply invites firms to go against the basic tenet of capitalism and gratuitously reduce their profits. Legislation to throw the junk food and soft drink pushers out of the schools and off the airwaves while taxing such products as tobacco and alcohol would not only run counter to New Labour ideology but would also raise the awkward question of why, if it is a good idea, it was not done years ago.

Part V

The Demands of Social Justice

An indifference to inequality, as the foreign observers remark, is less the mark of particular classes than a national characteristic. It is not a political question dividing parties, but a common temper and habit of mind which throws a bridge between them. Hence even those groups which are committed by their creed to measures for mitigating its more repulsive consequences rarely push their dislike of it to the point of affirming that the abolition of needless inequalities is their primary objective, by the approach to which their success is to be judged, and to the attainment of which other interests are to be subordinated. When the press assails them with the sparkling epigram that they desire, not merely to make the poor richer, but to make the rich poorer, instead of replying, as they should, that, being sensible men, they desire both, since the extremes both of riches and poverty are degrading and anti-social, they are apt to take refuge in gestures of deprecation. They make war on destitution, but they sometimes turn, it seems, a blind eye on privilege.

R. H. Tawney

13

Pathologies of Inequality

In chapter 1, I mentioned as one of the questions that a theory of social justice must answer the following. Suppose that, in the midst of a rich society, there are people living in poverty, is the objection that inequality is wrong or only that poverty is bad? The problem that arises in sorting out these two answers is that either of them might be expressed by saying that justice demands more equality. For if poverty is to be eliminated, the money will have to come from those who have plenty of it. On one view, there is no need to go any further in reducing inequality. Thus, according to the Commission on Social Justice, whose (negative) contribution to the topic I analysed in chapter 1, people 'rightly think that redistribution of income is not an end in itself': rather, the only basis for such redistribution as is required is to meet 'the needs of the less fortunate'.[1] The alternative position is that reducing inequality is desirable – if not as an end in itself then as a necessary condition of achieving a number of valuable objectives.

On the first view, taxing the rich to relieve poverty is merely a regrettable necessity. If New Labour's dream (prefigured by the Commission) could be realized – if education and jobs could eliminate poverty – Robin Hood could be permanently retired. Unfortunately, however, providing more education and training to those with the least will not change the distribution of income unless the nature of the jobs available changes. But there is no mechanism for producing better jobs in response to better qualifications. A high level of qualifications merely ratchets up the qualifications that employers demand for any given job, regardless of the necessity for them. Underemployment – holding jobs for which one is overqualified – is already endemic. Thus, as André Gorz has pointed out, the high rate of unemployment among the unskilled is due . . . to the fact that (both in France and in Germany) one-third of skilled or highly skilled people are in unskilled occupations (for want of being able to find anything better) and have thus elbowed out those who ought normally to fill such jobs.[2]

The more training and education a population has, the more pronounced will be the phenomenon of underemployment.

[In the USA,] the average level of education in the low-wage labor market is considerably higher now than in earlier periods. [Since] 1979, the share of workers in the low wage sector with at least some college education has risen by 13.5 per cent. . . . This is, of course, simply the outcome of long-term educational upgrading of the labour market.[3]

Even in the 1980s 'about 20 per cent of college graduates were working at jobs that don't normally require a college degree'.[4]

The demand for labour of any particular sort depends on how many people of that sort it is profitable to employ, given the output and the technology. Providing the existing supply is adequate, more supply will not create more demand. As Alison Wolf has written: 'I find it hard to construct a convincing argument that more sixth-form qualifications and more degrees are needed so that people can stack shelves, swipe credit cards or operate a cappuccino machine effectively.' Pointing out that 'the fastest-growing job in the 1980s was "postman"' and that 'that of the 1990s looks like being "care assistant" in nursing homes and hospitals', she adds wryly that 'it is important to remember just how many jobs like this do exist, because to listen to a lot of rhetoric you would think that every semi-skilled or unskilled job was going to vanish tomorrow, if not early this afternoon'.[5] Similarly, in the USA 'among the ten occupations the Bureau of Statistics says will add the most jobs over the next ten years, five are low-wage positions, including retail salespersons, cashiers and home health aides.'[6] It is always worth remembering that, even if every adult had a PhD, there would still be a need for postmen and shop assistants. The result would simply be an updated version of the one in which there was 'The Noble Lord who rules the State / The Noble Lord who cleans the plate / The Noble Lord who cleans the grate'. Instead of Noble Lords, as in *The Gondoliers*, we would have 'The PhD who cuts the brain, the PhD who drives the train, the PhD who clears the drain', and so on.[7]

Let us define somebody as 'overeducated' for their job if 'others with the same qualifications are employed elsewhere for much more pay'.[8] Then, for the UK:

people who look at this issue in detail have almost unanimously concluded that, in this sense of the term, we definitely overeducate....
Spiralling numbers of people with formal qualifications mean that
employers can now insist on employees having more education than
in the past, and will also suspect that anyone without qualifications isn't
worth having. The result is that jobs which twenty years ago were done
by people who had left school at sixteen or eighteen now go only to
new entrants who have degrees.[9]

In most cases the jobs are the same and call for the same abilities,
and there is no evidence to support the idea that putting somebody
with more education in the same job will result in its being done
better.[10]

Thus, having more education pays off *for the individual* because
what matters is not how much you have but how much you have in
relation to others. But this is quite consistent with the possibility that
those with more education will be paid less now than those with less
education were paid before. And this is precisely what has in fact
been happening in America. Since the 1980s, wage rates over the
whole lower end of the range have been declining. Yet, 'the proportion of data-entry clerks with a high school diploma rose between
1989 and 1997 from 38 per cent to 50 per cent.' Comparable figures
for telephone operators were 26 per cent and 46 per cent and for elec-
tricians and telephone repairers from about a third to a half. Yet all
these (and other occupations with similar increases in qualifications)
exhibited 'greater than average declines in wages'.[11]

None of this should be taken to suggest that we need to rethink
the desirability of ensuring, as far as possible, that every child com-
pletes secondary education and that extra resources should be
devoted to the disadvantaged rather than (as is now typical) to the
most advantaged. What it does mean is that improvements in education plus incomes set by labour market earnings are no panacea. If
we accept that the distribution of income and wealth is unjust, and
that it would be more just if it were more equal, we cannot get around
the answer that money has to be redistributed from the rich to the
poor. That should be enough for anyone who accepts the premises
advanced in this book. I should like, however, to address those who,
for whatever reason, wish to maintain that poverty should be eliminated and that whatever redistribution is required to do so is just, but
that there is no case for being concerned with the distribution of
income and wealth beyond that.

I shall take up two versions of this. One follows the conception of
poverty in official use in America, and defines it in terms of the ability
to satisfy certain 'basic needs'. It is static in that 'basic needs' are

assumed not to change over time. Thus, the current poverty level in the United States is supposed to permit the purchase of goods and services of the same value as in the 1960s. In 1997, the poverty line stood at $313 per week for a family of four – a sum that is hard to conceive as providing everything necessary for even a spartan existence.[12] Even by this inhuman standard, the official statistics showed that 'more than 13 per cent of Americans fell below [it] in 1997, including about one out of every nine whites and one out of four African-Americans and Hispanics'.[13] For children under 18, the statistics were a good deal worse. One in five were living in poverty on this criterion: one in six white children and one in three African-American and Hispanic children.[14]

In practice, poverty has been defined 'as existing for a family if its income is less than three times the cost of a low-priced but nutritionally balanced food "basket"'.[15] The decision to set the poverty level at three times the cost of a minimal food budget was based on the assumption that a poor household spends a third of its income on food. Since the 1960s, the price of food has been kept artificially low by farm subsidies, while other costs, such as housing and energy, have risen faster. If the poverty index were updated to take account of this, it has been estimated that it would have to be increased to 50 per cent above its current level.[16] The failure to maintain even the purchasing power of the 1960s as the criterion for poverty is a grim reminder of the political invisibility of the poor in the United States.

In Britain, no mention of poverty was permitted while Margaret Thatcher was in power. New Labour concedes that there is such a thing and admits that it exists, with one-third of all children living in poverty. It also accepts that poverty should be defined not absolutely but relatively. However, it has not acted on the obvious implication that the rates of basic benefits should be indexed to the level of income. Until Mrs Thatcher, benefits were tied to earnings. She abolished the link, uprating benefits only in line with the cost of living. New Labour has refused to restore the link – still less to raise benefits to the level that they would now be at if the link to earnings (or, better, incomes) had been maintained. Thus, its actual policy rests on a notion of poverty as absolute rather than relative.

I do not in the least deny that poverty, defined as lack of basic necessities, is a great evil. It is shameful that in Britain, one of the richest countries in the world, people are having to choose 'between heating and eating' and that 1.4 million people are disconnecting themselves from the electricity supply because they cannot afford even the fixed costs, in addition to the 23,000 who have had their supplies cut off.[17] What is perhaps even more shameful is that the government itself 'has estimated that 20,000–50,000 people die every winter due to fuel poverty'.[18] I want to insist, however, that the whole idea of a standard of poverty unrelated to the incomes of others is nonsense. There is a commonplace view (accepted without question, for example, by Rawls) that, as long as you stay in the same place materially, you cannot be made worse off by falling further and further behind the majority of your fellow citizens. Against this, I maintain that becoming relatively worse off can make you absolutely worse off, in terms of opportunities and social standing.

Adam Smith pointed out that 'the ability to appear in public without shame' requires more in a more wealthy society: at a certain point, he suggested, a man needs a linen shirt to be respectably dressed. As living standards rose, it required more and more. In Smith's eighteenth century, everybody smelled (as Patrick Susskind reminds us unforgettably in *Perfume*), and had done in the West since the fall of the Roman Empire. In the course of the nineteenth century, standards of personal hygiene became higher, as cleanliness was claimed to be next to godliness. But only those with the resources (including the servants) to heat large amounts of water regularly could meet this norm, so everybody else could now be referred to contemptuously as 'the great unwashed' – a common expression of the time for the mass of the population. Thus, the standard of personal hygiene that had once been the norm became a source of social stigma. Today, when almost everybody can reach the norm, the inability to do so adds to the overall non-respectability of those without a roof over their heads.

Another example of the effects on the norm of a higher living standard is that of teeth, especially in the USA. Until some point after the Second World War, the alignment of people's teeth depended (for almost everybody except aspirant or actual film stars) on the work of nature. For some time now, however, to be snaggle-toothed is to be looked down on. But dentists are expensive, so rows of gleaming regular teeth are a middle-class prerogative. The result is that those whose behaviour has not changed with the times have lost social standing. More recently, the ante has been upped by increasing resort to cosmetic surgery. 'Some two million "procedures" were done in 1991, six times the number just a decade earlier', and this expansion has continued.[19] This is beneficial to those who have it (if it works) as long as the standard for appearance stays the same. But what happens is that the standard is raised: 'such procedures shift our frame of reference', so that 'an unusually large nose or protruding ears start to be perceived as disfigurements'.[20]

Again, if hardly anybody has a car, housing will be built in a way that enables it to be served by public transport, and the public transport will be forthcoming – for economic but even more for political reasons. When most people have cars, public transport decays, again more for political reasons than economic ones: those left stranded are a minority and, being poor or disabled, have little political clout even in relation to their numbers. Either ownership of a car or the price of a taxi to travel anywhere beyond walking distance can thus for many people become necessary for mobility. If almost everybody has a telephone, anybody who does not have one is left out of social arrangements and may well fail to be called for job interviews, since this is now commonly done by phone. Being able to follow what people are talking about used to require a radio; now it requires a television set. Being able to exchange presents is an element in social participation, but what counts as a present depends on the average wealth of the society. Similarly, the ability to have a meal in a restaurant is an important aspect of social inclusion, but what would have been an acceptable meal fifty years ago is now either completely unobtainable or would not be regarded as adequate by most people. The cheapest cuts of meat also become unobtainable: only in rural Louisiana have I seen a meat counter predominantly consisting of pigs' jowls, ears, and so on. These examples could be continued indefinitely, and readers will have no difficulty in thinking of many more. The implication of all this is that we can only define poverty in relative terms. One modest way of doing this is to define the poverty level as half of the median income in the society – that is to say, half of the income of the person halfway down the rank ordering of incomes. The rationale is that you are not excluded if the people in the middle of the income distribution have only twice as much as you have. On this criterion, the proportion of poor people in the USA in 1997 would go up from 13 per cent to over 23 per cent.[21] It would also (unlike the absolute poverty rate) have gone up continuously since 1967, when it was 18 per cent.[22]

A common response to this relativization of poverty is that it reintroduces egalitarianism by the back door. But the amount of redistribution required to eliminate poverty defined as a half or even as much as 60 per cent of the median income would in fact do very little to reduce incomes above the median. Thus, we should bear in mind, to begin with, that the median income in the United States (as in Britain) is much less than the average income. Squashing extra people up towards some fraction of the median income is therefore bringing them up to what is still a quite low level in relation to the national income as a whole. (The distance between the median and the average is simply a reflection of the degree of income inequality.) To eliminate poverty in America, then, not much of a dent would have to be made in the inequality that provides the richest fifth of the population with almost half the total national income, while the next richest fifth take almost a quarter, leaving only a little over a quarter to be shared out among the remaining three-fifths of the population.[23] Similarly, pushing up those at the bottom in Britain would not do anything much to reduce the enormous inequalities of income among those above the median. In fact, New Labour has lifted some people above the poverty line and brought others closer to it by increasing means-tested benefits. Yet simultaneously inequality has grown: 'The income gap is wider than ever, with the poorest 10% receiving 3% of UK income and the richest 10% getting more than a quarter.'[24] We are thus still left with the question of what is wrong with a society in which poverty has been eliminated but in which there are still very large inequalities above the level of the median income. From the perspective of this book, the obvious answer is that it is simply unjust. But both those who accept this answer and those who are unconvinced by it should be aware that inequality has undesirable consequences. I shall devote the rest of this chapter to spelling some of them out.

That inequality has effects on people that have nothing to do with poverty is illustrated by a point I made in chapter 6: average longevity declines all the way from the top to the bottom of the income distribution, so that even the very rich live longer than those who are merely rich. Status anxiety, as I argued, is one explanation of this. If you need only four bedrooms (at most) but your peers are all building houses with sixteen bedrooms, you feel that you have to have one too. But a community in which everybody has a house with sixteen bedrooms has its self-image threatened by some super-rich interloper who proposes to build one with sixty-four. Indeed, in a number of communities in places such as coastal Connecticut and Long Island, the inhabitants have banded together to try to use zoning rules to prevent such houses from being built. In Britain, too, as Anthony Sampson has pointed out, the building of houses on a deliberately ostentatious scale has now begun for the first time since the Edwardian era.[25] This is partly a matter of the rich having become richer, but it also, as Sampson suggests, reflects the self-confidence of the very rich, as in the Edwardian era, that they can afford to make a show of wealth. An especially nice irony is that, in its zeal to reward the successful, New Labour has not repealed 'Gummer's Law', the monstrous enactment by John Gummer (better known for his role in spreading BSE) that allows houses to be put up in areas of natural beauty where building would otherwise be prohibited, as long as they are *large* enough.[26]

The point here is often made in terms of 'positional goods', and this is a literal example: the super rich can not only build palatial houses, but they can also build them in places where nobody else would be allowed to do so! The essence of a positional good is that what matters is not how much you have but how much you have compared to other people. The wasteful competition for positional advantage can increase the danger for everyone, like an arms race. Sports Utility Vehicles (SUVs) now account for over a quarter of all passenger vehicles sold in the United States, up from 5 per cent in 1985.[27] 'What do people do with SUVs? Ninety-nine per cent drive them just like [ordinary] passenger vehicles.'[28] Why then do they buy them? SUVs get very poor mileage, which means that they cost more to run (as well as contributing to oil depletion and global warming). They are dangerous to their occupants because they are simply a body bolted onto a truck chassis, which is rigid and thus lacks the usual 'crumple zone' in front. They also have a high centre of gravity, which makes them 'more likely to roll over, a particularly deadly accident'.[29] But they are also immensely more dangerous to the occupants of cars:

> The problem is not just that SUVs and pick-ups [which have also increased their share of the market] are heavier than passenger cars. They also ride higher off the ground and often do not engage the most crash-resistant parts of cars, overriding their bumpers, or, even worse, smashing their front ends directly onto the heads of people in cars in side impacts. . . . [In side impacts,] a car's occupant is almost three times as likely to die if hit by an SUV rather than a car, and five times if hit by a pick-up, according to federal crash statistics. When an SUV or a truck hits a car, the driver is nearly 29 times more likely to die than the driver of the light truck, the figures show.

The comparable figure for an SUV is 21 times.[30] In the circumstances, it is scarcely surprising that the sales of cars have fallen from 71.1 per cent in 1985 to 45.4 per cent in 2004.[31] Everybody is less safe as a result, but with more and more unstable behemoths on the road, self-defence suggests that it is safer to drive one than drive a car.

We can restate the argument about education and equal opportunity using the concept of a positional good because, in the job market, what matters is not how much education you have but how much you have in relation to others. If half the population have a degree, then a degree will become the minimum qualification for entry-level positions in many jobs that previously would have been filled by those who had completed secondary education but gone no further. And if half the population have a degree of some sort, access to the more desirable jobs will depend on having attended an elite university. There are, as we have seen, many ways in which rich parents can buy their children the means to superior educational attainments, which will put them in a better position to get on to the elite university track. The greater the disparity in wealth, the greater the relative advantage of the rich over the rest. The rich can also provide their children with better access to desirable jobs than others with the same educational qualifications, through their contacts. Only a part of the transmission of privilege from one generation to the next is via education, and the more the ways of life of those in different strata diverge, the more exclusive the most useful contacts will be. (In 'modernized' Britain, the old informal processes are giving way to naked cash transactions: at one exclusive private school, a fundraising event auctioned off items donated by parents, among which were internships in merchants banks and similar institutions in the City of London.) The rich can also enable their children to make use of capital that nobody would lend them commercially or take financial risks that no prudent person without a guaranteed bail-out would be prepared to take. (I shall take this up further in the next chapter.) Thus, those who profess to care about equal opportunity must also be concerned with inequality.

While we should not underestimate the intrinsic advantages of washing machines, central heating and the like, we have to recognize that most goods have a positional aspect. And the wealthier the society becomes on average (even if the distribution of income remains the same), the larger the positional element will loom, as the ratio of show to usefulness increases. The cost of 'keeping up with the Joneses' thus rises in line with the standard of material prosperity. Achieving the same social standing as before costs more and more, but the additional expenditure may give negligible extra satisfaction if the money has gone on conspicuous rather than useful consumption. Satisfaction may even be decreased if the new, more expensive product takes more cost and effort to maintain it. But the problem of waste in the 'keeping it up' is exacerbated by increasing inequality, because most people aspire to a level a bit higher than their own.

As the gaps in income widen, the gaps between actual income and aspirational income widen too. Thus,

[Juliet Schor] describes how people used to aspire to a level only 20 per cent above what they actually had, but as income differentials widened during [the 1980s and 1990s], the 'aspiration gap' also widened. Survey data suggest that the incomes to which people aspired more than doubled between 1986 and 1994. As a result savings declined and debt increased.[32]

Borrowing has also increased in Britain in response to 'high expectations of how much is enough. A recent University of Cambridge study found that 57 per cent of people earning more than £35,000 believed they did not have enough money for essentials, while 40 per cent of those in the £50,000-plus bracket feel deprived'.[33] Obviously, the conception of 'essentials' and of what constitutes 'deprivation' have become completely detached from reality and are arrived at by comparisons with those who are even better off. A more equal society could create a sort of mutual disarmament in the struggle for status through material accumulation, allowing people to be more relaxed about their incomes and work less hard.

Crime is related to inequality as well as to poverty. This is a further indictment of inequality which relies not on its intrinsic injustice but on its consequences. Returning for a moment to the theme of the previous chapters, the 'personal responsibility' model consists of imposing draconian punishments on those convicted. But this is undermined by the very low detection rates. In Britain, there are now more police than at any time since 1993, yet the detection rate in England and Wales fell from 40 per cent in 1980 and 32 per cent in 1990 to 24 per cent in 2001; the Metropolitan Police solved 14 per cent of crime and 5 per cent of vehicle crimes. 'Detection', incidentally, does not mean conviction if the case went to court.[34] The figure of 'clear-up rates' is also inflated by the familiar practice of encouraging those facing conviction to take a look at the list of similar crimes committed in the area and take responsibility for as many as they feel like, on the understanding that they will not be charged with any additional offences.

We know quite a lot about the causes of crime. The 'public health' approach focuses on reducing the amount of crime by tackling the causes of crime. They boil down to the usual phenomena: poverty, inequality of income and status and unequal educational opportunity. Poverty and economic marginality obviously make crime more attractive. But inequality is independently significant. One researcher 'found that the extent of income inequality accounted for 35 per cent of the difference in homicide rates among the thirty-nine countries for which he had data'.[35] When we bear in mind how many potentially relevant ways there are in which countries differ – in wealth, availability of guns and the place of violence in their culture, for example – it is striking that an association this high comes through.

Within the USA, however, the amount of variance in factors such as these is much reduced, and here we find a very strong association between the degree of inequality within a state and its homicide rate, which remains significant after taking account of the extent of poverty within it.[36] The familiar processes of stigmatization and despair no doubt play their part here.

More generally, we may follow Robert Putnam in hypothesizing that much of the relation between crime rates and inequality flows through 'social capital': levels of trust (which are strongly correlated with equality in an American state) and complex social relations that bind people together.[37] But governments cannot do much directly about social capital whereas they have it in their power to reduce inequality. Putnam, in the final 'What should we do?' chapter of his *Bowling Alone*, astonishingly fails to mention reducing inequality in the USA even though this is the answer that stares you in the face when you read his book. Instead, he makes the bizarre suggestion that what America needs is more religious revivalism – a 'Great Awakening' – this in the country that is already out of sight in terms of religiosity and religious 'joining' in comparison with any country in continental Western Europe, all of which are far more equal than America and have immensely lower crime rates.[38]

Margaret Thatcher was no fan of the social sciences. Her government did its best to avoid collecting, or (if it could not avoid that) publishing inconvenient statistics. It also mandated that the Social Sciences Research Council (significantly renamed the Economic and Social Research Council) should not support any research that could not be proved to contribute to increasing the national income. At the same time, she was a born social scientist in producing an unusually decisive natural experiment: what happens when inequality in a society increases enormously over twenty years? The answer is that, from 1987 onward, violent crime rose at an unprecedented rate.[39] This can be explained partly as a direct effect of inequality, as those at the bottom felt increasingly alienated and dispossessed. But it has also been shown that the reason that the surge in crime lagged behind the big increase in inequality from 1980 onward was that it took that long for children who were violent to grow up enough to get into the crime statistics. There is a study that 'provides very convincing evidence that the extraordinary rapid rise in "violence against the person" was directly attributable to widening income differentials'. This occurred because 'violent young men were often violent as children' and 'the most important risk factors are parental irritability and disharmony, as well as depression and violence consequent upon relative poverty.'[40] In this context, it is significant that domestic violence has increased to two and a half times the amount it was twenty years ago.[41] (This figure may be inflated by an increased tendency for it to be reported or admitted in surveys, but it seems extremely implausible that the whole increase is simply an artefact.) The amount of violence among young men is remarkable: for those in the 16–24 age group, 'one in seven is a victim of violent crime each year', according to the British crime survey for 2001–2.[42]

Presumably, the amount of Original Sin in the population does not vary over time, so it can hardly explain why crime rates change. Similarly, the genetic characteristics of the population are extremely stable over a period of, say, twenty years. That rules out a genetic explanation of crime, since an explanation must be able to explain changes in the crime rate. To the extent that criminal behaviour 'runs in families', there are several reasons. If a very poor educational level is associated with crime, it is likely that a child will have a similar level to that of its parents, or at any rate stay in the same place within the distribution of educational attainments. More generally, the environment of the child – the nature of the home and the neighbourhood – will be the same as that of the parents. Roman Catholicism also 'runs in families', but, as I suggested earlier, not even the most rabid genetic determinist would claim that there must in that case be a gene for it.

My final charge against inequality is its deleterious effects on the functioning of democratic political systems – and, indeed, any system in which the government responds to the demands of the wealthy and powerful. This point, already brought up in chapter 6, can be stated using the positional goods terminology: in politics, what matters is not how much your group has but how much it has in relation to others. In the United States 'three quarters of total political campaign contributions to presidential and congressional elections are from families with incomes over $200,000 a year'.[43] To show how this skews the political system, it should be noted that in 1997 'the top one per cent [of households] included all households with after-tax incomes of above $246,000'.[44] The super rich also subvert democracy by their control over the media. 'Increasingly [in the USA] they are dominated by a few large corporations, typically headed by some of the richest men and women in America. Steve Case of AOL-Time Warner, Rupert Murdoch of News Corp and the sisters who own the Lox media empire.'[45] The same is true in Britain, partly thanks to New Labour's waiving limits on cross-media ownership for the benefit of Rupert Murdoch.

I shall return to this topic in chapter 17, but we can easily trace the consequences in public policy. I pointed out in chapter 1 that about half of all the benefits of President Bush's tax cut proposals would accrue to those in the top 1 per cent of the population and that most of the remainder would go to those in the top 10 per cent. Similarly, the Labour government has left intact all the loopholes that make death duties effectively a voluntary tax, even while, in its first four years, the amount of wealth needed to get into the *Sunday Times* list of the richest thousand people in England increased to three times as much as before. It also, extraordinarily, raised extra money for the health service from earned income alone (via national insurance contributions), so that unearned income made no contribution whatsoever. At the same time, party membership has fallen to almost half the number in 1997 and a number of trade unions have reduced their contributions in protest against government policies, thus making the Labour Party ever more dependent on wealthy donors.

Perhaps in the long run even more baneful is

> the increasing ability of the super-rich to separate themselves from the lives of ordinary people, whether in leisure or work, when the gap between the rich and poor is widening. . . . Many of the new country mansions [rising in England] seem to be making statements about this need for segregation.[46]

Living unimaginably different lives from those in the middle, let alone at the bottom, and with a new confidence that they will be able to pass on their wealth to their children, the very rich today neither sympathize with the lot of the poor nor fear that they or their descendants may have to share it.[47] It is worth emphasizing how far and how rapidly those at the top have pulled away from the rest. Thus in the USA 'the estimated purchasing power of the top 1 per cent rose by 157 per cent between 1979 and 1997, while the median household's purchasing power rose by only 10 per cent'.[48] The result was that 'the share of after tax income going to the top 1 per cent of American households almost doubled between 1979 and 1997'.[49]

Those at the top have similarly pulled away during the same period in Britain, as the result of big tax reductions, extra loopholes in estate taxation (so that all agricultural land is now exempt) and enormous increases in pre-tax incomes at the top, dramatized by the year-on-year surge in company directors' pay, virtually regardless of the performance of their companies. These increases parallel those in the United States, where a survey of 365 of the largest companies showed that, between 1990 and 1998, average pay (including the value of stock options) rose from just under $2 million a year to over $10 million a year. 'The average CEO compensation was . . . 419 times the pay of the average blue-collar worker in 1998.'[50] By 2003 it had risen to 531 times the average.[51]

A greater degree of inequality may also change the nature of politics in another way, and one that makes even policies aimed at ending poverty more difficult to enact. The anger and frustration of those in the middle may be turned not against the rich, who are practically invisible in their country houses, gated communities and exclusive institutions, but against the poor and (a usually overlapping category) those belonging to racial minorities. As Ian Shapiro has said: 'Hatred of welfare stems from the perception that most recipients are undeserving. Media portrayals of the very poor as disproportionately black and lazy reinforce the perception – as does the act of criminalizing the poor.'[52] In Britain (and elsewhere in Europe), the resentment and insecurity of those in the middle, or even quite a long way below the middle, can be diverted into ethnic scapegoating. The enthusiasm for the 'politics of identity' among many of those who think of themselves as being on the left plays directly into the hands of those who like to see the people in the lower ranks of the social order fight one another rather than make common cause against the rich.[53] Thus, inequality should concern even those who are concerned directly only with poverty in virtue of its impact on politics.

As I have said, the arguments in this chapter are designed to appeal to people who are unconvinced that social justice has any direct connection with equality, as well as those who accept that it has. I could say, in fact, that I have simply been filling in Tawney's reference to the 'repulsive consequences' of inequality. The more unequal a society becomes in terms of income and wealth, the more the connection between wealth and status is tightened, so that people who make valuable contributions to the life of the mind, to the arts, or to the well-being of their fellow citizens (teachers and nurses for example) tend to be accorded relatively low social standing unless they also make money. At the same time, those who make large amounts of money without any of those achievements have become objects of admiration. (Where would magazines like *Hello* be if it were otherwise? Nobel Prize winners need not apply.) The effects on attitudes are powerfully illustrated in the research carried out over a period of forty years by Alexander Astin and his colleagues. 'Since the mid-1960s, [they] have been asking 200,000 first-year college students in the United States what is important to them in life' and have found that 'the percentage who believe that it is very important or essential to "be very well off financially" has risen from just over 40 per cent to over 70 per cent.'[54]

To the extent that this high valuation of wealth arises from the increase in inequality, we have another way in which inequality makes people ill, and may afflict those further up in the income dis-

tribution more than those further down. An American study of adolescents found that those who put a priority on getting rich were enormously more likely than others to be diagnosable as suffering from
'depression, anxiety, attention deficit disorder, and behaviour disorders, as well as more long-standing personality disorders such as
narcissism, obsessive behavior and paranoia'.[55] Of course, correlation
is not causation, but the mass of international evidence collected by
Tim Kasser in his book *The High Price of Materialism* does suggest
that attaching happiness and self-esteem to the possession of material goods for their own sake is liable to endanger mental health:
'Contemporary American culture leads many people to work overtime and go into debt [and] . . . the price of overwork and debt is
stress.'[56] Those who place a high value on wealth are also found, not
very surprisingly, to place a low 'emphasis on personal relation-
ships', while their 'contributions to their community decline'.[57] This
kind of social isolation has been shown in study after study to create
psychological problems.

In essence, the social pathology of a highly unequal society consists in the destructive effect that inequality has on social solidarity:
the sense that those who live together share a common fate and
should work together. Disregard for the interests of others becomes
the norm. Just one example – but a telling one – is driving habits.
Between 1987, when I returned to Britain from America, and 1998
when I left again, I observed a remarkable increase in aggressive
driving and hostility to pedestrians. And some statistics cited by
Robert Putnam about motorists' observance of stop signs are a staggering indication of the decay in the level of public morality in the
USA: 'In 1979, 37 per cent of all motorists [at certain intersections in
suburban New York] made a full stop, 34 per cent a rolling stop, and
29 per cent no stop at all. By 1996, 97 per cent made no stop at all
at the very same intersections.'[58] The collective indifference to the
welfare of others expressed to an increasingly pathological degree in
public policy during these years has thus been accompanied by this
remarkable rise in the extent to which individuals showed a similar
lack of care.

As the sense of social responsibility withers, so too do levels of
trust in others decline. American data that extend over the relevant
time period suggest that views about the honesty of others appear to
reflect the social conditions under which people grew up:

[I]n the 1970s roughly 75 per cent of those born between 1930 and 1945
[the years of the New Deal and the Second World War] believed in the
essential honesty of others, and their views changed little over subse-

quent decades. Roughly 60 per cent [of those born between 1946 and 1960] agreed in the 1970's that 'most people are honest', and their views were unchanged in the late 1990s. Finally . . . Americans born after 1960 were not out of adolescence until the mid-1970s.

They thus grew up in the early years of what has been called the 'mean season' in American politics, and were also, of course, exposed to the Watergate scandal. Hardly surprisingly, then, 'ever since this cohort began to reach adulthood in the mid-1980s', roughly half of them have denied that 'most people are honest'.[59]

The same downward trend in trust reveals itself in Britain in an even more extreme form, and this makes sense because Britain started from a much higher level of equality and welfare state provision than the USA in the second half of the 1940s and then got worse at an accelerating rate, especially since the advent of Margaret Thatcher in 1979. The extent of the moral rot induced by these changes was shown clearly in a study by David Halpern, a Cambridge academic who was also, ironically, 'a member of the Downing Street strategy unit, Tony Blair's personal think tank'.[60] This study 'show[ed] that in the late 1950s, 60% of the population believed that other people "could generally be trusted". In the early 1980s the figure stood at 44%. [In 1993, it had] dropped to 29% and [was] thought still to be falling.'[61] Britain showed the biggest increase in mistrustfulness between 1983 and 2001 among eleven countries studied (most in Western Europe, but including Mexico, Japan and America). Northern Ireland (counted separately), the Republic of Ireland and the USA are the only other countries in which mistrust has increased at all, while those with strong welfare states and egalitarian policies on incomes have shown increases in trust from already high levels: up to 70 per cent in the three Scandinavian countries. Even more significantly, the Netherlands, the only country to have actually increased the level of social protection in the period, has witnessed by far the biggest increase in trust: from 40 per cent to 60 per cent in less than twenty years.[62]

Just as the first class passengers got most of the lifeboats on the *Titanic*, the very rich may be able to look with equanimity upon the disintegration of the social bond and all its attendant evils, because they can buy their way out of them. But everybody else has a stake in reducing inequality, as distinct from relieving poverty. Of course, anyone who has bought into the ideas about meritocracy and personal responsibility that I have been attacking in this book will believe that unequal outcomes are morally justified. But that still leaves open the question of the amount of inequality that is justified.

Let us leave planet Earth behind us for a moment and imagine a society in which something approximating equal opportunity had been achieved. As I pointed out in chapter 2, we would then have to take up the independent issue of the amount of inequality that would be consistent with social justice. There would still be no reason for accepting the assumption of the meritocrats that any size of reward is justifiable as long as there has been fair competition for it. The same point can therefore be made to those who believe that the conditions for justifying economic inequalities exist now. If you are impressed with the case I have been making here about the bad consequences of inequality, the question you should ask is: what is the smallest extent of inequality that can be squared with justice? On that stringent criterion, you could hardly find differences in personal merit capable of justifying a scale of inequality that would tear apart the fabric of society.

There is one final question to be asked, even though it is entirely hypothetical. If we had achieved a society in which the material conditions for equal opportunity had been achieved, would this justify inequalities that would undermine equal opportunity for the next generation? I assume that the material conditions for equal opportunity would call for more equality than that necessary to stave off the social pathologies described in this chapter. But I do not know (nor can anyone) what would be the acceptable limits, as long as everyone had access to comprehensive public services of high quality. I believe, however, that the extent to which unequal financial rewards could be attributed purely to different choices made from an equal choice set could never be very great. Bad luck such as illness and good luck such as being in the right place at the right time would still intervene, and it is hard to see how the forces making for cumulative inequalities could be completely eliminated. Equal opportunity at the starting gate – if it were ever achieved – could therefore be replicated for subsequent generations.

14

Wealth

It is one of the great mysteries of our time that, when political philosophers address themselves to the topic of social justice and money, they almost invariably focus on one question: the justifiability or otherwise of unequal earnings, which they tend to equate with earnings from paid employment. This may reflect the fact that academics are paid employees and, in that capacity, have a personal stake in questions about the justifiability of their earning a lot more than garbage collectors and a lot less than most of their undergraduates (if they are at an elite university) will be earning within five or ten years of graduation. An issue of particular poignancy for academics in the UK is that their pay has fallen so far in relation to other professionals, even in the public sector: it has roughly halved in relation to that of civil servants in the last thirty years.

However, earnings are only one source of income, so that even if we are concerned with no more than the distribution of income, this enquiry falls short. The share of earnings in the national income has declined in almost all rich countries in the past twenty years – and even more dramatically in some third world countries that have fallen into the clutches of the IMF. It is therefore no longer true to say (to the extent that it ever was) that unearned incomes are a relatively unimportant contribution to the distribution of income.[1] There is, moreover, a particularly good reason for paying attention to unearned incomes: they are much more unequally distributed than earnings, and thus add a lot to the overall income inequality within any rich country by increasing the number of very high incomes. Even among those who recognize that the distribution of income is a wider issue than the distribution of earnings, we can find economic inequality discussed as if wealth were of no significance in itself.[2] The explanation of this may be that everything of significance about inequalities of wealth is assumed to be captured by their contribution to inequalities of income. This is very far from the truth.

One reason is that a great deal of wealth may not give rise to income, as conventionally measured: if you own an island in the Caribbean, a mansion in Belgravia, an estate in the country and a collection of Picassos, the financial income liable to tax may be only a fraction of what it would be if this same amount of wealth were drawing investment income. We could impute an income based on the enjoyment of this wealth, and tax that too, but this is not done.[3] A partial move in this direction was represented in the British tax system by Schedule A, which was based on the value of people's houses and thus rendered taxation more equitable between those who owned their accommodation and those who rented it. But the revenue it raised was allowed to fall to a derisory level by not keeping the tax in line with rises in house prices, and it was eventually dropped. The principle was, nevertheless, valid and the only reason for confining it to houses, as against other forms of property, was their visibility and ease of assessment.

Another reason for distinguishing between wealth and income, as conventionally measured, is that capital gains are distinguished from income. Even if we forget about imputed income from the value of possessions, we must at least define your annual income as the amount that you could have spent during the year and still have been as well off at the end as you were at the beginning. On this criterion, if your Gainsborough is worth a million pounds more at the end of the year than it was at the beginning, your income for the year from this source alone was a million pounds. There is no principled basis for the distinction between capital gains and income. Yet no country taxes unrealized capital gains, and even realized capital gains are either untaxed or almost everywhere given favourable treatment in comparison with other income.[4] In the United States, holders of wealth have been even further privileged by the elimination of the tax on dividends. The gains from this bizarre reversal of elementary social justice are, it need hardly be said, distributed immensely unequally: 'The top 1 per cent of households owned 42 per cent of all stocks [in 1998], the top 5 per cent two-thirds, the top 10 per cent almost 80 per cent, and the top quintile almost 90 per cent', leaving 10 per cent to the remaining four-fifths of the population.[5]

Even those who believe social justice to be concerned only with poverty should take account of asset poverty as well as lack of income. Almost 40 per cent of the American population would not be able to survive on their financial assets for three months at the poverty level (which, it will be recalled, is extraordinarily low); if we include equity in a house, the proportion falls to a quarter, but comparing 1998 with 1983, this is a 14 per cent increase.[6] In Britain, a study published in 1998 estimated that in twenty years the proportion of households with no assets had risen from 5 per cent to 10 per cent.[7] Assets matter for a reason I have already given: a measure of income that excludes assets is misleading. For example, if you own your own house, you do not have rent or mortgage payments to meet, so you are better off on a given income. But assets are also important because they provide a measure of independence, a cushion against adversity, and an opportunity to make one-off capital payments that would otherwise be impossible. Thus 'both income and assets are important measures of well-being'.[8]

But the unequal distribution of wealth, as well as asset poverty, should also concern even those who do not regard it as a matter of social justice, for the reasons given in the previous chapter. In the United States, between 1983 and 1998, those in the top 1 per cent 'received 53 per cent of the total gain in marketable wealth over the period. The next 19 per cent received 38 per cent while the bottom 80 per cent received only 9 per cent.'[9] The wealth of the bottom 40 per cent declined.[10] As a result, 'in 1998 the top one per cent held 38 per cent of total household wealth and 47 per cent of financial wealth.'[11] In Britain, 'the Inland Revenue estimate that the share of marketable wealth of the top 10 per cent rose from 49 per cent to 52 per cent between 1982 and 1996, while the share of the top 50 per cent rose from 91 per cent to 93 per cent', thus leaving half the population to share out the remaining 7 per cent.[12]

Wealth inequality is far greater than income inequality. In 1998, while the top 1 per cent in the United States had 38 per cent of the total wealth, as we have seen, the top 5 per cent of families made off with 'only' 21 per cent of the total income between them.[13] Those who are persuaded that – even leaving aside issues of social justice – we should be concerned with great inequalities, must take seriously the extreme and growing inequality of wealth. For all the ill-effects on the social fabric represented by income inequality are much greater in the case of wealth inequality. One obvious reason is that the inequality is larger. But in addition, wealth, as against income alone, greatly enhances the forces making for all the pathologies that I have pointed out. Thus, the feeling of those at the top that they are insulated from the vicissitudes of the rest of their society is much greater if their advantage consists of great wealth. Equally clearly, the distorting effect of inequality on politics is accentuated by inequality of wealth as against income. For example, candidates for mayor in New York City can draw on public funding as long as they keep their total campaign expenditure within a set limit. This is as close as it is possible to get to a level playing field without contravening an infamous Supreme Court decision (*Buckley* v. *Valeo*) that prohibits caps on spending. By drawing on his huge private fortune, however, one of the candidates was able to exceed the limit without any public funding, and duly became Mayor Bloomberg. Further, extremely rich individuals can create right-wing organizations with their own money. We shall see in chapter 17 how profoundly this has shaped the way in which Americans (and by the spread of the same ideas, British people) understand the social world.

With the runaway incomes at the top end, the number of extremely rich people can be expected to continue to expand rapidly. Between 1989 and 1998, the number of households worth a million dollars increased by 58.2 per cent, the number with five million increased by 154.7 per cent and the number with ten million or more by 269.1 per cent, putting almost 240,000 households in that happy position.[14] A similar increase in wealth at the top has occurred in Britain. The *Sunday Times*'s 'Rich List' for 2002 put the amount required to get into the list of the thousand richest at £35 million – three times the amount required when New Labour assumed office in 1997, as I observed earlier.

In addition to the bad consequences of extremely unequal holdings of wealth, there is, of course, its intrinsic injustice. Not a great deal needs to be said in support of this claim. Great wealth arises either from enormous earnings or from profits that have been accrued during one's lifetime or from inheritance – with the original amount expanded in each case by investment. In fact, studies of those who become rich have found that in most cases (though not all) they started with a substantial sum. It is often said that 'the first million is the hardest', and if you start with that, or even a substantial amount of it, you are way ahead. The most recent available figures on wealth in Britain (from October 2003) put the Duke of Westminster at the top 'with an investment property portfolio of £5bn – one seventh of the total £35bn held collectively by the top 200'.[15] Of the next four families, three are aristocratic and owe their fortunes to inheritance.[16] The Duke of Westminster's money ultimately derives from his family's ownership of three hundred acres in what became Mayfair and Belgravia, the most exclusive locations in London.[17] Notice, incidentally, that the estimate is not of the Duke's total wealth, but only of his 'investment property portfolio'. That this huge amount of wealth has been passed on through the generations is a vivid illustration of the negligible effects of death duties on those who take good legal advice. Indeed, there are so many loopholes that they are understood by those in the know to be in essence a 'voluntary tax'. (It may be recalled from chapter 1 that the main concern of the Commission on Social Justice about death duties was that they hit those who failed to make the right arrangements in good time.) In the United States, too, good advice can minimize the impact of death duties, but if the currently legislated phasing out of death duties is carried through, the very wealthy will not even have that amount of trouble.

There are two possible ways in which taxes and state payments can narrow the wealth gap. One is to make the rich less rich; the other is to provide wealth, or the possibility of acquiring wealth, to those with little or none. Clearly, transferring wealth from those who have it to those who do not would do both at once. But the funding for increasing assets could come from anywhere, while taxes on wealth could be (and usually are) lumped in with other revenues. To illustrate the first case: the British government proposes a 'baby bond' that would mature into a modest sum and a 'savings gateway' that would match savings up to a certain limit. But there is no suggestion that it will be paid for by raising more money from death duties or by a tax on wealth, so it will have to be paid for out of general taxation. (The amounts are so trivial that this hardly matters, but it would for serious money.)

Within the current world economic order, there is only limited scope for radical equalization by taxing the rich. With regard to wealth taxes, the problem can be illustrated by noticing the remarkable gap between ends and means in a systematic study of wealth in America, Edward Wolff's *Top Heavy*. The subtitle of this book is *The Increasing Inequality of Wealth in America and What Can Be Done about it*. Since he is silent on possible schemes for narrowing the gap by pushing up those at the bottom, Wolff is obliged to pin his hopes on reducing wealth at the top. The method he proposes is the introduction of a wealth tax in addition to death duties, which raised only $24.1 billion in 1998 (as against income tax proceeds of $737.5 billion), and which he makes no proposals about altering. The Swiss wealth tax system, he says, 'seems to provide the most reasonable amount of revenue generated.'[18] This would, he estimates, raise rather more than twice the amount of death duties – $52 billion.[19] But death duties are, as I have observed, a joke and Wolff himself remarks on 'the small amount of revenue generated'.[20] That Wolff's proposed wealth tax would also not raise much is scarcely surprising in that the maximum rate would be 0.3 per cent, and this would start at only

$1.66 million![21] Wolff does not explain why this proposal is reasonable. If we should be concerned about the extent of inequality, as Wolff says we should, it is totally unreasonable. For it does nothing to reduce existing inequality, and does not even hold out the hope of doing much to reduce the rate at which the very rich pull away from the rest of the population. As Wolff himself says: 'Even the top marginal tax rate of 0.3 per cent would reduce the average yield on personal wealth by only 9 per cent.'[22] This is obviously a mere flea bite.

The Swiss system, which Wolff adopts as his model, has the most negligible rates that exist in any of the eleven Western European countries that have one. Several have rates around 2 per cent, either at a flat rate above a certain threshold or rising to that level.[23] The highest top rate is 3 per cent in Sweden, but there is a provision that total tax cannot exceed 80 per cent of income.[24] This deals with the objection that taxes might exceed total income, but there is no good reason for treating this as an objection. As I pointed out earlier, someone whose wealth is held almost entirely in assets that do not generate income (as conventionally measured) should be paying an amount of wealth tax that vastly exceeds his income. This is one of the main reasons for holding that a wealth tax is an indispensable demand of social justice. Be that as it may, limiting the maximum paid in wealth tax to only a proportion of income has the effect that no wealth tax, whatever its nominal rates, can actually reduce the size of large fortunes. It is hardly surprising that the wealth tax makes for only an insignificant increase in total tax revenues in Sweden. Although Wolff does not explain why he does not propose a lower threshold and a higher tax rate, the way in which the higher Western European tax rates cluster around two per cent may be suggestive of practical limits. I shall return to this later.

From the point of view of social justice, the case for death duties is unanswerable. But they would have to be very high indeed to prevent fortunes from growing, unless they were regarded as a mere supplement to a heavy wealth tax. If we assume that on the average thirty years or so elapse before the inheritors of wealth pass it on to their heirs, that is thirty years in which to build the fortune back up to replace the bite taken out of it by death duties. Even if three-quarters of the Duke of Westminster's estate were taken in death duties, his heirs would have only to invest as shrewdly as he has done to make it up. Reformers tend to be so modest in their demands that even closing existing loopholes would still render death duties no more than an inconvenience. David Nissan and Julian Le Grand, whose proposal for a capital grant I shall discuss in a moment, say that 'an ideal system would have rates that most regard as reasonable, to minimise incentives for avoidance or evasion'.[25] But what the wealthiest people regard as reasonable must be very little on this criterion, since most tax due now is avoided or evaded. What Nissan and Le Grand suggest is that existing loopholes should be closed, including the obvious one that gifts are not included, leaving 'a modest tax on gifts and bequests'.[26] What this comes to is a tax raising about a quarter of the total of estates and lifetime gifts.[27] Perhaps this would require rates that were rather more than 'modest' on very large fortunes, but they assure their readers that this would be 'far from penal taxation'.[28] (It will be recalled from chapter 1 how what used to be the slogan of the right has now permeated political discourse.) To be fair to the authors, however, they do not claim that the gap between rich and poor is to be narrowed by reducing wealth at the top.

If we ask why nobody is prop osing a serious effort to reduce inequality by ensuring (say) that nobody has more than a few million pounds or dollars, the answer is, I suppose, apparent to everyone. I shall not take up the general objection that social justice is impracticable until chapter 16, but it seems reasonable to treat this as a special case. If one country gets too far out of line with the rest, the very rich will simply relocate themselves, whether the threat comes from a heavy wealth tax or high rates of death duty. There are, of course, already 'tax exiles' taking advantage of low-tax havens, but at some point we would be looking at 'capital flight' on such a massive scale that the economy would be in danger of grinding to a halt. At the same time, there is no reason for accepting the idea that taxes should be set at whatever rate maximizes revenue: the point at which a further increase in the take from those liable to tax is more than offset by the reduction in the tax base arising from an additional shift of assets out of the country. For the object is not to maximize revenue but to reduce inequality as far as possible.

If I am correct in arguing that the pathologies of inequality outlined in the previous chapter are especially strongly driven by inequalities of wealth, it would surely be worth quite a lot to reduce the number and size of large fortunes. An improvement in social justice would also, of course, be brought about if rates of wealth tax and of gift and inheritance tax were pushed up to levels that would really reduce large fortunes, even if they would drive out some very rich people. There would need to be two conditions for this exodus to have the right result. The first is that any family whose members become tax exiles by moving substantial assets out of the country would have to be permanent exiles, with no right to return except for very brief periods on compassionate grounds – to visit dying relatives or attend funerals, for example. The other would be that nobody domiciled outside the country for tax purposes should be permitted to make any contribution to a political party or cause, advertise any except strictly commercial messages or own any newspapers, journals or television stations. Best of all, no doubt, would be an international accord eliminating large fortunes everywhere, but the kind of national-level action that can be taken should not be held hostage to such an uncertain future. Currently, despite an earlier promise by the Chancellor of the Exchequer, nothing has been done about the loophole that allows some 60,000 extremely rich foreigners to claim non-domicile status and pay no taxes. The case against change is said to be that there would be an 'exodus', but this would be something to welcome, since it would reduce wealth inequality at no cost.[29]

Even if we were to give up on the possibility of promoting equalization by greatly reducing the amount of wealth at the top, we could still take measures to increase the ownership at the bottom. Of course, people must have enough to live on and some over before it makes any sense to talk about their acquiring assets. But public policy should then focus on building up the assets of the poor. In America $3 billion a year goes in tax breaks and incentives for asset development, 90 per cent of it going to households making over $50,000 a year.[30] If instead this was made available to the poorest 100 million Americans, it would come to $3,000 a year per head, which would at least be something. However, the crucial condition for it to make sense to acquire assets is that the whole culture of means-testing, which includes restrictions on assets in both Britain and the United States, has to go. Benefits for unemployment and state pensions, for example, have to be regarded as entitlements, which should be unaffected by other income or by ownership of assets. This is the normal practice on the continent of Europe, whether the system is one of social insurance, straightforward universal benefits or some combination. Otherwise, it would be irrational for anyone who has good reason for expecting to require means-tested benefits to accumulate assets. Moreover, if (as in Britain) the basic state pension is very low and the rest made up by means-testing, a small private pension may provide no advantage because it simply reduces the size of the supplement.[31] This, however, anticipates the discussion of income in the next chapter, so I shall leave it until then.

A way of rescuing some elements of equal opportunity despite gross inequalities of wealth would be to provide each person with a capital grant at the age of (say) 18. The logic of this is that a relatively small capital sum (by the standards of the rich) has the potential to make a big difference to the set of opportunities available. As we have seen, the ideology that underwrites unequal outcomes insists that poor people are poor simply because they make dumb choices from the opportunities open to them. But the options open to those who can count on parental backing for investments in acquiring personal capital or undertaking risky ventures are entirely different from those without this assurance. Thus, as two eminent sociologists, John Goldthorpe and Robert Erikson, say:

> [C]hildren from less advantaged origins may have good reasons to avoid high-risk alternatives, even if risk aversion is equally distributed across classes. We would emphasize in this respect not only differences in current levels of income but, further ... differences in economic security, stability and prospects that [are] the main sources of class advantage or disadvantage.[32]

In the absence of any prospect of being bailed out by your parents, it may be, as they suggest, that it is rational to adopt a safe educational strategy – 'for example, opting for a vocational rather than an academic course that carries higher risks of failure, even though, for a working class child, this is not best suited to achieving upward mobility.'[33] This explains why, as they say, *'even when the level of demonstrated ability is held constant*, children of more advantaged class origins take more ambitious educational options – for instance stay on at rather than leave school or choose academic rather than vocational courses – than do children of less advantaged origins'.[34]

Wealth is of critical importance here. If your parents (or grandparents) are prepared to finance some years of very low and precarious earnings, you can enter an occupation with big eventual rewards that is simply not open to others. In Britain, the starkest illustration of this is provided by the careers of barristers, who are hired by the prosecution or defence in the higher tiers of the court system, and solicitors, who mostly do conveyancing and such like, plus appearing in lower courts. Being a solicitor is a safe occupation and can be entered without parental support. Leading barristers, in contrast, make literally millions of pounds a year, but may well have made almost nothing for several years before they got themselves established. I shall argue in the next chapter that, unless enormous rewards are taxed, they are both socially wasteful and socially unjust; but there will always be risky options and relatively safe options, and lack of access to wealth forecloses the first set. For even those who are willing to go into debt to engage in risky ventures may well find out that they cannot do so. You may be willing to borrow money in the hope of big eventual gains, but the bank that you ask for a loan from is likely to think differently.

I have already said something about the proposal made by David Nissan and Julian Le Grand for increasing the yield of death duties. They calculate that this would cover the cost of a £10,000 payment. An alternative American proposal, put forward by Bruce Ackerman and Anne Alstott, is for a much more substantial sum, $80,000, to be funded by a 2 per cent tax on all forms of wealth in excess of $80,000.[35] Since I have already discussed both forms of tax, I shall focus here on the idea of a capital grant.

Both proposals are for a universal grant. One argument for this is practical: if the size of the grant were made dependent on assets, whose assets should be counted? Few 18-year-olds have significant assets. (If some do as the result of gifts from parents or grandparents, these would stop in response to the scheme.) If grandparents as well as parents are counted, how are they to be factored in, and what happens if they do not in fact provide the help that those with any given level of wealth are expected to give? But the main point, for both sets of proponents, is that 'universal benefits contribute to the sense of national community, whereas targeted ones can be socially divisive'.[36] This is a point that I shall take up generally in the next chapter, but it seems to be absolutely right to say that the grant should be regarded as part of the national patrimony.

If it is to serve the purpose of providing opportunities for everyone that are now available only to children of wealthy parents, how large must the grant be? One approach would be to ask how much money the children of millionaires have transferred to them between the ages of (say) 18 and 25. If everyone received this sum at 18 (or between 18 and 25), we could say that everybody starts with the same amount that the children of a millionaire start with now. Unfortunately, we could still not say that (everything else being equal) the child of poor parents would have opportunities equal to those enjoyed by the children of millionaires now. As I shall explain, however, the reasons for this would also apply to a capital grant of any size.

Neither of the proposals I have mentioned follows this route. The figure of £10,000 proposed by Nissan and Le Grand appears to be arrived at by seeing what size of capital grant could be funded by closing loopholes in death duties, but this seems arbitrary: if more money was needed, the rate of death duties could be increased and a wealth tax could be introduced, for example. I do not see how £10,000 could be adequate to fund even one of the uses they offer as examples, even if their cost was unaffected by the introduction of the capital grant. £10,000 does not seem much to cover 'the start-up costs of a small business' or 'to "buy" or subsidize jobs which function as training for professions'. Another proposed use of the money is to provide 'the down-payment on a flat purchase'.[37] Even with the proviso that the capital grant leaves costs unchanged, it must be doubted that £10,000 is all that would be required to enable a swathe of additional young people to buy anywhere to live, at any rate in London or the whole south-east of England. 'Because of the house price explosion, fewer than 40% of new households (only 22% in London) can now afford a mortgage.'[38]

At current prices, the size of the 'down-payment' that most of those excluded from the housing market would need would have to amount to a substantial proportion of the price of a flat. But here we must challenge (not only in this case) the assumption that the introduction of capital grants would leave everything else as it is now. It is, in other words, a fallacy to assume that the opportunities provided by £10,000 (or £20,000 or £30,000) in a world in which only a minority of children have access to such sums of money would be provided by the same sum in a world in which everyone had access to it. To do so is to ignore the logic of positional goods introduced in the previous chapter. At any given time, the housing stock is fixed, so housing is a positional good: no influx of new money will house anybody extra (unless there is a lot of unoccupied housing in areas that offer jobs), and those who buy property will do so by outbidding other aspirants. They will, we can confidently predict, overwhelmingly be the ones whose parents can afford to give them enough to win in the auction – in other words, the ones who win now.

Only if the influx of new money were matched by a fast enough increase in the supply of housing would the iron logic of positional goods analysis be rendered irrelevant. In the UK, the minister with responsibility for housing has set up a task force to advise on housing policy (a concept that must make Blair wince), whose 'research . . . shows that around 120,000 new homes are needed annually, "far in excess of current provision", to meet the need for new affordable housing'.[39] Under these conditions, it may be that a sum of money to provide a down-payment would make a difference to the ability to buy housing. But we should be clear that the capital grant would play a relatively minor role in relation to a revolution in housing policy: one that, in contrast to the neglect of the past thirty or more years, was based on the premise that the government bears the responsibility for seeing that the population is decently housed.

This point has, of course, far wider ramifications: for any positional good, no level of capital grant can do anything about the fact that those with access to private wealth will always be able to outbid those who have to rely on the universal handout, however generous it may be. We are simply kidding ourselves if we think that this is a painless substitute for equalization of wealth. There is no threshold of an 'adequate' capital grant if those with access to more can still stay ahead. Firms that now pay nothing for induction into the business will ask for money; those that now ask for money will demand a nicely calculated increase, and so on. Business ventures may be less subject to the problem, but the large proportion of new ventures that go bust in their first year would probably increase even further, and it would be the relatively undercapitalized ones (i.e., those reliant on the capital grant) that would be the most likely to go to the wall.

One other use that Nissan and Le Grand propose for their capital grant is 'to contribute to fees and maintenance costs of higher or further education'.[40] They also say that, as a result of the capital grant, 'higher education subsidies can be further reduced without making anyone worse off'.[41] However, a government-sponsored survey has found that already 'poor students leave university with average debts of over £10,000, despite taking on more paid work and spending less than better off counterparts'.[42] Thus, their £10,000 capital grant would be wiped out, even without any increase in tuition fees, and even though many are working at jobs during the academic term for numbers of hours that reduce their opportunities to get the degree results that their wealthy peers can get with the same level of ability and the same amount of total (academic and non-academic) effort. Unsurprisingly, 'students from better off homes avoided high debts thanks to savings and "generous financial support"'.[43] I doubt if these 'savings' come from working in a supermarket: they doubtless came from money supplied earlier on, so they need not be counted separately.

Suppose that the tuition fees at elite universities were to increase by £5,000 a year and the capital grant were to rise to from £10,000 to £25,000, then students with no other support would still finish a three-year course with nothing. And if they wanted to give themselves the opportunity to succeed enjoyed by those helped out by their parents, they would still have to go into debt to avoid the need to take paid employment during term. School-leavers with no parental support might well prefer to take a place at a cheaper university so as to avoid this debt or even have some of the capital grant left at the end. Thus we would still have reproduced the class-based difference in choices resulting from lack of parental capital that I discussed earlier.

I need add little about the American proposal put forward by Bruce Ackerman and Anne Alstott. Its rationale is essentially that it is unfair that tuition fees for higher education are heavily subsidized by states and that some federal money is to be paid to college students with poor parents, while those who do not enjoy the benefits of higher education do not receive the equivalent in cash. 'Joe Six-Pack is every bit as much of an American as Joe College. And for the first time, his equal claim to citizenship will be treated with genuine respect.'[44] And 'the comparison . . . helps us set the standard.'[45] They set the level of their capital grant at $80,000, which (at 1997 prices) was 'enough to pay for four years' tuition at the average private college in the United States'.[46] They explain that this 'is the appropriate benchmark' because they 'expect tuition at public universities to rise substantially'.[47] However, this $80,000 would not contribute to maintenance costs, and it seems remarkably unlikely that there are enough 'good summer jobs' that pay so well as to enable a student without parental support to 'graduate debt-free (more or less)'.[48] It is interesting to contrast this optimism with their subsequent estimate that someone who had attended a community college – the lowest tier with low tuition fees – would have used $30,000 already after taking a two-year course.[49]

Leaving this aside, Ackerman and Alstott seem quite content with the thought that all the other advantages that can be claimed for a capital grant will be denied to those college graduates with no possibility of parental support, because all or most of their $80,000 will have been wiped out by tuition fees. This indifference seems to be based on an excessively rosy view of the value of a degree. (See the previous chapter.) It serves to emphasize the sharp contrast between, on the one hand, the position of those who have no capital left (or are in debt) with no prospect of parental capital and, on the other, the position of those whose parents, having saved the $80,000 they might now be paying in fees, are in an even better position to fund risky ventures, help with house purchase and so on.

The problem is especially acute because Ackerman and Alstott's examples of the way in which those who do not go to college might use their $80,000 show that they anticipate that it may have to be swallowed up in meeting the deficiencies of American public provision in cash and kind. For example, it might have to deal with the destitution that now faces the unemployed, make up for the lack of paid maternity leave or pay pre-school fees for children – and in this context we might bear in mind that fees for the best ones are higher than those charged by Harvard.[50] I fail to see why these expenses might not also have to be borne by college graduates. From the point of view of social justice, I would suggest that immunizing people against these risks and costs should have much higher priority than a capital grant that would be a random and often inadequate substitute for dealing with such issues.

I have concentrated on the limitations of the capital grant idea because I think it is important to show that, even with it, the opportunities open to those with access to parental wealth would be quite different from the opportunities open to those who had nothing but the grant to rely on. That is not to say that it would not level the playing field a little, and be worth doing. But the great enemy of social justice remains the vast inequality of wealth and its tendency to increase. Questions of taxation and questions of the capital grant should therefore be separated. Wealth taxes and estate taxes need to be made as tough as is feasible, and the level of the capital grant should be determined independently. But what the level should be is not even worth thinking about in the absence of information about the policy for funding higher education. And I am not going to be such a fool as to step into that minefield at the end of a chapter that has, I hope, made its point about its subject.

15

Jobs and Incomes

Political philosophers tend to think that there are only two significant questions to be asked about justice in relation to jobs. The first is: who should get jobs and on what criteria? The narrow conception of equal opportunity set out in chapter 4 calls for the most qualified candidates to get the job. We know that even this limited demand is not met, because the rate at which privileged positions are passed on from parents to children can be accounted for only partially by the superior education obtained by children whose parents are wealthy or have high status jobs. But we cannot stop there. Qualifications for good jobs, in turn, should arise from equal opportunities to obtain them. We know that this condition does not hold, and could never hold fully because, even under the most favourable conditions, there would still be congenital handicaps, diseases and injuries that would hold some people back. Social justice demands compensation for such disadvantages. It does not demand the impossible. It is clear from the discussion in Part II, however, that in societies such as Britain and the United States institutions badly fail to bring about as much equality of opportunity as is feasible. Even if perfect 'meritocracy' were achieved, in the sense that jobs invariably went to the most qualified applicants, it follows that the distribution of success in achieving high incomes and high status would still not be in accordance with the requirements of social justice.

In this context, it is hard to see why so much attention has been paid by philosophers to programmes that are intended to appoint American blacks to positions for which they are well qualified, even if they are not the most qualified applicants. This is no more than a small recognition of disadvantages at earlier stages. It has to be conceded that this kind of 'affirmative action' has done nothing for high school dropouts or those who graduated from a high school with minimal literacy and numeracy skills. (The addition of a certain score on standardized tests as a condition of graduation, as in New York State, will simply create a class of those who complete high school with no diploma.) Thus, affirmative action does nothing to address the most potent single source of unequal opportunities, which lies in the destructive environment and poor schools of the inner-city ghettoes. Despite this enormous limitation on its contribution to social justice as conceived here, it is clear that overall opportunity to get a good job can be made less unequal by affirmative action. The creation of a solid black middle class within thirty years is something in which Americans can take legitimate pride. It is yet another sign of the baneful effects of the ideology that I have been attacking in this book that so many people regard it as socially unjust because it involves violating the narrow conception of equal opportunity whose obfuscatory nature I pointed out in chapter 4.

Although there is plenty of room for arguing about implementation, there is no deep issue of principle involved, so I shall move on to the second question to which political philosophers devote a lot of attention: the justification of differences between the pay of different jobs. I believe that my discussions of equal opportunity and meritocracy should have established the conclusion that social justice can give us guidance only about local and limited comparisons. For example, somebody who voluntarily works more hours than another at the same job should be paid more; somebody who works 'unsocial hours' should be paid more than somebody doing the same kind of job during normal hours; somebody who works under unpleasant or hazardous conditions (e.g. on a North Sea oil rig) should be paid more than somebody employing comparable skills onshore. These can all be regarded as cases in which people have made different choices from the same set of options and the one who has taken the less attractive alternative can justly claim compensation for so doing. However, extra pay for higher qualifications, for all the reasons already given, is highly suspect as an implication of social justice. It can, again, be used only locally among people some of whom have taken the trouble to acquire some qualifications, while others who could have done so with the same amount of effort chose not to. The implications for any broader inequalities in earnings is that they cannot be squared with social justice, though it is usually assumed that there are practical necessities that require more inequality. I shall challenge this assumption in the next chapter.

If the two questions usually asked were the only ones worth asking, there would be nothing else to be said about jobs. In fact, there is still almost everything to be said. Perhaps because academics enjoy a good deal of autonomy and generally find their jobs enjoyable on balance, political philosophers are amazingly oblivious to the fact that the great majority of paid employment is a form of servitude and that those who undertake it are driven into it by sheer economic necessity. In the USA, the screw has been tightened in the past twenty years. As a result of falling wage rates, family incomes have been maintained (if at all) only by a lot more women taking full-time jobs. Surveys asking women why they have jobs show that 'virtually all the increase in full-time employment of women over the past twenty years is attributable to financial pressures, not personal fulfilment'.[1] Moreover, in countries with weak unions, poor labour protection laws and low or non-existent unemployment benefits, such as the USA and, to a somewhat lesser extent, Britain, employers have the power to force employees to work long hours on pain of losing their jobs. In America, 73 per cent of employees would prefer to work fewer hours for less pay.[2]

This, incidentally, helps to put the vaunted national income per head of the USA into perspective: the GDP (gross domestic product) per capita of the USA was $32,184 in 1998, compared with $21,132 in France and $23,010 in Germany. But this is accounted for by the extraordinarily long hours worked (about fifty hours a week on average), the very short paid holidays and the relatively high participation rate in the labour market.[3] What really matters is production per hour, which was higher in a number of Western European countries (including France and Germany) than in the United States.[4] In recent years, the official figures for American productivity have picked up, but both the numerator and the denominator are suspect. Estimated growth has been heavily concentrated in computers and similar devices, but this estimate depends on questionable assumptions about the relation of quality improvements to the output of goods and services.

> If [a 2004] $1,000 PC is twice as fast as last year's then, according to conventional logic, its 'real' value is twice the 2003 model's. . . . If you are typing letters and sending email, the speed increase hardly makes a difference. But to the official US accountants, the matter is settled. The logic ripples throughout the statistical apparatus.[5]

What makes all this particularly fishy is that 'even enthusiasts concede that productivity in heavy computer-using industries – such as finance, business services and communications – has either been increasing very slowly or declining'.[6] I think most academics who have been in the business long enough to make the comparison would agree that it takes a lot longer to deal with mail since email became standard because there is so much more of it. Extrapolating from this experience, I find nothing paradoxical in the idea that faster or more sophisticated means of communication could actually cause less to get done.

If the output is systematically overestimated, the input – the total number of hours worked – is systematically underestimated. For those who are not paid by the hour, the bureau of labour statistics (BLS) simply makes up an average number of hours worked per week. 'The BLS assumes that executives in the hi-tech sector work normal 35 or 40 hour weeks. To anyone in the industry, that assumption is hilarious.'[7] For hourly-paid workers, the BLS simply takes the hours reported by employers; but these are the hours they pay for, which may bear little relation to the hours actually worked. 'One of the undisputed stars of the productivity revolution is the huge retail chain Wal-Mart, which has repeatedly been sued for requiring its "associates" to work long after they have clocked off for the day.'[8] (In some cases, this violation of federal law has been compounded by locking the doors, in violation of basic fire safety requirements.) In addition, Wal-Mart, along with numerous other retail firms, has simply deleted hours for which employees had clocked in electronically. 'In interviews, five former Wal-Mart managers acknowledged erasing time to cut costs. . . . "We were told we can't have any overtime," [one] said.'[9] Even 'Wal-Mart executives' admitted that the company had 'cheated workers for years' by crediting those who forgot to clock in after their lunch break with only three hours for the day instead of seven.[10]

Provided that people are not forced into working long hours by low pay rates and lack of other income support, they tend to turn higher productivity into more leisure rather than more pay. In Western European countries with high levels of productivity and much shorter hours than the USA (and Britain), the work/leisure balance still appears to be too biased towards work. In the Netherlands, 70 per cent of women and 17 per cent of men work part time for proportionately less pay, and even then 22 per cent of the men working full time say they would like to change to part time.[11] Most jobs are boring and monotonous, provide little or no scope for creativity, and require subservience to superiors. That the interesting, creative and autonomous jobs almost invariably pay more than the rest is an additional injustice. But the injustice on which I want to focus here is the power relation itself and the consequent degradation of a large part of the population.

The power of the employer rests ultimately on the right to hire and fire. This right can be circumscribed by legislation and also inhibited by strong trade unions. In both Britain and the United States unions have declined dramatically in their numbers and also in their ability to win cases under labour laws. In both countries, the decline in unions is to a great extent due to anti-union legislation in the Thatcher and Reagan years and anti-union administration of what legislation there is. But it also owes a lot to the collapse of employment in the manufacturing industry, which has traditionally been well unionized, and its replacement by jobs in the service industry, whose employees are much harder to organize. As I mentioned in chapter 2, the average size of a firm has decreased alongside this development, and this itself militates against unionization. It has been estimated that a quarter of the increase in inequality of earnings in both countries in the past twenty years can be accounted for by the greater weakness of unions, and, as a result, the increased vulnerability of workers.[12]

As far as legislation is concerned, the USA has no job-protection legislation, and Margaret Thatcher passed nine measures all intended to weaken the position of workers. Even then, Tony Blair goes around berating other EU countries on their need for more 'labour flexibility', which means (among other things) that it is easy for employers to get rid of workers without compensation or payment in lieu of accrued benefits. The power of employers to drive down wages beyond a certain point can be limited by a statutory minimum wage. In the USA, the real value of the minimum wage has been allowed to fall by 27 per cent since the 1960s, with the consequence that now more than a fifth of full-time workers are making less than the officially defined poverty level – almost double the proportion of thirty years ago.[13] And in Britain the Labour government brought in a comprehensive minimum wage (after the minimum wage in catering and agriculture had been abolished by the Thatcher government), but at a level that was applauded by business for making virtually no difference – which was indeed the government's criterion in implementing it.

Admittedly, the threat of dismissal that hangs over all employees can be carried out in any specific case only at some cost to the employer. The replacement will have to be acquired, acclimatized and perhaps trained for the specific requirements of the firm.[14] Moreover, even if the current worker is less good than the best that might be obtained, there exists no selection procedure to ensure that the new employee will, even after all the costs have been borne, be any better than the present one. However, to the extent that threats are effective, they need not be carried out, which provides the employer with the best of all worlds: the advantages of being able to hold the threat over the heads of the workers without the costs associated with carrying it out. As an alternative to the approach that keeps the threat of dismissal in the background, an employer can choose to rule entirely by fear, and throw out employees regularly simply to make the threat of unemployment more salient. Thus, the president of General Electric recommends firing 10 per cent of the company's employees each year automatically – *pour encourager les autres*, as Voltaire said of the execution of Admiral Byng. This strategy is especially attractive where there is a large pool of available labour, the job requires only minimal ability and training, and where monitoring is either unnecessary or easy. A perfect example is working at a check-out counter, and it illustrates vividly the tyranny that these conditions make possible. Thanks to electronics, the job of checking out purchases has been deskilled because it is no longer necessary to calculate change; it is not even necessary to speak the same language as the customers – as anybody who goes shopping in New York will be able to testify. A further twist is that, with cash registers connected to a central computer, the management can easily monitor the average time per transaction taken by each worker.

Karl Marx could sit in the British Museum and build his indictment of capitalism on Blue-Books – official government publications about working conditions. Nowadays, we have to rely on scholarly research or reports of personal experiences. Barbara Ehrenreich's description of the conditions and pay in a number of jobs performed by millions of Americans illustrates the degradation they experience.[15] I have already mentioned in chapter 12 the written tests administered by firms, and we can add drug tests to that as an initial intrusion. But these are nothing to the humiliating and repressive conditions on the job. Some employers require their workers to work straight through an eight-hour shift with no break for eating and a tiny crevice of autonomy.[16] Until 1998, there was not even a federal requirement that employers be permitted to go to the toilet – and in a book published the year before that, the authors wrote:

> While we were dismayed to discover that workers lacked an acknowledged right to void at work, [the workers] were amazed by outsiders' naive belief that their employers would permit them to perform this basic function when necessary. . . . A factory worker, not allowed a break for six hour stretches, voided into pads worn inside her uniform.[17]

Summing up, Barbara Ehrenreich wrote: 'What surprised and offended me most about the low-wage workplace . . . was the extent to which one must surrender one's basic civil rights and – what boils down to the same thing – self-respect.'[18] Even talking to other employees may be prohibited – presumably to head off any risk of joint action.[19]

> Any dictatorship takes a psychological toll on its subjects. If you are treated as an untrustworthy person – a potential slacker, drug addict, or thief – you may begin to feel less trustworthy yourself. If you are constantly reminded of your lowly position in the social hierarchy, whether by individual managers or by a plethora of impersonal rules, you begin to accept that unfortunate status.[20]

What has been called 'management by stress' extends up the occupational ladder as a more ruthlessly exploitative style of management has grown in both America and Britain, 'in which workers in a variety of industries are being squeezed to extract maximum productivity, to the detriment of their health'.[21] As early as the late 1970s, an American management consulting firm advertised its services in these terms: 'We will show you how to screw your employees (before they screw you) – how to keep them smiling on low pay – how to manoeuver them into low-pay jobs they are afraid to walk away from – how to hire and fire so you always make money.'[22] In both the United States and Britain, study after study has documented 'rising stress and a matching sharp decrease in job satisfaction in the last decade'.[23] Thus, even if the increased pressure on workers increased productivity and even if the proceeds were not drained off by increased profits and outlandish pay at the top, the net result would still be an enormous deterioration in the quality of tens of millions of lives. I pointed out in chapter 6 the deleterious effects on health that accompany humiliation, lack of control and uncertainty about future employment. *The Lancet* – the leading UK medical journal, hardly a hotbed of radicalism – ran an editorial entitled 'Why Business is Bad for Health' that summed up the current state of knowledge:

> The re-engineering of corporations may sound progressive, especially to shareholders, but the apparent price workers pay is an undercurrent of anxiety and diminished loyalty and commitment, their morale eroded by a chaotic and dysfunctional work environment in which individuals are discounted or devalued altogether. . . . A recent study showed that workers who kept their jobs during a major downsizing were twice as likely to die from cardiovascular disease, perhaps triggered by work stress.[24]

The power that employers can exercise over workers increases with the unemployment rate. But even if there are relatively few who (given the alternatives) want a job and do not have one, there is still ample justification for fear that it will not be possible to replace an existing job with another on the same level. Thanks to the massive over qualification of contemporary workforces, Marx's 'reserve army of the unemployed' is augmented by the reserve army of the under-employed, any of whom are ready and willing to replace anyone whose job becomes vacant. Further, the more unattractive the alternative to having a job is, the greater the fear of losing it. In most continental European countries, workers can count on unemployment benefits which maintain a high proportion of their incomes for a substantial period.[25] Unemployment thus does not have a catastrophic effect on income. In Britain, contrastingly, unemployment benefit has fallen from a little over 20 per cent of average earnings when Margaret Thatcher came to power to about 12 per cent now.[26] A variant on the 'work-welfare' system is to require the unemployed to undertake training, even if it is badly done and leads, at best, to a qualification for a job of the kind for which there are no vacancies.[27] In the United States, with the 'end to welfare as we know it', the coercion of the poor takes an extraordinarily naked form, and any job – however degrading and poorly paid – becomes better than none, as we saw in chapter 11.

The power of employers also increases to the extent that additional benefits are attached to the job. Thus, occupationally linked pension schemes make the employee's pension depend on the firm's not reneging on its undertaking and not going bankrupt. The United States has vividly illustrated the latter, while in Britain, a number of firms have unilaterally scrapped retirement benefits linked to pay because they have failed to make sufficient provision to fund them and refuse to cut into profits to do so now. Since trade union negotiators have year after year accepted lower pay in return for these schemes, this is straightforward cheating. (The amount forgone can be illustrated by the willingness of union negotiators to accept pay reductions in return for employers who have retained such schemes for existing employees not closing them to new entrants.) In a number of countries, occupational pensions operated by individual firms are replaced by a state-run top-up scheme which achieves the same ends but in a way that removes discretion from the hands of individual employers. Of course, this still ties the level of pension to earnings, but in a way that reduces the power of employers. Uniquely in the United States, health insurance is tied to jobs, and employers are free to determine what proportion of their workforce will be covered. The proportion has been going down, which makes the retention of jobs in the core workforce even more of an imperative.[28] Even when an employer offers some health plan to an employee, it is entirely discretionary in terms of what it costs and what it covers. One insurance company advertises 'benefits tailored to your company's needs' – not to your employees' needs, which could not even begin to be met on the sort of premiums quoted.[29]

There is a further benefit that may be attached to a job, this time by the state: the United States and Britain both have systems whereby low pay is initially added to and then after a certain point tapers off. Some political philosophers who favour more equality have welcomed this system, but this illustrates the typical short-sightedness of which I complained at the beginning of this chapter. For it could meet with approval only by somebody who thought of jobs purely as sources of income instead of setting them within the context of the capitalist system as one founded on unequal power. What such top-up payments do is subsidize an employer to get people to work at extremely unattractive jobs for extremely low pay.[30] The decision of the employer to take someone on thus triggers a payment by the state which makes the job (supposedly) enough to live on. The result is to increase the power of the employer yet further, because it enables the government to demand that people take these jobs or lose their claim to unemployment benefit. The effect of payments contingent on holding a job is the precise opposite of an unconditional payment to everybody, which would strengthen the bargaining position of workers.

If we want social justice, we have to reduce the importance of having paid employment. There are two reasons for this. The first is that, the less intimidating the threat of being unemployed, the more choosy workers can be and the more employers will have to make their jobs attractive. The second is that there is no adequate justification for large inequalities of earnings – so the smaller the part played by earnings in people's standards of living, the more just is the society. This means that many of the most important resources and opportunities should be available to all without any conditions. Universal benefits – in cash and kind – can provide a social bond instead of the 'us' and 'them' sentiments fostered, as we saw in chapter 11, by means-tested benefits targeted at the poorest and most vulnerable members of society. In-kind benefits should include comprehensive free health care and education from infancy through secondary school. Another quite different sphere in which high-quality universal provision is essential to reduce inequalities in people's opportunities arising from unequal incomes is public transport.

The provision of public transport cannot be left to the profit motive, and this is well understood on the continent of Europe. Trains and buses must run regularly, early and late, whether or not they attract many passengers. If people are to be able to rely on public transport, what is essential is its *availability*. Buses with one or two passengers on the excellent New York bus network are evidence that the system is working. Of course, public transport must also be affordable by those with the lowest incomes, and this means that it has to be heavily subsidized: in Italy, for example, the extensive train system collects only around 10 per cent of its costs in fares, and any system that is going to be cheap and reliable will have to do the same. Nobody should be shut off from full participation in their society by their being unable to afford, or unable to drive, a car. In addition, to anticipate chapter 17, nothing less than the survival of human life is at stake in the continued rise of worldwide 'greenhouse gas' emissions, and any serious attempt to deal with the problem entails the phasing out of the private car. Of course, all this costs money, but this has to be offset against the savings on cars, roads and traffic congestion, as well as the cost (human even more than financial) of injuries and deaths caused to pedestrians, cyclists and motorists by the private car.

The natural extension of universal provision of public services is to provide everyone with an individual unconditional income – a basic income – that would enable them to get by, and letting them build on this themselves. Of course, this would have to be paid for with taxes. But even quite high marginal income tax rates would always leave people better off with earnings, even small ones, than without. This would avoid the problem of all systems of benefits conditional on lack of other income: that a job has to be paid enough to make it worth taking. As we have seen, compulsion and the lowering (or abolition) of the income guarantee have been the responses to this. But a basic income avoids the problem altogether by eliminating this 'poverty trap'. It is essential that the basic income should be paid to individuals. The case for taxing people on their own income, and not making one family member's tax bill dependent on another's, applies here with equal force. It is only because notions of equity are left behind and replaced by questions about relieving poverty at the lowest possible cost that the incomes of couples are pooled for the purpose of establishing benefit levels. This has perverse effects by making the incentive for one member of a couple to work depend on what the other does. For example, the British earned income tax credit comes into effect if one person works sixteen hours a week, but is reduced for each hour that the other member of the couple works, disappearing when the other person is working twenty-four hours a week. This is obviously crazy, if the object is to provide everybody with an assured income to which they can add by their own effort. Pensioners are similarly treated as consumption units rather than as citizens with separate individual rights, both for the basic state pension and for income supplements.

Means-testing is expensive to administer, whereas a universal income is as simple to pay as are more familiar universal child benefits and pensions. But that is only the beginning of the objections to means-testing. Because of the high withdrawal rates of means-tested benefits, they encourage the non-reporting of earnings. A lot of so-called 'benefit fraud' consists of this, and the criminalization of a whole section of the population would cease if the basic payment was unconditional. An encouraging sign of the potential acceptability of a basic income is that a great deal of middle-class housework, odd jobs, gardening, and so on is paid on a cash basis, with both parties perfectly well aware that this is a way of enabling people on means-tested benefits to supplement their incomes. I believe that it is very rare for either side to think that they are doing anything wrong.

A further serious problem with means-testing is the extraordinary complexity that it can generate. In both the United States and Britain, the incomes of those in the bottom third of the income distribution depend in a bewildering variety of ways on individual and family earnings, unearned income, savings and then, in addition, a plethora of in-work, out-of-work benefits (different depending on a host of factors) and post-retirement payments coming from a number of sources according to different rules. In Britain, the incomprehensibility of the system as a whole led to the House of Commons Security Committee being told in 1999: 'if you teach social security to lawyers and welfare rights workers, you have to go through it about four times before they understand it, and then you give them a little example to work out and they all get it wrong.'[31] If lawyers and welfare rights workers get a simple example wrong immediately after four or so explanations, it is hardly surprising if the front-line troops manning the counters (now operating from behind perspex screens to protect them from the often justified rage of their 'clients') make so many mistakes – almost always by denying people benefits to which they have a right.

What about the people who are supposed to claim the benefits in the first place? Bear in mind that, in the nature of the case, many of them will be among the least educated members of the population – including the shameful proportion who are functionally illiterate. Many of them will be trying to juggle two jobs and children, so they are hardly in a position to find out about benefits and fill out complex forms. Many will be elderly and perhaps also sick: not all of them can count on help in making claims.[32] A means-tested benefit that is claimed by two-thirds of those eligible to receive it is considered a big success, while 'in the most well-regulated countries, studies have shown that means-tested schemes have take-up rates as low as 20 per cent'. Just to take one example, the government introduced a new tax credit for pensioners in October 2003; in April 2004, the take-up rate was 2.9 million people out of 4.9 million eligible. A large proportion of those who did get anything were either underpaid or overpaid. Altogether, it is not surprising that the House of Commons public accounts committee described the whole thing as 'nothing short of disastrous'.[33]

Those who embrace the cult of responsibility will have a hard time making the case that the low take-up of some means-tested benefits is the responsibility of those who fail to claim for reasons such as this. However, a convenient way of avoiding the admission that the system is at fault is to claim that lack of take-up arises because some people are too proud or obstinate to apply. If we translate this into honest English, what it means is that people who believe that they should get a decent amount of money as a right are unwilling to be put in the humiliating position of having to beg for a little extra by revealing to some official details of their circumstances that they quite correctly believe to be their own business. It is known that such people do exist – and why not? They are simply a further illustration of what is wrong with means-tested benefits.

Once people are stuck in the net of means-tested benefits, they have little opportunity or incentive to add to their incomes. Whereas an unconditional income guarantees freedom to add to it, means-testing really does create 'welfare dependency'. The problem lies not in the existence of a state income-support system, but in the form it takes. A further objection to means-testing is that it also involves asset-testing, and thus makes saving or private pension policies pointless unless one is confident of not becoming dependent on means-tested benefits. Only an unconditional income can avoid this problem. Although there is a bogus debate among academics about 'basic income versus capital grant', only an unconditional income can make a capital grant work as it is supposed to. I pointed out in the previous chapter that it would subvert the rationale of a capital grant if it had to fill in for unemployment insurance or paid maternity leave. Equally, it would lose much of its point in a regime of asset-tested benefits. The British government's half-baked version of a capital grant – small sums to be invested by parents in, it suggests, the stock market – will fail precisely those whom it should be intended to help most. For its proposal envisages that the savings of those who do not immediately get a job will be used to pay the means-tested benefit for the unemployed. 'That means that an 18-year-old who can't find work will have his or her mini lottery prize snatched back by another arm of government.'[34] If a capital grant is to yield any of its promise as a way of enabling people to start small businesses and take chances, it is essential that its recipients must be able to count on enough money to live on both while they are getting the project set up, and in the event that it fails.

To conclude this discussion of the virtues of basic income, I shall tie up this chapter by arguing that it is the most practicable (perhaps the only practicable) way of counteracting the excessive power of employers over workers. As Philippe Van Parijs, the best-known defender of basic income, has said, it gives 'the least well endowed greater power to turn down jobs that they do not find sufficiently fulfilling, and thereby creat[es] incentives to design and offer less alienating employment'.[35] There would still, as I have emphasized, be a strong incentive to get a job, but the compulsion to take just any job would disappear. Much of the increased stress generated by low-paid jobs has been the result of reducing the number of people doing the same work. Employers would not only find it necessary to spread the work around more, but they would also not be able to change their employees' shifts without consultation and good notice. Since people would not need to be able to live solely on their pay, not only could more workers be employed in existing jobs, but also jobs that have disappeared in Britain, but which might well be attractive, could make a reappearance. An example would be the reintroduction of station-masters at small stations: many travellers at night would be reassured by the presence of somebody on the premises with access to a telephone. Nobody would accept 'zero hours' contracts, making themselves available for an unknown number of shifts at unknown times. The 'cost savings' to large organizations that have been achieved by contracting services out have simply been achieved by reducing the pay and conditions of employees. Thus, the chief executive of a private care home company that had just achieved record profits said that local authority-run care homes cost more because they were 'overstaffed' and enjoyed 'all those pensions, holidays, sick pay, overtime pay and so forth'.[36] With any luck, a company like this would go bankrupt, because it would have no employees.

With cost savings at the expense of workers eliminated, the many advantages to an organization of the management's having direct control over what goes on would return to the fore. To turn over the cleaning of a hospital or the maintenance of a rail system to a firm whose management is interested only in doing as little as possible for the money and whose labour force is underpaid, overworked, commonly untrained and unmotivated by any future prospect is literally to invite lethal consequences – a truth that Railtrack in Britain has acknowledged by getting rid of the practice of subcontracting maintenance.

Although, as I have emphasized, social justice is about high incomes as well as low ones, getting rid of poverty – measured in relative terms – is also of critical importance. Taking as the standard the now accepted European definition of poverty as standing at 60 per cent of the median income, Britain had almost the highest level in the European Union at 22 per cent, while Denmark had only 9 per cent and Finland only 10 per cent in 1997.[37] Clearly, money needs to be shifted around on a serious scale, and the only reliable way of doing it is to provide a basic income: child allowances sufficient to keep children above the poverty line and incomes for adults set at the appropriate level.

I have focused here on Britain rather than the United States, because the debate has been carried on almost exclusively in Western Europe. Further, the British government does in principle accept that it should be getting rid of poverty. But it is clear that its measures have been hopelessly inadequate, in addition to all the counterproductive efforts of trying to do it by adding more and more means-tested benefits: between 1997 and 2001, the proportion of the population in poverty declined only by a very small number in relation to the total.[38] During the same period, the continued trend for incomes at the top to pull away from the rest, combined with the unchanged top rate of income tax, resulted in inequality actually increasing.[39] A basic income would solve both defects simultaneously, since it would automatically keep everybody out of poverty, while the rates of income tax required to fund it would inevitably reduce inequality.

In America, the introduction of a basic income (accompanied by high-quality public services of the kind I outlined earlier) would, of course, be even more important than in Britain, because poverty (by any standards, but especially by the relative one I have followed) is more dire and the 'end of welfare' makes even more intense the compulsion to work long hours, do more than one job, put up with arbitrary changes in shifts and generally accept working conditions that no free agent would dream of putting up with. But to get basic income on to the political agenda would require that the abuse of the principle of personal responsibility must be vanquished. That is why arguments of the kind put forward in this book need to be made over and over again.

Can any society really afford to offer an unconditional income to everyone? Can the money be found for high-quality public services? Can we, in other words, afford social justice? I shall take up that question in the next chapter.

16

Can We Afford Social Justice?

Is social justice, as conceived of in this book, utopian? Utopias such as William Morris's *News from Nowhere* were quite popular in the late nineteenth century. The twentieth century has more characteristically produced dystopias – possible futures to be avoided – such as Aldous Huxley's *Brave New World* and George Orwell's *Nineteen Eighty-Four*. Michael Young's *The Rise of the Meritocracy* was intended as a dystopia but has been regarded by some as a utopia; conversely, B. F. Skinner's *Walden II* was intended as a utopia but has been almost universally treated as a dystopia.[1] Utopias and dystopias have in common that they are static: once in being, there is nothing to change them into anything else. This is no drawback with dystopias, whose especial horror lies in their stability. But a utopia with no place for creativity – beyond that of the author who created it – by its nature cannot be an attractive prospect.

The principles of social justice laid out in this book are not open to any such objection. They are not, and are not intended to be, a blueprint for a perfect society. Different societies could be socially just to the same degree while differing in innumerable ways. While principles of social justice offer criteria for judging institutions, they leave it as an open question what institutional changes would move a certain society in the right direction starting from its current state. Experience – including the lessons learned from reforms already introduced that were intended to produce a more just society – is bound to introduce new perspectives. Institutions will also have to adapt to new conditions, including new knowledge and new technologies. Even where I have pushed for a certain line of development, such as on basic income, I do not intend to suggest that it will be best in all possible societies or that somebody may not have a better idea any day now.

There is another sense in which principles of social justice might be criticized as utopian. To realize social justice, high-quality public provision and approximate material equality are necessary. But is this feasible? What is being asked here is not self-evident. One question that could be being asked is about the political feasibility of social justice, whether in the USA and Britain or in the world as a whole. This is still ambiguous unless we specify the time scale we have in mind. Is it within the realm of possibility that an American president with a majority in both Houses of Congress will at any time soon get busy enacting any programme that would get the country significantly closer to social justice? No. Will a government of either of the major parties in Britain do so in the next few years? No. But extend the time horizon and the question becomes more interesting. I shall address the political prospects for social justice in Part VI, and for now leave that question on one side.

For the purpose of this chapter, I shall take the import of the question to be: 'Is social justice economically feasible?' If we take it to mean 'Is it feasible in one country?' then the answer depends to quite a large extent on what happens outside the country. Measures that were binding on all members of the European Union, for example, would reduce the constraints on individual countries within it. Much more broadly, the current international economic regime is designed to replicate on a world scale the most abhorrent features of American society. A fundamental change in the whole system of global governance to control the power of capital rather than to maximize it would obviously make an enormous difference. The immense inequalities between the incomes of countries cannot possibly be explained by different choices from a common set of options, and are themselves unjust. But global inequality also makes the achievement of social justice especially problematic within poor countries.

For a country such as India, for example, the elimination of the evil of sheer stark poverty has to be regarded as the top priority. In the absence of large-scale international transfers – and the resources getting to the right people – this is going to have to be brought about by raising the national income. Social justice would suggest that those with high incomes (by Indian standards) should be taxed quite heavily to contribute to the alleviation of poverty. But the extent to which this can be done is limited by the mobility of labour. As long as the USA, in particular, continues to make up for its extraordinarily poor record in training professionals (apart from lawyers and business school graduates) by hiring them from poor countries such as

India, the possibility of pursuing social justice domestically in India is severely constrained by the threat of a massive 'brain drain'. The worst off people in India are better off with doctors, engineers and other trained professionals being retained than they would be without them. 'In Bangalore, the "Silicon Valley of India", highly skilled computer software designers . . . earn[ed] an average of $960 a month [in 1993], one eighth of the comparable American wage.'[2] But in a country in which the average income is a lot less than that per *year*, this is still, comparatively speaking, a lot of money. If they are allowed to keep a lot of it, these software designers can live a pretty comfortable life – especially if it is true that the biggest luxury of all is being able to have full-time domestic servants – and still contribute something. But at some point (a long way before taxes reduced their incomes to, say, three times the average) emigration would surely become very attractive. Considerations of social justice therefore have to give way before the need to head off a 'brain drain'.

Another way of saying this is that the extreme inequality of earnings in the United States infects the rest of the world, by setting limits on the amount of redistribution other countries can carry out. However, in rich countries the terms of the trade-off are far less onerous, if we are concerned with total production – an assumption whose relevance to these countries I shall go on to challenge. Preventing a brain drain might with some effort be adduced for a ratio (in 2000) of 57:1 in Brazil and 45:1 in Mexico between the average pay of chief executive officers (CEOs) and that of the average employee. But it could hardly explain why the US ratio was 531:1 and why Britain's CEOs needed 25:1, while those in France, Germany and Japan rubbed along with 16:1, 11:1 and 10:1 respectively.[3] 'There is little global market in British managers. People don't want ours and we don't often recruit from abroad: 86% of FTSE [firms included in the *Financial Times* index of stock market prices] CEOs come from the UK, another 6% from the EU (many from Ireland) and 8% from the US and the rest of the world.'[4]

There are two ways in which countries such as Britain and the United States might be unable to afford social justice. One is that the high level of universal public services called for would be too expensive. Almost any level would be 'too expensive' if service provision is inseparable from waste, so that it will not offer value for money. The other way in which social justice might be unfeasible is that the economy of a relatively equal society (especially one with a basic income above the poverty line) might collapse because the motivation to work would be inadequate.

As a preface to the first point, I want to make a crucial distinction between two 'costs' of social justice: that between public expenditures and transfers. Public expenditures are real costs in the sense that they use resources that could otherwise have been at the disposal of individuals. If a country spends money on the military, the police, the prison service, social work, education and medical care, for example, that is money that is subtracted from the flow of total disposable income. Transfers, in contrast, leave total disposable income almost exactly the same: their only cost in terms of lost individual consumption is that of collecting and disbursing the money.

Taxes such as income tax, value added tax and national insurance (which is effectively a tax on workers) do not cost a lot to collect as a proportion of the sums raised. A wealth tax could be introduced with a high enough threshold that only a few thousand people would be involved, then extended downwards. Gift and inheritance taxes are not particularly expensive to collect. 'Green' taxes on carbon emissions, fertilizer run-off, noise generation, vehicle use and other kinds of anti-social behaviour would require an administrative apparatus to monitor them. But it should be borne in mind here that the object is not simply to raise taxes but to change behaviour, and that everybody gains from that. As far as payments are concerned, the cost of dispensing them as a proportion of the money paid out varies enormously. Means-tested benefits, especially if they are contingent on satisfying some further condition such as disability, can cost up to 10 per cent of their value, whereas universal child allowances cost less than 1 per cent, and basic income would be similar. If, as I suggest, social justice requires universal payments, the distribution costs would be minute: this includes the capital grants proposed in chapter 14.

Means-tested benefits also cost a lot to enforce, because the widespread paranoia about 'welfare cheats' – 'they' are defrauding 'us' – leads to a lot of effort being put into detecting what is usually simply a matter of people not declaring earnings that would be subject to tax rates as high as 100 per cent. Universal benefits would eliminate any distinction between 'us' and 'them', and the only personal taxes would be income tax, wealth tax, gift tax and inheritance tax. Income tax is currently underenforced, in Britain and far more so in America. Tax inspectors recover in unpaid taxes hundreds of times what it costs to employ them, which shows how much undetected fraud exists. The moral as well as the economic feasibility of a just society depends on its being a general presumption that people will pay what they owe. But even if it were decided to spend, say, 5 per cent of income tax revenues on enforcement (especially ensuring compliance among those with the highest incomes), the amount collected from any set of tax rates would be much higher. Equally importantly, the burden would be spread much more fairly, since most large-scale tax evasion occurs among the self-employed, especially if they turn themselves into corporations.

Of course, public services and transfers both require that the money for them should be raised. But I must again emphasize that there is all the world of difference between tax money that is paid straight back to people to a large extent (in the case of universal benefits, often the same people who paid it) and tax money that is used for the consumption of real resources. Even the eminent economist Robert Solow committed the error of treating them in the same way when he wrote that the 'cost' of a low level introductory basic income of $150 per month would be $380 billion, which he compared with the similar amount spent on the military.[5] But what this really means is that the military budget was at that stage taking $150 per month from the pocket of every American, so that eliminating it would pay for a basic income at that level. Incidentally, although Solow was writing as recently as 2000, the United States was spending on 'defence' three years later around $550bn a year and rising, which would fund a basic income of almost half as much again – around $220 a month.[6] Since then the cost has risen yet further. If it were reduced so that America were merely spending more than any other country instead of having a larger budget than the next twenty-five countries combined, the windfall would make a very tidy start.

As far as public services are concerned, there is really not much to say here except that countries can afford any amount of them that they are prepared to pay for. (There is a wide range within Western Europe, for example.) However, there are two further points worth making. The first is that we should distinguish between public services that do harm and public services that do good. I am interested in improvement (in both scope and quality) of those that do good: health care and all kinds of services to enable the elderly and sick to live independent lives, education (at all ages for more hours a day and providing more help), social work, drug rehabilitation, and so on. But a great deal of American and (to a somewhat smaller extent) British public expenditure is devoted to doing actual or potential harm: prisons and the military are the prime examples. As far as prisons are concerned, I cited numerous studies in chapter 7 showing that benign intervention in areas such as education, housing and help with drug problems would save many times their cost because of the consequent lower expenditure needed for prisons. Drastically reducing the use of custodial sentences, which generate high rates of recidivism, would also make for a great saving. More than anything else, perhaps, the legalization of marijuana in the United States, and taking a public health rather than a punitive approach to other drugs, would have the prospect of halving the prison population all by itself: the United States has more people in jail on drug offences than all those in jail in Western Europe on all offences put together. (In addition, of course, if we are talking about ways of raising money, taxing marijuana along similar lines as tobacco would transfer the profits now made illegally to the coffers of the state.)

We should also bear in mind that a more just society will be one that breeds less crime, given what we know about the well-established link between inequality and crime. Moreover, if an adequate basic income replaced the subsidization of bricks and mortar, everybody would have a choice of housing, and the existing subsidized housing (housing estates, 'projects' in America) would have to be either razed to the ground or spruced up to be attractive. Left to its own devices, the housing market would be too sluggish in responding to a situation in which everybody could afford decent housing, so a vigorous government building programme would be needed. But there would be great advantages for everyone because the maintenance of social control depends on the dispersion of disruptive families. Getting away from a situation virtually guaranteed to create juvenile delinquency by concentrating problem families in 'sink' estates or projects would therefore reduce the adult crime rate. The freedom offered by a basic income would decrease crime in another way. There is, as I pointed out in chapter 5, a well-established link between the absence of parents in the evenings and at night, educational failure and suspension from school followed by a turn to crime. If parents were in a position to refuse jobs that were inconsistent with their responsibilities to their children, this downward spiral could be stopped right at its source.

A completely wasteful, and very expensive, use of tax money that is not simply a cash transfer, though it is not exactly a public service, is the subsidization of farming by the United States and the European Union. As we have seen, the surplus produce is dumped abroad at below the cost of production and has ruinous effects on farmers in poor countries. Getting rid of the whole system would therefore be a major contribution to global justice in addition to yielding sizeable revenues for other purposes.

In addition, a redistribution of income and power would save on education and health care. Adequate nutrition, healthy housing and enough parental time off work would improve lifetime health and also throw less of a burden on the educational system, from its earliest stages. Again, better-educated parents make for healthier as well as better-educated children, so we have a virtuous circle. Moreover, a society with a high economic floor and a much looser connection between money and status would be one in which the diseases due to stress (especially coronary heart disease) would be less common. Alleviation of stress by smoking, drug-taking and eating would also be far less necessary, while a responsible society would accept that so-called 'lifestyle choices' are to a large extent manipulated by companies selling unhealthy food and would take remedial action. Prevention is far more effective than (attempted) cure – and prevention mostly requires cash transfers, whereas cure absorbs real resources.

The starvation of the beneficial public services in Britain and (even more) in the United States is thus not as much a matter of underspending on public services overall but rather of the way in which the money is allocated. I have argued that a more just society and a more just world would make possible a massive shift of resources – which is not to say that a large reallocation would not be possible right now. I have also suggested that, in a socially just society, some of the remedial functions of the public services would be less needed. Even so, the provision of universal high-quality services would no doubt increase the share of the national income devoted to public expenditures. However, we must offset against this the amount that people would not have to spend on private consumption. As we have seen, the frantic (and expensive) efforts of parents to give their children an edge in terms of school results arises from the enormous spread of pay at the top of the income distribution. If that were to go, all this wasteful competition for positional advantage would lose its force, and private schools could become an eccentric luxury for those who could still afford them, as long as the public school system provided uniformly high-quality education. Similarly, if the publicly provided health service were of uniformly high quality, the incentive to opt out would be far less, and if incomes were more equal the possibility of doing so would be less as well.

I have argued that social justice requires that access to the means of mobility should be the prerogative of everybody, which entails reliable and comprehensive public transport running from early morning until late at night, if not twenty-four hours a day. The phasing out of the private car (necessary in any case, as I shall argue in Part VI) will obviously save an enormous amount – some public savings in the form of roads, but most of it private: the cars themselves and their maintenance and insurance, the fuel with which to run them, and the immense cost (even if it is not strictly monetary in most cases) of road congestion. Needless to say, the reduction to a fraction of its present level in the incidence of deaths and injuries sustained by car users, cyclists and pedestrians must also count as an immense benefit.

At this point, I suppose it is necessary to say a word about the idea that public expenditures are necessarily wasteful. Curiously, the enormous cost overruns in procurement that are routine in the military somehow do not lead to the conclusion that its budget should be slashed. But whenever Conservative politicians maintain that they can cut taxes without reducing public services, it is always by 'cutting bureaucracy and waste', while Labour politicans try to square the circle in the same way when explaining how they will be able to improve the quality of public services without having to increase taxes to pay for them.[7] If it has any meaning, it is that the pay and conditions of public service workers will be forced down even further.

Measured against some standard of perfection, all organizations are to some degree wasteful, and there is no reason in general for large public services to be more wasteful than large private organizations. Where a direct comparison can be made, public organizations come out rather well. Thus, the system of health care insurance in America needs so much paperwork that all doctors appear to need a staff to deal with it at their end, while at the other end is a huge and unnecessary bureaucracy engaged in deciding who gets paid what. A system in which every injection has to be put on some patient's bill is obviously grossly inefficient. Indeed, the American system is so expensive that, when NAFTA eliminated tariffs, American business representatives complained of unfair competition from Canada, because American employers were burdened with high medical insurance premiums – and even those extend only to a (decreasing) proportion of the workforce, while the coverage offered has deteriorated. The 'internal market' in the NHS, which introduced a watered-down version of this craziness, resulted instantly in the employment of large additional numbers of managers and a lot of highly paid accountants to try to make it work.

No British reader will need to be reminded of the fiasco of ignoring the wisdom of impeccably right-wing governments on the continent (such as the Swiss) in keeping the railways state-owned. The advantages of having a single organization for all aspects of the operation is obvious. But no less obvious should be the advantage of having a public service run by people whose duty is to users – to provide a good and safe service – rather than those whose duty is (as things stand) wholly to make the largest possible profit for their shareholders. Driven by some death wish (not for their own: ministers have official cars), the New Labour government insisted, in the face of overwhelming public opposition and expert advice, on the privatization of the London Underground, leading to two crashes within three days, both due to faults in the track – hardly unconnected with the reduction of safety inspections from every day to every third day.[8] An official inquiry into one of these accidents 'blamed cost-cutting and a "short-term attitude" towards repairs'.[9]

Of course, public services will always generate some 'waste' in the form of buying things that do not perform as expected, stockpiling too many of some item with a limited life, and so on. In a large organization, these sums may look significant, even though they amount only to a minuscule fraction of the budget. But waste in this sense is inherent in all consumption, public or private. Hands up all those who have never bought a pair of shoes that turned out to be uncomfortable or an appliance that never gets used. And how many people could be confident that a diligent search of their home would not turn up an excess supply of something that seemed like a good idea at the time? The ideologues of the market somehow assume that money in private hands can never be wasted, but we all know too well that this is not so. An attempt to compare systematically the proportion of resources wasted in public and private hands would be interesting, but a priori it seems to me overwhelmingly likely that private consumption wastes more for two main reasons. First, far more private purchases are one-offs, whereas public consumers can learn from trial and error. And, second, public spenders can afford to hire experts to choose their purchases.

Public expenditure might be wasteful in a different way if it failed to give value for money. But it is no easy matter to say what precisely is the value of the service delivered, reduced to money terms, so that it can be compared to the cost. One method, especially beloved by economists, and supposedly 'objective', is that a publicly supplied good is wasted if the person who gets it would rather have had the amount it cost to provide it as cash. The trouble is that nobody believes in the relevance of this criterion – except, maybe, economists whose professional indoctrination has been so strong as to suppress all traces of common sense. We do not think that somebody scheduled for a hip replacement should be able to demand to be allowed to hobble around instead and spend the amount saved on gin. Nor do we care whether or not a schoolchild (or its parents) would sooner have the money than the education. We support the provision of public goods because we have decided, collectively, that they supply services that we believe ought to be available to every citizen. What people would be prepared to spend themselves is not absolutely irrelevant to such a judgement, but it is far from decisive. If we had a much more equal distribution of income, we would not be faced with cases in which very poor people are getting public services whose cost they would sooner take as cash.

Undeniably, public provision may be wasteful in the sense that, having decided that it should be provided, we think that more is being provided than it is worth our paying for collectively. I have suggested that, in this sense, a large part of the health care budget is wasted on desperate, hi-tech methods of keeping people alive for a last few weeks or months in a miserable state. Similarly, although those who are retarded for neurological reasons should certainly have more than the average amount spent on their education, at some point it would make sense to switch to compensating them directly for their lack of equal opportunity. The right-wing press in Britain also likes to pretend that many public sector activities are completely pointless. Rupert Murdoch's *Sunday Times* had a reporter waste public money by applying for sixty public-sector jobs. Since the reporter pretended to find the job descriptions either incomprehensible or too hilarious to be worth describing usefully, it is not possible to form a precise view of the value of some of these jobs. But it is hard to see why it would not be a good idea for a local authority to give somebody the job of devising policies to reduce smoking and to ensure the enforcement of existing ones. Similarly, it is not difficult to see why any public body (starting with the police force) might need an anti-racism officer. Some initiatives were rather imaginative. On a number of social indicators, the most deprived area in Britain is Knowsley, near Liverpool. I confess that I am unable to see why it should be so funny to appoint somebody to a job there working with 'problem fathers' and showing them how they might relate better to their children. Similarly, a 'food availability officer' (how comical!) is a reasonable public response to the problem I referred to in chapter 6, of the unavailability of healthy food in poor areas. And, given the baffling benefits system that I referred to in the last chapter, I do not see how anybody could doubt the value of a 'welfare rights officer' to advise people of their entitlements. An encouraging sign that public money is not being wasted is that this pseudo-applicant, whose incompetence was demonstrated by his inability to understand the jobs or their significance, was not offered any of them.[10]

The second question about the feasibility of social justice is whether the high levels of taxation needed to fund high-quality public services and the transfers necessary to give everyone an income above the poverty line would cause the economy to collapse. I shall take up three questions. First, would an increase in the total tax burden be ruinous? Second, would a severe reduction in net inequality remove incentives to work? And third, would a basic income pose specific problems for production?

As far as the first question is concerned, the total tax take varies widely among rich countries, which tend to stay in roughly the same rank order from year to year. In 2000, taxation as a share of GDP was estimated by the OECD to be 35 per cent in America and 41 per cent in Britain, leaving most Western European countries ahead, with Germany, the Netherlands, Italy, Austria, Belgium and Finland over 45 per cent, while Norway, France, Denmark and Sweden exceeded 50 per cent.[11] In 2003, the Treasury was taking 'quiet satisfaction' in Britain's taxes having been only 35.9 per cent of GDP in the previous year. Though low growth had held down tax receipts in the Eurozone countries, the same countries were still above Britain, with Sweden (outside the Euro) at the top with 50 per cent.[12] Despite the absurd monetary and fiscal rules of the Euro, the countries that spend more than Britain are still mostly better off, and have in the past had faster economic growth while a higher proportion of the GDP has gone into taxes.

A government committed to social justice would be deeply ashamed of having reduced the take in taxes and would be aiming to move as fast as possible up the league table to the Swedish level or beyond. It would be especially mortified at the fact that the share paid by business had also fallen, and that at a footling 7.1 per cent was lower than that in any other of the twelve EU countries.[13] Instead, 'the government claimed victory' over the CBI (Confederation of British Industry) in proving that Britain was a low tax country: clearly, the implications of this for all those living in poverty and suffering from poor public services were of no interest in comparison.[14] As far as the United States is concerned, the scope for spending more is almost unlimited, and the grim state of affairs described in this book is especially understandable when we recall how far the already hopelessly inadequate budget is biased towards internal and external repression. (The same is, to a smaller extent, also true in Britain.)

We can discard the problem of the share of taxes in GDP, though it may be worth leaving it with a remark that a country in which people are healthy and well educated and in which the state spends a lot of money on the infrastructure clearly has a headstart. The incentive argument for inequality has been quite successfully propagated by its beneficiaries and is widely believed. Yet there is little empirical support for it – provided, of course, that people do actually get paid for working. The best evidence from the United States suggests that higher taxes have little effect on work effort.[15] One reason is that there

are income effects that may make work more attractive as well as substitution effects that will tend to make leisure more attractive. People
'may have some target income in mind. They may have a house in a
particular area and a car in mind. They will work as long as it takes to
earn such an income. If the Chancellor [of the Exchequer] takes some
of their income away they may work even longer.'[16]

Robert Frank and Philip Cook, in their powerfully argued book
The Winner-Take-All-Society, show how high taxes on very high earnings 'would not reduce but actually increase economic efficiency!'[17]
This is because most very high earnings accrue to those who can bring
in a lot more money than others by being among a small group of
those who can add a lot to profits. This has always been true of film
stars, though it was less so when the grip of the Hollywood film
studios held down competition. But it has now spread far more
widely. Publishers are looking for the next blockbuster novel, and the
huge advances paid to the best prospects squeeze out worthy books
that would previously have been published. Television creates a
demand for super-leagues made up of elite football clubs, and these
are prepared to pay vast sums for a player who adds greatly to their
attractiveness to viewers. CDs concentrate royalties on a handful of
the best-known performers, whereas it would earlier have been possible for more musicians to make a living from personal performances. A day trader who is 1 per cent better than the person next
to him may now be worth a thousand times more as a result of electronic transactions and the enormous expansion of financial markets:
the ratio of dollars turned over in real trade to dollars turned over in
world financial markets has leapt from a ratio of 1:13 in 1979 to a
ratio of 1:65 now. These are all winner-take-all markets, which generate a huge gap between the winners and others who are almost as
good (in whatever way is relevant) but are far less well paid.

This is another illustration of the importance of positional goods.
Thus, to take a familiar example, what matters in a case fought under
the Anglo-American adversary system is not having a good lawyer
but having one better than the other side's. When a lot is at stake, it
is worth a firm's paying a lot to prevail. The top rates charged by tax
QCs (the elite barristers in the UK) have risen between 2001 and
2003 from £1,000 to £2,000 an hour, and 'a number of QCs specializ-
ing in tax, commercial law, and chancery (wills, property and trusts)
pocket as much as £2m a year'. The author of the survey stated the
classic positional goods explanation: that clients believe that it is
worth getting the best in 'bet-the-company' cases.[18]

Even if most of these very high earnings were taxed, the same
people would probably practise, but it would be even better for the

economy if some of these talents were redirected towards more socially useful occupations. Law is (like trading on the stock market) a zero-sum game, and the purposes of justice would be just as well served with well-matched advocates of less than superstar quality. But what is even worse than the misallocation of talent at the top is the misallocation of efforts to get to the top. Thus, as Frank and Cook say, 'our national income would be higher if some students abandoned their ambitions to become multimillionaire plaintiffs' attorneys in favour of the more modest but more predictable paychecks of electrical engineers'.[19] They call the excessive competition generated by a few jackpots 'overcrowding', and argue that 'the effect of higher taxes on these incomes would be to reduce the overcrowding problem'.[20] Ironically, then, the objection from the point of view of economic efficiency is that 'the relevant incentives in winner-take-all markets are often too large', producing waste through 'excessive entry and effort on the part of the contestants'.[21]

The huge rewards paid to chief executive officers and other top executives are justified as providing them with 'incentives'. In practice, however, the performance targets that have been declared are often adjusted downward if the company's shares fall, so that officers do not suffer as they were supposed to, or even gain. Coca-Cola's board, for example,

> set aside for [its new director, Douglas N. Daft] a million shares of stock, worth almost $60 million at the time, but said he could have them only if Coke's earnings per share grew at least 20 per cent a year over the five years beginning Jan. 1 2001. . . . Herbert Allen, the investor who was chairman of Coke's pay panel, praised the targets then as proof that executives and shareholders would prosper together or not at all. In April 2001, however, just four months into the five-year period, Mr Daft and the rest of Coke's management announced they would not meet the goal. The next month, the company's directors made sure that Mr Daft would not suffer financially because of the shortfall [by the simple expedient of lowering the target].

By the end of the year, Coke's stock had fallen 23 per cent while Mr Daft's pay rose by 47 per cent to $74.2 million.[22] The hollowness of the claim that large quantities of stock options provide incentives for top executives has been exposed by the lack of relation between the size of their holdings and the company's performance. If anything the effects of stock options are perverse, encouraging directors to push up the value of the shares artificially over one quarter, and then cash in and get out, rather than focus on the long-term future of the company.[23]

Finally, what about a basic income pitched at 60 per cent of average income? This seems very likely to lead to changes in the behaviour of the people whom we saw working grotesque hours that are at times harmful to their children. Mothers (even fathers) and other carers might well stay at home more, perhaps resulting in the proliferation of part-time jobs, since these would be the only way for employers to attract workers. All these seem to be desirable changes. But 60 per cent of the average income is not a lot. It is not likely to be an amount that anyone with the ability to get a decent job would settle for, so it would be surprising if many people would give up paid employment to pursue other goals. But those who did might well be performing valuable tasks in voluntary organizations or in innumerable other ways. Moreover, one of the advantages of a basic income is that it gives people a chance to drop out of paid employment for a time so as to work on getting some new qualification or simply expanding their intellectual horizons.

One idea that has been mooted is that the receipt of the basic income should be conditional on evidence of having engaged in one or more of a broadly defined list of valuable activities. This kind of 'participation income' would have the disadvantage of requiring some monitoring, but it would deal with the objection that some people would simply scrounge off the efforts of others, putting nothing back in return. The concept of 'rights and responsibilities' does have a genuine application here: it is quite reasonable that the right to a basic income as a citizen should be associated with a responsibility to the community.

What the effects of a poverty-level basic income would be can obviously only be speculative. But no country is going to introduce a basic income at that level straight off, so there would be plenty of time to observe incremental effects and fine-tune the next stage in the light of experience gained. The most likely way of getting to a basic income would be first to make the child benefit and the pension enough to live on without requiring any means-tested benefits. I have already argued that there are overwhelming reasons for doing this. The disabled, whose benefit level is now a disgrace in Britain, should also obviously be included. This would leave the able-bodied in between the two age limits, and the next stage might be a move over not too many years to 30 per cent of the median income, in other words half the full basic income. At this level, it would still need means-tested topping-up for those without other income. However, it could replace the Earned Income Tax Credit by putting a floor under everybody's earnings and would thus achieve at any rate some of the advantage of reducing the power of employers. They would simply have to pay enough to make it worthwhile to work, allowing for their employees already being halfway to the poverty line.

It is reasonable to suppose that a poverty level basic income supported by high and progressive taxes would reduce total production. But here I shall anticipate my next chapter and say that total production has to come down anyway. Under the present type of economic system, this would result in a large number of additional people becoming unemployed. Since jobs that have been transferred to lower-paid countries will in any case have continued to disappear, the prospect for a society without a basic income would be dismal. Yet there would still be plenty of things that people could do for one another that would be useful, but would not pay enough to count as paid employment in the conventional economy. With a basic income sufficient to keep everybody out of poverty, there would be no such problem. Nobody would be forced into idleness as the price of drawing unemployment benefit. Existing jobs could be spread around further, more low-paid but attractive jobs could be created (as I suggested in the previous chapter), the voluntary sector could expand and the burden of caring for an ageing population shared round more equitably.

The question that should be asked is: can we *not* afford social justice? By largely detaching income from employment, we can get off the treadmill mentality that tells us that we have to have economic growth simply to maintain employment levels. With much greater equality, we can cut back on the waste generated by feverish competition for a slight edge in education and jobs and the self-defeating effort inherent in the pursuit of goods for their positional value. We can also have a more peaceful society, as a result of the inclusiveness produced by the combination of income security and access on the same terms as everyone else to schools, hospitals, transport and all the other public services.

Once we recognize that we have reached the limits of production – indeed overstepped them to a degree that threatens the very survival of the human race – nobody can say that his being rich does not make anyone else poorer. In a finite world, everything that anyone has is something that others cannot have. Greed cannot be sanctified – as it has been since Adam Smith – by saying that it is in the longer run for the greater good of all. I can do no better than end this chapter by quoting what John Maynard Keynes wrote in 1930:

> When the accumulation of wealth is no longer of high social importance, there will be great changes in the code of morals. We shall be able to rid ourselves of many of the pseudo-moral principles which

have hag-ridden us for two hundred years, by which we have exalted some of the most distasteful of human qualities into the position of the highest virtues. We shall be able to afford to dare to assess the money-motive at its true value. The love of money as a possession – as distinguished from the love of money as a means to the enjoyments and realities of life – will be recognised for what it is, a somewhat disgusting morbidity, one of those semi-criminal, semi-pathological propensities which one hands over with a shudder to the specialists in mental disease. All kinds of social customs and economic practices, affecting the distribution of wealth and of economic rewards and penalties, which we now maintain at all costs, however distasteful and unjust they may be in themselves, because they are tremendously useful in promoting the accumulation of capital, we shall then be free, at last, to discard.[24]

Part VI

The Future of Social Justice

Say not, the struggle naught availeth,
The labour and the wounds are vain
The enemy faints not, nor faileth
And as things have been they remain.

If hopes were dupes, fears may be liars; . . .
Arthur Hugh Clough

17

The Power of Ideas

'A journey of a thousand miles', said Mao, 'begins with a single step.' But before even that first step can be taken, an essential condition has to be met. You have to want to set out on the journey. Perhaps you do not have much of an idea of the eventual destination: you may want to see how things go, and decide at each stage where to head for next. But you must at least have enough of an idea about the way ahead to have the confidence to believe that that first step will be in the right general direction. The failure of the left in America and Britain (which has nothing to do, of course, with whatever electoral successes the Democratic or Labour parties may have achieved) stems above all from the lack of any sense of purpose. It is not worth raising questions about progress until an articulate form is given to discontent with the status quo and the direction in which things are moving. People have to know that there is a rational, principled basis for dissatisfaction – outrage indeed – at what has been done and is being done to our societies and our world.

Where the left has failed, the right has succeeded to an extraordinary degree. The epicentre of right-wing propaganda is the United States, where a network of lavishly financed foundations, and the books and journals that they promote at enormous expense, have rationalized all the most mean-spirited impulses of affluent American whites. The real breakthrough can be traced to Charles Murray's *Losing Ground*, which argued that 'welfare' destroyed character, that it encouraged women (understood to be black women) to have children for the sake of drawing bigger welfare payments, and that it should be abolished.[1] Its success is undeniable, but what made this book so popular? And why, although its slipshod arguments have been exhaustively refuted by serious academics, has this criticism had virtually no public impact?

Murray's ability to stay one jump ahead of his critics dates right back to the launch of the book. An especially clever ploy was to hold a so-called 'seminar', which had the unusual feature that 'well-known columnists and other members of the media' were paid between $500 and $1,500 to participate. This was, in fact, 'simply a chance for Murray to sell his idea to the punditocracy without having to respond to difficult queries that might have been posed by a competent economist'.[2] But none of this would have done any good (nor would the thousands of free copies mailed out to other opinion-makers) unless the book's message had chimed in with what the pundits – who proceeded to sell the message in turn – wanted to hear. And they struck a responsive chord in their readers, for a reason that Murray himself explained with disarming frankness in his pitch to publishers: ' "Why can a publisher sell it?" he asked. "Because a huge number of well-meaning whites fear that they are closet racists, and this book tells them that they are not. It's going to make them feel better about things they already think but do not know how to say." '[3] Murray's next foray, *The Bell Curve*, completed the job and made racism itself respectable, if we take racism to consist in a belief in the genetic inferiority of blacks. This was equally well promoted, equally flawed, refuted with equal thoroughness and – for the same reasons as before – just as successful.

The left has one enormous advantage over the right: the case for radical change of the kind advocated in this book can be shown to flow from widely accepted premises without any need to indulge in obfuscation or lies. All that has to be done is to clarify the logical implications of the principles that people maintain they espouse and relate them to the facts. In contrast, the only honest case that can be made for the agenda of the right is that it suits the people who benefit from it very nicely. The left's advantage is offset, however, by the relative sophistication of its ideas. It is not only that they demand institutions that are more complex than those supported by crude pro-marketeers. More significantly in the present context, they also require a more complex understanding of society than do the nostrums of the right. Any fool can comprehend the notion that the rich are rich because of their personal merits, while the poor are poor because of their lack of merit. Of course, only a fool would believe it, but the truth of the matter cannot be conveyed without invoking the concept of a basic structure of society imposing strong constraints on the choices of people located in different positions within it. Only when this has been established does it become possible to advance the argument that a great deal of collective intervention in the market and its distributive outcomes is needed to bring about any semblance of the 'level playing field' that we all profess to believe in.

It is a commonplace of liberal thought that, in the long run, it is ideas and not interests that rule the world. Supposing this to be true, it does not necessarily have the comforting implications that are customarily drawn from it. It is assumed that, in the 'marketplace of ideas', good ideas will drive out bad, even if they run counter to vested interests. But what if that marketplace is so rigged that good ideas never get a hearing? What if the vested interests own the media, finance the hired guns such as Murray, and fill the airport bookshelves with superficially authoritative books? They can then establish the bounds of legitimate discourse about public policy on their own terms. And this is much more insidious than the kind of crude censorship practised by the Soviet state, which was apparent to everybody. There is, indeed, a 'hidden hand', but it is not the one that, according to Adam Smith, brings public benefits from competition. Rather, it is one that produces the appearance of competition without the substance.

The old quip (originally due, I believe, to George Bernard Shaw) that the only way of enjoying the freedom of the press is to own one has never been more apt. At the time of writing, three-quarters of the press in Britain is controlled by three men: Rupert Murdoch (*The Sun*, *The Times* and the *Sunday Times*), Lord Rothermere (*The Mail*) and Conrad Black (*The Telegraph*).[4] All these newspapers slant the news to suit the political agenda of their proprietors. Beneficiaries of injustice throughout history have realized that the best way of hanging on to their privileges is to divert hostility onto foreigners, and with various degrees of subtlety the message is put across in these newspapers that the United Kingdom is under constant siege from all kinds of outsider, epitomized by 'Europe'. The attempt to undermine support for the public services, an example of which I gave in the previous chapter, is also a staple. In the USA, a book entitled *The Media Monopoly* counted fifty companies that controlled the flow of media to the public in 1985; today the number is six.[5] Not all of them are, let it be conceded, as avowedly intended to sway public opinion as Rupert Murdoch's television and print media (including the Fox TV channel and the *New York Post*). But all are owned by individuals or corporations that have no interest in upsetting the apple cart.[6] There is little need for direct censorship because self-censorship becomes instinctive: '[T]he reporter, the editor, the producer, and the executive producer all understand implicitly that their jobs depend in part on keeping their corporate parents happy.'[7] Even the so-called

Public Broadcasting Service in America depends heavily on corporate sponsorship, in return for (relatively discreet) advertising and – more important – the ability to determine what gets broadcast. For example, a talk show, *Think Tank*, is hosted by a notorious hard-line conservative and largely funded by three of the major right-wing foundations.[8]

It is important to realize that the domination of radio talk shows by uncouth, rabid extremists, and the somewhat more civilized television panels in which four right-wingers sit around and reinforce one another's prejudices, would not have been possible until after 1987. Before this, the Federal Communications Commission's rules for the renewal of a licence depended on 'strict adherence to the . . . Fairness Doctrine as the single most important requirement of operation in the public interest'.[9] This required, as the US Supreme Court put it in upholding the doctrine, 'a free exchange of opposing views, with roughly equal time given to all sides, if demanded, on the public airwaves'.[10] The Reagan-appointed FCC repudiated any such notion explicitly: '[T]he perception of broadcasters as community trustees should be replaced by a view of broadcasters as marketplace participants.'[11] But there is no competitive market, thanks to successive moves by the FCC to permit ever greater concentration of ownership.[12]

The left is also weakened by the disarray of the trade union movement – fragmented, shrinking and even then increasingly representative of middle-class workers rather than those who are the poorest and most marginalized. These are almost completely non-unionized while forming an ever-larger proportion of the labour force as casualization and involuntary 'self-employment' become the preferred way of cutting costs. The long-term unemployed, the permanently disabled, the single mothers at home with their children – indeed, the young and the old except in as far as they form part of the concern of current union members – are left out altogether in the calculus of trade union leaders, to the extent that they focus solely on the protection of their members' interests. The American labour movement has not for a very long time (with a few exceptions) regarded it as a part of its function to articulate and publicize an alternative vision of society. The recrudescent ideology of individualism, with its concomitant implications that the members of a society owe nothing to one another and that personal merit determines success or failure, has thus had an unopposed hearing. Trade unions in Britain have, in contrast, seen themselves in the past as having a broad political role. Indeed, the Labour Party was founded as the political branch of the 'labour movement'.

Unfortunately, however, British trade unions have never appreciated that to play a political role they need to devote resources to developing a capacity for politically relevant analysis. This failure has had momentous consequences because the trade union movement now finds itself devoid of the means to provide a counterweight to the common ideology promoted by the press and the politicians. This could be done only if the TUC had invested in creating the kind of in-house expertise that is needed to sustain a more radical programme against the arguments that the government can so readily summon up. High-ranking civil servants would not have got where they are unless they had (or acted as if they had) the right beliefs, so they do not need to be cajoled into providing their political masters with appropriate briefings. This support can be topped up *ad lib* – at the taxpayers' expense – by the in-house collections of experts that the government maintains and by individual 'policy advisers'. All this is, of course, to leave out the adverse publicity that any radical idea will attract in either Britain or the USA, without any prompting from the government, from the right-wing think-tanks and the media.

To appreciate the culpability of the trade unions for the hegemony of right-wing ideas, it is instructive to contrast Britain and the USA with Sweden. There, the peak organization of the manual workers' unions, the LO, started in the 1930s to hire some of the best brains in the country to develop a comprehensive alternative to the commonplaces of pro-market ideology. In particular, it attracted a succession of brilliant economists who were able, by the sheer power of applied intellect, to orientate the whole public debate so that those who opposed their ideas were put on the defensive: the whole game was played in the other side's half of the field. In contrast, President Clinton's policy of 'triangulation' – which essentially amounted to getting elected as a Democrat and then behaving like a Republican – was directly responsible for the inability of the Democrats in Congress to mount any coherent opposition to even the most outrageous moves by the Bush administration to favour corporations and extremely rich individuals. Indeed, a number of Democrats persistently vote with the Republicans – quite sincerely in as far as they share their underlying beliefs. Nobody has suggested that taxes should actually be raised to pay for education, health care and enough money for everyone to live on decently, or that 'defence' spending should be cut drastically to help fund domestic programmes. Rather, the only argument has been about how much taxes should be cut and how much more money should be committed to the project of empire. That craven acceptance of the other side's agenda illustrates perfectly the triumph of the ideas of the right.

Similarly, what should already have become clear is that the whole premise underlying New Labour politics is the polar opposite of that on the basis of which the Labour Party was founded: that the interests of labour and capital are necessarily opposed to one another and the Labour Party's job is to support those of labour. At the Annual Dinner of the Confederation of British Industries, Tony Blair presented his credentials by pledging himself to 'a good climate for business and a tax system which rewards success'.[13] He also boasted that 'it is this government, this New Labour government, that has cut capital gains tax further than ever before. We have been listening to business'.[14] And listening to good effect: 'Business leaders recognize that what New Labour is saying fits exactly with current thinking in industry.'[15] I mentioned earlier that the Labour Party was originally conceived of as the political wing of the labour movement, and, whatever its failings, it at least knew which side it was supposed to be on.

An instructive contrast: one of the highest priorities of the 1945 Labour government, pressed from within the Cabinet by Ernest Bevin (the Transport and General Workers' Union boss) was 'decasualization'. The most notorious example of casual labour was the way in which dockworkers stood around in pens every morning waiting to see if they would be picked for work that day or would have to go back home with no pay. There is no difference between this and 'zero-hours' employment – a perfectly legal device – which is an entirely one-sided contract: people hold themselves ready to be called in for work at short notice and are paid only for the hours they actually work. Substituting the telephone for physical presence makes the process invisible but even more servile, because at least a docker knew at a set time whether the rest of the day was (albeit involuntarily) his or not. In the bad old days before the pursuit of profit was allowed to become so completely untrammelled by any considerations of decency or humanity, people had proper employment contracts that guaranteed a weekly wage for a certain number of hours of work, and it was up to the management to operate within this constraint. This is precisely the kind of thing that New Labour denounces in the name of 'flexibility'.

The dominance of two major parties in Britain and the USA is a fact, and so is their ideological similarity. This has a disastrous effect on the scope of public debate because the result is that ideas outside the tiny range spanned by the parties scarcely get a look-in. On the continent, with its multi-party systems, the defection of Social Democrats from the pursuit of social justice has less pernicious effects because there are other political parties, with more radical platforms, and these parties are capable of gaining votes, sometimes seats, and sometimes even a share in government. A remarkable illustration of the effects of this proliferation of parties bidding for the votes of disillusioned Social Democrats was the elimination of Lionel Jospin, the Socialist candidate, in the first round of the French presidential elections in 2003. Many people who would have gritted their teeth and voted for him in the second ballot, on the assumption that the choice would lie between him and Chirac, expressed their dissatisfaction with the government that he had led by giving their votes to other parties on the first round. In the end, it turned out that so many did so that Jospin failed to come in second and, as a result, to qualify for the second ballot.

Even where there are relatively few parties, Greens have seats in some national legislatures, Norway has its Left Socialists, and so on. In contrast, dissident voices are silenced by the two-party system in the United States, which is stabilized against third-party threats by the first-past-the-post system (still also maintained in Britain, despite promises of reform), and the deliberate creation by state legislatures of safe seats in the House of Representatives for members of both parties. In the 2002 presidential election, Ralph Nader was completely shut out of the televised presidential debates, in spite of polls showing that he had a substantial following. Moreover, the United States is 'alone among 146 countries, according to one study, in refusing to provide free television time to political candidates'.[16] Furthermore:

> a key provision [in proposals for campaign finance reform in 2002] that would have forced the networks to offer candidates their least expensive advertising rates [was] originally passed by the Senate by a 69 to 31 margin, [but] died in the House of Representatives following a furious campaign by the National Association of Broadcasters and the cable television industry.[17]

Nader's opportunity to get his message across was minuscule compared to that of the major parties, with their large contributions from corporations and rich individuals. Even so, and despite the fact that many people who would have voted for Nader in a two-ballot or preferential system felt constrained to vote for Gore, he obtained significant numbers of votes in some states. Perhaps equally significantly, 'he robbed the Democratic Party of much of its activist base', illustrating the discontent of many activists with 'New Democratic' policies.[18] In a system with multi-member constituencies – and any of the methods currently in use for turning votes into seats – there would without doubt be Green Party members of the House of Representatives from the states in which Nader showed the most strength. This would make it far harder for the media to ignore the Green agenda.

In Britain, the Liberal Democrats have a presence in Parliament, but function primarily as the alternative to the Conservatives in much of the south and west of England, differing little from Labour on socioeconomic issues though more concerned with civil rights. The necessity of gaining a plurality in a single constituency eliminates the possibility of minority positions such as that of the Greens being represented; all the other parties in the House of Commons are territorially based: regional (Scottish and Welsh nationalists) or regional/communal (parties in Northern Ireland). And as long as most Labour and Liberal voters are prepared to vote for whichever candidate has the best chance of beating the Conservative, the Labour and Liberal Democratic parties themselves are in effect regional parties, as I have already suggested.

In contrast to the United States, Britain still has a rule that the broadcast media should be 'impartial'. However, this in practice means only that the positions of the two major parties (with an occasional sound-bite from the Liberal Democrats) should be covered. It is not taken to mean that the full spectrum of positions held by well-supported organizations such as Greenpeace or the RSPCA have to be heard, or that anti-government trade union leaders (representing millions of members) must have a voice. This would not be so stultifying if the parties were themselves pluralistic, since even the official understanding of 'impartiality' would require the airing of some range of ideas. Margaret Thatcher realized how she could make this work to her advantage by smiling upon (without actually endorsing) reports from right-wing think-tanks advocating more extreme developments of the themes of marketization and privatization – in the schools, the hospitals, the prisons, the civil service and anywhere else that human ingenuity (divorced from common sense) could contrive to push them. As she correctly calculated, the wilder the proposals that could be got into the arena of public discourse, the more the 'middle ground' would shift to the right. She could then adopt policies that were in fact very extreme while leaving everybody relieved that she had not accepted other proposals that were even more batty. Of course, Labour could do the same thing in reverse by stimulating and giving favourable attention to proposals far to the left of its own positions. But the non-right-wing think-tanks tend to look only at technical adjustments to the status quo, and the only permissible speculations are those that involve more extreme versions of New Labour policies.

A highly instructive episode occurred when Peter Hain, the Leader of the House of Commons, let the *Daily Mirror* publish part of a draft speech calling for 'a grown up and honest debate on tax', and Tony Blair took time out from an EU summit meeting in Salonika to phone him up and tell him to take it out. The passage that replaced it in the final draft of the lecture can only have been dictated by Blair himself and obviously came straight from the heart:

> Let me make it clear, as the Prime Minister has done today [i.e. on the telephone]. We will not raise the top rate of tax and there is no going back to the old days of punitive tax rates to fund reckless spending. In fact, income tax has fallen under Labour.[19]

Hain had not even made any concrete proposals, merely called for the subject to be openly discussed within the Labour Party. And his main idea appears to have been not to increase taxation or shift it away from low-income taxpayers, but to raise the threshold of the present 40 per cent tax rate, on the ground that it 'now catches far too many middle income employees, including teachers and police officers.'[20] The only way of funding the loss from this would be, he cautiously put it, for 'those at the very top of the pay scale contributing more'.[21] Getting more from the very rich to help those in the middle (actually those well above median earnings) is scarcely a revolutionary notion, but it 'had broken New Labour's great tax taboo', and that was enough to make Blair incandescent with rage.[22] The replacement that he made up, with the incantation of 'punitive taxation' (a notion whose nonsensical nature I pointed out in chapter 1) and its presupposition that any additional public spending must be 'reckless', could equally well have come from the lips of Margaret Thatcher in her heyday.

It is easy to understand the dynamics of a situation in which the official New Labour line (to which everyone has to adhere) is fanatically opposed to any hint of higher income tax rates, while the Conservatives are happy with the inheritance of Margaret Thatcher's tax system but make noises from time to time about lowering taxes. As two social scientists have said: 'By moving the centre ground of public opinion to the right, Mr Blair has also moved it closer to the ideology of the Conservatives.'[23] Thus, the twentieth report of the British Social Attitudes Survey published in 2003 found that 'between 1996 and 2002, Conservative attitudes to redistribution stayed much the same, with about one fifth in favour, whereas Labour support dropped from 58% to 49%.'[24] Perhaps we should, if anything, be surprised that seven years of a debate with only one side represented has not had a greater effect.

Precisely the same dynamic has been at work for many years now in the United States. I have already illustrated the process with the case of Charles Murray. More generally, 'conservatives have spent billions during the past decade, both to pressure the mainstream media to move rightward and to create their own parallel media structure, which serves the same purpose as it provides an alternative viewpoint both to the faithful and the gullible'.[25] What is crucial here is that this elaborate structure of extreme right broadcast and print media, interlocking and mutually reinforcing, 'is considered to be one of two – or perhaps two and a half – legitimate poles in the spectrum of American media discourse. Its power of gravity pulls the center rightward and leaves liberals off in outer space.'[26] Indeed, in the paranoid world that these zealots have created, it is now claimed to be an act of treason to raise critical questions about American institutions at home and American policy abroad. Liberals (in the American sense) are not just in outer space: they have been defined as aliens.

This is all pretty gloomy. Can anything more be said? I shall show in the following chapters that there is much more to be said. The news is highly unsettling. But what it shows is that, whatever may happen in the future, the one thing it cannot be is a continuation of the status quo.

18

How Change Happens

Hopes would certainly be dupes if they depended on the belief that a sudden revelation will bring about the kinds of change called for by justice. But a book about social justice, as I suggested in chapter 1, would not be worth writing if its ambitions were circumscribed by the demands of 'political relevance', taking that to mean that it cannot be devoted to anything except putting forward a few technical fixes of the status quo. As Philippe Van Parijs has written:

> If a carriage is stuck in the mud and you want to get it moving in the right direction, the best policy is rarely to make everybody scrape under the wheels or push at the back. Some people should pull ropes some distance ahead, while others investigate routes further ahead.[1]

The power of the ideology that I depicted in the previous chapter cannot be denied. But no more can the inexorable forces that make the continuation of 'business as usual' totally impossible. Scarcely anybody denies the existence of resource depletion, population growth and global warming. But nowhere near so many people are aware of the size of threat they pose or of the scale and rapidity of the response that will be required to prevent the human race from reaching the point of no return. I shall lay out the facts, as I have come to understand them, in the next chapter. These are the basis for well-founded fears, and those who belittle them are liars. But in the chapter that follows, which concludes the book, I shall argue that they provide some reason for hope. This is because the only steps that would be adequate to come to terms with the threat would unavoidably enhance the cause of justice both in the world as a whole and within individual countries.

The power of ideas – in this case alternatives to the prevailing ideology – can be driven by a sense of crisis.

> We may yet change course, and looking into the abyss may be just the motivation we need. But we're not going to make it unless we set off, quite explicitly, to build a fair world. In this sense, global warming is as much an opportunity as it is a threat. . . . The global-warming crisis is big enough to get our attention and, perhaps, to focus our minds, but it's nevertheless small enough to deal with. . . . All we have to do is face the facts.[2]

That the facts cannot fail to have radical implications for action is well understood by George W. Bush. On the tenth anniversary of the historic Earth Summit held in Rio in 1992, the world's leaders reassembled in Johannesburg to review progress (actually, regress) on stabilizing the environment, but Bush announced that he was not going to attend. It was explained by a spokesman that the summit's agenda 'strikes at the core values of the President'.[3] This may have been more revealing than intended. At any rate, the President's priorities were exhibited by the alternative use he made of the time: hosting a meeting of the most hawkish members of his entourage 'to discuss war on Iraq and other military adventures'.[4]

When he assumed office, Bush announced that he was repudiating the Kyoto Treaty on restricting greenhouse gas emissions because 'the science is uncertain'. He then asked the National Academy of Science to answer a series of questions which he undoubtedly hoped would take them several years to answer. Unfortunately for this ploy, the Academy fired back a report saying that the answers were already known, thanks to the prodigious efforts over many years of the International Panel on Climate Change (IPCC), sponsored by the United Nations, which brings together 'thousands of scientists from around the world in a tightly focused process designed to provide continually updated assessments of the threat, the science that allows us to know the threat, and the uncertainties of that science'.[5] Bush was therefore forced to concede that 'the National Academy of Sciences indicates that the [temperature] increase is due in large part to human activity'.[6] In fact the models used by the IPCC can fully explain the amount of global warming that has occurred, and very likely (as we shall see) underestimate the future amount. Bush's admission was, however, quickly left behind. The administration excised a 28-page section on climate change from an Environmental Protection Agency report, and the Agency has now decreed that carbon dioxide from industrial emissions – the main cause of global warming – is not a pollutant . . . The Bush administration appears to be guided by a memo by the political consultant Frank Luntz. 'Should the public believe that the scientific issues are settled, their views about global warming will change accordingly. Therefore, you need to make the lack of scientific certainty a primary issue in the debate', it said.[7]

This strategy is characteristic of the Bush administration, not only on global warming, but also on other issues awkward for its corporate sponsors such as workplace injuries and obesity.

More than 60 of the nation's top researchers, including 20 Nobel laureates, signed a report in late February 2004 charging that the Bush administration has misrepresented scientific findings . . . to support its policies. The report, published by the Union of Concerned Scientists, also recounted unusual steps by the administration to block appointments of qualified scientists to advisory panels because the candidates opposed the president's policies.[8]

The key is, again, Luntz's memo, in which he wrote: 'The scientific debate is closing [against us] but not yet closed. There is still a window of opportunity to challenge the science.'[9] It is not necessary to make the challenge plausible: the point is simply that the allegation of uncertainty provides an excuse for inaction.

So nervous was the Bush administration in the run-up to the 2004 election that it sent out 'a remarkable email to all Republican congressmen' advocating 'an age-old political tactic to deal with the tricky subject of global warming – deny, and deny aggressively. . . . It tells them how global warming has not been proved, air quality is "getting better", the world's forests are "spreading not deadening" . . . and the "world's water is cleaner and reaching more people."'[10] All of these assertions, as we shall see in the next chapter, are the exact opposite of the truth.

What I find immensely encouraging, however, is the level of concern among Bush's campaign managers about the dangerous potential of the truth. I believe that they are right to worry. There is already in existence an impressive network of organizations inspired by the conviction that things are going badly wrong. Susan George, for many years a writer of influential books on world inequality and its causes, has described the Global Justice Movement as 'a movement of popular education directed towards action'.[11] But people join it in the first place, she suggests, because of something as basic as a feeling that 'the bastards have gone too far'.[12] Or, as George Monbiot, another writer and activist, puts it: 'I think the great majority of people who have joined the movement started off with a vague sense that something was wrong, not necessarily being able to put their finger on what it was.'[13] The power of ideas is to convert an inchoate sense of anxiety into the pursuit of a concrete set of proposals.

The only way in which we can speculate fruitfully about the future is by consulting the past. It is true that we are facing an unprecedented situation, but all the major crises in history have been unprecedented to some degree or another. The current situation is not wholly without precedents from which we may be able to draw some useful lessons. The closest and most recent parallel is provided by the 1930s and '40s. Capitalism was discredited (even in the eyes of its remaining beneficiaries) by its performance, and was widely perceived as not only financially but also morally bankrupt. Then, as now, there were two alternative futures open. One – which appeared most likely at the time – was that Nazism and Fascism would sweep over the whole of Europe while the Japanese 'greater co-prosperity sphere' would extend to the whole of Asia. The United States (and probably Canada) would stay out of it, and in the rest of the Americas populist authoritarianism would spread out from Mexico and Argentina.

There were good reasons for expecting Britain and France to make a deal with Hitler. The best occasions for making a stand against him – his reoccupation of the Rhineland and his invasion of Czechoslovakia – had already been passed up. In Spain, the counterpart of 'appeasement' was 'neutrality' between the legitimate government and Franco's insurrection. This left the Germans and Italians free to supply Franco with equipment and try out the technique of terror bombing (on Guernica and other towns), while on the Republican side only the Soviet Union supplied any military aid, and that was of an order of magnitude less in quantity and quality. In Germany, capitalists had thrown in their lot with Hitler as their surest defence: why would not their counterparts in the remaining independent countries do the same?

In the event, a British government able and willing to resist was formed, and held on long enough for the United States to join the same side. And victory did not recreate the pre-war status quo but produced governments of the left in Britain and France. Even where this did not occur, the institutions characteristic of the post-war 'welfare state' were created, though each country built on its own earlier systems of provision. Thus, if there is any lesson to be learned, it is that a crisis will be resolved in a way that either smashes social justice completely or moves it a decisive step nearer to realization.

There was no inevitability, however, in the way in which the defeat of the Axis powers led to the election of a Labour government in Britain. In fact, most people expected that gratitude to Winston Churchill would put the Conservatives back in power. Moreover, in the last election before the war, in 1935, the Conservatives had had a very large majority, so a Labour victory would require an enormous swing. Why, then, did Labour in fact win by a large majority? The war created experiences that unavoidably had an unsettling effect on existing beliefs. The chances of war (whether or not you were bombed out as a civilian and where you were sent as a conscript) made dramatic the absurdity of the notion that how people fared depended on their own choices – a justification for the status quo as potent before the war as it has become again now. In the desperate struggle for survival, it was impossible not to realize the inefficiency, as well as the inequity, of a system that put boobies from public schools in charge of seasoned non-commissioned officers who had the 'wrong' class background.

All this, however, would by itself still have led only to 'a vague sense that something was wrong'. Crystallizing it into support for Labour occurred through a chain of events that started with the creation of the Left Book Club by the publisher Victor Gollancz in the 1930s. Subscribers received books bound in distinctive orange covers at regular intervals. These adopted a 'popular front' position, a broad church that could include Clement Attlee, the Labour leader, and those who (not unreasonably, given the Spanish situation) saw the Soviet Union as the only bulwark against Fascism and Nazism.

The second stage consisted in the role of the Education Corps in the Second World War. If members of the armed services (whatever their politics) were almost the only people not surprised by Labour's success, it was partly due to the line pursued consistently in the pamphlets put out by the Army Education Corps. It could be said that the Education Corps had a captive audience, but it was not in any position to engage in brainwashing: it had to persuade by starting from premises acceptable to its audience and then showing what conclusions they led to, taking into account the relevant facts. Schoolmasters must have made up a large part of the Corps, and one of them deposited a more or less complete cache of its pamphlets in the library of my grammar school. I have not needed to return to them, because the only point I want to draw from them is the one that impressed me at around the age of 15: how to do it. The strategy that I have tried to follow in this book is the one that I absorbed then.

You could not coherently criticize the German and Italian governments for denying liberty, equality and democracy to their own peoples without recognizing that Britain fell far short of the ideals being appealed to. The lesson to be learned is that those who are intent on establishing the acceptability of proposals for change should always seek to show that these proposals flow from principles that are implicit in positions that their interlocutors already hold. Thus, for example, it is extraordinarily hard to deny in the twenty-first century that racial discrimination practised by the police, the office of the Director of Public Prosecutions, the prison service and other public institutions is anything but abhorrent. Even newspapers that pander to the basest prejudices of their readers are not quite able to deny that. Instead, they claim (in the face of all evidence) that racial discrimination is not a systematic phenomenon – any such idea is 'political correctness' gone mad, their columnists thunder. The problem is merely one of a few 'rotten apples'. Another favourite move is to interview disaffected police officers – who obviously do not belong in the contemporary police force – and get them to say that 'morale' will suffer if they are liable to be disciplined for racist slurs or harassment and are made to report in detail on the circumstances of every 'sus' stop (interrogating somebody in the street on the basis of 'suspicion'), with details of the ethnic identity of the person involved.

The 'efficiency' of the police force, editorials warn their readers, is being undermined by busybodies, in other words top-ranking policemen who are taking the problem of racism seriously. But what could 'efficiency' mean in this context? How can we say that a police force is 'efficient' at doing its job if its members are free to employ racist epithets, make racially discriminatory use of their discretionary powers and refuse to make timely and strenuous efforts to investigate attacks (even fatal ones) on members of racial minorities? Only, it appears to me, if 'efficiency' is defined implicitly as looking after the interests of the kind of people who read such newspapers. But this simply amounts to reintroducing by the back door the legitimacy of racist behaviour by the police.

As well as appealing to premises that it was awkward to reject, the Education Corps employed a strategy that could be called 'letting the facts speak for themselves'. Of course, the facts never really speak for themselves: they always have to be interpreted against a background of assumptions that give them significance. For example, faced with the data on the scale of inequality in the distribution of wealth and income and the unequal quality of education, health care, and housing, somebody might simply draw the inference that there are a hell of a lot of lazy and feckless people around. It could not plausibly be denied that the carrots dangled in front of the most successful people in countries such as Britain and the USA have now been made so juicy that they must motivate anybody with a disposition towards greed. It does not follow that the carrots are juicy at the bottom: as I have observed, poor people face high marginal tax rates because of the level at which benefits are withdrawn if they acquire any other income. But then it is still possible (if that is the answer you want to reach) to conclude that the sticks are still not sharp enough to drive the rest of the population along the desired path. This leads logically to coercion – the 'work-welfare' system normal in the nineteenth century and now the great enthusiasm of the 'modernizers' in Britain and the USA. But it does not require a great deal of context-setting to draw people to the perception that inequalities of the kind I have mentioned cannot come about on the basis of freely made choices from fair opportunities.

If we ask what facts about the current situation can provide an impetus towards both global and domestic justice, there are three candidates that seem to me to stand out. First, there is the lethal cocktail of renewable resource depletion, population growth and global warming that the Bush campaign would like to wish out of existence. Second, the way in which the entire set of rules governing the international system works in the interests of the rich countries is by now well understood, and is at last meeting coherent resistance from the governments of poor countries. But this system does not spread the gains equally among those in the rich countries: on the contrary, most of the benefits accrue to the owners of capital. Others in the rich countries have a stake in curbing the mobility of capital and muzzling the threat of capital flight. Third, and generalizing this last theme, there exists a basis for a move towards greater social justice within both rich and poor countries. In some relatively poor countries, such as Brazil and Argentina, parties of the moderate left have won elections partly as a response to IMF policies, but also because internal inequalities are intolerable. In the rich countries, there is a widespread feeling that the economic system is corrupt, though this awaits mobilization.

Why, in this context, does social justice matter? It plays four roles, I suggest. The first, to which I referred at the beginning of this chapter, is that unless a programme can be crystallized around a coherent set of principles it is liable to become a mere shopping list, no more than the sum of a lot of sectional demands. The second important role of the idea of social justice is that it is capable of motivating people in a way that a demand put forward simply on the basis of interest is not. In particular, it helps to overcome the problem that, even if each of the members of a large group recognizes that some comprehensive change would be beneficial to all of them, that is not sufficient to make it in any single person's interest to make sacrifices to achieve it. Only when demands – for trade unions, for women to have the vote, for civil rights for blacks in the South, for example – are infused with a sense that justice is at stake do they achieve political weight.

Third, I need hardly point out that a sense of justice can motivate people who do not expect to gain personally from its realization. The anti-Apartheid movement, in which so many people outside South Africa participated, is a stirring example. The Civil Rights Movement in America also, of course, owed a lot to whites who knew they were risking life and limb to take part. An extension of this role of the idea of social justice – my fourth point – is that, once change has occurred, those who opposed it – or at least their descendants – have repeatedly exhibited a pattern of coming to accept that the new situation is just. Hardly any whites in the South thought slavery was wrong while it existed, as far as we can tell, yet I doubt if it now has even private defenders. In recent decades, opinion about legally enforced segregation seems to have shifted in a rather similar way. Votes for women was a demand that was still regarded as outlandish by a large majority of men (and a substantial minority of women) as recently as the early years of the twentieth century, yet it is now accepted as a totally commonplace implication of elementary justice. Similarly, colonialism was widely accepted (even by parties of the left) as unproblematic until the 1960s yet it would now find few defenders. Thus, a conception of social justice can stabilize changes even if they were originally brought about in the face of resistance that was thought to be morally justified.

19

Meltdown?

It is quite possible that by the year 2100 human life will have become extinct or will be confined to a few residual areas that have escaped the devastating effects of nuclear holocaust or global warming on a scale that has in the past wiped out almost all existing life forms. The standing threat to survival posed by nuclear weapons is all too familiar. I shall therefore pause here only to remark that a number of moves by the Bush Administration have greatly increased the probability of nuclear war. The contrast between the treatment of Iraq and North Korea sends an obvious message to every government in the world that it had better acquire nuclear weapons as fast as possible. And the Administration's repudiation of the ABM (antiballistic missile) Treaty, together with its avowed intention to dominate space so as to strike at any target without warning, can be construed only as an effort to insulate America against retaliation for destroying more countries by remote control.

At the time of writing, the outcome of the 2004 election is still in the future. But it would be foolish to imagine that much good can come of an election in which a large part of the Democratic candidate's pitch is that service in Vietnam makes him more qualified as a military leader than fighting an illegal war on the basis of fraudulent claims. The wheels are already beginning to fall off the project for making the twenty-first century 'the American century'. But it will not be repudiated, regardless of the identity of the White House's occupant. The only question is whether the undermining of international constraints on American freedom of action will be pursued relatively subtly (as by Clinton) or crudely. In many ways, the first is more dangerous because it makes the organization of international resistance more difficult.

For the purpose of this chapter, I shall focus on the threats I referred to in the previous one: resource depletion, overpopulation and global warming. Although renewable resources – especially fossil fuels – are often thought of as a serious problem, it is the exploitation of existing economically accessible reserves that will be catastrophic, rather than their exhaustion. Coal reserves would create more than 600 billion metric tonnes of carbon if burned, oil reserves more than 200 billion and natural gas just under 200: around 1,000 billion tonnes altogether.[1] Greenpeace, which advocates an attempt to keep global warming down to 1°C above its historic average, calculated in 1997 that this might be achieved only by burning less than a quarter of these reserves – ever – so that the rest would have to stay in the ground.[2] Given the havoc already wrought by a rise of 0.6°C, a rise of 1°C sounds like a prudent target. But it is now widely believed that things have already gone a lot too far for global warming to be checked at that level. The most recent estimates of the impact of atmospheric carbon dioxide on global warming (which I shall discuss shortly) suggest that even keeping global warming down to 2°C will be extraordinarily difficult to achieve and may also already be out of reach. The conclusion therefore remains: even keeping global warming down to three times its present level will require most of the economically exploitable fossil fuel reserves already discovered to stay in the ground.

The really bad news concerns what is happening to the soil, the oceans and sources of fresh water. The World Wildlife Fund's *Living Planet Report 2002* estimated that world consumption was 20 per cent above the earth's biological capacity, and that 'future projections based on likely scenarios of population growth, economic development and technological change' made it likely that consumption would amount to between 180 per cent and 220 per cent of the earth's biological capacity by the year 2050. 'Of course, it is very unlikely that the Earth would be able to run an ecological overdraft for another 50 years without some severe ecological backlashes undermining future population and economic growth. But it would be far better to control our own destiny than leave it to nature.'[3] To give a bit of reality to these figures, 'seventy per cent of the drylands used for agriculture – nearly a third of the world's land area – is threatened by being turned into desert. . . . The amount of agricultural land available for each person in developing countries has declined from 0.79 acres in the early 1960s to 0.51 acres and is expected to reach 0.39 acres by 2030', due to increased degradation of the soil and population growth.[4]

Once we factor in global warming, the prospects become far worse:

> Seas will rise by half a meter by 2080 purely on account of the fact that warmer water takes up more volume. But if we add on the probability of significant melting of ice sheets in Greenland and the potential destabilization of the Western Antarctic Ice Sheet, the rise would be considerably higher. A 3-foot or 1-meter rise would put paid to a full third of the world's croplands.[5]

The productivity of land not threatened by inundation will also be drastically reduced by global warming. The summer of 2003, with two hot dry months in northern Europe, reduced average EU grain production by 10 per cent but had far more severe effects further east: 75 per cent down in the Ukraine, an important producer, and 80 per cent in Moldova.[6] The amount of grain produced per person in the world is less than at any time in the past three decades (thus wiping out the 'green revolution') and stocks are at their lowest since records have been kept. 'Experts predict that the damage to crops will be even greater when the full cost of the heat is known. And they warn that this is just a foretaste of what will happen as global warming takes hold.'[7]

The oceans are in no better shape – a result of overfishing, exacerbated by immensely destructive methods of fishing that have been developed. For example, the use of dragnets can kill eight pounds of discarded fish for every pound of shrimp caught in the Gulf of Mexico, thus destroying the entire ecology of the region.[8] Overall, 'the magazine *Nature* . . . reported that 90 per cent of large fish stocks had been removed worldwide', and in many areas there are 'virtually no reproductive fish around', leading to a proposal for a complete ban on fishing in a third of the world's oceans.[9] Again, global warming is already giving a foretaste of its potential for making things a lot worse, with the result that even where conservation efforts are undertaken they are liable to be nullified. 'The North Atlantic . . . has less than 20 per cent of the fish it held in 1900.'[10] But in addition to the legacy of overfishing, 'the North Sea is undergoing "ecological meltdown" as a result of global warming, according to startling new research. Scientists say that we are witnessing a "collapse of the system", with devastating implications for fisheries and wildlife.'[11] The basic explanation for this is that cold-water plankton, whose incidence has been monitored for more than seventy years, have been driven hundreds of miles further north and replaced by 'smaller, warm-water species that are less nutritious.'[12] Despite a big reduction in fishing quotas, therefore, stocks of young cod are still at their lowest for twenty years.[13]

What happens in the oceans is important, but fresh water is an irreplaceable source of life. Where (as often occurs) rivers cross frontiers, we are already seeing severe conflicts arising between countries about the amount of water those upstream impound and how much they release for the use of those downstream. As Michael Klare observes in *Resource Wars*:

> [C]onflict over water has, in fact, been a feature of human behavior throughout history. In the Old Testament, for example, it is recorded that the Israelites could not enter the 'promised Land' – the fertile valleys of the Jordan River basin – until they expelled its original inhabitants.[14]

Plus ça change! To reverse the familiar saying, those who cannot forget the past are doomed to repeat it – with incalculable political consequences. ' "Water for Israel is not a luxury," former prime minister Moishe Sharett once asserted . . . "Water is life itself." '[15] The obvious implication is that water should be shared equitably, with everybody's fundamental needs satisfied before anybody enjoys an abundance. Few countries have accepted this elementary principle, least of all Israel.

Although a number of countries have threatened to go to war over water, the one clear case in which control over water was

> a factor in igniting . . . full-scale conflict [was] the Six Day War of 1967, when the Arab League, angered at Israel's construction of its National Water Carrier, which had appropriated much of the water of the Jordan River for use in Israel, began to dig canals to divert two Jordan tributaries. . . . Israelis immediately shelled and destroyed both projects. The attacks by Syria, Egypt and Jordan that eventually followed had many causes, but water remained a priority for both sides. Before it ended, Israel had blown up a dam that Syria had been constructing on the Yarmouk River and annexed the Golan Heights; it took the West Bank of the Jordan, along with one-third of the Kingdom's most fertile land; and it seized from Egypt both Gaza and the Sinai Peninsula.[16]

Significantly, the only area that was not an additional source of water supply was the Sinai, which it relinquished relatively early.[17] Since then, the inequitable sharing of water has reached quite amazing proportions. 'At the mercy of Israel on the Jordan, and Syria on the Yarmouk, the people of Jordan have less water than any place in the Middle East.'[18] In the Occupied Territories:

[M]any villages, without any water supply, are forced to collect occasional rainwater in cisterns and barrels or to wait for deliveries from trucks. In recent years, the lack of water has shriveled Arab farms in the West Bank. Now less than 4 per cent of these farms are irrigated. Wells here are drying up because Israeli settlers' deep wells and powerful pumps drain the water while Palestinians are forbidden to dig new wells or even deepen old ones. In the words of one Palestinian, 'No one can accept that he does not have water to drink and his neighbor has a swimming pool.'[19]

Conflict can only become more intense as population expands (much of it in water-poor areas) while salination and pollution destroy more supplies of usable water. Continued (and probably accelerating) warming will create more evaporation. More importantly, the further breakdown of the systems that shift the atmosphere and the oceans around the globe will greatly exacerbate the unreliability of the seasonal rainfalls upon which many people rely for harvests. 'Some 261 large rivers pour from one nation into another', and disputes over the waters of the Nile and of the Tigris and Euphrates area are already straining relations to breaking point.[20]

It has been impossible to discuss the impact of resource depletion without already bringing in population growth and global warming. Let me now address these explicitly. As far as population is concerned, the most recent 'median variant' figure of the United Nations puts it at 9.3 billion in 2050 and still growing.[21] Some of this increase, ruinous to the future of the planet as it will be, is almost unavoidable. For while, in the affluent countries, population tends to be stable or (in the absence of immigration) declining slightly, this means that an increasing proportion of the world's population is in poor countries. And many of these have had such a rapid growth over recent decades that half of their populations are currently under the age of 15. If, starting tomorrow, every fertile woman in these countries had two children who survived their first year (i.e. less than the long-run replacement rate), their populations would still increase greatly before eventually stabilizing and then falling. Short of the universal adoption of the Chinese one-child-per-woman policy in all countries with rising populations, there are only three plausible ways in which the world population will fail to grow: the classic triad of war, pestilence and famine. These will have to carry off billions of people to bring the population back to its current level or below. We are adding 'ninety million people a year. Think of a million lives lost in a famine or war – those numbers are replaced in four days.'[22]

However, if the population does stabilize, the experience of wealthy countries shows that the same forces will continue working to bring it down. As recently as 1830, world population was only one billion, and it then took until 1930 to climb to two billion. The main reason for the small number of years now between each further increase of a billion (the last took twelve years) is, of course, that any given rate of increase will add a billion faster the larger the population is to begin with.[23] But the same logic of compound interest works equally well on the downward slope. It may be too optimistic to hope to get back to a world population of a billion in less than two hundred years. But the closer to it the human race gets, and the quicker, the less pressure it will put on the environment and the greater the chances of human life surviving over the thousands of years that may still be just within the realm of possibility.

I have already touched on pestilence and famine, and I talked at the beginning of this chapter about war. Barring major catastrophes, then, world population will continue to grow. But it would be an error with incalculable consequences to be fatalistic: far below the projected number I cited, population growth could be stopped and reversed. I shall discuss solutions (and their implications for justice) in the next chapter. But it is worth making it clear here that liberal rights do not include the right to reproduce. As John Stuart Mill explained definitively in *On Liberty*, creating additional human beings is an act that has repercussions for the whole society – and nowadays, we can add, the whole world. It is therefore totally inappropriate to regard it as lying within that 'private sphere' within which the wishes of the principals should be paramount.[24]

An argument against concern with population growth in poor countries that has been made by their governments ever since the Rio Earth Summit, and taken up by some well-meaning but muddled people in the West, runs along the following lines. The average Indian, it is said, contributes only a twentieth as much to global warming as the average American, so it is absurd to say that population growth threatens the global ecology. There are two objections. First, the quadrupling of the Indian population to a billion since Independence is still equivalent to almost 40 million Americans or 100 million West Europeans.[25] Thus, the argument is misguided, because the effects are not trivial. It is also self-contradictory, because the same people also want to insist that India should have the chance to become a far more prosperous society. Under these circumstances, an extra Indian will become more and more significant as a contributor to global warming, as well as pressing yet harder on the world's dwindling resources.

Failure to control the number of births imperils future improvement of the human lot in more ways than are immediately apparent.

For example, much of the surge of population in the third world has arisen from western-funded measures for eradicating mosquitoes (the vectors of malaria and other diseases), the elimination of small-pox, and other life-saving public health measures. It has become a commonplace, even in gatherings of rich countries' governments, that much more along the same lines could be done about reducing disease (including AIDS) at a cost that would be trifling, in relation to their countries' combined national incomes. But this well-intentioned humanitarian intervention will serve only to make matters worse, creating far more human misery in the long run, unless it is accompanied by the even more vigorous pursuit of measures to counteract the yet further increase in world population that it would bring about.

Furthermore, the increase in population in poor countries greatly exacerbates the problem of dealing equitably with global warming. Any just solution – and any solution that has any hope of acceptance by the world's poor countries – must accommodate their industrialization. Countries such as China and India will never accede to any system of quotas for the emission of greenhouse gases that locks them in permanently as poor relations. And industrialization, even if it is close to eschewing fossil fuels, will still have to mean that their use by these countries will increase in relation to that of rich countries. Thus, if global emissions have to be cut to, say, an eighth of their present level, the rich countries will have to cut down to vastly less than an eighth of their present levels to make room. But no country, North or South, can reasonably be expected to agree to any pact under which a country that fails to contain its population growth as much as possible can make indefinite demands for greater emission quotas corresponding to its population. It is impossible to imagine any agreement on equal quotas per head of population on any terms that did not fix each country's entitlements at a certain date with no subsequent adjustments except to take account of emigration and immigration. But the difficulty of getting an agreement will be a good deal greater if there continue to be countries in which the average woman has six or more children.

Finally, global warming. As I have already mentioned, when he assumed office, George W. Bush announced that he was repudiating the Kyoto Treaty because 'the science is uncertain'. But the only room for uncertainty is about the size of the effects: what is the precise relation between the emission of greenhouse gases and their concentration in the atmosphere? how much global warming will any given concentration of greenhouse gases eventually bring about? and what will be the effects on the planet of any degree of global warming?

However, when the future of the planet is at stake, we should surely adopt the 'precautionary principle' and act on the assumption that the least favourable estimates are correct. After all, in deciding whether or not to take out an umbrella, we do not make a 'median estimate' of the probability of rain and take an umbrella only if we think it is more likely to rain than not: we take one if we think that there is any plausible chance of its raining. One fact that is undeniable is that global warming is occurring. When the IPCC showed that temperatures have risen above those of the past thousand years, sceptics suggested that the earth was cooler then than in the period before, but drilling cores deeper into the ice has extended the same conclusion back to two thousand years.[26] Another fact, which scarcely anybody not in the pay of an oil company denies, is that greenhouse gases have to be implicated, because (as one scientist put it) 'if you look at the natural ups and downs in the temperature, you'll find nothing remotely like what we're seeing now'.[27]

Although there are a variety of greenhouse gases, carbon dioxide is by far the most important, because it takes much longer to dissipate. The implication is that 'if we were to stop putting any more carbon dioxide or other industrial gases into the air today . . . temperatures would continue to rise for another 40 years'.[28] The only question is, then, how much temperatures will rise, since we are obviously going to go on dumping some greenhouse gases into the atmosphere for quite a while yet, come what may.

The most likely answer is: a lot. Only a complete reversal of current trends can hope to limit the increase in average temperatures to a 2°C rise above the historical norm (that is to say 1.4°C above the present level). Carbon dioxide concentration is measured in parts per million (ppm) and has already risen from a preindustrial 270 ppm to 370 ppm. The IPCC estimate, which needs to be revised downwards (as we shall see), was that a concentration of 450 ppm would keep global warming down to no more than 2°C. It is now clear that the IPCC was too complacent about the prospect of such a rise. But even fixing the level at 450 ppm would require fast and radical action. 'Total global greenhouse gas emissions must soon drop to 60 to 80 per cent below their 1990 levels.'[29] It was this year – 1990 – that was chosen as the baseline year for the Kyoto Protocol, but global emissions since then have in fact greatly increased, so the reduction from the present level must be correspondingly greater.

To complete the sequence, we need to ask about the effects of global warming. The answer is alarming enough – even for the present level of greenhouse gas concentration and the increase in average world temperatures so far arising from it. It has always been understood that global warming would manifest itself most dramatically in an increase in the number and severity of extreme events. In early July 2003, the World Meteorological Organization issued an unprecedented statement taking 'the view that events this year in Europe, America and Asia are so remarkable that the world needs to be made aware of it immediately'. Hurricanes, heavy rainfall of catastrophic proportions and record temperatures have reached unprecedented levels, it said, and will increase with global warming.[30] A leading scientist suggested that events anticipated for twenty to thirty years' time were already happening, and that 'a worst case scenario' may be the correct one in that climate change may be 'proceeding much faster and stronger than expected'.[31]

The IPCC's last prediction of possible temperature rises by the end of the century suggested that they would not exceed 5°C, but 'a recent conference of leading atmospheric scientists in Berlin concluded that the IPCC's models may have underestimated the effect of atmospheric soot, the airborne industrial waste of the past'.[32] Without that mitigating factor, the Earth might have warmed up three times as much as it has.[33] The cleaning up of particulate emissions from coal-fired power stations will, as it works its way through the processes of atmospheric change, make the skies clearer: improvements in the local environment will thus, paradoxically, make the global situation much worse. Similarly, the haze from forest fires will diminish in time, if only because almost all the forests have already been burned in large areas of the world. The net result is that average global temperatures could rise by 7°C to 10°C by the end of the century.[34]

As the temperature rises, 'large-scale discontinuities' become more probable. The IPCC has suggested that the probability starts to increase sharply after a rise of 3.5°C.[35] But this estimate again appears to be too optimistic. Western Europe will have temperatures like those found at the same latitudes in Russia and Canada (Siberia and the Northern Territories) if the thermohaline circulation – the movement of enormous volumes of water in the oceans over great distances – collapses. But this is already beginning to occur as a result of the mere 0.6°C rise we have experienced so far. The northward movement of the Gulf Stream has to be compensated by an equivalent move south of cold water, and measurements at one point in the flow 'show that the outflow has fallen by 20 per cent since 1950, which suggests a comparable reduced inflow from the Gulf Stream'.[36] This is a direct result of global warming manifested in 'large-scale melting of Arctic ice and the consequent pouring of huge volumes of fresh water into the North Atlantic'. It already constitutes itself as a threat to the survival not only of polar bears but also of the Inuit, as each year there is less ice, and what there is forms later and melts earlier.[37]

The Antarctic is also melting fast. On the basis of ice cores, research published in the journal *Science* concluded that 'between 1841 and 1950 there was very little change but there is a marked decline in sea ice distribution since 1950 of about 20 per cent'.[38] Since the annual melting of the pack ice – from more than 7 million square miles in winter to 1.5 million in summer – plays a large part in the thermohaline circulation, a big reduction in the amount of sea ice is ominous. But it is in line with the observation that 'average temperatures on the Antarctic peninsula have risen by 3°C in the past 50 years'.[39] The melting of sea ice does not affect the sea level, but the melting of land ice is, of course, another matter. If the West Antarctic ice sheet (the smaller of the two that cover the continent) melts, the result will be an increase of eighteen feet in the sea level.[40] Nobody is suggesting that this is going to happen soon, but the 'precautionary principle' suggests that a disaster of this magnitude cannot be risked.

Since snow reflects sunlight, the exposure of land will speed up global warming further. But there are a number of other and more alarming ways in which the process can be self-reinforcing if certain thresholds (whose level is uncertain) are passed. The decomposing matter trapped in permafrost could be laid bare and release 'enormous quantities of carbon dioxide and methane into the atmosphere'.[41] Since buildings erected on the permafrost are already collapsing, this is not a far-fetched scenario. Another possibility is that what is left of the Amazon rain forest could die back due to drought, thus turning it into a source of greenhouse gases rather than a sink.[42] The most cataclysmic prospect is that vast stores of methane hydrate – a super-greenhouse gas – that are currently frozen under the oceans will, when global warming has reached some point, rise to the surface and dissipate themselves into the atmosphere.[43] There is a growing body of scientific opinion that attributes the end of the Permian era 251 million years ago to global warming caused initially by huge volcanic eruptions that triggered off the release of methane hydrate from the oceans. The Permian period was one of flourishing plant and animal life and ended, as the almost complete lack of fossils shows, cataclysmically, with 90 per cent or more of species wiped out. 'Suddenly the events of a quarter of a billion years ago begin to look very topical indeed. One of the possible endings of the human story has been told. Our principal political effort must now be to ensure that it does not become set in stone.'[44]

20

Justice or Bust

Over the next fifty years, renewable resources will continue to become scarcer, world population will grow and global warming will have more and more adverse effects. The only alternative is a nuclear holocaust, which I would not recommend as a solution. Leaving that aside, the question left is whether the dismal prospect that I laid out in the previous chapter will be left to play itself out to the end, or whether the steps needed to control the situation (which will become more drastic for every year that they are postponed) will be taken.

What makes the choice even more stark than it might already appear is that ecological breakdown can scarcely fail to be accompanied by political breakdown. In *Leviathan*, Thomas Hobbes said that, in conditions of anarchy, life would be 'poor, nasty, brutish and short'. But in the seventeenth century anarchy would have been tempered by a population that was not excessive, a relatively small human impact on either the earth or its atmosphere, and average temperatures within a range that supported human life and that of other species. International anarchy will be far less benign in a future world containing in excess of ten billion occupants, with average temperatures far above the historical norm and suffering a crisis in renewable resources. In addition to deaths as a direct or indirect consequence of wars fought over the control of natural resources – water supplies, cultivable land, marine life and (in the world that will be created by the continuation of 'business as usual') oil – hundreds of millions of additional people will die each year from lack of drinking water and sanitation, starvation and the spread of tropical diseases to ever wider areas.[1] The instability will be reinforced by the number of refugees created by global warming, as their living places disappear under the rising seas and as drought and desertification make agriculture impossible. 'There are already more [of these refugees] than their "political" counterparts – 25 million, according to the last estimate, compared to around 22 million conventional refugees at their highest point in the late 1990s. By 2050, mostly due to the effects of global warming, there could be more than 150 million.'[2]

This figure, from 2002, already looks much too low, as the changes previously predicted for decades ahead have already manifested themselves. A Pentagon study carried out in 2004 talks about drops in average temperature of 6°C in Britain and Scandinavia within twenty years. It is similarly alarmist about the sea level, predicting that it will increase so much as to make Bangladesh uninhabitable. It puts the number of people who will face famine in the hundreds of millions. The report was commissioned by the Pentagon's Office of Net Assessment, whose job it is to weigh risks to national security, and that is its focus. It 'predicts that abrupt climate change could bring the planet to the edge of anarchy as countries develop a nuclear threat to defend dwindling food, water and energy supplies.'[3] As things become more desperate, the report predicts, riots and internal conflict will tear apart India, South Africa and Indonesia. To sum up: 'Disruption and conflict will be endemic features of life.'[4]

If the future is Hobbesian, the distribution of goods will depend on the distribution of the means of coercion and extraction. In such a world, there can be no place for justice. I do not regard it as part of my task to forecast whether that will in fact be the future or whether a less reckless course will be taken. The hope that I wish to offer is a contingent one. It is this: *if* the second path is followed, it will have four positive implications for justice. First, the policies needed will in themselves be in line with the requirements of global justice. Second, these changes will have knock-on effects that are likely to amplify the improvement in justice. Third, the new international and domestic institutions that will have to be created to implement the needed changes will be able to be put to use in order to make distribution more just in other ways as well, and it will be very hard to provide any coherent rationale for failing to use them in this way. Finally, the kind of mobilization that will have to occur can scarcely fail to have a momentum leading to changes beyond those strictly required for stabilization. I shall not be able to defend these four theses systematically in the pages of this book that remain. I shall therefore content myself with offering illustrations, some based on firmly established data and others to varying degrees speculative.

I shall begin with population. Suppose we ask: how can the increase in world population be contained below the currently predicted levels by means other than war, pestilence and famine (to which we may add inundation)? The conventional wisdom used to be that the 'demographic transition' from a high to a low birth rate had to wait on the achievement of a certain level of economic development. But this analysis rested on a confusion between correlation and causation. A finer-grained analysis shows that there are specific factors associated with reductions in birth rates. The most important is the autonomy – which entails the education – of women. The second most important thing is to make having children expensive: we know that (even with reasonable child allowances), the prohibition of child labour and the requirement – effectively enforced – that all children go to school until the age of 16 will infallibly affect the calculus facing couples. (Clearly, the first condition – education for girls – requires the universality postulated in the second, since anything short of universal education will leave out girls.) However, in a country like India, in which two-thirds of the women (and one-third of the men) are illiterate, and the promise of free education has never been anything like met, achieving these goals will demand large funds from the countries that can afford to provide them.

A very important motive for having a lot of children – and especially male children – is that, in the absence of a guaranteed state pension in old age, children are a form of insurance against destitution – at any rate as long as there is a strong norm that children must, if necessary, make large sacrifices of their own and their own children's interests in order to support aged or ailing parents. Universal pensions are very rare in poor countries, and, again, the money for them is going to have to come from the rich ones, simply because there is nowhere else for it to come from.

It is clear that everything that needs to be done to hold down population growth will at the same time contribute to the cause of justice. But my second thesis is also illustrated by this case, because educating women and giving them more autonomy is bound to change the dynamics of the society – not immediately, perhaps, but certainly in a time measured at most in decades. And these social, economic and political ramifications of the original change must necessarily work themselves out in a way that will make relations between men and women more just.

In the previous chapter, I discussed conflicts over the distribution of water, which are bound to go on getting more intense. Both population growth and global warming make the available resources even less than they would otherwise be, so failure to keep these forces in check will make the Pentagon report's doomsday scenario more probable. But significant deterioration in the availability of water is bound to occur, even in the most optimistic scenario. Since the world is already exceeding its carrying capacity in relation to all renewable resources, conflicts will not be confined to those arising over the distribution of water. Defusing these conflicts requires an international body with powers to enforce the distribution of these scarce resources equitably. Giving priority to needs over wants must mean that the lot of those who now have least must improve in comparison with the lot of those who now have most, which is what justice demands.

This is, as far as it goes, another illustration of the first thesis. But the relevance of the third thesis comes in when we ask why the scope of the principles that are called upon in crises should not be extended. And the answer is, as far as I can see: no reason at all. If the atmosphere is to be treated as a global commons on which everybody has an equal claim, why should countries that are lucky enough still to have fertile soil and a climate suitable for growing valuable crops be able to appropriate all the benefits? Why should not countries' with arid conditions and poor soil share in the product? The same goes for countries that still have harvestable fish within their 200-mile limits. And there is no rational basis for leaving out natural gas, oil and minerals. I need not enlarge on the implications that this principle would have for global justice. The institutional point is simply that any world authority with the capacity to impose its decision in relation to actively contested disputes over the sharing of water, fisheries and other renewable resources would also have the capacity to carry through a plan for the more systematic redistribution of the benefits flowing from control of natural resources.

Global warming is a problem so challenging that it will hardly come as a surprise if I suggest that it illustrates all four theses. The obvious question which has to be addressed first is: what, on the best scientific evidence available, would be the rate at which carbon emissions would have to be cut to avoid a dangerous increase in average global temperatures? The answer is, unhappily, that there is no 'safe' trajectory, no guaranteed 'soft landing'. The present level is already melting the ice at the poles, interfering with the thermohaline circulation and causing droughts, floods and hurricanes on an unprecedented scale. If the average temperature were merely to stay where it is now, these trends would continue. But there is nothing we can do to avoid an increase over the next forty years because of the length of the carbon cycle and, we can add, the effect of clearer skies. The only question is, therefore, as I pointed out in the last chapter, what we would have to do about greenhouse gas emissions to keep temperatures down to an acceptable level.

But acceptable to whom? If they take the problem seriously at all, politicians in the rich countries operate on the basis that a 2°C increase (1.4°C over the present level) would be acceptable. But this number is driven by politics: you start by deciding how much you could cut emissions and still have a chance of staying in office, take the most wildly optimistic estimate of the relation between greenhouse gases and climate change and when you crank all that through you come out at 2°C. 'In 1996, the European Environmental Council (EEC) decided that the global average surface temperature increase should be held at a maximum of 2°C above the preindustrial level, and that as a consequence the CO_2 concentration had to be held below 550 ppm.'[5]

I showed in the previous chapter that a 2°C target is dangerously high. If the Gulf Stream does not disappear as a result of such an increase and if the polar ice does not melt too much, the rich countries may be able to adapt. They would have to evacuate some areas (the Dutch government is already making plans), build enormously expensive defences to protect the rest from flooding and revamp large parts of the drainage system. The British government's Office of Technology produced a report prepared by sixty experts warning that:

> disasters will be inevitable, no matter what we do. . . . Parts of cities may have to be demolished to make room for flood reservoirs or green corridors to take the water away. . . . The southeast, and all estuaries with a potential for tidal surge, are also high risk. . . . Large farmed areas might either be lost to the sea or sacrificed for coastal defence. . . . The areas of the country most vulnerable to river and flash flooding because of crumbling Victorian sewers are the cities and towns between Lancashire and the Humber, including Manchester, Bradford and Leeds.[6]

For the rest, the rich countries will have to add to the costs of abandonment and construction those that simply have to be absorbed. To give one example, claims for storm and flood damage in Britain have 'doubled between the five years to 2003, compared with the previous five years', according to the Association of British Insurers.[7] They can only go on up, whatever is done, in future. But the rich countries could afford to absorb such losses. The South is far less well placed to cope. China, Bangladesh and India have millions of people who could not be defended at any expense against an increase in the sea level of even two or three feet, and there is nowhere that they could be relocated. An argument has been put forward (whether sincerely made or not) that the North should go on pursuing economic growth at any cost to the climate so that it can afford to help the South. Quite apart from the fact that the North would suffer economic losses off-setting any gains, the whole idea is totally unrealistic because the ele-mental forces unleashed by global warming make any human efforts to control them seem puny in comparison. You might as well propose keeping the thermohaline circulation going by installing giant pumps all along its major routes.

Despite the dire consequences (even if things turn out relatively well) from a 2°C rise in average temperatures, it may be unavoidable. The IPCC's 'high' estimate of the impact of CO_2 on climate change, when factored in with other greenhouse gases, had the implication that the level required to stabilize the average temperature at 2°C above the historical norm is around 350 ppm – below the current 370 ppm.[8] And it must be borne in mind that that estimate was made when the consensus view was that a 5°C rise by the end of the century was the maximum that could be expected even from 'business as usual', whereas this has now gone up to a range of 7°C–10°C. In its Second Assessment Report, the IPCC put forward at its best guess that the concentration of CO_2 consistent with a 2°C temperature increase was 450 ppm. Its Third Assessment Report, in 2001, changed this to its 'median' estimate, but no longer endorsed it.[9] It is, on the basis of current knowledge, a good deal too low. The implication is that the figure of 550 ppm still current among politicians as a concentra-tion consistent with a 2°C rise is totally discredited scientifically. Its survival can be attributed only to the fact that politicians – not only George Bush – are not prepared to face the realities of global warming. The British government is no stranger to wishful thinking, so it is quite in character that it still maintains this as its target.[10]

The author of 'A Modest Proposal to Save the Planet' cites and criticizes the government's target but proposes only 450 ppm instead as 'the maximum concentration in the atmosphere that can be con-sidered safe'.[11] No doubt he intended the title 'Modest Proposal' to be ironic, echoing Swift's 'Modest Proposal', but it is in fact modest to a fault. There is, to repeat, no 'safe' level, and 450 ppm is likely to be very dangerous indeed, leading to global warming well in excess of 2°C, which in turn will enhance the probability of catastrophic 'discontinuities' of the kind outlined in the previous chapter. Never-theless, even achieving that modest target will require a revolution in the way in which the world – North and South alike – does business.

There is (as with all the other parameters) a wide range of uncer-tainty about the reduction in carbon emissions that would be needed to stabilize the concentration of carbon dioxide at 450 ppm. The IPCC's Third Assessment Report suggested that, in the worst case scenario, world emissions of carbon would have to come down from about eight gigatonnes to about three by 2050.[12] In view of the advances in understanding that have occurred since then, we can be pretty sure that the worst case scenario is actually worse than this. Since 450 ppm is very probably too high to keep warming down to 2°C, and 2°C looks as if it will be far worse than it seemed when the standard was adopted, reducing carbon emissions to two gigatonnes – cutting them to a quarter – makes more sense as an objective. Even then, we must bear in mind that this constitutes a massive violation of the 'precautionary principle' – but we must also bear in mind that the principle may be literally inapplicable here because it is possible that the average temperature would rise to a dangerous level even if emissions of carbon fell to zero tomorrow and stayed there for a long time.

Divided between 6.3 billion people, 2 billion tonnes of carbon in 2050 is around 0.3 tonnes per head. Of course, the population will be bigger then, but I have argued that current numbers should be taken as the basis for national allocations. (The equity of that proposal, however, depends on the rich countries implementing all the policies that I proposed to keep the increase down.) To put this figure into perspective, China is already well over the limit, while the rest of Asia (minus Japan) is not far off. Africa is the only continent well below. At the other end of the scale, the United States has to get its emissions down to about 5 per cent of the current level, Australia and Canada to about 6 per cent and the other industrialized countries to about 12 per cent on the average.[13]

Reductions would, of course, be phased in over a period, but would still have to come down fast to hit the target. The rich countries would have time to adapt, and could also cushion the blow, especially at the beginning, by buying unused quotas from other countries. This option would fade away as quotas dropped and countries in surplus, such as India, increased their production. The answer has to lie first in more energy-efficient production and building. This painless (though not cheap) move would by default probably enable the profligates to reach the emission level of the other rich countries. Fossil fuels would have to give way rapidly to renewable sources of energy, generating electricity from the sun with photovoltaic cells and the wind with turbines. Research and investment in capturing the unlimited power of the waves and the tides would have to become a priority. In the end, however, we cannot get round the fact that all of this put together would not be anywhere near enough without a change in the way of life in rich countries. Cars will no longer be possible except for short trips and electrically powered trains will have to be the primary means of long-distance travel. (Laying the tracks over existing motorways would help to achieve both ends simultaneously.) Air travel is especially pernicious because it pumps carbon dioxide straight into the upper atmosphere, but it also just produces too much carbon to be consistent with a low-emissions regime.[14] The end of flaging would mean that the pace of life would have to slow down, making it less stressful.

What would this do for justice? First, and most obviously, treating the atmosphere as a global commons to be divided up equally would itself constitute a just distribution of a scarce resource. Second, there would be brisk bidding for surplus emissions quotas by the rich countries, which would make for redistribution towards poor countries. Third, over and above this, the rich countries would have to pay for the poor countries to industrialize using renewable energy, because there is no alternative. China is the most striking illustration. Its 'primary energy source, and its dirtiest is coal, which accounts for 70 per cent of its power supply.'[15] With the economy booming, the Prime Minister is calling for 'the development of large coal mines' and 'the exploration and exploitation of petroleum' as well as making deals with oil producers elsewhere.[16] As a result, 'experts predict that by 2020 China could pass the United States to become the biggest source of carbon dioxide'.[17] But the planet cannot manage with one United States, let alone two. No deal that has built into it the implication that countries such as China and India are forever condemned to be poor relations can be realistic. Hence, 'even in a world dominated by the North and its corporations, the South commands the vast power of historical inertia. Its trump, quite simply, is that there must be massive cascades of clean-energy development in the South, because without them there will be a global ecological disaster.'[18]

My second thesis is that an effective response to the threats I have identified is bound to have desirable consequences over and above the direct ones. Let me offer three reasons in this case. First, a quota for the carbon emissions of each country has to be implemented by its government. Pricing cannot do the job in the rich countries because a 'carbon tax' that would clear the markets at progressively lower levels of carbon per head would enable those with high incomes to scoop the pool, leaving the rest without electricity, gas and oil. As in Britain during and after the Second World War, only a rationing scheme can enable a short supply to be shared so that everyone has enough. Then, it was most importantly food and clothing; now it is claims over carbon. The obviously fair method – and the only one that has any chance of acceptance – is to give all adults the same share, with children getting a smaller allowance according to age. A proposal for implementing this is to take the half of emissions attributable to individual consumption (domestic, travel and so on) and issue everybody with a 'smart card' that would deduct an amount from their annual quota every time they engaged in a carbon-producing transaction.[19] Unused quotas could be bought by those who had the money, and this would clearly bring about some redistribution of income. More significantly, however, it would make money less important, because those with a lot of it would still find that they were severely constrained in the ways in which they could spend it. The most carbon-free expenditure in an economy that is heavily biased towards fossil fuel energy is personal services. But how many haircuts, manicures and yoga lessons can one person manage?

Second, the constituency for social justice is, as I have emphasized throughout, swelled by a sense of common fate and drained by a feeling that you can buy your way out of trouble. If 'contraction and convergence' occurs, it must force a recognition of common fate. More concretely, the revival of public transport at the expense of the private car replaces isolation and a competition for road space with social mixing and no chance of stealing a march on others. I need not enlarge on the third point, because I have already made it in chapter 16. We can afford social justice once we give up on the chimera of economic growth, because the argument that we must have inequality to provide incentives (which may not even be true, anyway) ceases to have any weight.

My third thesis is that the institutions needed to deal with the problems are bound to extend their scope in ways that are likely to further justice. There has to be a new world authority replacing the IMF, the World Bank and the WTO, with a constitution that is in some way representative. It is surely clear that the model of the IMF and the World Bank, which are completely controlled by the rich countries and dominated by the United States, is inappropriate. But the WTO, which requires unanimity among all the countries within it, is not a practicable framework. It is not my job to produce blueprints: there are plenty around already and once scrapping the existing institutions and replacing them has been recognized as an imperative, there would be plenty more. The essential point is that the new organization has to make population, renewable resources and global warming central to its mission. Considerations of trade and aid have to be subordinated to those, and existing policies may need to be reversed. International trade is inseparable from transporting goods long distances, for example, but the control of global warming means that the consumption of locally produced goods has to be promoted.

The spillover effect is that any international decision-making body that is not dominated by the rich countries will inevitably reflect the interests of the other 80 per cent of the human race. The WTO has a notional decision rule of 'one country one vote', as I have said, but in practice it has been dominated by the rich countries, whose representatives meet to concoct an agenda and then do their best by threats and bribes to ram it through. Some slight indication of the potential for cooperation among poor countries was provided by the WTO meeting at Cancún in September 2003. For the first time, a group of twenty-one populous poor countries – including China, India and Brazil – succeeded in maintaining a common front, despite all efforts to intimidate or buy off individual members. 'Suddenly the proposals for global justice that relied on solidarity for their implementation can spring into life.'[20] Admittedly, all that has happened so far is that the 'G21', followed by many other poor countries, refused to consider a set of proposals to eliminate even more of the means by which they could maintain control of their economies, and insisted that there should be serious discussion of the rich countries' tariffs and agricultural subsidies. But the Brazilian foreign minister claimed that 'we have gained the political initiative. . . . We are optimistic for the medium and long run. We will have an increased capacity to negotiate and if a deal comes it will . . . service the global system as a whole.'[21] Whatever the eventual outcome, this was 'the most significant change in the WTO's balance of power for 50 years'.[22]

Finally, I come to my fourth thesis. This is that the political forces that would be required to bring about the kinds of change needed would also carry over to advance justice in other ways. It is apparent that the major parties of government in western societies are incapable of taking bold and decisive action. They will have to be either transformed or replaced. As I have argued, this is where ideas make a difference, because only an alternative vision of the future can provide the impetus. And that vision must, I suggest, be built around the idea of social justice. Let me return again to the analogy of the 1930s. Increasing disillusion with the mainstream parties is manifesting itself in falling electoral turnout and the shift of votes to smaller parties. But disillusion can, as we know, be channelled into racism and xenophobia instead of the pursuit of a renewed social democratic agenda. I cannot say which way things will go. But I do wish to claim that only the second path is consistent with human survival.

An encouraging sign is the level of outrage that has been generated by the corruption and the sheer naked greed displayed by so many of those to whom the current system provides a great deal of discretionary power. Everybody now understands the point made in chapter 16: that executives boost the value of their stock options by concealing bad news about their company and selling out before it goes bankrupt. In 1999 and 2000, for example, ten chief executives cashed in £525 million of shares that shortly thereafter fell to anything between 5 per cent and nothing. Sixty chief executives made £2.7 billion between them before the market crashed.[23] As Joseph Stiglitz pointed out, privatization is pushed on poor countries as a way of avoiding government corruption:

> But I'm not sure these private sector advocates quite had in mind the abilities that American corporate capitalism has demonstrated so amply recently: corruption on an almost unfathomable scale. They put to shame those petty bureaucrats who stole a few thousand dollars or even a few million. The numbers bandied about in the Enron, World-Com and other scandals are in the billions, greater than the GNP of many countries.[24]

Similarly, the lack of connection between directors' pay and the performance of their companies in both Britain and the United States has been so frequently reported that it has presumably sunk into everybody's consciousness. Equally striking has been the mismatch between their pay generally and any plausible criterion. Thus, in 2002, average pay in Britain rose by 3.2 per cent, share prices dropped by 24.4 per cent and chief executives' pay rose by 23 per cent. 'The value of the companies in the FTSE-100 index had tumbled almost 50 per cent from their peak three years earlier. Over the same period, however, boardroom pay advanced by more than 84 per cent.'[25]

All this makes nonsense of any idea that market economies pay people for creating value, or for their performance. How deep this goes as a basis on which to build a movement for social justice is hard to say. But an American survey found in 2002 that '66 per cent of workers said they trusted their employers just some or not much at all'. In response to another question, '50 per cent of non-union workers [said] that they wanted to join a union, the highest level in three decades'. Thus 'the nation may have reached a watershed in which workers conclude that they need collective protections to safeguard them from predatory executives and economic downturns.'[26]

Similarly, many people – by no means all rich – have lost money from having put their trust in insurance or stock market advisers, in the integrity of those running companies and in the accountants who were supposed to guarantee that integrity. The losers include people who were sold insurance policies that were supposed to pay off their mortgages, and will now come nowhere near, and those who relied on advice from brokers resting on supposedly impartial assessments that were manipulated for the firm's profit. There are also those whose occupational pensions have been wiped out by the bankruptcy of their employers, and those whose employers, having failed for years to put enough into their pension funds to meet their obligations, now claim that they cannot afford to do so.

Where does all this leave us? The physics and the politics of global warming are both shrouded in uncertainty. We may already be past the point of no return. Some further global warming will occur whatever we do, and that may be enough by itself to set off an uncontrollable acceleration in the rate at which greenhouse gases build up in the atmosphere. The British government's chief scientist, Sir David King, has warned that it is 60 million years since the concentration of carbon dioxide in the atmosphere was as high as it is now. Then, it soared to a completely unsustainable 1,000 parts per million. ' "No ice was left on earth. Antarctica was the best place for mammals to live, and the rest of the world would not sustain human life," he said.'[27] We can only hope that this fate can still be averted by timely and drastic action to conserve energy and replace fossil fuels by renewable sources.

If that is so, there is room for politics to make a difference. But will the human race make good use of whatever breathing space is left? We should not forget how often the world outlook changed in the course of the twentieth century.

> In 1910, Europeans were confident of the peace-causing benefits of economic interdependence and the irrationality of armed conflict. By the late summer of 1914, Europe's great powers were at war. The United States enjoyed prosperity and optimism during the second half of the 1920s. By 1933, the world was well into a painful depression, Hitler was in control of Germany, and the century was fast headed toward its darkest moments. In early 1945, the United States was busy building a postwar partnership with the Soviet Union, US forces were rapidly demobilizing, and the American people were looking to the United Nations to preserve world peace. Within a few short years, the Cold War was under way and the United States and Soviet Union were threatening each other with nuclear annihilation.[28]

We can add to that list of rapid and unforeseen changes the end of colonialism and the collapse of the Soviet Union. The need for another revolution should be obvious to all those who are not wilfully blind. It is not, I fear, probable. But without doubt it is possible.

Postscript, 3 November 2004 Tony Blair and George W. Bush make perfect foils because of their sublimely unselfconscious reproduction of the clichés that pass for thought in the political discourse of their respective countries. But while these ideas prevail, no politician will advance social justice. Bush picked up a lot of votes as the champion of 'moral values'. Kerry might have changed the terms of the debate by contrasting the claims of unborn babies with those of the millions of real children whose lives could be saved by substantial foreign aid and cheap imported drugs. Again, 'family values' are mocked by the desperate conditions in which many American children live. Social justice was already defeated in the campaign; the result made only a marginal difference.

Notes

Preface

1 Brian Barry, *Culture and Equality: An Egalitarian Critique of Multi-culturalism* (Cambridge: Polity, 2001; Cambridge, Mass.: Harvard University Press, 2001).
2 Brian Barry, *Justice as Impartiality* (Oxford: Clarendon Press, 1995).
3 I expand on these themes in a lengthy reply to critics of *Culture and Equality* in 'Second Thoughts – and Some First Thoughts Revived', pp. 204–38 in Paul Kelly, ed., *Multiculturalism Reconsidered* (Cambridge: Polity, 2002).

Chapter 1 Why We Need a Theory

1 George Orwell, *Collected Essays, Journalism and Letters*, ed. Sonia Orwell and Ian Angus, vol. 1 (London: Secker & Warburg, 1968), pp. 23–30: pp. 25–6.
2 Survey evidence shows that 'just price' thinking of this kind is still prevalent in contemporary market societies. Thus 82 per cent of respondents said that it would be 'unfair' for a hardware store to raise the price of snow shovels from $15 to $20 the morning after a large snowstorm, whereas 79 per cent said it would be fair if a grocer who had had to pay 30 cents more for lettuce due to a short-term failure of supply raised the price by the same amount. Similarly, 75 per cent thought it would be fair for a landlord to raise the rent when the lease became due for renewal to reflect increased costs, whereas 91 per cent found it unacceptable for the landlord to increase the rent simply because he had discovered that the tenant had taken a job closer by and would therefore be reluctant to move. Daniel Kahneman, Jack L. Knetch and Richard Thaler, 'Fairness as a Constraint on Profit Seeking: Entitlements in the Market', *American Economic Review*, 76 (1986),

pp. 728–41. See also, for the translation of such ideas into regulatory regimes, Edward E. Zajac, *The Political Economy of Fairness* (Cambridge, Mass.: The MIT Press, 1995).

3 *Social Justice: Strategies for National Renewal*, The Report of the Commission on Social Justice (London: Vintage, 1994).

4 Ibid., pp. 17–18.

5 Ibid., p. 17.

6 Ibid., p. 391.

7 Ibid., table 1.1, p. 29.

8 Ibid., p. 28.

9 Ibid., p. 379.

10 David Firestone, 'With Tax Cuts Passed, Republicans Call for More', *New York Times*, 24 May 2003, p. A12.

11 *Social Justice*, p. 377.

12 Ibid., p. 378.

13 There are too many instances to cite, but see especially the attack on the 'Levellers' on pp. 110–13 of ibid.

14 Ibid., p. 390.

15 'A maximum tax bill would reinforce a commitment to fair taxes, while ensuring that any other tax reforms did not impose an excessive burden on any particular group [i.e. the extremely rich – B.B.]. The maximum tax bill should certainly be no more than 50 per cent.' Ibid.

16 Paul Johnson and Frances Lynch, 'Sponging off the Poor', *Guardian*, 10 March 2004, p. 15.

17 Alistair Beaton, *The Little Book of New Labour Bollocks* (London: Simon and Schuster, 2000), 'Glossary'. To mark the tenth anniversary of the Report, the body responsible for it (the IPPR) commissioned a follow-up study which concluded (in July 2004) that, after two terms of New Labour government, the Commission's conception of social justice was no closer to fulfilment than it had been before. To fail when measured against such pitifully undemanding goals is a remarkable (negative) achievement.

18 For an extended discussion of this issue, see Brian Barry, 'The Welfare State versus the Relief of Poverty', *Ethics*, 100 (1990), pp. 503–29; reprinted in Robert Goodin and Alan Ware, eds., *Needs and Welfare* (London: Sage, 1990), pp. 73–103.

19 Firestone, 'With Tax Cuts Passed . . .'. The study was carried out by the Urban-Brookings Tax Center.

20 David Firestone, '2nd Study Finds Gaps in Tax Cuts', *New York Times*, 1 June 2003.

21 Firestone, 'With Tax Cuts Passed . . .'.

22 Ibid.

23 John Tierney, 'Republicans Explain an About-Face', *New York Times*, 24 May 2003, p. A12.

24 Philip E. Mella, lead letter in *Wall Street Journal*, 2 June 2003, p. A17, published under the title 'The Politics of Economic Envy and Distortion'.

25　Ibid.
26　Ibid.
27　Ibid.
28　John Roemer, 'Socialism's Future: An Interview with John Roemer', *Imprints*, 3 (1998), pp. 4–24: p. 23.

Chapter 2　The Machinery of Social Injustice

1　David Donnison, 'Act Local: Social Justice from the Bottom Up', Commission on Social Justice Discussion paper No. 13 (1994), reprinted in Jane Franklin, ed., *Social Policy and Social Justice: An IPPR Reader* (Cambridge: Polity, 1998), pp. 134–53. 'The Machinery of Social Injustice' is the heading of the first section of the paper (p. 134).
2　Ibid., p. 134.
3　Ibid.
4　Annette Lareau, *Unequal Childhoods: Class, Race, and Family Life* (Berkeley and Los Angeles: University of California Press, 2003), p. 29.
5　Joseph Stiglitz, 'Corporate Corruption', *Guardian*, 4 July 2002, p. 15.
6　Kurt Eichenwald: 'Clay Feet: Could Capitalists Actually Bring Down Capitalism?' *New York Times*, 30 June 2002, section 4, pp. 1 and 5; quotation from Rohatyn on p. 9 of Gretchen Morgan, 'Rebound from Ruin, if not from Mistrust', *New York Times*, 30 June 2002, section 3, pp. 1 and 9.
7　John Rawls, *A Theory of Justice* (Cambridge, Mass.: Harvard University Press; Oxford: Clarendon Press, 1971). Anyone wishing to follow this up should try to get hold of the original version, not the one being put out now by Harvard University Press, some of which is a mess because of changes subsequently introduced by Rawls.
8　The *cognoscenti* will know of whom I am talking. For others, the names will be of no interest.
9　The United States has the most highly qualified experts in the instruction of torture in the world: those who gave instruction at Fort Benning in Georgia to 'some 60,000 Latin American special forces, paramilitaries and intelligence agents in the black arts of terrorism'. Two-thirds of the army officers who committed the worst atrocities in El Salvador were graduates, and in Chile they ran Pinochet's secret police. 'In 1996, the US government was forced to release copies of the school's training manuals, which recommended blackmail, torture, execution and the arrest of witnesses' relatives.' John Pilger, 'The Great Charade', *Observer*, 14 July 2002, p. 29.
10　Samuel Johnson, *Taxation No Tyranny; An Answer to the Resolutions and Address of the American Congress*, pp. 411–55 in *Political Writings*, ed. Donald J. Greene (New Haven, Conn.: Yale University Press, 1977), p. 454.
11　Marquis de Condorcet, 'On the Admission of Women to the Rights of Citizenship', pp. 91–6 in Keith Michael Baker, ed., *Condorcet: Selected Writings* (Indianapolis: The Bobbs-Merrill Co., 1976).

12 George Orwell, 'Charles Dickens', pp. 454–504 in Sonia Orwell and Ian Angus, eds., *The Collected Essays, Journalism and Letters of George Orwell* (Harmondsworth, Mddx: Penguin Books, 1970), vol. I, p. 456.

13 Ibid., p. 457, emphasis in original.

14 Ibid.

15 Ibid., p. 458.

16 Charles Dickens, *A Christmas Carol*, pp. 45–134 in Michael Slater, ed., *The Christmas Books*, vol. I (Harmondsworth, Mddx: Penguin Books, 1971), pp. 133, 50.

17 Ibid., pp. 46, 119–20.

18 The organization was the Red Cross, whose mission is disaster relief, and which provides money only to meet temporary needs wherever tents and soup kitchens are not the more feasible option. Having made no undertakings about the disbursement of any contributions it received after September 11, its officers naturally sought to keep most of the money as a reserve to be used in doing its job as the occasion demanded. However, an outcry from donors forced the Red Cross to pass the money along to people who had suffered in some way from the attacks, despite the lavish compensation that they were already guaranteed.

19 For example, the amounts spent on 'vengeful giving' were instead of those usually given to charitable causes, with the result that any number of worthy organizations faced bankruptcy. Even more grotesquely, a charity that raises money by promising to spend it on projects benefiting the poorest people in the poorest countries actually cut down on this work in order to 'initiate new programming in New York City to address psychosocial trauma in the wake of the [World Trade Centre] tragedies' (Mercy Corps Annual Report, 2001).

Chapter 3   The Scope of Social Justice

1 The skulduggery perpetrated by the United States government in trying to force poor countries to accept genetically modified varieties of their agricultural staples arises from the fact that giant American companies such as Monsanto and Cargill (lavish contributors to the Bush coffers) cannot make money if people simply plant unpatented seeds that produce plants whose seeds can in turn be planted next year. The point is that 'GM technology permits companies to ensure that everything we eat is owned by them. They can patent the seeds and the processes that give rise to them. They can make sure that crops can't be grown without their patented chemical. They can prevent seeds from reproducing themselves.' George Monbiot, 'Starved of the Truth', *Guardian*, 9 March 2004, p. 15. However, the WTO Agreement on 'Trade Related Aspects of International Property Rights' (TRIPS) is so broadly drawn that it opens up the possibility of farmers growing traditional crops having to pay royalties to an agribusiness company in the USA, with the connivance of the US Patent Office. See Matthew

Clement, 'Rice Imperialism: The Agribusiness Threat to Third World Rice Production', *Monthly Review*, February 2004, pp. 15–22.

2   Roger Thurow and Scott Miller, 'As US Balks on Medicine Deal, African Patients Feel the Pain', *New York Times*, 2 June 2003, pp. A1, A9. 'Wealthier countries . . . promised in Doha, Qatar, to loosen patent restriction [on drugs] in order to ease shortages and reduce prices. . . . But last September, when all the other 143 countries in the World Trade Organization had lined up behind a new plan on the trade of medicines, the US blocked the proposal', p. A1. The US instead cut the scope to twenty 'infectious diseases', thus leaving out 'heart-related problems, diabetes and chronic respiratory diseases' that form the staple of third world medical problems.

3   For examples of the disastrous effects of IMF nostrums in Malawi, Ghana, Ethiopia, the Philippines and Mexico, see Fred Magdoff, 'A Precarious Existence: The Fate of Billions', *Monthly Review*, February 2004, pp. 1–14: pp. 5–7. An insider's view of these policies is offered by the former Chief Economist of the World Bank, Joseph Stiglitz, in his *Globalization and Its Discontents* (New York: W. W. Norton, 2002).

4   David Munk, 'Lula's Dreams for Brazil are Delayed as the Realities of Power Hit Home', *Guardian*, 31 December 2003, p. 12.

5   Ibid.

6   Ibid.

7   Fiona Macaulay, Institute of Latin American Studies in London, quoted in ibid.

8   Larry Rohter, 'Brazil's War on Hunger Off to a Slow Start', *New York Times*, 30 March 2003, p. A12.

9   Ibid.

10   Tony Smith, 'A Philanthropy Rush in Corporate Brazil', *New York Times*, 30 March 2003, p. BU5.

11   Ibid.

12   Michael W. Weinstein, 'The Aid Debate: Helping Hand or Hardly Helping?' *New York Times*, 26 May 2002, section 4, p. 3.

13   Charlotte Denny and Larry Elliot, '100m More must Survive on $1 a Day', *Guardian*, 19 June 2002, p. 24.

14   For a useful account of some of the more important cases, which emphasizes the way in which aid and IMF policies have contributed to ethnic divisions (such as that leading to the civil war in Sri Lanka), see Milton J. Esman and Ronald J. Herring, eds., *Carrots, Sticks and Ethnic Conflict: Rethinking Development Assistance* (Ann Arbor, Mich.: University of Michigan Press, 2001).

15   'According to the IMF's Trade Restrictiveness Index . . . countries like Mali, Mozambique, and Zambia are considerably more open than the EU and the US.' John Vidal, 'Trade not Aid', *Guardian*, 27 May 2002, p. 17. Much good it does them in the face of restrictions on their exports!

16   In an interview with David Held, abbreviated in *Times Higher Education Supplement*, 7 April 2003, in full in OpenDemocracy.net.

17   Ibid.
18   Ibid.
19   Ibid.

Chapter 4   Why Equal Opportunity?

1   Annette Lareau, *Unequal Childhoods: Class, Race and Family Life* (Berkeley and Los Angeles: University of California Press, 2003), p. 5.
2   Ibid.
3   Tom McArthur, *Oxford Guide to World English* (Oxford: Oxford University Press, 2002), p. 41.
4   *The Oxford Dictionary of Quotations*, ed. Angela Partington (Oxford: Oxford University Press, 4th revised edn, 1996), p. 428.
5   R. H. Tawney, *Equality* (New York: Capricorn Books, 1961 [1931]), p. 108.
6   Benjamin I. Page and James R. Simmons, *What Government Can Do: Dealing with Poverty and Inequality* (Chicago: University of Chicago Press, 2000), p. 50.
7   Sanders Korenman and Christopher Winship, 'A Reanalysis of *The Bell Curve*: Intelligence, Family Background and Schooling', pp. 137–78 in Kenneth Arrow, Samuel Bowles and Steven Durlauf, eds., *Meritocracy and Economic Inequality* (Princeton, NJ: Princeton University Press, 2000), Appendix B, pp. 168–75.
8   Alan Travis, 'Letwin Sees "Neighbourly Society" as the Way to Beat Crime', *Guardian*, 9 January 2002, p. 4.

Chapter 5   Education

1   David Miliband, 'Class Haunts the Classroom', *Guardian*, 18 September 2004, p. 27. It is worth noting that Miliband wrote this as Minister for School Standards.
2   Donald T. Simeon and Sally M. Grantham McGregor, 'Nutrition and Mental Development', pp. 1457–66 in *The Cambridge World History of Food*, vol. II (Cambridge: Cambridge University Press, 2000), pp. 1457–8.
3   Ibid., p. 1459.
4   Martha A. Field and Valerie A. Sanchez, *Equal Treatment for People with Mental Retardation: Having and Raising Children* (Cambridge, Mass.: Harvard University Press, 1999), table 3.1, p. 27.
5   John Posen, 'Bad NY Air Damaging to Infants, Study Says', *Columbia Spectator*, 16 February 2004, pp. 1 and 10: p. 10.
6   Juliana A. Maantay, 'Zoning, Equity and Public Health', pp. 228–50 in Richard Hofrichter, ed., *Health and Social Justice: Politics, Ideology, and Inequity in the Distribution of Disease* (San Francisco: Jossey-Bass, a Wiley Imprint, 2003), p. 239.
7   Ibid.

8   Ibid., p. 237. Toxic waste dumps are a general health hazard. 'A study of 23 sites in Britain, Denmark, France, Belgium and Italy compared the incidence of chromosomal abnormality [such as Down syndrome] within 1.9 miles of hazardous waste sites and between 1.9 and 4.3 miles. The researchers found that after adjusting for maternal age and socioeconomic factors, chromosomal abnormalities were 40% more likely to occur within the two-mile zone. . . . In 1988, the same researchers reported a 33% higher risk of non-chromosomal abnormalities – defects in gene components which cause problems such as spina bifida and cleft palate.' James Meikle, 'Birth Defects Rise Near Toxic Waste Dumps', *Guardian*, 25 January 2002, p. 7.

9   Maantay, 'Zoning, Equity and Public Health', p. 239. See also Vicki Been, 'What's Fairness Got to Do With It? Environmental Justice and the Siting of Locally Undesirable Land Uses', summarized in Frank Ackerman et al., eds., *The Political Economy of Inequality* (Washington, DC: Island Press, 2000), pp. 255–9.

10 Janet C. Gornick and Marcia M. Meyers, 'Support for Working Families: What We Can Learn From Europe about Family Policies', pp. 90–107 in Robert Kuttner, ed., *Making Work Pay: America after Welfare* (New York: The New Press, 2000), p. 100.

11 David K. Shipler, 'Total Poverty Awareness', *New York Times*, 21 February 2004, p. A15. Because living in slum housing is associated with so many factors that make for dropping out of school, it is hard to isolate the effect of just one factor, and this estimate may be too high. But the deleterious effects of even low concentrations of lead are well established.

12 Betty Hart and Todd R. Risley, *Meaningful Differences in the Everyday Experience of Young American Children* (Baltimore, Md.: Paul H. Brookes Publishing Co., 1995), p. 193.

13 Annette Lareau, *Unequal Childhoods: Race, Class and Family Life* (Berkeley and Los Angeles: University of California Press, 2003), n. 4, p. 290. The whole of this book is relevant to the topic, tracing with a wealth of detail the way in which class advantages and disadvantages are transmitted.

14 Hart and Risley, *Meaningful Differences*, pp. 132–3.

15 Ibid., p. 133.

16 Ibid., pp. 144–6.

17 Ibid., pp. 198–9.

18 Ibid., p. 146.

19 Children's Defense Fund, 'Child Care Basics', April 2001, <www.childrensdefense.org/earlychildhood/childcare/basics.asp>.

20 Karen Schulman, *The High Cost of Child Care Puts Quality Care Out of Reach for Many Families* (Washington, DC: Children's Defense Fund, 2000), p. 9.

21 Ibid.

22 Gornick and Meyers, 'Support for Working Families', p. 102.

23 Ibid., p. 103.

24 Children's Defense Fund, 'Child Care Basics'.
25 Ibid.
26 Ibid.
27 Ibid.
28 Schulman, 'The High Cost of Child Care', p. 6.
29 Ibid., p. 3.
30 Ibid., p. 4.
31 Ibid., p. 3.
32 Children's Defense Fund, 'Child Care Basics'.
33 Ibid.
34 Harold L. Wilensky, *Rich Democracies: Political Economy, Public Policy and Performance* (Berkeley, Calif.: University of California Press, 2002), p. 277. On a 5-point scale, the USA and the UK both ranked next to bottom on child-care arrangements in comparison with other rich countries.
35 Polly Toynbee, 'Talking is Not Enough', *Guardian*, 19 March 2004, p. 15.
36 Simeon and McGregor, 'Nutrition and Mental Development', pp. 1458–9.
37 Jody Heymann, 'Can Working Families Ever Win?' *Boston Review*, 27(1) (Feb/March 2002), pp. 4–13: p. 8.
38 Ibid., figure 6, p. 10.
39 Gary Orfield, 'Policy and Equity: Lessons of a Third of a Century of Educational Reforms in the United States', pp. 401–26 in Fernando Reimers, ed., *Unequal Schools, Unequal Chances: The Challenges to Equal Opportunity in the Americas* (Cambridge, Mass.: Harvard University Press, 2000), p. 404.
40 Ibid.
41 Ibid., p. 417.
42 Both quotations from Field and Sanchez, *Equal Treatment*, p. 23.
43 Ibid., p. 29.
44 Ibid.
45 Ibid., p. 26.
46 Ibid., p. 25.
47 See Shipler, 'Total Poverty Awareness', for a connection between 'maternal stress' and diminished IQ.
48 Orfield, 'Policy and Equity', p. 404.
49 Ibid., p. 417.
50 Field and Sanchez, *Equal Treatment*, p. 32.
51 Glenn C. Lowry, *The Anatomy of Racial Inequality* (Cambridge, Mass.: Harvard University Press, 2002), tables 6 and 7, pp. 180 and 181.
52 Julian E. Barnes, 'Unequal Education', *US News and World Report*, 22 March/29 March 2004, pp. 67–75: table on p. 69.
53 Hart and Risley, *Meaningful Differences*, p. 183.
54 Ibid., pp. 202 and 203.
55 Ibid., p. 206.
56 Ibid., pp. 207–8.

57   See Field and Sanchez, *Equal Treatment, passim*.
58   'All the parents we observed wanted their children to be successful students and productive citizens': Hart and Risley, *Meaningful Differences*, p. 210.
59   Ibid., p. 213.
60   Polly Toynbee, 'Going Nowhere', *Guardian*, 2 April 2004, p. 15.
61   Ibid.
62   Jo Blunden, 'Mobility has Fallen', *Centre Piece* (Centre for Economic Performance, London School of Economics, vol. 7, no. 2, Summer 2002), pp. 8–13: p. 13.
63   David Walker, 'New Breed of Middle Classes Closes Ranks', *Guardian*, 18 May 2002, p. 9.
64   'Oh Lords, Oh Derry', extract from Robin Cook's diaries, *Sunday Times*, 12 October 2003, pp. 1 and 2 of 'News Review': p. 2.
65   Nicholas Barr and Iain Crawford, 'Myth or Magic', *Guardian Higher*, 2 December 2003, p. 20.
66   Carole Leathwood, 'A Critique of Institutional Inequalities in Higher Education (or an Alternative to Hypocrisy for Higher Educational Policy)', *Theory and Research in Education* 2 (2004), pp. 31–48: table 1, p. 35. The actual figures are: Oxford 12.2, Cambridge 11.9, Imperial 8.1, North London 22.8, Guildhall 20.5 and Thames Valley an extraordinary 35.
67   Walker, 'New Breed of Middle Classes Closes Ranks'.
68   Leathwood, 'A Critique of Institutional Inequalities', table 2, p. 37. (The classes are IIIM, IV and V.)
69   Ibid., p. 41.
70   Will Woodward, 'UK Spending on Education Lags behind Rivals', *Guardian*, 14 June 2002, p. 8.
71   Phil Revell, 'Poor Little Rich Schools', *Guardian* (Education), 23 April 2002, p. 2.
72   Ibid.
73   Howard Glennerster and William Low, 'Education and the Welfare State: Does it Add Up?', pp. 28–87 in John Hills, ed., *The State of Welfare: The Welfare State in Britain since 1974* (Oxford: Clarendon Press 1990), p. 52.
74   Ibid., p. 53. Even more outrageously, private schools have been given generous sums of money from the national lottery: two grants of £500,000 for a sports hall and a tennis centre, the latter to a school miles away from the nearest town and whose 'prospectus makes no mention of community use of its facilities'. Eton College – the richest of the public schools – got £3.8 million for a rowing lake and sports centre open to the public but on its own grounds and with free access to its pupils. Revell, 'Poor Little Rich Schools'.
75   Woodward, 'UK Spending'.
76   Jenni Russell, 'Pay as You Learn', *Guardian*, 8 April 2002 (G2), pp. 2–3: p. 2.
77   Ibid.

78 Ibid.
79 Ibid.
80 Patrick Wintour, 'Bold No. 10 Idea for Tax and Schools', *Guardian*, 27 April 2001, p. 1.
81 Lucy Ward, 'Parents Will Bribe or Blag Children's Way to Best Schools', *Guardian*, 19 April 2004, p. 3.
82 Ibid.
83 Orfield, 'Policy and Equity', p. 418.
84 Will Woodward, 'London Schools Supremo to Woo Rich Parents', *Guardian*, 2 July 2002, p. 9, quoting Stephen Twigg, then junior education minister with special responsibility for London.
85 Fiona Millar, 'Admissions Impossible', *Guardian* (Education), 11 November 2003, p. 2.
86 Ibid.
87 Russell, 'Pay as You Learn', p. 3.
88 Lucy Ward, 'Help for Popular Schools Risks "Spiral of Decline"', *Guardian*, 14 October 2003.
89 Ibid.
90 Ibid.
91 Ibid.
92 Orfield, 'Policy and Equity', p. 412.
93 Ibid.
94 For an analysis of what is taught in these schools, see chapter 6 of my *Culture and Equality* (Cambridge: Polity Press, 2001; Cambridge, Mass.: Harvard University Press, 2001).
95 US Department of Education statistics, which may be found at <www.policyalmanac.org/education/archive/privateschools.pdf>.
96 Nancy Folbre, 'Leave No Child Behind?' pp. 68–77 in Kuttner, ed., *Making Work Pay*, p. 71.
97 Lisa W. Foderaro, 'Using Love, and Chess Lessons, to Defy Theories on Race and Test Scores', *New York Times*, 7 April 2002, p. 33.
98 Summary of Douglas S. Massey, 'The Age of Extremes: Concentrated Affluence and Poverty in the Twenty-First Century', pp. 155–88 in Ackerman et al., eds., *The Political Economy of Inequality*, p. 157.
99 Ibid., p. 156.

Chapter 6 Health

1 First quotation from Richard Hofrichter, 'Preface', pp. xvii–xxi in Hofrichter, ed., *Health and Social Justice: Politics, Ideology and Inequity in the Distribution of Disease* (San Francisco: Jossey-Bass, a Wiley Imprint, 2003), p. xviii; second quotation from the Acheson Report: D. Acheson, *Independent Inquiry into Inequalities in Health* (London: Stationery Office, 1998), p. 7, quoted in Hilary Graham, 'From Science to Policy: Options for Reducing Health Inequalities', pp. 522–41 in Hofrichter, ed., *Health and Social Justice*, p. 538.
2 Graham, 'From Science to Policy', p. 538.

3   Ronald Dworkin, 'Justice in the Distribution of Health Care', pp. 203–22 in Matthew Clayton and Andrew Williams, eds., *The Ideal of Equality* (London: Macmillan, 2000), p. 205.

4   John Aubrey, *Brief Lives*, ed. Oliver Lawson Dick (London: Penguin Books, 1987), p. 234.

5   William Muraskin, 'Nutrition and Mortality Decline: Another View', in *The Cambridge World History of Food* (Cambridge: Cambridge University Press, 2000), vol. 2, pp. 1389–97: p. 1390.

6   James S. House and David R. Williams, 'Understanding and Reducing Socioeconomic and Racial/Ethnic Disparities in Health', pp. 89–131 in Hofrichter, ed., *Health and Social Justice*, p. 97, citations suppressed.

7   Arline T. Geronimus, 'Addressing Structural Influences on the Health of Urban Populations', pp. 542–56 in Hofrichter, ed., *Health and Social Justice*, p. 544.

8   House and Williams, 'Understanding and Reducing Socioeconomic and Racial/Ethnic Disparities in Health', figure 3.8, p. 112. The numbers are for 1990, but the same general picture continues to be accurate.

9   Richard Wilkinson, *Unhealthy Societies: The Afflictions of Inequality* (London: Routledge, 1996), p. 67.

10 Christopher Jencks, 'Does Inequality Matter?' pp. 49–65 in *Daedalus*, Winter 2002, p. 61.

11 Richard G. Wilkinson, *Mind the Gap: Hierarchies, Health and Human Evolution* (London: Weidenfeld and Nicolson, 2000 and New Haven, Conn.: Yale University Press, 2001), p. 5.

12 Will Hutton, 'The Truth about Ageing', *Observer*, 6 October 2003, p. 24.

13 Howard Glennerster, *Understanding the Finance of Welfare: What Welfare Costs and How to Pay for it* (Bristol: The Policy Press, 2003), p. 67.

14 Wilkinson, *Unhealthy Societies*, p. 5.

15 Ibid.

16 For discussion of this issue and possible changes in international law to cope with it, see Thomas Pogge, *World Poverty and Human Rights* (Cambridge: Polity, 2002), ch. 6.

17 Glennerster, *Understanding the Finance of Welfare*, p. 65; emphasis in original.

18 John Carvel, 'Rich Patients get Better NHS Care', *Guardian*, 7 November 2003, p. 10.

19 Sarah Boseley, 'Rich Benefit Most from Improved Treatment of Cancer, say Scientists', *Guardian*, 10 March 2004, p. 5.

20 Ibid. Blacks in the United States are disadvantaged in remarkably similar ways. 'A 2002 Institute of Medicine report points out that blacks are less likely to receive appropriate cardiac medications or be referred for coronary artery bypass surgery. If they have kidney problems, they're less likely to receive dialysis or a transplant. Studies have shown that doctors dispense lower dosages of pain medicine to

African-Americans. According to the Institute's report, blacks receive lesser medical care regardless of their income and whether they have health insurance.' *Newsday*, 9 March 2004, p. B47.

21 This problem could be fixed by making the ability to communicate a prerequisite for gaining a medical qualification and by setting up an inspectorate to observe interactions between doctors and patients so as to tell them how to do better. The trouble is, of course, that patients' advocacy groups represent the articulate middle class, leaving the victims of class-related inequalities in health care without a voice. This is a pattern we have already seen and will see more of as this book progresses.

22 For a discussion of this point, see pp. 37–8 of my *Culture and Equality* (Cambridge: Polity, 2001; Cambridge, Mass.: Harvard University Press, 2000).

23 Quotation from Wilkinson, *Unhealthy Societies*, p. 92.

24 John W. Lynch et al., 'Income Inequality and Mortality: Importance to Health of Individual Income, Psychosocial Environment, or Material Conditions', pp. 217–27 in Hofrichter, ed., *Health and Social Justice*, figure 7.1, p. 220.

25 Ibid., figure 7.2, p. 221.

26 Wilkinson, *Mind the Gap*, p. 5.

27 Wilkinson, *Unhealthy Societies*, figure 5.1, p. 73. The gradient was continuous over all the twelve groups into which the population was divided, with one exception. If we thought that material deprivation was the driving force behind the relation, we would expect any inconsistency to come somewhere in the top half of the income distribution, whereas the only group that was out of line was the group one from the bottom.

28 Ibid., figure 5.8, p. 88.

29 Ibid., p. 193.

30 Ibid., p. 179.

31 Ibid. This will come as no surprise to those who recall Adelaide's lament in *Guys and Dolls* (first produced in 1950), in which she summarized a physiology textbook by saying that under conditions of chronic insecurity 'a person could develop a cold'.

32 Ibid., p. 194.

33 Ibid., p. 195.

34 Ibid., p. 196.

35 Ibid., p. 195.

36 Richard Levins, 'Is Capitalism a Disease? The Crisis in Public Health', pp. 365–84 in Hofrichter, ed., *Health and Social Justice*, p. 373.

37 House and Williams, 'Understanding and Reducing Socioeconomic and Racial/Ethnic Disparities in Health', table 3.1, p. 90.

38 Lynch et al., 'Income Inequality and Mortality', figure 7.2, p. 221.

39 House and Williams, 'Understanding and Reducing Socioeconomic and Racial/Ethnic Disparities in Health', p. 107. Internalized racism is also, of course, bad for health through its contribution to poverty: if

you are told you are rubbish so often that you believe it, you are hardly going to achieve anything. (See ibid. for this point.)

40   Wilkinson, *Unhealthy Societies*, p. 178.
41   Ibid.
42   Ibid., p. 53.
43   Ibid.
44   Ibid., p. 107.
45   Sarah Kuhn and John Wooding, 'The Changing Structure of Work in the United States: Implications for Health and Welfare', pp. 251–65 in Hofrichter, ed., *Health and Social Justice*, p. 254.
46   Wilkinson, *Unhealthy Societies*, p. 196.
47   Jencks, 'Does Inequality Matter?' p. 60.
48   Randeep Ranesh, 'The Last Thing on their Minds', *Guardian*, 13 May 2004, p. 15.
49   Ibid.
50   Juliana A. Maantay, 'Zoning, Equity and Public Health', pp. 228–50 in Hofrichter, ed., *Health and Social Justice*, p. 243.
51   Lynch et al., 'Income Inequality and Mortality', p. 222.
52   See Wilkinson, *Unhealthy Societies*, Part III.
53   See my 'Social Exclusion, Social Isolation and the Distribution of Income,' pp. 13–29 in John Hills, Julian Le Grand and David Piachaud, eds., *Understanding Social Exclusion* (Oxford: Oxford University Press, 2002).
54   Robert W. Fogel and Chulhee Lee, 'Who Gets Health Care?', *Daedalus*, Winter 2002, pp. 107–18: p. 115.
55   Brian Deer, 'American Health Care goes on the Critical List', *Sunday Times*, 2 September 1990, p. 11.
56   Ibid.
57   Marcia Sherman, 'Doubts on Mammograms do not Affect their Use', *New York Times*, 23 June 2002, section 15, p. 2.
58   Ibid.
59   Ibid.
60   'Medical decisions are not always made for medical reasons. . . . We [in the USA] do a lot more implanting of pacemakers than Europe and perform more caesarian sections and hysterectomies.' Hospitals buy expensive equipment to compete with other hospitals (which thus generates excess capacity) and then have to pay for it by charging insurance companies for unnecessary use. Further, 'to keep the "batting average" high, [a] surgeon has to perform [several hundred] operations [a year of a particular kind] . . . so there's an incentive to keep both surgeons and machines working.' Levins, 'Is Capitalism a Disease?' pp. 371, 372.
61   Denise Grady, 'Oops Wrong Patient: Journal takes on Medical Mistakes', *New York Times*, 18 June 2002, section 4, pp. 1 and 6.
62   Levins, 'Is Capitalism a Disease?' p. 372.
63   Sarah Boseley, '1 m Patients "Suffer Harm in Hospitals"', *Guardian*, 19 June 2002, p. 4.

64 Daniel Wikler, 'Personal Social Responsibility for Health', *Ethics and International Affairs*, 16 (2002), pp. 47–55: p. 49.

65 Ibid., p. 53.

66 Ibid., p. 52.

67 Greg Critser, *Fat Land: How Americans Became the Fattest People in the World* (Boston: Houghton Mifflin, 2003), pp. 129–30.

68 Wikler, 'Personal Social Responsibility for Health', p. 50.

69 This is not to deny, of course, that the total effects on health of environmental factors for any particular person depend on the interaction between it and that person's genome. (See chapter 9.) But the entire analysis here is carried out at the level of groups. Conceivably, there is a group-wide genetic basis for the weight (see text below) of the inhabitants of certain islands in the South Seas, but this kind of explanation would be a desperate resort as an explanation of group differences in health within countries such as Britain and America. Positive evidence for the failure of this hypothesis is that people who lose well-paid employment and start living in poverty and insecurity start to exhibit just the same traits as those who were poor all along.

70 Wilkinson, *Mind the Gap*, p. 65.

71 Describing life working in a chronically understaffed cheap restaurant, Barbara Ehrenreich says of a table adjacent to the toilets that its function is 'to house the ashtrays in which servers and dishwashers leave their cigarettes burning at all times, like votive candles, so that they don't have to waste time lighting up when they dash back here for a puff'. When she complains that the lack of any breaks in an eight-hour shift leaves no time for eating, one of her fellow server replies, 'Well, I don't understand how *you* can go so long without a cigarette.' Barbara Ehrenreich, *Nickel and Dimed: On (Not) Getting on in America* (New York: Henry Holt and Co., 2001), pp. 30, 32.

72 Levins, 'Is Capitalism a Disease?' p. 380.

73 Wilkinson, *Unhealthy Societies*, pp. 185–6.

74 Ibid., p. 188.

75 Severin Carrell, 'Comfort Eating Releases Chemicals that Fight Stress', *Independent on Sunday*, 14 September 2003, p. 5.

76 Norman Peccarano, quoted in ibid.

77 Ibid.

78 Wilkinson, *Unhealthy Societies*, p. 186.

79 Critser, *Fat Land*, p. 116.

80 Beezy Marsh, 'Obesity: New Child Alert', *Daily Mail*, 8 October 2003, pp. 1 and 6: p. 6.

81 Ibid.

82 Critser, *Fat Land*, p. 116.

83 Ibid., p. 5.

84 Ibid., p. 120.

85 Ibid., p. 123.

86 Ibid.

87 Ibid.

88   Ibid., p. 121.
89   Greg Critser, 'New Front in Battle of the Bulge', *New York Times*, 18 May 2003, WK, p. 7.
90   Ibid.
91   Ibid.
92   Ibid.
93   Eric Schlosser, *Fast Food Nation: The Dark Side of the All-American Meal* (New York: HarperCollins, 2002 [2001]), p. 57.
94   Ibid., p. 52.
95   Ibid.
96   Ibid., p. 55.
97   Ibid., p. 56.
98   Ibid., p. 55.
99   Ibid., p. 56.
100 Critser, *Fat Land*, p. 114.
101 Sean Poulter, 'Junk the Food Ads: Children "at Risk" from Hard Sell', *Daily Mail*, 21 July 2003, p. 13.
102 Ibid.
103 Quoted in Tim Kasser, *The High Price of Materialism* (Cambridge, Mass: The MIT Press, 2002), p. 91.
104 The connection between fast food and calorie intake is amazingly close: a study of 50,000 American adolescents found that those who ate three or more fast-food meals a week (a fifth of the total) averaged a daily intake of 2,752 calories, while those who ate one or two averaged 2,192 and those who ate none averaged 1,952 (Critser, *Fat Land*, p. 115).
105 Ibid., p. 28.
106 Sean Poulter, 'The Ice Creams that Pack a Cool 1000 Calories', *Daily Mail*, 26 July 2003, p. 35.
107 David Adam, 'Super Calorific Ice Cream Can Contain Staggering Amounts of Fat', *Guardian*, 25 July 2003, p. 2.
108 Ibid.
109 Jo Revill, 'Cadbury's Condemned Over School Sports Sweetener', *Observer*, 30 March 2003, p. 25.
110 Ibid.
111 David Gow and Larry Elliot, 'PM Seeks Industry Support for Reforms', *Guardian*, 18 November 2003, p. 19.
112 Levins, 'Is Capitalism a Disease?'

Chapter 7   The Making of the Black Gulag

1   Loïc Wacquant, 'Deadly Symbiosis: Rethinking Race and Imprisonment in Twenty-First Century America', *Boston Review*, 27(2), April/May 2002, pp. 23–31: p. 27.
2   Bernard E. Harcourt, 'Policing Disorder', *Boston Review*, 27(2), April/May 2002, pp. 16–22: p. 20.
3   Ibid., p. 21.

4   David Cole, *No Equal Justice: Race and Class in the American Criminal Justice System* (New York: The New Press, 1999), p. 50.

5   Ibid., p. 144.

6   Ibid., p. 156.

7   Ibid., p. 8.

8   This does not mean (as some commentators ignorantly suggested) that those in favour of acquittal thought it less likely that Simpson was guilty than that he was innocent. All they (we) had to hold was that, whether through incompetence or fraud, the police had rendered the material evidence unreliable – and, in the absence of an eye-witness, that was all the prosecution had.

9   Marc Mauer, *Race to Incarcerate* (New York: The New Press, 2001 [1999]), p. 162.

10   Ibid., pp. 84–5.

11   Ibid., pp. 81–3.

12   Ibid., p. 85. The lawyers did finally win expenses and overheads in addition to the fee, but only a highly dedicated lawyer would fight a capital case all out for that.

13   Ibid., p. 86; internal quotation from study cited.

14   Ibid., pp. 78–9.

15   Erin Texeira, 'Study on Blacks: Gains but still Shortages', *Newsday*, 25 March 2004, p. A5.

16   Ibid., p. 145.

17   Ibid.

18   Jerome J. Miller, 'Tracking Racial Bias' (summary of his *Search and Destroy: African-American Males in the Criminal Justice System* (Cambridge: Cambridge University Press, 1996), ch. 2), pp. 259–62 in Frank Ackerman et al., *The Political Economy of Inequality* (Washington DC: Island Press, 2000), p. 261.

19   Cole, *No Equal Justice*, p. 145; see this page also for more detail.

20   Miller, 'Tracking Racial Bias', p. 261.

21   Ibid., p. 262.

22   Wacquant, 'Deadly Symbiosis', p. 28; emphasis in original.

23   David Sheff, 'The Good Jailer', *New York Times Magazine*, 14 March 2004, pp. 44–7: p. 46.

24   Cole, *No Equal Justice*, p. 146.

25   Ibid., p. 147.

26   Ibid.

27   Ibid., p. xi.

28   Ibid., p. 148.

29   Ibid.

30   Al Baker, 'Fees, as Surely as Taxes, will Rob the State of Jobs, Critics of Pataki Budget Say', *New York Times*, 16 February 2003, p. 38.

31   Cole, *No Equal Justice*, p. 144. As Jeremy Bentham first pointed out, penalties should be graduated so that someone who commits one crime is not given an incentive to commit a greater one. Here, it is worth killing any number of police officers to avoid arrest for a drug offence,

32   Ibid., p. 145.
33   Department of Justice, Bureau of Justice Statistics, 27 July 2003: <www.ojp.udoj.gov/bjs/pub/press/p02pr.htm>.
34   Ibid.
35   Brent Staples, 'Growing Up in the Visiting Room', *New York Times Book Review*, 21 March 2004, p. 7.
36   Cole, *No Equal Justice*, p. 148.
37   Wacquant, 'Deadly Symbiosis', p. 23.
38   Ibid.
39   Ibid.
40   Fox Butterfield, 'Prison Rates among Blacks Reach a Peak, Study Finds', *New York Times*, 7 April 2003, p. A12.
41   Mauer, *Race to Incarcerate*, p. xii.
42   Staples, 'Growing Up in the Visiting Room'.
43   Jennifer Gonnerman, 'Life Without Parole', *New York Times Magazine*, 19 May 2002, pp. 40–4: p. 44.
44   Wacquant, 'Deadly Symbiosis', p. 30.
45   Gonnerman, 'Life Without Parole', p. 43; see also Wacquant, 'Deadly Symbiosis', p. 30 for more detail on the legislative history of this exclusion.
46   Gonnerman, 'Life Without Parole', p. 43.
47   Wacquant, 'Deadly Symbiosis', p. 28.
48   Fox Butterfield, 'Freed from Prison, but still Paying a Penalty', *New York Times*, 20 December 2002, section 1, p. 18.
49   Ibid.
50   Wacquant, 'Deadly Symbiosis', p. 28.
51   Butterfield, 'Freed from Prison'.
52   Stephen Burd, 'Seeking Redemption for a Drug Law', *The Chronicle of Higher Education*, 5 April 2002, pp. A17–19: p. A17.
53   Ibid.
54   Gonnerman, 'Life Without Parole', p. 42.
55   Wacquant, 'Deadly Symbiosis', p. 29.
56   Gonnerman, 'Life Without Parole', p. 42.
57   Ibid., p. 43.
58   Ibid., p. 41.
59   Mauer, *Race to Incarcerate*, p. 187. For a sophisticated discussion of the implications of this for the American system of governance, see Leonard C. Feldman, 'Redistribution, Recognition and the State: The Irreducibly Political Dimension of Injustice', *Political Theory*, 30 (2002), pp. 410–40.
60   *New York Times*, editorial: 'Former Felons have a Right to Vote', 17 October 2002, section A, p. 32. Quite apart from the other banana republic aspects of the presidential election in Florida, the Governor did his best for his brother by hiring a firm to disqualify as many additional blacks as possible. One strategy was to remove blacks who were actually eligible to vote from the electoral rolls without notifying them. By the time they found out at the polling station, it was too late.

61   Ibid., p. xii.
62   Ibid., p. 10.
63   Ibid.
64   Mauer, *Race to Incarcerate*, p. 195.
65   Cole, p. 192.
66   Gonnerman, 'Life Without Parole', p. 44.
67   Ibid.
68   A big contribution to the glut of heroin is the replacement of the Taliban regime in Afghanistan by the northern warlords, who regard the growing of opium (banned by the Taliban) as a major source of revenue.
69   Stephen Labaton, 'Downturn and Shift in Population Feed Boom in White-Collar Crime', *New York Times*, 2 June 2002, pp. 1 and 31: p. 1.
70   Ibid.
71   Ibid., p. 32.
72   Ibid.
73   Alan Travis, 'Ministers Act over Bursting Prisons', *Guardian*, 9 March 2004, p. 6.
74   Martin Bright, 'One in 100 Black Adults Now in Jail', *Observer*, 30 March 2003, p. 20.
75   Hugh Muir and Rebecca Smithers, 'Ethnic Minority Pupils Get More Help', *Guardian*, 23 October 2003, p. 8.
76   Alan Trevis, 'Courts Told "Jail Fewer Children"', *Guardian*, 5 September 2002, p. 11.
77   Nick Paton Walsh, 'Ethnic Timebomb in our Jails', *Observer*, 24 June 2001, p. 12.
78   Richard Ford, 'Judges are "not Trusted to Jail Criminals"', *The Times*, 7 June 2003, p. 1.
79   'A Costly Waste of Time', *Guardian* editorial, 2 July 2002, p. 15.

Chapter 8   The Idea of Meritocracy

1   Michael Young, *The Rise of the Meritocracy, 1870–2033* (London: Thames and Hudson, 1958).
2   David Miller, *Principles of Social Justice* (Cambridge, Mass.: Harvard University Press, 1999), p. 177.
3   Michael Young, 'Down with Meritocracy!', *Guardian*, 29 June 2001, p. 17.
4   I should say that David Miller, whose definition of meritocracy I quoted, does acknowledge inequality of opportunity as an issue (*Principles of Social Justice*, pp. 180–1) but he says that almost nothing can be done about it and he does not regard it as impugning the validity of the principle that 'merit' should be rewarded.
5   Michael Frayn, '. . . To Each According to his Ability', pp. 140–3 in *On the Outskirts* (London: Collins, 1964), p. 140.
6   Ibid.
7   Ibid., p. 141.

8   Ibid., p. 142.
9   Roland Benabou, 'Meritocracy, Redistribution and the Size of the Pie',
     pp. 317–39 in Kenneth Arrow, Samuel Bowles and Steven Durlaf, eds.,
     Meritocracy and Economic Equality (Princeton, NJ: Princeton Uni-
     versity Press, 2000), p. 319.
10   Ibid.
11   Adam Swift, *Political Philosophy: A Beginners' Guide for Students and
     Politicians* (Cambridge: Polity, 2001), p. 41.
12   Young, *The Rise of the Meritocracy*, p. 74.
13   Ibid., p. 86.
14   Quoted in Richard Lewontin, 'Race and Intelligence', in Ned Block
     and Gerald Dworkin, eds., *The IQ Controversy: Critical Readings*
     (London: Quartet Books 1977), p. 82.
15   Quoted in Ned Block and Gerald Dworkin, 'IQ, Heritability
     and Inequality', in Block and Dworkin, eds., *The IQ Controversy*,
     p. 473.
16   Harry Brighouse, *School Choice and Social Justice* (Oxford: Oxford
     University Press, 2000), p. 138. I should make it clear that this is only
     one component in Brighouse's own conception of equal educational
     opportunity.
17   Leon Kamin, who unmasked Burt, provides a succinct summary of the
     case against him in 'Heredity, Politics and Psychology I', pp. 242–64 in
     Block and Dworkin, eds., *The IQ Controversy*.
18   Kitcher, *Vaulting Ambition: Sociobiology and the Quest for Human
     Nature* (Cambridge, Mass.: The MIT Press, 1985), p. 2. The epigraph to
     Part III is drawn from this admirable book.
19   Ibid., p. 1.

Chapter 9   The Abuse of Science

1   Richard Herrnstein and Charles Murray, *The Bell Curve* (New York:
     Free Press, 1994), p. 101.
2   James R. Flynn, 'IQ Trends over Time: Intelligence, Race and Meri-
     tocracy', pp. 35–60 in Kenneth Arrow, Samuel Bowles and Steven
     Durlauf, eds., *Meritocracy and Economic Inequality* (Princeton, NJ:
     Princeton University Press, 2000), p. 46.
3   Professor John Ermish, quoted in David Walker, 'New Breed of Middle
     Class Closes Ranks', *Guardian*, 18 May 2002.
4   Flynn, 'IQ Trends over Time', p. 47.
5   Ibid., p. 46.
6   Herrnstein and Murray, *The Bell Curve*, p. 101.
7   Michael Young, *The Rise of the Meritocracy, 1870–2033* (London:
     Thames and Hudson, 1958).
8   Michael Young, 'Down with Meritocracy!' *Guardian*, 29 June 2001,
     p. 117.
9   Young, *The Rise of the Meritocracy*, pp. 111, 108.
10   Flynn, 'IQ Trends over Time', table 3.3, p. 52.

11 Philip Kitcher, *Vaulting Ambition: Sociobiology and the Quest for Human Nature* (Cambridge, Mass.: MIT Press, 1985), p. 335.
12 Martha A. Field and Valerie A. Sanchez, *Equal Treatment for People with Mental Retardation* (Cambridge, Mass.: Harvard University Press, 1999), p. 49.
13 Ibid.
14 Mary Jo Bane and Christopher Jencks, 'Five Myths about your IQ', pp. 325–38 in Ned Block and Gerald Dworkin, eds., *The IQ Controversy* (London: Quartet Books, 1977), p. 328.
15 'In general, differences in IQ account for less than 10 per cent of the variation in actual job performance. In many situations, there is no relation at all between a man's IQ and how competent he is at his job.' Ibid., pp. 327–8.
16 I discuss this point at some length in my *Culture and Equality: An Egalitarian Critique of Multiculturalism* (Cambridge: Polity, 2001; Cambridge, Mass.: Harvard University Press, 2001), pp. 100–2.
17 Stephen Jay Gould, 'Curveball', pp. 11–22 in Steven Fraser, ed., *The Bell Curve Wars: Race, Intelligence and the Future of America* (New York: Basic Books, 1995), p. 15.
18 Ned Block, 'How Heritability Misleads about Race', *Cognition*, 56 (1995), p. 106.
19 Ibid., p. 105.
20 My jaundiced attitude to selection on the basis of a test carried out at the age of 11 may be fuelled, I confess, by having only just scraped through the 11+ examination myself. Although scores were not disclosed, this can be deduced from the fact that all my classmates who passed were allocated to their first or second choice school (the two local schools that were chosen by everybody), whereas I was assigned to a school halfway across London in an area which very likely did not produce a high ratio of 11+ passes and hence had spare capacity.
21 Richard C. Lewontin, 'The Analysis of Variance and the Analysis of Causes', pp. 179–93 in Block and Dworkin, eds., *The IQ Controversy*.
22 I should emphasize that this applies only to moral and political philosophers. Those who actually study the subject, such as Ned Block and Philip Kitcher, are entirely another matter.
23 Block, 'How Heritability Misleads about Race', p. 103.
24 Ibid., p. 125.
25 Quoted by Field and Sanchez, *Equal Treatment for People with Mental Retardation*, p. 75.

Chapter 10   Responsibility versus Equality?

1 Thomas Hobbes, *Leviathan*, ch. 32.
2 Janet Browne, *Charles Darwin: The Power of Place* (New York: Alfred A. Knopf, 2002), p. 176.
3 *Oxford Book of Quotations*, ed. Angela Partington (Oxford: Oxford University Press, 1996), p. 27.

4 'Genetics of Behaviour', pp. 284–6 in Richard L. Gregory, ed., *The Oxford Companion to the Mind* (Oxford: Oxford University Press, 1987), p. 284.
5 'Galton', pp. 282–3 in ibid.: p. 283.
6 'Genius', p. 286 in ibid.
7 'Galton', p. 283 in ibid.
8 Ibid. George Bernard Shaw springs to mind as an indefatigable publicist for the religion of improvement in the characters of future generations, though he rejected the key Darwinian idea that acquired traits could not be transmitted.
9 This disparagement of technical skill remains pervasive. Alison Wolf, in her book *Does Education Matter?* (London: Penguin, 2002), devotes a chapter to the efforts of successive governments for the past 130 years to upgrade the quality and status of vocational qualifications, under the telling title 'A Great Idea for Other People's Children'. In the past twenty-five years, during which a whole alphabet soup of qualifications has come and gone, vocational equivalents of academic GCSE and A level examinations (taken at 16 and 18 respectively) have continued to be pursued by children who did not do well enough at the age of 14 to get into the academic stream but did not want to drop out of school. These vocational qualifications have never gained the 'equal standing' promised by the Conservatives in 1991 or 'as much status and esteem as academic [qualifications]' promised by Labour in 2001 (both quoted in ibid., p. 56). The latest gimmick is a proposal that 'vocational GCSEs and A levels would lose [the] vocational prefix to establish parity' (*Guardian*, 22 January 2003, p. 8). Wolf said in 2001 that she would be 'willing to bet a large sum' on the failure of 'vocational GCSEs ... *avowedly* aimed at low-achieving young people [to] achieve "parity of esteem" with academic qualifications' (*Does Education Matter?*, pp. 96, 97; emphasis in original). I find it hard to believe that the decision to abolish the prefix 'vocational' puts her in any danger of losing her bet. It is an indication of the government's belief in the efficacy of 'spin' that it should imagine that the deletion of a word will solve the real problem.
10 In practice, those women who suffered sterilization (in addition to permanent institutionalization) were often simply unwed mothers or other people who were for some reason or other inconvenient to their relatives. The landmark case – that of *Buck* v. *Bell*, which established the constitutionality of compulsory sterilization – was a case in point: 'In fact it appears that the woman forcibly sterilized in that case did not have retardation. Like many persons placed in institutions for the 'feeble-minded' at that time, she was an unwed mother. But her pregnancy did not even show she was 'promiscuous', a characteristic then associated with retardation; it was the result of rape [by] a relative of the same woman who had her committed to the state institution.' Martha A. Field and Valerie A. Sanchez, *Equal Treatment for People*

with Mental Retardation (Cambridge, Mass.: Harvard University Press, 1999), p. 68.

11 George Orwell, *The Collected Essays and Letters*, ed. Sonia Orwell and Ian Angus (Harmondsworth, Mddx: Penguin, 1970), vol. 3, pp. 1 and 30. Even so, writing on the eve of the 1945 general election Orwell revealed his lack of faith in 'the masses' by holding on to his long-standing prediction that the Conservatives would win.

12 'My faith sustains me, because I pray daily . . .' Elizabeth Bumiller, 'Aides say Bush Girds in Solitude, not in Doubt', *New York Times*, 9 March 2003, pp. 1 and 22: p. 22.

13 Jimmy Carter, 'Just War – or a Just War?', *New York Times*, 9 March 2003, p. 13.

14 'Could 75 to 80 per cent of the believers in Armageddon have voted for Bush? It appears so.' Quotation from Kevin Phillips, *American Dynasty: Aristocracy, Fortune and the Politics of Deceit in the House of Bush* (New York: Viking, 2004), quoted in a review by Paul R. Krugman, 'The Wars of the Texas Succession', *New York Review of Books*, 26 February 2004, pp. 4–6: p. 5.

15 James Boswell, *Life of Johnson*, ed. R. W. Freeman (London: Oxford, 1970), p. 411.

16 For an excellent discussion of all the points raised here, see Marc Fleurbaey, 'Equality of Resources Revisited', *Ethics*, 113 (2002), pp. 82–105, esp. p. 84.

17 Gordon Marshall, Adam Swift and Stephen Roberts, *Against the Odds? Social Class and Social Justice in Industrial Societies* (Oxford: Clarendon Press, 1997), Appendix J (pp. 244–9): table J1, p. 246.

18 Samuel Bowles and Herbert Gintis, 'The Inheritance of Inequality', *Journal of Economic Perspectives*, 16 (2002), pp. 3–30: p. 3.

19 Horatio Alger, Jr., *Ragged Dick and Struggling Upward* (Harmondsworth, Mddx: Penguin Books, 1986), 'Introduction' by Carl Bode, pp. ix–xxi: p. ix.

20 *Struggling Upward*, pp. 33–80 in ibid., p. 280.

21 Bode, 'Introduction' in ibid., p. ix.

Chapter 11   Rights and Responsibilities

1 Actually, the remark is attributed to him in one of the original *Fabian Essays*. Even if apocryphal, however, it has become so famous that it must have struck a chord. See *The Oxford Dictionary of Quotations*, p. 323, *sub* Harcourt.

2 *The Cambridge Biographical Encyclopaedia* says that is what he is 'best remembered for', though I am not sure how many people remember him at all. See p. 423 *sub* Harcourt.

3 Ed Vulliamy, 'Bush Squirms in Sleaze Scandal', *Observer*, 14 July 2002, p. 12.

4 Ibid.

5 Ibid.

6　Ibid.
7　Ibid.
8　Ibid.
9　Ibid.
10　Eric Alterman, *What Liberal Media? The Truth about Bias and the News* (New York: Basic Books, 2003), pp. 172–3.
11　Tony Blair, 'My Vision for Britain', *Observer*, 10 November 2002.
12　Paul R. Krugman, 'The Wars of the Texas Succession', *New York Review of Books*, 26 February 2004, pp. 4–6: p. 4.
13　Paul Brown, 'Pollution Still Pays as Firms Shrug Off Fines', *Guardian*, 31 July 2003, p. 9.
14　Ibid.
15　Ibid.
16　The repertoire included the murder of striking workers by mercenaries such as the notorious Pinkerton Agency or by local police acting at the behest of the owners.
17　S. N. Behrman, *Duveen* (New York: The Little Bookroom, 2003; originally published in articles in the *New Yorker*, 1951 and 1952), p. 133.
18　Martin Kettle, 'We Have a Minimum Wage – Now Let's Set a Maximum', *Guardian*, 21 May 2003.
19　Ibid.
20　Deborah Orr, 'A Divided Nation – and the Rifts are Growing', *Independent*, 20 May 2003, p. 10.
21　Andrew Clark, 'Ladbroke Grove Train Company Pleads Guilty', *Guardian*, 11 December 2003, p. 9.
22　Ibid.
23　Orr, 'A Divided Nation – and the Rifts are Growing'.
24　Ibid.
25　Angela Philips, 'Children First', *Guardian*, 30 July 2003, p. 15.
26　Ibid.
27　Ibid.
28　Ibid.
29　Jody Heymann, *The Widening Gap: Why America's Working Families Are in Jeopardy and What Can be Done About It* (New York: Basic Books, 2000), p. 136.
30　Christopher D. Cook, 'Plucking Workers', pp. 157–64 in Christopher Caldwell and Christopher Hitchens, eds., *Left Hooks, Right Crosses: A Decade of Political Writing* (New York: Thunder's Mouth Press/Nation Books, 2002), p. 158.
31　Ibid., pp. 158–9.
32　Ibid., p. 157.
33　George Orwell, *Nineteen Eighty-Four* (London: Secker and Warburg, 1951), p. 220.
34　Ibid., p. 221.
35　Quoted in Desmond King, *Actively Seeking Work: The Politics of Unemployment and Welfare Policy in the United States and Britain* (Chicago: Chicago University Press, 1995), p. 176.

36 Ibid., p. 168.
37 Blair, 'My Vision for Britain'.
38 'Benefit Cuts for Tenants "Insulting" ' in British Roundup, *Guardian*, 31 July 2003, p. 9.
39 Patrick Wintour, 'Benefit Cut for Nuisance Tenants Scrapped', *Guardian*, 26 November 2003, p. 2.
40 Ibid.
41 John Carvel, 'U-turn on Benefit Cut for Neighbours from Hell', *Guardian*, 28 January 2004, p. 6.
42 Ibid.

Chapter 12   Irresponsible Societies

1 Catherine Bennett, 'Is Jail the Answer for Fatal Negligence?', *Guardian*, 25 September 2003, G2, p. 5.
2 Ibid.
3 Ibid.
4 Barbara Ehrenreich, *Nickeled and Dimed: On (Not) Getting by in America* (New York: Henry Holt, 2001), pp. 15, 48.
5 Daniel Wikler, 'Personal and Social Responsibility for Health', *Ethics and International Affairs*, 16 (2002), pp. 47–55: p. 48.
6 Barry Schwartz, *The Paradox of Choice: Why More is Less* (New York: HarperCollins, 2004), p. 26.
7 Ibid., pp. 26–7.
8 Ibid, p. 27.
9 Ibid.
10 Ibid., p. 28.
11 Ibid., p. 29.
12 Jenni Russell, 'Parental Choice: Tutor, Find God, Appeal, Move or Pay', *Guardian*, 14 February 2004, p. 18.
13 Patrick Wintour, 'Byers Pushes for More Choice in Public Services', *Guardian*, 6 April 2004, p. 8.
14 Ibid.
15 Nina Bernstein, 'Once Again, Trying Housing as a Cure for Homelessness', *New York Times*, 23 June 2000, pp. 29–30: p. 29.
16 Ibid.
17 Ibid., p. 30.
18 Ibid.
19 Ibid.
20 Ibid.
21 Ibid., quotation from Marybeth Shinn.
22 Ben Summerskill and Dino Mahtani, 'Homelessness in Drugs Epidemic', *Observer*, 14 July 2002, p. 12.
23 Ibid.
24 Ibid.
25 Eric Klinenberg, *Heat Wave: A Social Autopsy of Disaster in Chicago* (Chicago: Chicago University Press, 2002), p. 30.

26   Ibid., p. 79.
27   Ibid., p. 80.
28   Ibid.
29   Eric Klinenberg, 'Baked to Death', *Guardian*, 20 August 2002, G2, pp. 12–13: p. 12.
30   Ibid.
31   Klinenberg, *Heat Wave*, pp. 47–78.
32   Ibid., pp. 155–6.
33   Ibid., p. 130.
34   Ibid., p. 134.
35   Ibid., p. 132.
36   Ibid., p. 133.
37   Klinenberg, 'Baked to Death', p. 12.
38   Klinenberg, *Heat Wave*, p. 214.
39   For a full analysis of this process, see ibid., ch. 4, 'Governing by Public Relations'.
40   Klinenberg, 'Baked to Death', p. 12.
41   Ibid.
42   Klinenberg, *Heat Wave*, p. 179.
43   Ibid., pp. 143–4.
44   Patrick Wintour, 'Cabinet Weighs up Tactics on Hunting Issue', *Guardian*, 19 November 2003, p. 13.
45   Sarah Hall, 'Labour Considers Ban on Junk Food Ads During Children's TV', *Guardian*, 31 May 2004, p. 3.
46   Ibid.
47   Ibid.
48   Ibid.

Chapter 13   Pathologies of Inequality

1   Commission on Social Justice, 'The Justice Gap', Discussion Paper No. 1, reprinted as ch. 2 in Jane Franklin, ed., *Social Policy and Social Justice* (Cambridge: Polity, 1998), p. 46.
2   André Gorz, *Reclaiming Work: Beyond the Wage-Based Society* (Cambridge: Polity, 1997), pp. 81–2.
3   Jared Bernstein, 'Two Cheers for The Earned Income Tax Credit', pp. 153–63 in Robert Kuttner, ed., *Making Work Pay: America after Welfare* (New York: The New Press, 2002), p. 160.
4   David R. Howell, 'Institutional Failure and the American Worker: The Collapse of Low-Skill Wages', pp. 214–17 in Frank Ackerman et al., *The Political Economy of Equality* (Washington DC: The Island Press, 2000), p. 216.
5   Alison Wolf, *Does Education Matter? Myths about Education and Economic Growth* (London: Penguin Books, 2002), pp. 48–9.
6   Bernstein, 'Two Cheers for The Earned Income Tax Credit', p. 160.
7   Sir W. S. Gilbert, *The Savoy Operas* (London: Macmillan, 1968), p. 528.
8   Wolf, *Does Education Matter?*, p. 50.
9   Ibid., p. 51.

10 Ibid., p. 52.
11 Howell, 'Institutional Failure and the American Worker', p. 193.
12 Frank Ackerman, 'Poverty, Inequality and Power, Overview Essay', pp. 143–51 in Frank Ackerman et al., eds., *The Political Economy of Equality*, p. 147.
13 Ibid.
14 Ibid.
15 Ibid., p. 145.
16 Frances Fox Piven and Richard Cloward, 'Poor Relief and the Dramaturgy of Work', pp. 162–6 in Ackerman et al., eds., *The Political Economy of Equality*, p. 164.
17 Juliette Jowit, 'Millions Live without Water, Gas or Power', report by The National Consumers Council, *Observer*, 14 September 2003, p. 13.
18 Ibid.
19 Robert H. Frank and Philip J. Cook, *The Winner-Take-All Society: Why the Few at the Top Get so Much More than the Rest of Us* (London: Penguin Books, 1995), p. 176.
20 Ibid., p. 177.
21 Frank Ackerman, 'Unequal Earnings: Theory versus Reality', pp. 1–10 in Ackerman et al., eds., *The Political Economy of Equality*, p. 3.
22 Ibid.
23 Ibid.
24 John Carvell, 'Support For Higher Taxes Doubles', *Guardian*, 9 December 2002, p. 7 (the figures are for 2002).
25 Anthony Sampson, 'The New Edwardians', *Observer*, 14 July 2002, p. 18.
26 Ibid.
27 Danny Hakim and Norm Alster, 'Lawsuits: This Year's Model', *New York Times*, 30 May 2004, section 3, pp. 1 and 9: p. 9.
28 Ibid.
29 Ibid.
30 Ibid.
31 Ibid.
32 Richard Wilkinson, *Mind the Gap: Hierarchies, Health and Human Evolution* (New Haven, Conn.: Yale University Press, 2001), p. 30. The reference is to Juliet Schor, *The Overspent American: When Buying Becomes You* (New York: Basic Books, 1998).
33 Hester Lacey, 'How Well Do You Know Your Children?' *The Independent on Sunday*, 14 December 2003, pp. 16–17: p. 17.
34 Tom Robbins and Mark Ludlow, 'Crime Detection Rates Decline by up to a Third', *Sunday Times*, 30 June 2002, p. 10.
35 Richard G. Wilkinson, *Unhealthy Societies: The Afflictions of Inequality* (London: Routledge, 1996), p. 156.
36 Ibid., pp. 155–6.
37 Robert D. Putnam, *Bowling Alone: The Collapse and Revival of American Community* (New York: Simon and Schuster, 2000), pp. 308–9.
38 Ibid., pp. 408–9.

39   Wilkinson, *Unhealthy Societies*, p. 162.
40   Ibid.
41   Mary Riddell, 'Be Afraid, but not too Afraid', *Observer*, 14 July 2002, p. 28.
42   Alan Travis, 'Abrupt End to Six-Year Fall in Crime', *Guardian*, 12 July 2002, p. 1.
43   Jeff Maddick, 'The Power of the Super-Rich', *The New York Review of Books*, 18 July 2002, pp. 25–7: p. 26.
44   Christopher Jencks, 'Does Inequality Matter?', *Daedalus*, Winter 2002, pp. 49–65: p. 49.
45   See Maddick, 'The Power of the Super-Rich', p. 26.
46   Sampson, 'The New Edwardians'.
47   See Ian Shapiro, 'Why the Poor Don't Soak the Rich', *Daedalus*, Winter 2002, pp. 118–28: p. 120.
48   Jencks, 'Does Inequality Matter?', p. 49.
49   Ibid.
50   Frank Ackerman, 'New Paths to the Top: CEO and Celebrity Compensation', pp. 61–77 in Ackerman et al., eds., *The Political Economy of Equality*, pp. 64–5.
51   Gretchen Morgerson, 'Explaining (or not) Why the Boss is Paid so Much', *New York Times*, 25 January 2004, section 3, p. 1.
52   Shapiro, 'Why the Poor Don't Soak the Rich', p. 123.
53   See ibid., pp. 122–3 and also my *Culture and Equality* (Cambridge: Polity; Cambridge, Mass.: Harvard University Press, 2001), esp. ch. 8.
54   Cited in Tim Kasser, *The High Price of Materialism* (Cambridge, Mass.: The MIT Press, 2002), p. 104.
55   Ibid.
56   Ibid., p. 82.
57   Ibid., p. 64.
58   Putnam, *Bowling Alone*, p. 143.
59   Ibid., pp. 140–1.
60   Cited in John Elliott and Lauren Quinitanco, 'Britain is Getting More Suspicious', *Sunday Times*, 18 May 2003, p. 5.
61   Ibid.
62   Ibid.

Chapter 14   Wealth

1   Thus, in Germany, unearned income accounted for 22 per cent in 1978, while in 1994 the corresponding proportion was 33 per cent. André Gorz, *Reclaiming Work: Beyond the Wage-based Society* (Cambridge: Polity, 1999), p. 17.
2   A good example is the article discussed in Part II by Christopher Jencks on 'Does Inequality Matter?', *Daedalus*, Winter 2002, pp. 49–65.
3   One way of looking at it is that the billionaire would have a very large income if he chose to hold his wealth in the form of financial assets.

Ideally, it should be irrelevant to his tax liability that he prefers to enjoy it in the form of pictures and properties instead. For all this means is that he gets more enjoyment from owning these than he would get from the investment income he could have as an alternative.

4   See Edward N. Wolff, *Top Heavy: The Increasing Inequality of Wealth in America and What Can Be Done about it* (New York: The New Press, 2002), p. 48, table 7–1, and p. 49.
5   Ibid., p. 28.
6   Ray Boshara, 'Poverty is More than a Matter of Income', *New York Times*, 29 September 2002, WK, p. 13.
7   David Nissan and Julian Le Grand, 'A Capital Idea: Helping the Young to Help Themselves', pp. 29–41 in Keith Dowding, Jurgen de Wispelaere and Stuart White, *The Ethics of Stakeholding* (London: Palgrave, 2003), pp. 31–2.
8   Boshara, 'Poverty is More than a Matter of Income'.
9   Wolff, *Top Heavy*, p. 14.
10 Ibid., pp. 8–9.
11 Ibid., p. 8.
12 Nissan and Le Grand, 'A Capital Idea', p. 30.
13 Wolff, *Top Heavy*, p. 38.
14 Ibid., p. 15.
15 Mary O'Hara, 'Landed Gentry Top Property Rich List', *Guardian*, 11 October 2003, p. 30, data from *Estates Gazette*.
16 Ibid.
17 *The Sunday Times*, 'Rich List', 7 April 2002 (supplement).
18 Wolff, *Top Heavy*, p. 60.
19 Ibid.
20 Ibid., p. 66.
21 Ibid., p. 60.
22 Ibid., p. 74.
23 Ibid., p. 45.
24 Ibid., pp. 44–5.
25 Nissan and Le Grand, 'A Capital Idea', p. 36.
26 Ibid.
27 Ibid.
28 Ibid.
29 Ken Maguire, 'Brown Urged to Keep Tax Loophole Pledge', *Guardian*, 19 March 2004, p. 4.
30 Boshara, 'Poverty is More than a Matter of Income'.
31 The general point is raised in John Hills, 'Inclusion or Insurance? National Insurance and the Future of the Contributory Principle', London School of Economics: CASE paper 68, May 2003.
32 Robert Erikson and John H. Goldthorpe, 'Intergenerational Inequality: A Sociological Perspective', *Journal of Economic Perspectives*, 16 (2002), pp. 31–44: pp. 33–4.
33 Ibid., p. 42.
34 Ibid., p. 41; emphasis in original.

35 Bruce Ackerman and Anne Alstott, *The Stakeholder Society* (New Haven, Conn.: Yale University Press, 1999).
36 Nissan and Le Grand, 'A Capital Idea', p. 33; Ackerman and Alstott, *The Stakeholder Society*, pp. 184–7.
37 Nissan and Le Grand, 'A Capital Idea', pp. 38–9.
38 'Challenging Thatcher's Legacy', *Guardian*, 19 November 2003, G2, p. 8.
39 Ibid.
40 Nissan and Le Grand, 'A Capital Idea', p. 38.
41 Ibid., p. 35.
42 Lucy Ward, 'Poor Students Shoulder Debt for Learning', *Guardian*, 19 November 2003, p. 6.
43 Ibid.
44 Ackerman and Alstott, *The Stakeholder Society*, p. 56.
45 Ibid., p. 58.
46 Ibid. (The 1997 date is suggested by p. 238, n. 24.)
47 Ibid., p. 239, n. 29.
48 Ibid., p. 58.
49 Ibid., p. 71.
50 See ibid., p. 68 for the first example, p. 69 for the other two.

Chapter 15   Jobs and Incomes

 1 Robert D. Putnam, *Bowling Alone: The Collapse and Revival of American Community* (New York: Simon and Schuster, 2000), p. 179.
 2 André Gorz, *Reclaiming Work: Beyond the Wage-Based Society* (Cambridge: Polity, 1997), p. 64.
 3 Will Hutton, *The World We're In* (London: Little Brown, 2002), p. 164.
 4 Christopher Jencks, *'Does Inequality Matter?'* pp. 49–65 in *Daedalus*, Winter 2002, table 2, p. 54.
 5 Doug Henwood, 'US Miracle is based on Longer Hours for Less Pay', *Guardian*, 2 February 2004, p. 15.
 6 Ibid.
 7 Ibid.
 8 Ibid.
 9 Steven Greenhouse, 'Time Records often Altered, Job Experts Say', *New York Times*, 4 April 2004, pp. 1 and 22: p. 22.
10 Ibid.
11 Gorz, *Reclaiming Work*, p. 101.
12 Richard B. Freeman and Lawrence F. Katz, 'Rising Wage Inequality: The United States versus Other Advanced Countries', pp. 21–5 in Frank Ackerman et al., *The Political Economy of Equality* (Washington DC: Island Press, 2000), p. 24.
13 See Jared Bernstein, 'Two Cheers for the Earned Income Tax Credit', pp. 154–63: p. 161; and David Howell, 'Skills and the Wage Collapse', pp. 181–95: p. 181; both in Robert Kuttner, ed., *Making Work Pay: America after Welfare* (New York: The New Press, 2002).

14 'Spherion [a recruiting firm] estimates that the turnover of one job, on average, costs a company 1.5 times an employee's annual salary.' David Koeppel, 'The New Cost of Keeping Workers Happy', *New York Times*, 7 March 2004, p. BU11.
15 Barbara Ehrenreich, *Nickel and Dimed: On (not) Getting By in America* (New York: Henry Holt, 2001).
16 Ibid., p. 12.
17 Ibid., n. 5. p. 37.
18 Ibid., p. 208.
19 Ibid., p. 209.
20 Ibid., p. 210.
21 Ibid., n. 4, p. 35.
22 David M. Gordon. 'Wielding the Stick', pp. 18–21 in Ackerman et al., ed., *The Political Economy of Equality*, p. 18.
23 Polly Toynbee, *Hard Work: Life in Low-Pay Britain* (London: Bloomsbury, 2003), p. 218.
24 Cited in Stefan Fern, 'Let's Give Change a Rest', *Guardian*, 31 May 2004, p. 15.
25 Gorz, *Reclaiming Work*, p. 20.
26 John Hills, *Exclusion or Insurance? National Insurance and the Future of the Contributory Principle* (London School of Economics, CASE-paper 68, 2003), p. 8.
27 See Desmond King, *Actively Seeking Work? The Politics of Unemployment and Welfare Policy in the United States and Great Britain* (Chicago: University of Chicago Press, 1995).
28 Abby Ellin, 'For Many, Full-Time Work Means Part-time Benefits', *New York Times*, 17 August 2003, section 10, pp. 1 and 3: p. 1.
29 Full-page advertisement by HIP in *The Wall Street Journal*, 3 March 2004, p. B2A. Most of the page is occupied by a photograph of somebody (presumably a company director) with a big grin on his face explaining how he got the costs so low. He has plenty to grin about – provided, of course, that his own medical insurance is in an entirely different league.
30 'Back in 1968, full-time work at the minimum wage put a worker with two children about $1,300 above the poverty line. [With] the EITC . . . her family's income once again surpasses the poverty line, in this case by a few hundred dollars. Over the past three decades, the cost of maintaining an antipoverty wage has been shifted from employers to taxpayers.' Bernstein, 'Two Cheers for the Earned Income Tax Credit', p. 162.
31 Hills, *Exclusion or Insurance?*, p. 4.
32 Guy Standing, *Beyond the New Paternalism* (London: Verso, 2002), p. 98.
33 Sarah Hall, 'Tax Credit System Branded a Disaster', *Guardian*, 22 April 2004, p. 9.
34 'Bonds Unlikely to Set the Children Free' (no author credited), *Guardian*, 13 November 2003, p. 21.

35   Philippe Van Parijs, 'A Basic Income for All', pp. 3–26 in Joshua Cohen and Joel Rogers, eds., *What's Wrong with a Free Lunch?* (Boston: Beacon Press, 2001), p. 21.
36   Toynbee, *Hard Work*, p. 206.
37   Tony Atkinson, 'How Basic Income is Moving Up the Policy Agenda: News from the Future', paper for BIEN conference, 12–14 September 2002, figure 3.
38   David Piachaud and Holly Sutherland, *Changing Poverty post-1997* (London School of Economics: CASEpaper 63, November 2002).
39   Andrew Shepherd, 'Inequality under the Labour Government' (London: Institute for Fiscal Studies Briefing Note 33, 2003), p. 4.

Chapter 16   Can We Afford Social Justice?

1   As Avishai Margalit has pointed out, Orwell and Skinner both postulate a society whose members are deliberately controlled. 'The most one can aim for is to replace negative, aversive stimuli by overt positive ones', *The Decent Society* (Cambridge, Mass.: Harvard University Press, 1996), pp. 72–3.
2   Commission on Social Justice, *Social Justice: Strategies for National Renewal* (London: Vintage 1994), extracts in ch. 1 in Jane Franklin, ed., *Social Policy and Social Justice* (Cambridge: Polity, 1998), pp. 17–18.
3   Gretchen Morgenson, 'Explaining (or not) Why the Boss is Paid so Much', *New York Times*, 25 January 2004, section 3, p. 1.
4   Polly Toynbee, 'Fat Cats' Pay is the Result of Greed, not Competition', *Guardian*, 24 December 2003, p. 16.
5   Robert Solow, 'Forward', pp. ix–xvi in Joshua Cohen and Joel Rogers, eds., *What's Wrong with a Free Lunch?* (Boston: Beacon Press, 2001), p. xiii.
6   George Monbiot, 'State of War', *Guardian*, 24 October 2003, p. 25.
7   Simon Walters, 'IDS and Howard Split over Tax Cuts', *Mail on Sunday*, 5 October 2003, p. 2; Gordon Brown's electioneering promise in 2004 to improve public services without raising taxes.
8   Zoe Williams, 'These Aren't Accidents', *Guardian*, 23 October 2003, p. 25. As she points out, the reduction in frequency of inspections was introduced just before privatization – obviously to make investment look more attractive. This is perhaps even more eloquent of the clash between profit and safety.
9   Kevin Maguire, 'Passengers Face Tube Chaos in Safety Row', *Guardian*, 21 November 2003, p. 7.
10   Gareth Walsh, 'Fancy a Rubbish Job?' *Sunday Times*, 13 July 2003, News review, pp. 1–2.
11   Benjamin I. Page and James R. Simmons, *What Government Can Do: Dealing with Poverty and Inequality* (Chicago: University of Chicago Press, 2000), p. 133.
12   Larry Elliott, 'Brown Claims Tax Victory over CBI', *Guardian*, 23 October 2003, p. 21.
13   Ibid.

14 Ibid.

15 Page and Simmons, *What Government Can Do*, pp. 131–4.

16 Howard Glennerster, *Understanding the Finance of Welfare: What Welfare Costs and How to Pay For It* (Bristol: The Policy Press, 2003), p. 48.

17 Robert H. Frank and Philip J. Cook, *The Winner-Take-All Society: Why the Few at the Top Get So Much More than the Rest of Us* (London: Penguin Books, 1995), p. 21.

18 Clare Dyer, 'Number of QCs Earning £1m a Year up by 25%', *Guardian*, 22 October 2003, p. 7.

19 Frank and Cook, *The Winner-Take-All Society*, p. 9.

20 Ibid., p. 21.

21 Ibid., p. 212.

22 David Leonhardt, 'Coke Rewrote Rules, Aiding its Boss', *New York Times*, 7 April 2002, section 3, p. 6. Coke was only one of numerous examples. For a general account, see David Leonhardt, 'Did Pay Incentives Cut Both Ways?' *New York Times*, 7 April 2002, section 3, pp. 1, 6 and 7.

23 David Altman, 'How to Tie Pay to Goals instead of the Stock Price', *New York Times*, 8 September 2002, p. BU4. 'In fact, stock option grants have become so large in the last decade that executives have become wealthy by selling just a fraction of their holdings during a stock-price run-up that turns out to be fleeting': David Leonhardt, 'Tell the Good News. Then Cash In', *New York Times*, 7 April 2002, section 3, pp. 1 and 5: p. 1.

24 John Maynard Keynes, 'Economic Possibilities for our Grandchildren', pp. 321–7 in *Essays in Persuasion*, vol. IX, *The Collected Writings of John Maynard Keynes* (London: Macmillan, 1972), p. 329.

Chapter 17   The Power of Ideas

1 Charles Murray, *Losing Ground: American Social Policy 1950–1980* (New York: Basic Books, 1984).

2 Eric Alterman, *What Liberal Media? The Truth about Bias and the News* (New York: Basic Books, 2003), p. 92.

3 Quoted in ibid., p. 90.

4 Black's insensate greed (of the kind to be discussed in chapter 20) has resulted, as this goes to press, in his being forced out. His replacement by two brothers (the Barclays) scarcely constitutes an access of pluralism, and their editional appointments indicate that a strong right-wing line will be maintained.

5 Alterman, *What Liberal Media?*, p. 22.

6 'The two heads of AOL Time Warner . . . took home a combined $241 million in 2001. Michael Eisner of Disney pulled down nearly $73 million. Leave aside the fact that stocks of each of these companies performed miserably in the same years, something you will probably not find discussed much in the myriad media properties they control. Ask yourself if the men and women who earn numbers like that are

really sending forth aggressive investigators of financial and political malfeasance . . .?' Ibid., p. 27.

7   Ibid., p. 23.
8   Ibid., p. 87.
9   Ibid., p. 71.
10   Ibid.
11   Ibid.
12   Rules to deregulate media ownership to a point at which both print and television media could both be concentrated in the hands of a few giant corporations, adopted by the FCC in 2003, were so outrageous that a majority of a Senate committee made up of members of both parties voted to overturn them. Stephan Labaton, 'Senate Moves to Restore FCC Limits on the Media', *New York Times*, 5 June 2003, pp. C1 and 8.
13   The full sentence runs: 'Enterprise should be encouraged through a good climate for business and a tax system which rewards success; and an active welfare state that moves people off benefit and into work.' Tony Blair, speech at the annual dinner of the CBI, 17 May 2000. Quoted in Alistair Beaton, *The Little Book of New Labour Bollocks* (London: Simon and Schuster, 2000), n.p.
14   Extract from same speech, ibid., n.p.
15   Ibid., n.p.: speech in the Assembly Rooms, Derby, 18 January 1996.
16   Alterman, *What Liberal Media?*, p. 26.
17   Ibid.
18   Ibid., p. 149.
19   Michael White, Sarah Hall and Larry Elliot, 'Hain Forced to Retreat on Rich Tax', *Guardian*, 21 June 2003, pp. 1 and 2: p. 1.
20   Ibid.
21   Ibid.
22   Ibid.
23   John Carvel, 'Support for Higher Taxes Doubles', *Guardian*, 9 December 2003, p. 9. Quotation from John Curtice and Stephen Fisher.
24   Ibid.
25   Alterman, *What Liberal Media?*, p. 227.
26   Ibid., p. 259.

Chapter 18   How Change Happens

1   Philippe Van Parijs, 'Reply', pp. 121–7 in Philippe Van Parijs et al., *What's Wrong with a Free Lunch?*, ed. Joshua Cohen and Joel Rogers for *Boston Review* (Boston: Beacon Press, 2001), pp. 124–5.
2   Tom Athanasiou and Paul Baer, *Dead Heat: Global Justice and Global Warming* (New York: Seven Stories Press, 2002), pp. 148–9; emphasis suppressed.
3   Geoffrey Lean, 'How to Save the World in 10 Days', *The Independent on Sunday*, 25 August 2002, p. 18.

4   Ibid.
5   Athanasiou and Baer, *Dead Heat*, p. 30.
6   Ibid., p. 31 (speech by George W. Bush on 11 June 2001).
7   Andrew Gumbel, 'US Says CO_2 is not a Pollutant', *The Independent on Sunday*, 31 August 2003, p. 17.
8   Jeffrey Brainard, 'How Sound is Bush's "Sound Science"?' *The Chronicle of Higher Education*, 5 March 2004, pp. 18 and 20: p. 18.
9   Antony Barnett, 'Bush Attacks Environment "Scare Stories"', *Observer*, 4 April 2004, p. 15.
10 Ibid.
11 Cited in Mike Bygrave, 'Where Have All the Protesters Gone?', *The Observer*, 14 July 2002, pp. 24–6: p. 24.
12 Ibid.
13 Cited in ibid.

Chapter 19   Meltdown?

1   Dinyar Godrej, *The No-Nonsense Guide to Climate Change* (Oxford: New Internationalist Publications Ltd., 2001), p. 123.
2   Ibid., p. 122.
3   WWF, *Living Planet Report 2002*, Summary, p. 1.
4   Geoffrey Lean, 'The Issues', *Independent on Sunday*, 25 August 2002, p. 20.
5   Godrej, *The No-Nonsense Guide*, p. 60.
6   John Vidal and Heather Stewart, 'Europe's Harvest Crisis', *Guardian*, 3 September 2003, p. 1.
7   Geoffrey Lean, 'Hot Summer Sparks Global Food Crisis', *Independent on Sunday*, 31 August 2003, p. 4.
8   Thurston Clarke, review of Richard Ellis, *The Empty Ocean* (Washington DC: Island Press, 2003), *New York Times*, 25 May 2003, p. 13.
9   Severin Carroll, 'Ban Fishing in Third of all Seas, Scientists Say', *Independent on Sunday*, 31 August 2003, p. 7.
10 Stephen M. Meyer, 'End of the Wild: The Extinction Crisis is Over. We Lost', *Boston Review*, 29 (April/May 2004), pp. 20–5: p. 25.
11 Richard Sadler and Geoffrey Lean, 'North Sea Faces Collapse of its Ecosystem', *Independent on Sunday*, 19 October 2003.
12 Ibid.
13 Ibid.
14 Michael T. Klare, *Resource Wars: The New Landscape of Global Conflict* (New York: Henry Holt, 2002 [2001]), p. 38.
15 Ibid., p. 141.
16 Diane Raines Ward, *Water Wars: Drought, Flood, Folly and the Politics of Thirst* (New York: Riverhead Books, 2002), pp. 180–1.
17 Ibid., p. 181.
18 Ibid., p. 205.

19 Ibid.
20 Ibid., p. 188; for Turkish appropriation of the waters of the Tigris and Euphrates, see pp. 188–95; for the Nile, see pp. 196–202.
21 Tom Athanasiou and Paul Baer, *Dead Heat: Global Warming and Global Justice* (New York: Seven Stories Press, 2002), n. 3, p. 162.
22 Ward, *Water Wars*, p. 3.
23 Ibid.
24 John Stuart Mill, *On Liberty*, in *On Liberty and Other Writings*, ed. Stefan Collini (Cambridge: Cambridge University Press, 1989). 'The fact itself, of causing the existence of a human being, is one of the most responsible actions in the range of human life', and thus controls on the creation of human life 'do not exceed the legitimate powers of the state': p. 108.
25 Athanasiou and Baer, *Dead Heat*, figure 1, p. 22.
26 Ian Sample, 'Not Just Warmer: It's the Hottest for 2000 Years', *Guardian*, 1 September 2003, p. 3.
27 Ibid.
28 Geoff Jenkins, 'Head of the Meteorological Office's Climate Prediction Programme', quoted in Robin McKie and Mark Townsend, 'Sweltering Nation on Brink of Heat Record', *Observer*, 10 August 2003, p. 6.
29 See Athanasiou and Baer, *Dead Heat*, p. 15, and *passim*.
30 Michael McCarthy, 'Reaping the Whirlwind', *Independent*, 3 July 2003, p. 1.
31 John Vidal, 'Global Warming may be Speeding, Fears Scientist', *Guardian*, 6 August 2003.
32 Ibid.
33 Michael Meacher, 'Apocalypse Soon', review of Mark Lynas, *High Tide: News from a Warming World* (London: Flamingo, 2004) in *Guardian*, 24 March 2004, p. 13.
34 Vidal, 'Global Warming may be Speeding'; Meacher, 'Apocalypse Soon'.
35 Athanasiou and Baer, *Dead Heat*, pp. 42–3.
36 Bill McGuire, 'Will Global Warming Trigger a New Ice Age?' *Guardian*, 'Life', 13 November 2003, p. 8.
37 Paul Brown, 'Global Warming is Killing us Too, say Inuit', *Guardian*, 11 December 2003, p. 4.
38 David Fickling, 'Shrinking Ice in the Antarctic Sea "Exposes Global Warming"', *Guardian*, 15 November 2003, p. 16.
39 Ibid.
40 Godrej, *The No-Nonsense Guide*, p. 30.
41 Ibid.
42 Meacher, 'Apocalypse Soon'.
43 Godrej, *The No-Nonsense Guide*, p. 27.
44 George Monbiot, 'Shadow of Extinction', *Guardian*, 1 July 2003, p. 19.

Chapter 20   Justice or Bust

1   According to a joint report by the World Health Organization, the UN Environment Programme and the World Meteorological Programme, climate change has 'already brought about a noticeable increase in malnutrition as well as outbreaks of diarrhoea and malaria, the three "big killers" in the poorest countries in the world'. Paul Brown, 'Global Warming Kills 150,000 a Year', *Guardian*, 12 December 2003, p. 19.

2   Geoffrey Lean, 'The Issues', *Independent on Sunday*, 25 August 2002, p. 20.

3   Mark Townsend and Paul Harris, 'Now the Pentagon Tells Bush: Climate Change will Destroy Us', *Observer*, 22 February 2004, p. 3.

4   Ibid.

5   Tom Athanasiou and Paul Baer, *Dead Heat: Global Justice and Global Warming* (New York: Seven Stories Press, 2002), pp. 43–5.

6   Paul Brown, 'It's Too Late, Climate Change Floods are Inevitable – No Matter What', *Guardian*, 22 April 2004, p. 3.

7   Rupert Jones, 'Global Warming will Hit Insurance Costs', *Guardian*, 8 June 2004, p. 13.

8   Athanasiou and Baer, *Dead Heat*, pp. 45–8.

9   Ibid., pp. 48–9.

10 Mayer Hillman, 'A Modest Proposal to Save The Planet', *The Independent Review*, 27 May 2004, pp. 1–7: p. 6.

11 Ibid.

12 Ibid., pp. 52–3.

13 Dinyar Godrej, *The No-Nonsense Guide to Climate Change* (Oxford: New Internationalist Publications, 2001), p. 104.

14 Hillman, 'A Modest Proposal', p. 6.

15 Jim Yardley, 'China's Economic Engine Needs Power (Lots of It)', *New York Times*, 14 March 2004, WK, p. 3.

16 Ibid.

17 Ibid.

18 Athanasiou and Baer, *Dead Heat*, p. 120; italics suppressed.

19 See Hillman, 'A Modest Proposal', for this idea.

20 George Monbiot, 'A Threat to the Rich', *Guardian*, 16 September 2003, p. 21.

21 Philip Thornton, 'Developing Countries Hail G21 as a "coup of genius"', *Independent*, 15 September 2003, p. 17.

22 Charlotte Denny and Larry Elliot, 'G21 Alliance of the Poor Fights Subsidies Deal', *Guardian*, 15 September 2003, p. 16.

23 Stephen Grey and Michael Gillard, 'Named: Bosses who Made Billions by Selling Before Shares Crashed', *Sunday Times*, 6 October 2002, p. 13. (When even the Murdoch press starts to put out incendiary stories like this, it is hard to deny that there is something in the air.)

24 Joseph Stiglitz, 'Corporate Corruption', *Guardian*, 4 July 2002, p. 15.

25 Julia Finch and Jill Treanor, 'Boardroom Pay up 23 per cent', *Guardian*, 31 July 2003, p. 1.

26 Stephen Greenhouse, 'Update on Capitalism: What do you Mean by "Us", Boss?' *New York Times*, 1 September 2002, WK, p. 3.
27 Geoffrey Lean, 'Why Antarctica will soon be the *Only* Place to Live', *The Independent on Sunday*, 2 May 2004, p. 1.
28 Charles A. Kupchan, *The End of the American Era* (New York: Vintage Books, 2003 [2002]), p. xvii.

Index

legal responsibilities of, 147–8,
157
management techniques of, 204–6
and pensions, 158–9, 207, 272
social responsibilities of, 144–5,
148, 154–5, 165, 165–6
and stock options, 227, 271, 304
n. 23
and taxation, 225
and workplace safety, 156–7
Byers, Stephen, 159

Cadbury, 93, 165
California prison system, 98–9
capital
movement of, 29
capital gains, 187
capital grants, 193–4, 195–9, 211–12
capitalism, 16
crisis of (1930s), 246
crisis of (current), 16, 270–2
and social justice, 5, 93–5, 145,
216
carbon emissions, *see* global
warming, and emissions targets
Carlyle, Thomas, 24
CBI, *see* Confederation of British
Industry
charity, 24, 25
capriciousness of, 24, 25, 276
nn. 18 & 19
and deserving/undeserving poor,
132–3, 152
Chicago
heat-wave deaths in, 161–2,
163–4
child care, 52–4, 60, 149
children, 17, 41–2
advertising directed at, 90, 91–2
disadvantaged, 14–15, 45, 47–8,
49–50, 54–9, 68–9
and environment, 122–3, 123
table 1, 124–5, 126
as 'insurance' for parents, 263
IQ testing of, 113, 114, 115–16,
120–1, 123
obesity in, 89, 89–90, 92

and parental input, 42, 50, 51–2,
54–5, 69
personal responsibility of, 46,
59–60, 136–7
and social hierarchy, 17, 41
China
and carbon emissions, 268
as leader of 'G21', 270
liberal rights, absence of in, 22–3
Chirac, Jacques, 32, 239
choice
and inequality, 65, 75, 137
and personal responsibility,
136–41, 154–5
and public services, 65, 75, 137,
159
Churchill, Winston, 247
citizenship
classes of, 23
Civil Rights Movement (USA), 250
climate change, *see* global warming
Clinton, Bill, 149, 237
Clough, Arthur Hugh, 133, 231
Coca-Cola
and executive remuneration, 227
in schools, 90
Commission on Social Justice
(Britain), 6–9, 10, 14, 169, 190
communications
and productivity, 203
Condorcet, Marquis de, 23
Confederation of British Industry
(CBI), 147–8, 225
Conservative Party (Britain), 241,
247; *see also* Thatcher,
Margaret
Cook, Philip, *see* Frank and Cook,
The Winner-Take-All Society
Cook, Robin, 61
corporations, *see* businesses
corruption, 74, 142–3, 227, 270–1
cosmetic surgery, 173
crime
Conservative explanation of, 45
education, lack of, and, 95, 100–1,
103, 104
inequality and, 178–80